T0321898

Web Semantics for Textual and Visual Information Retrieval

Aarti Singh
Guru Nanak Girls College, Yamuna Nagar, India

Nilanjan Dey
Techno India College of Technology, India

Amira S. Ashour
Tanta University, Egypt & Taif University, Saudi Arabia

V. Santhi
VIT University, India

A volume in the Advances in Data Mining and Database Management (ADMDM) Book Series

www.igi-global.com

Published in the United States of America by
IGI Global
Information Science Reference (an imprint of IGI Global)
701 E. Chocolate Avenue
Hershey PA 17033
Tel: 717-533-8845
Fax: 717-533-8661
E-mail: cust@igi-global.com
Web site: http://www.igi-global.com

Library of Congress Cataloging-in-Publication Data

Names: Singh, Aarti, 1980- editor. | Dey, Nilanjan, 1984- editor. | Ashour, Amira, 1975- editor. | Santhi, V., 1971- editor.
Title: Web semantics for textual and visual information retrieval / Aarti Singh, Nilanjan Dey, Amira S. Ashour, and V. Santhi, editors.
Description: Hershey, PA : Information Science Reference, [2017] | Includes bibliographical references and index.
Identifiers: LCCN 2017002958| ISBN 9781522524830 (hardcover) | ISBN 9781522524847 (ebook)
Subjects: LCSH: Semantic Web. | Information retrieval. | Multimedia systems. | Image processing--Digital techniques. | Big data.
Classification: LCC ZA4240 .W43 2017 | DDC 025.042/7--dc23 LC record available at https://lccn.loc.gov/2017002958

British Cataloguing in Publication Data
A Cataloguing in Publication record for this book is available from the British Library.

Table of Contents

Preface xiii

Acknowledgment xix

Section 1
Tools and Techniques of Information Retrieval

Chapter 1
Scope of Automation in Semantics-Driven Multimedia Information Retrieval From Web 1
Aarti Singh, Guru Nanak Girls College, Yamuna Nagar, India
Nilanjan Dey, Techno India College of Technology, India
Amira S. Ashour, Tanta University, Egypt

Chapter 2
Information Retrieval Models: Trends and Techniques 17
Saruladha Krishnamurthy, Pondicherry Engineering College, India
Akila V, Pondicherry Engineering College, India

Chapter 3
A Study on Models and Methods of Information Retrieval System 43
Manisha Malhotra, Chandigarh University, India
Aarti Singh, Guru Nanak Girls College, Yamuna Nagar, India

Section 2
Associating Semantics With Information

Chapter 4
Technique for Transformation of Data From RDB to XML Then to RDF 70
Kaleem Razzaq Malik, University of Engineering and Technology Lahore, Pakistan
Tauqir Ahmad, University of Engineering and Technology Lahore, Pakistan

Chapter 5
Conversion of Higher into Lower Language Using Machine Translation 92
Raghvendra Kumar, Lakshmi Narain College of Technology, India
Prasant Kumar Pattnaik, KIIT University, India
Priyanka Pandey, Lakshmi Narain College of Technology, India

Section 3
Extracting Knowledge From Information

Chapter 6
Knowledge Discovery From Massive Data Streams 109
Sushil Kumar Narang, SAS Institute of IT and Research, India
Sushil Kumar, IIT Roorkee, India
Vishal Verma, MLN College, India

Chapter 7
Knowledge Discovery and Big Data Analytics: Issues, Challenges, and Opportunities 144
Vinoth Kumar Jambulingam, VIT University, India
V. Santhi, VIT University, India

Section 4
Suggested Reading: Applicability of Semantics-Driven Contents

Chapter 8
Web Semantics for Personalized Information Retrieval 166
Aarti Singh, Guru Nanak Girls College, Yamuna Nagar, India
Anu Sharma, ICAR-IASRI New Delhi, India

Chapter 9
Semantic Web-Based Framework for Scientific Workflows in E-Science 187
Singanamalla Vijayakumar, VIT University, India
Nagaraju Dasari, VIT University, India
Bharath Bhushan, VIT University, India
Rajasekhar Reddy, VIT University, India

Chapter 10
State-of-the-Art Information Retrieval Tools for Biological Resources 203
Shashi Bhushan Lal, ICAR-Indian Agricultural Statistics Research Institute, India
Anu Sharma, ICAR-Indian Agricultural Statistics Research Institute, India
Krishna Kumar Chaturvedi, ICAR-Indian Agricultural Statistics Research Institute, India
Mohammad Samir Farooqi, ICAR-Indian Agricultural Statistics Research Institute, India
Sanjeev Kumar, ICAR-Indian Agricultural Statistics Research Institute, India
Dwijesh Chandra Mishra, ICAR-Indian Agricultural Statistics Research Institute, India
Mohit Jha, ICAR-Indian Agricultural Statistics Research Institute, India

Chapter 11
Role of Social Networking Sites in Enhancing Teaching Environment 227
Singanamalla Vijayakumar, VIT University, India
Vaishali Ravindra Thakare, VIT University, India
Amudha J, VIT University, India
S. Bharath Bhushan, VIT University, India
V. Santhi, VIT University, India

Compilation of References 244

About the Contributors 280

Index 288

Detailed Table of Contents

Present digital information driven society is a part of Semantic Web, where focus is on returning relevant information to the users, in response of their searches. Research community had been doing great efforts to associate semantics with textual information since early 2000. However, there had been tremendous growth in capturing, sharing, storing and retrieving photographs and multimedia contents on the web in last one decade. This has drawn attention of research community for embedding semantics with multimedia contents while storing, so as to lead efficient retrieval of these contents later on. This chapter focuses on presenting need of associating semantics with images, initially various techniques of image retrieval are elaborated. Existing techniques of embedding semantics in images are analyzed, further scope of automation in associating semantics with images is explored considering software agent technology as instrument.

Chapter 2

Information retrieval is currently an active research field with the evolution of World wide web. The objective of this chapter is to provide an insight into the information retrieval definitions, process, models. Further how traditional information retrieval has evolved and adapted for search engines is also discussed. The information retrieval models have not only been used for search purpose it also supports cross lingual translation and retrieval tasks. This chapter also outlines the CLIR process in a brief manner. The tools which are usually used for experimental and research purpose is also discussed. This chapter is organized as Introduction to the concepts of information retrieval. Description of the information retrieval process, the information retrieval models, the role of external sources like ontologies in information retrieval systems. Finally the chapter provides an overview of CLIR and the tools used in developing IR systems is mentioned. Further the latest research directions in IR is explained.

Chapter 3

Information Retrieval (IR) is the action of getting the information applicable to a data need from a pool of information resources. Searching can be depends on text indexing. Whenever a client enters an inquiry into the system, an automated information retrieval process becomes starts. Inquiries are formal statements which is required for getting an input. It is not necessary that the given query provides the relevance information. That query matches the result of required information from the database. It doesn't mean it gives the precise and unique result likewise in SQL queries. Its results are based on the ranking of information retrieved from server. This ranking based technique is the fundamental contrast from database query. It depends on user application the required object can be an image, audio or video. Although these objects are not saved in the IR system, but they can be in the form of metadata. An IR system computes a numeric value of query and then matches it with the ranking of similar objects.

Section 2
Associating Semantics With Information

Chapter 4
Technique for Transformation of Data From RDB to XML Then to RDF.......... 70
Kaleem Razzaq Malik, University of Engineering and Technology Lahore, Pakistan
Tauqir Ahmad, University of Engineering and Technology Lahore, Pakistan

This chapter will clearly show the need for better mapping techniques for Relational Database (RDB) all the way to Resource Description Framework (RDF). This includes coverage of each data model limitations and benefits for getting better results. Here, each form of data being transform has its own importance in the field of data science. As RDB is well known back end storage for information used to many kinds of applications; especially the web, desktop, remote, embedded, and network-based applications. Whereas, EXtensible Markup Language (XML) in the well-known standard for data for transferring among all computer related resources regardless of their type, shape, place, capability and capacity due to its form is in application understandable form. Finally, semantically enriched and simple of available in Semantic Web is RDF. This comes handy when with the use of linked data to get intelligent inference better and efficient. Multiple Algorithms are built to support this system experiments and proving its true nature of the study.

Chapter 5
Conversion of Higher into Lower Language Using Machine Translation 92
Raghvendra Kumar, Lakshmi Narain College of Technology, India
Prasant Kumar Pattnaik, KIIT University, India
Priyanka Pandey, Lakshmi Narain College of Technology, India

This chapter addresses an exclusive approach to expand a machine translation system beginning higher language to lower language. Since we all know that population of India is 1.27 billion moreover there are more than 30 language and 2000 dialects used for communication of Indian people. India has 18 official recognized languages similar to Assamese, Bengali, English, Gujarati, Hindi, Kannada, Kashmiri, Konkani, Malayalam, Manipuri, Marathi, Nepali, Oriya, Punjabi, Sanskrit, Tamil, Telugu, and Urdu. Hindi is taken as regional language and is used for all types of official work in central government offices. Commencing such a vast number of people 80% of people know Hindi. Though Hindi is also regional language of Jabalpur, MP, India, still a lot of people of Jabalpur are unable to speak in Hindi. So for production

those people unswerving to know Hindi language we expand a machine translation system. For growth of such a machine translation system, used apertium platform as it is free/open source. Using apertium platform a lot of language pairs more specifically Indian language pairs have already been developed. In this chapter, develop a machine translation system for strongly related language pair i.e Hindi to Jabalpuriya language (Jabalpur, MP, India).

Section 3
Extracting Knowledge From Information

T.S. Eliot once wrote some beautiful poetic lines including one "Where is the knowledge we have lost in information?". Can't say that T.S. Eliot could have anticipated today's scenario which is emerging from his poetic lines. Data in present scenario is a profuse resource in many circumstances and is piling-up and many technical leaders are finding themselves drowning in data. Through this big stream of data there is a vast flood of information coming out and seemingly crossing manageable boundaries. As Information is a necessary channel for educing and constructing knowledge, one can assume the importance of generating new and comprehensive knowledge discovery tools and techniques for digging this overflowing sea of information to create explicit knowledge. This chapter describes traditional as well as modern research techniques towards knowledge discovery from massive data streams. These techniques have been effectively applied not exclusively to completely structured but also to semi-structured and unstructured data. At the same time Semantic Web technologies in today's perspective require many of them to deal with all sorts of raw data.

The era of big data has come with the ability to process massive datasets from heterogeneous sources in real-time. But the conventional analytics can't be able to manage such a large amount of varied data. The main issue that is being asked is how to design a high-performance computing platform to effectively carry out analytics on big data and how to develop a right mining scheme to get useful insights from voluminous big data. Hence this chapter elaborates these challenges with a brief introduction on traditional data analytics followed by mining algorithms that are suitable for emerging big data analytics. Subsequently, other issues and future scope are also presented to enhance capabilities of big data.

Section 4
Suggested Reading: Applicability of Semantics-Driven Contents

This chapter explores the synergy between Semantic Web (SW) technologies and Web Personalization (WP) for demonstrating an intelligent interface for Personalized Information Retrieval (PIR) on web. Benefits of adding semantics to WP through ontologies and Software Agents (SA) has already been realized. These approaches are expected to prove useful in handling the information overload problem encountered in web search. A brief introduction to PIR process is given, followed by description of SW, ontologies and SA. A comprehensive review of existing web technologies for PIR has been presented. Although, a huge contribution by various researchers has been seen and analyzed but still there exist some gap areas where the benefits of these technologies are still to be realized in future personalized web search.

In the future generation, computer science plays prominent role in the scientific research. The development in the field of computers will leads to the research benefits of scientific community for sharing data, service computing, building the frameworks and many more. E-Science is the active extending field in the world by the increase data and tools. The proposed work discusses the use of semantic web applications for identifying the components in the development of scientific workflows. The main objective of the proposed work is to develop the framework which assists the scientific community to test and deploy the scientific experiments with the help of ontologies, service repositories, web services and scientific workflows. The framework which aims to sustenance the scientific results and management of applications related to the specific domain. The overall goal of this research is to automate the use of semantic web services, generate the workflows, manage the search services, manage the ontologies by considering the web service composition.

With the advancements in sequencing technologies, there is an exponential growth in the availability of the biological databases. Biological databases consist of information and knowledge collected from scientific experiments, published literature and statistical analysis of text, numerical, image and video data. These databases are widely spread across the globe and are being maintained by many organizations. A number of tools have been developed to retrieve the information from these databases. Most of these tools are available on web but are scattered. So, finding a relevant information is a very difficult, and tedious task for the researchers. Moreover, many of these databases use disparate storage formats but are linked to each other. So, an important issue concerning present biological resources is their availability and integration at single platform. This chapter provides an insight into existing biological resources with an aim to provide consolidated information at one place for ease of use and access by researchers, academicians and students.

In recent days, most of the academic institutions across the world understand the usefulness of social networks for teaching and learning. In general, information is being transferred across the world for multiple purposes in different aspects through social media networks. In academic environment to enhance the teaching and learning processes social media networks are used to greater extent. Researchers

Preface

WWW has become currently an inseparable part of our life. Today we are living in digital society, where large amount of multimedia information is produced and stored daily. Retrieving relevant information from these large repositories is a challenging task. The present web generation, namely Web 2.0 focuses on embedding semantics with information. It is called as Semantic Web i.e. meaning oriented web, which means rather than returning information based on keyword matching, information would be returned on the basis of its context. Recently, the web includes text as well as images, audio, video and many other forms of unstructured data generated from messengers.

The semantic web term was coined in 2001, since then lot of research work had been done towards architecture of semantic web, towards developing methods and techniques for embedding semantics with textual information. However, since last one decade there had been tremendous growth in capturing, sharing and retrieving photographs, audio and video data on the web. With widespread popularity of handheld smart mobile devices and availability of Internet anywhere, anytime has led to this growth of multimedia data. There is also increase in attempt of retrieving such information; however retrieving relevant multimedia information from web is still very tough task due to the lack of sufficient information about uploaded multimedia contents. Now, research community has started putting efforts towards incorporating semantics with multimedia contents so that relevant contents may be retrieved in future searches. For associating semantics with pictures, their low-level features need to be extracted and to be expressed in words. Further, automation of this process is very much desired, considering the frequency of contribution on the web.

Consequently, there is an urgent need for an edited collection elaborating techniques of embedding semantics with multimedia information. Specially, techniques for automatic semantic annotation of images must be presented.

OBJECTIVE OF THE BOOK

Objective of this book is to present existing methods and techniques of associating semantics with textual and visual information. Techniques used for associating semantics with information at low level are also elaborated. Methods used for extracting knowledge from web and techniques used for this purpose are explained. Further, extracting knowledge from Big-data available on web, significance of such knowledge discovery and challenge's prevailing needs to be focused. This book also aims to present various application areas of semantics oriented multimedia information.

ORGANIZATION OF THE BOOK

This book is comprised of 11 chapters arranged in four sections. Section 1 comprises of three chapters and focuses on methods and techniques of semantic information retrieval from textual contents as well as multimedia contents. Second section contains two chapters that provide low level details of associating semantics with information. The third section focuses on extracting knowledge from multimedia information through providing techniques for knowledge discovery from textual data as well as from big data present on the web. The fourth section of the book includes four chapters, which illustrating various dimensions of applicability of semantic based contents in present digital society. The summary for the book organization is as follows.

Section 1: Tools and Techniques of Information Retrieval (Chapters 1-3)

This section highlights the information retrieval techniques, which are currently an active research field with the evolution of World Wide Web.

Chapter 1: This chapter focuses on the elaborating techniques that are available for embedding meaning with textual and visual information. It includes several image retrieval process and techniques and also outlines intelligent software agents, which can be used for automatic context based image retrieval.

Chapter 2: This chapter included an insight into the information retrieval definitions, process and models. The authors addressed the traditional information retrieval procedures with adopted search engines. Furthermore, the CLIR process is introduced in brief. The role of external sources such as ontologies in information retrieval systems are also entails.

Chapter 3: This chapter highlighted the existing methods for information retrieval, such as the basic model, Boolean model, vector space model, latent semantic, and the probabilistic model. All these methods own pros and cons based on the kind of information that the user requires. Furthermore, the authors discussed the IR capabilities along with the text based and content based information retrieval methods that used for extracting the information. The authors established that the CBIR is more efficient and effective than the TBIR with accurate results. The evaluation of ranked and unranked retrieval result which retrieved after a query is also addressed.

Section 2: Associating Semantics With Information (Chapters 4-5)

The semantic information is the entry part that defines the different attributes for an entry. The main goal of this section is to establish the concept of semantic information firmly on using mapping techniques.

Chapter 4: This chapter discussed the importance of better mapping techniques for Relational Database (RDB) to Resource Description Framework (RDF). It represented the limitations and benefits of the data model to achieve superior results. Each transformed data form has its own significance in the field of data science. For example, the RDB can be employed in several applications especially the web, desktop, remote, embedded, and network-based applications. Although, the EXtensible Markup Language (XML) is involved for data for transferring among all computer related resources regardless of their type, shape, place, capability and capacity due to its form is in application understandable form. The authors established that the proposed RDF can be used to achieve the nearest form of maximized customization when transforming one data model to another.

Chapter 5: Word Sense Disambiguation (WSD) is complex as it handles full language complexities to identify the meaning of words in context in a computational manner. This chapter proposed an exclusive approach to expand a machine translation system beginning higher language to lower language. Since Hindi is considered the regional language in India, a machine translation system has been proposed. An apertium platform has been used, where a lot of language pairs more specifically Indian language pairs. In this chapter, a machine translation system has been developed for strongly related language pair i.e Hindi.

Section 3: Extracting Knowledge From Information (Chapters 6-7)

The era of big data leads to the ability to process massive datasets from heterogeneous sources in real-time. But the conventional analytics can't be able to manage such a large amount of varied data. This section is concerned with the data discovery concept and tools.

Chapter 6: Knowledge Discovery is a significant process for finding new knowledge about an application domain from large data volumes for making decisions and strategies in related application areas. It has several applications in numerous scientific and business domains; however, the World Wide Web is one of the most fertile areas for data mining and knowledge discovery research as it contains huge amount of information. Web mining is the application of data mining techniques to discover and analyze potentially useful information from Web data. This chapter included a comparison of popular knowledge Discovery process models, where new types of data, new applications, and new analysis demands continue to emerge leading to novel data mining and knowledge discovery tasks. Finally, the authors depicted that the future seems to be dazzling for knowledge discovery. Increasing computational power and continuous creative solutions will be certainly revolutionizing the way for the data mining and information processing.

Chapter 7: This chapter addressed the different techniques that can be applied to design a high-performance computing platform for effective analytics on big data. In addition, the right mining schemes to get useful insights from voluminous big data are also included. The authors elaborated these challenges with an initial briefing about traditional data analytics followed by the mining algorithms that are suitable for emerging big data analytics. Subsequently, other issues and future scope are also presented to enhance the capabilities of big data.

Section 4: Suggested Reading – Applicability of Semantics-Driven Contents (Chapters 8-11)

Chapter 8: This chapter has extensively discussed the synergy between Semantic Web (SW) technologies and Web Personalization (WP) for demonstrating an intelligent interface for Personalized Information Retrieval (PIR) on web. Adding semantics to WP through ontologies and Software Agents (SA) realizes several benefits, which are also included. A brief introduction to the PIR process is provided followed by description of SW, ontologies and SA. An inclusive review of the existing web semantics for PIR has been included.

Chapter 9: The progress in computers leads to research benefits of scientific community for sharing data, service computing, building the frameworks and many more. E-Science becomes an active extending field by the increase of the data and tools. The main objective of this chapter is to discuss the use of semantic web applications to identify the components in the development of scientific workflows. It developed a framework which assists the scientific community to test and deploy the scientific experiments with the help of ontologies, service repositories, web services and scientific workflows. The overall objective of this chapter is to automate the use of semantic web services, to generate the workflows and to manage the search services and the ontologies by considering the web service composition.

Chapter 10: This chapter focuses on finding relevant information from the biological databases that contain information and knowledge collected from scientific experiments, published literature and statistical analysis of text, numerical, image and video data. Several tools have been developed to retrieve the information from these databases. This chapter is concerned with the present biological resources and their availability and integration at single platform. It provides an insight into existing biological resources with an aim to provide consolidated information at one place for ease of use and access by researchers, academicians and students.

Chapter 11: This chapter is briefly describes the issues and challenges of the social networks for teaching and working insertion. The authors assessed the social media tools, specifically Facebook, Blogs, Google groups, SkyDrive and Twitter that are used by the teachers and the students as well for academic purposes. Further, the relationship between usage of SNS and academic performance of students has been tested statistically by views of teachers in most of the universities and with affiliated colleges.

This book is expected to assist researchers, academicians, technology developers and engineers working in the field of Web Semantics. Furthermore, the book provides insights and support executives concerned with recent web semantics technologies that have magnetized much attention. It addressed innovative conceptual framework for various applications. The book is expected to serve as a reference for the post-graduate students as it offers the requisite knowledge for understanding the knowledge discovery techniques along with different applications. This book is based on a research studies carried out by experienced academicians and is expected to shed new insights for researchers; academicians, students and improves understanding of Web Semantics.

Aarti Singh
Guru Nanak Girls College, Yamuna Nagar, India

Nilanjan Dey
Techno India College of Technology, India

Amira S. Ashour
Tanta University, Egypt & Taif University, Saudi Arabia

V. Santhi
VIT University, India

Acknowledgment

Discipline is the bridge between goals and accomplishment. - Jim Rohn

Writing a book is an intensive task, requiring long hours of attention and dedication. Firstly, we would like to express our sincere gratitude to *God* for blessing us with good health and high spirits to work on this project. While writing this book, all of us have taken out time by stealing it from our family and friends. Thus, we would like to thank our *families* for their patience and support all through various phases of compilation of this book. We would like to acknowledge support of our *students*, many of them contributed towards this book in some way. We dedicate this book to all of them!

We extend our sincere thanks to all the *authors*, who have contributed their valuable work for this book. Authors have contributed towards various dimensions of the theme of interest. We thank all authors for devoting their time, patience and perseverance and efforts towards this book. We strongly believe that this book will be a great asset to all researchers in this field!

We would like to express our gratitude to the *reviewers* who spared their precious time for reviewing the chapters of this book, gave constructive suggestions for improvement and assisted us in editing, proofreading and design, throughout this project.

We are grateful to the *IGI-publication team*, who provided us an opportunity to reveal our potential on this front. Constant cooperation and support rendered by them, is really appreciable and it's because of their support that we could complete this project in time. We extend our heartful thanks to the team for their trust in us and providing us all required resources well in time, which helped us managing this project in flexible manner.

Last but not the least; we would like to thank our *readers* for choosing this book. We hope it would be a useful resource in its domain.

Aarti Singh
Guru Nanak Girls College, Yamuna Nagar, India

Nilanjan Dey
Techno India College of Technology, India

Amira S. Ashour
Tanta University, Egypt & Taif University, Saudi Arabia

V. Santhi
VIT University, India

Section 1
Tools and Techniques of Information Retrieval

Chapter 1
Scope of Automation in Semantics-Driven Multimedia Information Retrieval From Web

Aarti Singh
Guru Nanak Girls College, Yamuna Nagar, India

Nilanjan Dey
Techno India College of Technology, India

Amira S. Ashour
Tanta University, Egypt

ABSTRACT

Present digital information driven society is a part of Semantic Web, where focus is on returning relevant information to the users, in response of their searches. Research community had been doing great efforts to associate semantics with textual information since early 2000. However, there had been tremendous growth in capturing, sharing, storing and retrieving photographs and multimedia contents on the web in last one decade. This has drawn attention of research community for embedding semantics with multimedia contents while storing, so as to lead efficient retrieval of these contents later on. This chapter focuses on presenting need of associating semantics with images, initially various techniques of image retrieval are elaborated. Existing techniques of embedding semantics in images are analyzed, further scope of automation in associating semantics with images is explored considering software agent technology as instrument.

DOI: 10.4018/978-1-5225-2483-0.ch001

INTRODUCTION

Semantics in web focus on extracting meaningful information from web. It involves methods and techniques which can help extract textual and visual contents based on context of user's search. Seed of web semantics was sown by Tim-Berner's Lee in 1990's when he coined the idea of semantic web (Lee, Hendler & Lassila,2001) as he could realize that with wide acceptance of WWW information overload would occur in future. Since WWW is an open system with no control on type, quality and amount of information been submitted by the participants, significance of this repository can only be retained if users are provided with relevant information in response to their searches. Due to the presence of vast volumes of textual and image based contents on web, manual access to every content is not possible which lead to development of application software termed as Search Engines which provided interface between users and ever-growing repository of information. Initially SEs were providing web pages based on keywords of search query only, thereby returning more number of irrelevant web pages. Subsequent researches focused on improving algorithms for searching, indexing and retrieval of information based on context of search. However, this also involves filtering of search results based on predefined contexts available with SE. If the context desired by the user is not defined in SE, then user will have to compromise as irrelevant results would be obtained. Solution to this problem is to embed meaning of information in web contents itself, which will help SE in better deciding when to return which contents to users.

Lot of research has been carried out towards embedding and extracting meaning of textual information i.e. information comprising of words. However, from last one decade, large amount of visual information is getting uploaded, stored and retrieved. With advent of mobile computing, internet and mobile phones have become important part of our lives and medium of internet access for all of us. Modern hand held mobile devices are equipped with camera to capture still photographs and high quality videography. People share photographs on social networking sites to express themselves. With trend of capturing photographs, search for images has also increased. 'One image can speak thousand words' this phrase is leading the society. Images are widely asked for education, entertainment, emotional expression and so on. With increased demand of images, need to index the images was felt. Today vast amount of images of various objects & places are available in various databases but searching and extracting relevant images is a prevailing issue. Although, research community is putting rigorous efforts towards developing techniques through which meaning of image contents can be extracted so that it may be stored with image itself and image may be retrieved based on its contents.

This chapter focuses on elaborating techniques available for embedding meaning with textual and visual information. Tim Berner Lee's vision of semantic web can only be realized fully when both textual and visual contents are semantic oriented and can be returned based on context of user's search.

IMAGE RETRIEVAL PROCESS AND TECHNIQUES

Image retrieval based on its contents is one of the earliest techniques which got popularity; Query by example is one such technique. However, user studies show that most users are interested in semantic entities rather than in visual appearance (Singhal & Shandilya, 2010). Thus based on interests, image retrieval can be classified in two categories:

- Content based image retrieval.
- Context based image retrieval.

Content Based Image Retrieval Methods

Content based image retrieval refers to all tools and techniques that help us organize digital images by their visual contents. Thus, it involves similarity functions, image annotation engines. Conventionally, image databases allow textual search on images using only meta data associated with them. However, practically all digital images don't have meta data associated with them and, textual search is not possible for images without meta-data. One solution is to manually annotate images with meta data based on information contained but considering the amount and frequency of images been uploaded on the web, manual annotation of all images doesn't seem feasible. Content based image retrieval overcomes this problem by searching and accessing images based on their low-level features using an example image.

Traditionally image retrieval involves segmenting the images based on their low-level features such as color, texture, shape and spatial locations. Images are segmented based on these features and stored for later retrieval based on same features. Feature extraction is utmost important for content based retrieval of images. As per Rui, Huang and Chang (1999) visual features of images may be classified as follows.

For content based image retrieval general features of images are important as they are independent of any domain and application. Brief description of extraction of these features is given below:

- **Color:** A prominent feature used for image retrieval. It is appealing compared to image background and is independent of image size and orientation. Many techniques are used for extracting/retrieving color of an image. Color histogram is most popular technique for this purpose. L1 and L2 metric are used

Figure 1. Classification of visual features of images

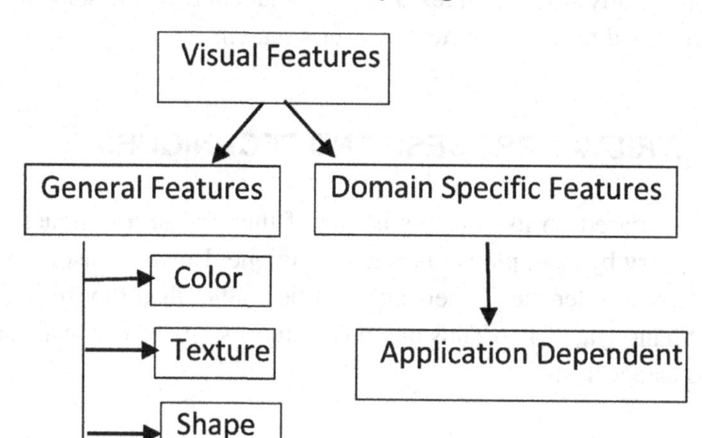

for comparing similarity of color histograms of two images. Cumulative color histogram technique provided improvement in color histogram technique. Apart from color histograms, color moments and color set techniques are also used in image retrieval. Color moments is based on the principal that any color distribution is characterized by its moments. Since most of information revolves around low level moments, thus only first, second and third level moments involving mean, variance and skewness are extracted for color feature representation. Color set is a technique facilitating search in large image collections. A color set comprises of collection of colors from a quantized color space. Color set results in binary feature vector facilitating binary search tree providing faster search for images.

- **Texture:** A uniform pattern, not generated from a single color or intensity. It is inherent property of every surface and provides important information about structural arrangement of any surface and its surrounding environment. Research towards texture extraction started in 1970's when Haralick & Shanmugam,(1973) proposed co-occurrence matrix for texture feature representation. Tamura, Mori & Yamawaki (1978) made important contribution in this direction by providing six properties for texture representation. All six properties namely coarseness, contrast, directionality, linelikeness, regularity and roughness are visually meaningful. Wavelet transform, KL expansion and Kohen maps are some techniques used for texture analysis. Wavelet transform has also been used for texture image annotation (Ma & Manjunath, 1995).

- **Shape:** Shape feature doesn't refer to shape of an image rather to the shape of a particular region being sought out. Shapes are extracted from an image using either segmentation or edge detection method also termed as region based and boundary based techniques. Segmentation method uses entire shape region. It is difficult to automate and requires human intervention. Edge detection uses outer boundary of the shape. It is appealing shape extraction technique, since edges give idea about shapes present in the image and is thus useful for segmentation, registration and identification of an object in it.

For characterizing shapes within images, reliable segmentation is utmost important without which the shape estimates are largely meaningless. A new technique termed as 'Normalized Cuts Partitioning Criterion (NCut)' has been proposed in (Shi & Malik,2000) which performs better than traditional bi-partitioning method, for segmenting an image. In Ncut method an image is considered as a weighted graph with vertex set V containing all pixels of the image and the edge weight $w(p,q), p \in V, q \in V$. $w(p,q), p \in V, q \in V$ presents the perceptual similarity between a pixel pair in some way. Now a cut indicates a partition of the nodes into disjoint subsets A and B s.t. $A \cap B = \varnothing, A \cup B = V$. $A \cap B = \varnothing, A \cup B = V$ .his method uses two terms called Cut and Association where

$$Cut(A,B) = \sum_{p \in A, q \in B} w(p,q).$$

$$Cut(A,B) = \sum_{p \in A, q \in B} w(p,q) \text{a}$$

$$Association(A) = \sum_{p \in A, r \in V} w(p,r).$$

$Association(A) = \sum_{p \in A, r \in V} w(p,r)$. based on these two terms NCut criteria is defined as:

$$NCut(A,B) = \frac{Cut(A,B)}{association(A)} + \frac{Cut(A,B)}{association(B)}.$$

any other techniques for efficient segmentation exist in literature such as K-way cut, textured image segmentation, Hidden Markov Random Fields and Expectation-Maximization algorithm, segmentation based on Mean shift procedure (Comaniciu & Meer, 2002) etc.

A Content based image retrieval (CBIR) system involves four major tasks

- **Data Collection:** Process of collecting images for database creation. Images may be collected from internet using web crawler or bot and may be collected from user activities.
- **Extracting Image Features and Creating Feature Database:** Collected images are analyzed and their low-level features are extracted and stored in the database for future usage.
- **Searching the Database Using Input Image Given by the User:** Such image databases are connected with a user interface, where user can input image to be searched. Low level features of input image are extracted and then compared with already stored images and several images with minimum similarity distance are retrieved from the database.
- **Process and Index the Retrieved Results and Present it to User:** The result images retrieved from the feature database are indexed by similarity distance and returned to the user.

Figure 2. Phases of CBIR system

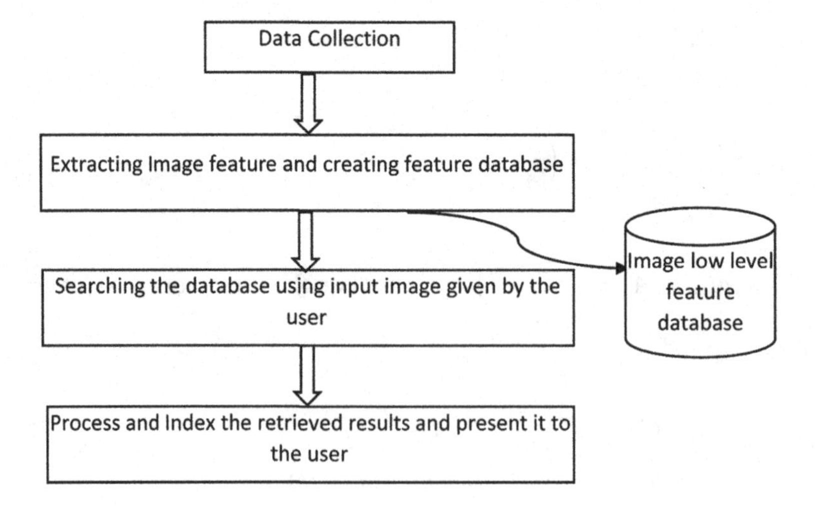

Context Based Image Retrieval

Apart from the low-level features of an image, some textual information might be associated with it. All information that doesn't come from visual properties of the image can be considered as the context of an image (Westerveld, 2000). For example, name of persons in the image, place where image was taken, occasion etc. can reveal information displayed in the image. Context based image retrieval can make use of annotations that were manually added for disclosing the images such as keywords, descriptions etc. or on collateral text that is inherently available with an image for example captions, subtitles, nearby text etc.

Latent Semantic Indexing (LSI) is an approach that has been proved successful in both monolingual and cross-lingual text retrieval. LSI uses co-occurrence statistics of terms to find semantics of document terms, thus using these techniques it is concluded that documents having similar terms are probably related. Using LSI, one can infer that a document containing words- reservation, room, shower and breakfast are related to documents about hotels, even though word 'hotel' is not mentioned in that particular document. Since LSI groups related concepts, it can help solve ambiguity problem.

Westerveld (2000) presented an LSI based approach to combine image low level features (content) and words from collateral text (context) into one semantic space. This approach highlighted that LSI can help uncover hidden semantics of images. This work indicated that using a combination of low level features and collateral text associated with images, better context based retrieval can be achieved.

Barnard, Duygulu, Forsyth, Freitas, Blei & Jordan (2003) highlighted that semantics should be associated with images as:

- Users request images both by object kinds and identities.
- Users request images both by what they depict and what they are about.
- Queries based on image histograms, texture, overall appearance etc. are becoming uncommon.
- Text associated with images is extremely useful in practice, as effective search can be performed on them.

Automatic annotation of images has attracted many researchers, many organizations such as newspaper had been annotating their image collections for internal usage (Markkula and Sormunen (2000), Armitage & Enser, (1997). However, this had been easy for newspapers since images usually have captions associated with them. Archivists received pictures and used to annotate them with words, likely to be useful in retrieving those images. Later, journalists or other users used to search the collections using those keywords only. However, this is manual process of image annotation. Two applications of automatic image annotation are browsing support (Barnard, Duygulu & Forsyth, 2001) and Auto-illustrate (Barnard and Forsyth, 2001). They proposed that similar images might be annotated with similar description to provide browsing support for users. While auto-illustrate tool can automatically suggest images provided block of text.

Text annotation of images can be either based on probability model or makes use of Boolean queries. Using probability model, one might predict text, in case images are provided. There are two ways of doing this, first is to predict annotation of entire image using entire information present. This task is specifically termed as 'Annotation'. Second method is to associate particular words with a particular shape or substructure in the image. This process is termed as 'Correspondence'. Figure 3 summarizes text annotation process:

Performance of annotation is fairly easy to evaluate automatically and thus it can work with large data sets, however it is difficult to evaluate performance of correspondence technique.

Figure 3. Phases of CBIR system

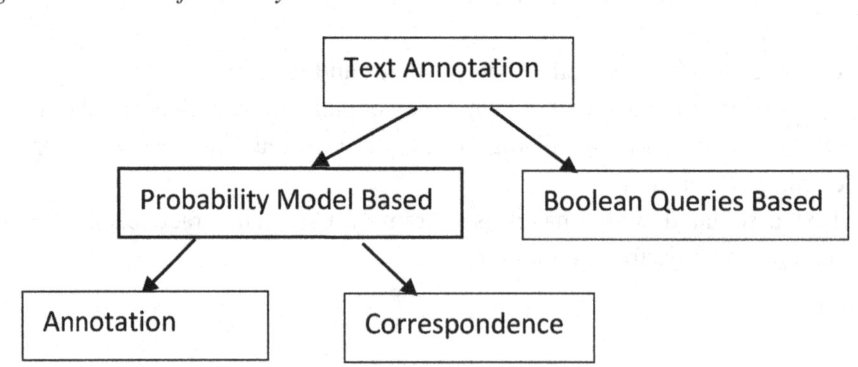

SOFTWARE AGENTS FOR AUTOMATIC CONTEXT BASED IMAGE RETRIEVAL

Although many efforts for automatic association between pictures and words (Barnard *et al.*, 2003) have been made, these methods require human intervention to some extent. However, considering large size of images on the web, there is dire need for automatic context based image retrieval. The same has been felt by research community and some efforts towards automatic annotation of images has been carried out. For instance, Henry Lieberman, Rosenziveig and Singh (2001) proposed an intelligent software image annotation and retrieval process, called an agent. Aria was developed using standard Java Swing editor coupled with a pane containing a custom-built image retrieval and annotation application. Authors used this agent with e-mail system, where as a user types some words this intelligent agent extracts keywords, search images having matching keywords from image database and displays those images in right side pane, from where user can easily use those images in his /her e-mail to make it effective. This system has been tested and provided promising results. ARIA can learn keywords based on user's selection and add them in image database for future usage.

Intelligent software agents belong to a promising technology that finds its roots in distributed artificial intelligence. The research in this direction started around 1970's when Carl Hewitt proposed an Actor system (Hewitt, Bishop, & Steiger, 1973) and defined actors with clear internal definitions with the potential to communicate with their peers in the system. The succeeding developments focused on making intelligent actors now known as software agents where the word agent has evolved from greek word 'agein', which implies to guide (Milojicic, 2000). The term is being explored by research fraternity continuously and many reports pertaining to the developments in agent oriented techniques that enable a more active role of the computers in knowledge acquisition have been contributed. In the domain of computer science, a software agent is a special software entity dedicated to perform an assigned task on behalf of a human or an object (Nwana, 1996). Franklin and co-authors define an agent as "special software entities carry out some set of operations on behalf of a user or another program with some degree of independence or autonomy, and in so doing, employ some knowledge or representation of the user's goals or desires" (Franklin & Graesser, 1996).

Software agents (Juneja, Singh, Singh & Mukherjee, 2016) are possessed with many useful attributes which make them appealing solution as background workers in web-based applications and in environments where large tasks need to be accomplished without human intervention such as image annotation and retrieval. Attributes of software agents are:

- **Autonomous**: An agent should be able to execute without the need for human interaction, although intermittent interaction may be required.
- **Social / Communicative**: An agent should have a high level of communication with other agents. The most common protocol for agent communication is the Knowledge Query and Manipulation Language (KQML) (Juneja, Jagga & Singh,2015), (Juneja, Singh & Jagga, April 2015).
- **Reactive / Responsive**: An agent should be able to perceive its environment and react to changes in it.
- **Proactive**: Proactive agents do not just react to their environment but can take active steps to change that environment according to their own desires.
- **Adaptive**: Adaptive agents have the ability to adjust their behavior over time in response to internal knowledge or changes in the environment around them.
- **Goal-Oriented / Intentions**: These agents have an explicit internal plan of action to accomplish a goal or set of objectives.

Now, in order to exhibit all the above stated features agents are possessed with ontologies. An ontology is explicit specification of domain of interest, it clearly specifies classes, functions, axioms and instances included in it, along with relationship among them. Actually, ontology can be considered as vocabulary of a domain of interest and it helps agents to communicate with their peers in cyber space, with clear understanding of terms being talked about. Ontologies belong to artificial intelligence domain and aim towards facilitating machine learning. Tim berners Lee in his vision of semantic web mentioned use of ontologies. Semantic web architectures presented by Lee and later improved by Gerber and his co-authors (Gerber, Barnard & Merwe, 2007), Gerber, Barnard & Merwe (2008)) clearly make use of Ontology (singh *et al.*, 2010) for semantics in web. Figure 4 given below presents comprehensive functional layered architecture of semantic web as presented by Gerber and his co-authors.

Ontology (Singh, Juneja & Sharma,2010) driven agents and multi-agent systems are widely deployed for information extraction from heterogeneous sources in present semantic web. Some efforts for ontology driven image annotations have also been made by researchers, for instance Hollink, Schreiber, Wielemaker & Wielinga, (2003) have proposed an ontology based tool for semantic annotation and search in collection of arts related images. Their work provided knowledge-engineering aspect such as the annotation structure and links between the ontologies. They have made use of four thesauri which are relevant for arts images. Their tool supports two types of semantic searches for images in the collection, first is the random search using any concept and second search option needs user to exploit the annotation template for search process.

Figure 4. Orthogonal layered Architecture for Semantic Web (Gerber, Barnard & Merwe, 2008)

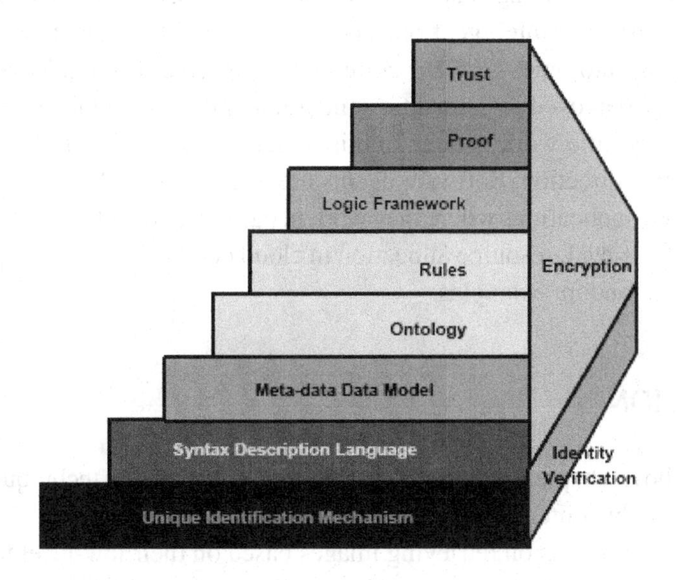

Schreiber, Dubbeldam, Wielemaker and Wielinga (2001) in their work explored the use of ontologies (Singh & Anand,2013) to index and search collection of photographs. Their work presented a multimedia information analysis tool for annotating images and searching on them. They have deployed photo annotation ontology and subject matter ontology. Prototype tool had been evaluated with existing search engines and usability analysis performed by small set of users. It was observed that subject matter description needed further improvement in case of images containing more than one agent. Authors emphasized that research on ontology mapping (Singh, Juneja & Sharma,2011) and merging was required for effective annotation of multimedia information.

Lieberman & Liu (2002) highlighted that people often wants to have meaningful connections between different media such as text and photographs. Traditional methods of image annotation used for this purpose lack knowledge about difference in vocabulary or semantic connections which are obvious for human beings but are not explicitly stated. Their work made use of world semantics i.e. concepts used in day -to-day life. Photo retrieval is performed by expanding keywords using spatially, temporally and socially related concepts. These expanded concepts are represented using concept node graphs, where nodes are commonsense relations and weighted edges represent commonsense relations.

From above discussion, it is clear, that use of ontology is advocated by researchers for annotation of images so as to facilitate their semantic retrieval. Software agents are artificially intelligent objects already present in semantic cyber space, which possess ontologies for their communication and working. Thus, intelligent agents may be deployed for semantic annotation, indexing and retrieval of images. Although, very little work is done in this direction but there is tremendous scope of work in this direction. Software agents are already been deployed for versatile internet based applications where they work in background and support automation, information retrieval, resource allocation in cloud computing and web personalization are some random examples.

DISCUSSION

From the above chapter, it is clear that there are two major techniques of image retrieval, namely content based and context based image retrieval. Content based image retrieval focuses on retrieving images based on their low-level features such as color, texture and shape features. Here relevant images are returned to the user, based on its similarity with an example image using low level feature similarity. Second technique i.e. context based image retrieval focuses on extracting relevant images based on meta data associated with them. Annotation is a technique of adding metadata with images. Literature survey indicated that research community is demanding for automatic methods of image annotation, however as on date there is no standard method for automatic annotation of images. This work also presented software agents and their potential for automation of image annotation process has been highlighted.

CONCLUSION

Images are more effective means of information exchange as compared to text. However, considering frequency of image upload on web, it is difficult to search a relevant image whenever it is desired. For complete realization of semantic web, images on the web must be embedded with metadata illustrating their contents, this will help in retrieval of relevant images at later stage. Many techniques for annotation of images had been proposed, however they require human intervention thereby lacking scalability. Some techniques for automatic annotation of images have also been proposed, however none provides complete automation suitable for vast repository of images on web. This work has highlighted potential of software agent technology for automatic annotation of images. Being inherently equipped with ontologies, agents are suitable for this job. They are already being deployed for automation of many web based applications, thus they have proved potential. Future work, aims towards proposing agent based mechanism for automatic annotation of images on web.

REFERENCES

Armitage, L. H., & Enser, P. G. (1997). Analysis of user need in image archives. *Journal of Information Science*, *23*(4), 287–299. doi:10.1177/016555159702300403

Barnard, K., Duygulu, P., & Forsyth, D. (2001). Clustering art. In *Computer Vision and Pattern Recognition, 2001. CVPR 2001. Proceedings of the 2001 IEEE Computer Society Conference on* (*Vol. 2*). IEEE.

Barnard, K., Duygulu, P., Forsyth, D., Freitas, N. D., Blei, D. M., & Jordan, M. I. (2003). Matching words and pictures. *Journal of Machine Learning Research*, *3*(Feb), 1107–1135.

Barnard, K., & Forsyth, D. (2001). Learning the semantics of words and pictures. In *Computer Vision, 2001. ICCV 2001. Proceedings. Eighth IEEE International Conference on* (Vol. 2, pp. 408-415). IEEE. doi:10.1109/ICCV.2001.937654

Comaniciu, D., & Meer, P. (2002). Mean shift: A robust approach toward feature space analysis. *IEEE Transactions on Pattern Analysis and Machine Intelligence*, *24*(5), 603–619. doi:10.1109/34.1000236

Datta, R., Joshi, D., Li, J., & Wang, J. Z. (2008). Image retrieval: Ideas, influences, and trends of the new age.[CSUR]. *ACM Computing Surveys*, *40*(2), 5. doi:10.1145/1348246.1348248

Deb, S., & Zhang, Y. (2004). An overview of content-based image retrieval techniques. In *Advanced Information Networking and Applications, 2004. AINA 2004. 18th International Conference on* (Vol. 1, pp. 59-64). IEEE. doi:10.1109/AINA.2004.1283888

Franklin, S., & Graesser, A. (1996, August). Is it an Agent, or just a Program?: A Taxonomy for Autonomous Agents. In *International Workshop on Agent Theories, Architectures, and Languages* (pp. 21-35). Springer Berlin Heidelberg.

Gerber, A., Van der Merwe, A., & Barnard, A. (2008, June). A functional semantic web architecture. In *European Semantic Web Conference* (pp. 273-287). Springer Berlin Heidelberg.

Gerber, A. J., Barnard, A., & Van der Merwe, A. J. (2007, February). Towards a semantic web layered architecture. In *Proceedings of the 25th conference on IASTED International Multi-Conference: Software Engineering. Innsbruck, Austria* (pp. 353-362). IASTED.

Haralick, R. M., Shanmugam, K., & Dinstein, I. H. (1973). Textural features for image classification. *IEEE Transactions on Systems, Man, and Cybernetics, 3*(6), 610–621. doi:10.1109/TSMC.1973.4309314

Hewitt, C., Bishop, P., & Steiger, R. (1973, August). A universal modular actor formalism for artificial intelligence. In *Proceedings of the 3rd international joint conference on Artificial intelligence* (pp. 235-245). Morgan Kaufmann Publishers Inc.

Hollink, L., Schreiber, G., Wielemaker, J., & Wielinga, B. (2003, October). Semantic annotation of image collections. In Knowledge capture (Vol. 2). Academic Press.

Juneja, D., Jagga, A., & Singh, A. (2015). A review of FIPA standardized agent communication language and interaction protocols. *Journal of Network Communications and Emerging Technologies, 5*(2), 179-191.

Juneja, D., Singh, A., & Jagga, A. (2015, April). Knowledge Query Manipulation Language (KQML): Recap. *IFRSA's International Journal of Computing, 5*(2), 54–62.

Juneja, D., Singh, A., Singh, R., & Mukherjee, S. (2016). A thorough insight into theoretical and practical developments in multiagent systems. International Journal of Ambient Computing and Intelligence.

Kekre, D. H., Thepade, S. D., Mukherjee, P., Wadhwa, S., Kakaiya, M., & Singh, S. (2010). Image retrieval with shape features extracted using gradient operators and slope magnitude technique with BTC. *International Journal of Computers and Applications, 6*(8), 28–33. doi:10.5120/1094-1430

Lee,, T. B., Hendler, J., & Lassila, C. (2001). The Semantic Web. *Scientific American, 5*(1), 36.

Lieberman, H., & Liu, H. (2002, May). Adaptive linking between text and photos using common sense reasoning. In *International Conference on Adaptive Hypermedia and Adaptive Web-Based Systems* (pp. 2-11). Springer Berlin Heidelberg. doi:10.1007/3-540-47952-X_2

Lieberman, H., Rozenweig, E., & Singh, P. (2001). Aria: An agent for annotating and retrieving images. *Computer*, *34*(7), 57–62. doi:10.1109/2.933504

Ma, W. Y., & Manjunath, B. S. (1995, October). A comparison of wavelet transform features for texture image annotation. In *Proceedings of the 1995 International Conference on Image Processing* (Vol. 2). IEEE Computer Society. doi:10.1109/ICIP.1995.537463

Markkula, M., & Sormunen, E. (2000). End-user searching challenges indexing practices in the digital newspaper photo archive. *Information Retrieval*, *1*(4), 259–285. doi:10.1023/A:1009995816485

Milojicic, D. (2000). Agent systems and applications. *IEEE Concurrency*, *8*(2), 22–23. doi:10.1109/MCC.2000.846190

Newsam, S., Sumengen, B., & Manjunath, B. S. (2001). Category-based image retrieval. In *Image Processing, 2001. Proceedings. 2001 International Conference on* (Vol. 3, pp. 596-599). IEEE. doi:10.1109/ICIP.2001.958189

Nwana, H. S. (1996). Software agents: An overview. *The Knowledge Engineering Review*, *11*(03), 205–244. doi:10.1017/S026988890000789X

Rui, Y., Huang, T. S., & Chang, S. F. (1999). Image retrieval: Current techniques, promising directions, and open issues. *Journal of Visual Communication and Image Representation*, *10*(1), 39–62. doi:10.1006/jvci.1999.0413

Schreiber, A. T., Dubbeldam, B., Wielemaker, J., & Wielinga, B. (2001). Ontology-based photo annotation. *IEEE Intelligent Systems*, *16*(3), 66–74. doi:10.1109/5254.940028

Shi, J., & Malik, J. (2000). Normalized cuts and image segmentation. *IEEE Transactions on Pattern Analysis and Machine Intelligence*, *22*(8), 888–905. doi:10.1109/34.868688

Singh, A., Anand, P. (2013). State of Art in Ontology Development Tools. *International Journal of Advances in Computer Science & Technology,* 2(7), 96-101.

Singh, A., Juneja, D., & Sharma, K.A. (2010). General Design Structure of Ontological Databases in Semantic Web. *International Journal of Engineering Science and Technology,* 2(5), 1227-1232.

Singh, A., Juneja, D., & Sharma, K. A. (2011). Design of An Intelligent and Adaptive Mapping Mechanism for Multiagent Interface. *Proceedings of Springer International Conference on High Performance Architecture and Grid Computing (HPAGC'11)*, 373-384. doi:10.1007/978-3-642-22577-2_51

Singhai, N., & Shandilya, S. K. (2010). A survey on: Content based image retrieval systems. *International Journal of Computers and Applications*, *4*(2), 22–26. doi:10.5120/802-1139

Tamura, H., Mori, S., & Yamawaki, T. (1978). Textural features corresponding to visual perception. *IEEE Transactions on Systems, Man, and Cybernetics*, *8*(6), 460–473. doi:10.1109/TSMC.1978.4309999

Wang, C., Zhang, L., & Zhang, H. J. (2008, July). Learning to reduce the semantic gap in web image retrieval and annotation. In *Proceedings of the 31st annual international ACM SIGIR conference on Research and development in information retrieval* (pp. 355-362). Singapore:ACM. doi:10.1145/1390334.1390396

Westerveld, T. (2000, April). Image retrieval: Content versus context. In *Content-Based Multimedia Information Access* (pp. 276–284). Le Centre De Hautes Etudes Internationales D'informatique Documentaire.

Chapter 2
Information Retrieval Models:
Trends and Techniques

Saruladha Krishnamurthy
Pondicherry Engineering College, India

Akila V
Pondicherry Engineering College, India

ABSTRACT

Information retrieval is currently an active research field with the evolution of World wide web. The objective of this chapter is to provide an insight into the information retrieval definitions, process, models. Further how traditional information retrieval has evolved and adapted for search engines is also discussed. The information retrieval models have not only been used for search purpose it also supports cross lingual translation and retrieval tasks. This chapter also outlines the CLIR process in a brief manner. The tools which are usually used for experimental and research purpose is also discussed. This chapter is organized as Introduction to the concepts of information retrieval. Description of the information retrieval process, the information retrieval models, the role of external sources like ontologies in information retrieval systems. Finally the chapter provides an overview of CLIR and the tools used in developing IR systems is mentioned. Further the latest research directions in IR is explained.

DOI: 10.4018/978-1-5225-2483-0.ch002

INTRODUCTION

Information retrieval(IR) is a field concerned with structure, analysis, storage, organization searching and retrieval of information[Salton,1968]. With the abundant growth of information of web the information retrieval models proposed for retrieval of text documents from books in early 1960's has gained greater importance and popularity among information retrieval scientist and researchers. Today search engine is driven by these information retrieval models.

The fundamental research of information retrieval system focused on searching and retrieving documents relevant to the user information need expressed in the form of query. The challenge lies in retrieving most relevant documents from large corpus by processing the unstructured query. Eventually the information retrieval systems have been designed and researched for retrieving non textual content like video, images, audio and music.

The major issues in IR research is

- **Relevance:**
    - The relevance refer to the retrieval of the information which could be text, audio, image or video from the information sources as requested by an user. The relevance of the retrieval results is user centric as the perspective of relevance varies from one user to other.Designing information retrieval algorithms to retrieve user relevant documents and achieving better retrieval effectiveness is a real challenge.
- **Expression of User's Information Need:**
    - The expectation of the user posing a query could be to expect the information what he/she had in his/her mind. But the problem lies in whether the user expresses his/her needs correctly and precisely. An exact match of the user query to the document may not fetch the relevant documents. The terms used to express the user need in the form of query may not be present in the vocabulary/thesaurus/knowledge source and in literature this is reported as vocabulary mismatch problem or sparse data problem. Though the query given by an user is expanded using the vocabulary the vocabulary must be updated to reflect the terms, phrases currently practiced/used by the user community.Another reason which reduces relevance is that most of the information retrieval systems ignore linguistic relevance and they fetch documents based on the statistical properties.Hence the design of information retrieval systems should take into consideration the linguistic features and user context to fetch more relevant documents /information even though the user query is expressed with less preciseness.

- **Evaluation:**
  - Evaluation is another crucial issue in information retrieval systems. The documents retrieved are ranked by the order of the relevance to the user query. Hence researchers need to evaluate their information models using well known performance like precision, recall, f-measure and recall. The TREC document collections with relevance judgments also aid in evaluation of information retrieval models and techniques.

This chapter is organized as five sections Section I introduces the concepts of information retrieval. Section II describes the information retrieval process. Section III outlines the information retrieval models; Section IV explains the role of external sources like ontologies in information retrieval systems. Section V provides an overview of CLIR and finally the tools used in developing IR systems is mentioned. Further the latest research directions in IR is explained

DEFINITIONS OF INFORMATION RETRIEVAL

Definition 1 [Salton, 1968]

Information retrieval is a field concerned with the structure, analysis, organization, storage, searching, and retrieval of information.

Definition 2 [Christopher Manning et Al., 2009]

Information Retrieval (IR) is finding material (usually documents) of an unstructured nature (usually text) that satisfies an information need from within large collections (usually stored on computers)

INFORMATION RETRIEVAL (IR) MODEL DEFINTION

An information retrieval model is a mathematical framework for defining the search process. An information retrieval model describes the representation of the documents, information need expressed in the form of query, its relevance to the information searched for (which varies as it may be topic centric or user centric) and ranking of the retrieved documents.

Moreover, an information model predicts and explains what a user will find relevant given the user query. The correctness of the model's predictions can be tested in a controlled experiment mostly all the information retrieval models rank the documents retrieved. Few models are simple which do not provide ranking of the documents

INFORMATION RETREIVAL MODELS, ISSUES

Information Retrieval (IR) Models

An information retrieval model is a mathematical framework for defining the search process. An information retrieval model describes the representation of the documents, information need expressed in the form of query, its relevance to the information searched for(which varies as it may be topic centric or user centric) and ranking of the retrieved documents.

Moreover, an information model predicts and explains what a user will find relevant given the user query. The correctness of the model's predictions can be tested in a controlled experiment mostly all the information retrieval models rank the documents retrieved. Few models are simple which do not provide ranking of the documents.

Information Retrieval Process

In general in the information retrieval process the basic task is to search for information. When it is search task it sounds simple as we would have been familiar with utilities and commands like 'grep' to perform a search. In information retrieval the search task is defined is little complicated because of the following issues

- **Increased Search Scope:** Search task scope is large as the search task has to be performed on large collections of documents which range from trillions to quintillions of collections. Two issues is of importance here
    - one the speed with which has to be performed
    - how accurate the search results are ?
- **Efficiency and Semantics of the Query Expression:** The user's information need is expressed usually as a query. The query terms of the query expression are formulated using operators. The semantics of the operators are defined precisely and interpreted exactly by the ir engine. If the semantics is simple and weak it affects the search results.

- **Achieving the Best Retrieval Effectiveness:** An IR process should not only return a collection of documents in response to a query posed by a user, it should also be capable of ordering the results of the retrieval process. In other words the documents are to be ranked. The ranking need to be accurate, satisfying the user's information need.

Tasks in an Information Retrieval Process

1. **Query Formulation Task:** Information need is expressed as a query. Query is usually expressed a collection of terms connected with or without operators (depending on the IR model chosen).
2. **Pre-Processing the Documents and Queries:** The documents have to be pre-processed for identification of key index terms. The query expression has to be pre-processed to identify the significant query terms.
3. **Creation of Index of the Documents:** This can be done either on the fly or as an offline process. The indexing process influences the search time.
4. **Matching Process:** The query significant terms are matched against the documents and the results are returned to the searcher. The matching process is carried out using the similarity measures.
5. **Evaluation of the Retrieval Results:** The relevance of the retrieval results is evaluated.
6. **Ranking:** Using the similarity measures the retrieval results is ranked.
7. **Relevance Feedback:** Using this process the user is involved in identifying the relevant and irrelevant documents and based on this the query reformulation is carried out. This query reformulation helps to improve the retrieval effectiveness.

Before discussing the IR models let us understand what is meant and what could be seen as a document. Document is mostly referred as a textual piece of information which is usually unstructured and sometimes seems to be semi structured. Examples of documents includes web pages, email, books, news stories, scholarly papers, text messages, word document, power point presentations, forum postings, patents, im sessions, etc. All the above mentioned examples are referred as documents as they have few common properties like major content of them include text data which possess few metadata information like title, author, dates(i.e. Date of publication, date of sending an email message etc.,) subject, sender or owner of the content etc., now we have a question in our mind.

Figure 1. IR System Architecture

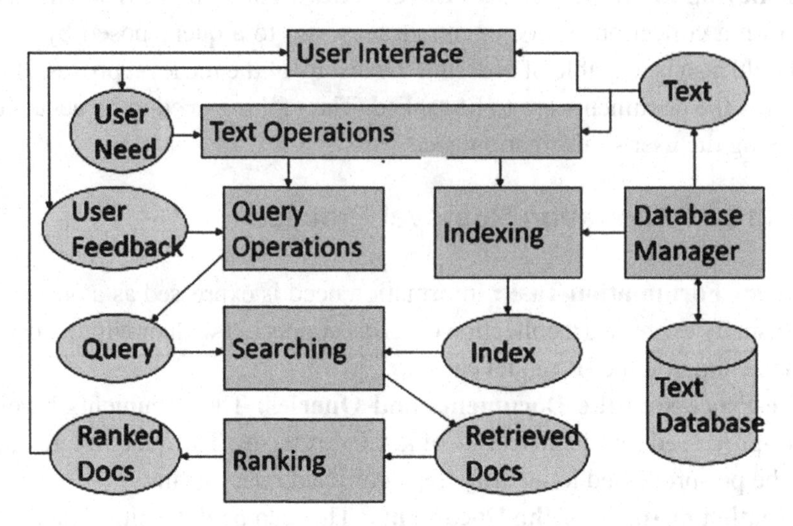

IS DATA RETRIEVAL AND DOCUMENT RETRIEVAL SAME OR DIFFERENT?

There is a subtle difference both retrieval process retrieves information. Data retrieval retrieves structured information and document or information retrieval retrieves unstructured information. Examples of data retrieval include answering a structured query like " find the account numbers having balance > Rs.2000000". In this data retrieval process the balance field values are compared against the value specified in the query and it is retrieved and presented to the user. Examples of information retrieval include answering a query like "find the bank scandals in north and western India reported in the newspapers". This query has to be processed against a news collection corpus and textual comparison is involved which is unstructured processing of queries on a text collection to answer the query asked for. Moreover the retrieved text from the news collections may be duplicated, sometimes irrelevant. Hence it is understood the retrieval process is slightly difficult than normal data retrieval.

Now let us have an overview of the classical IR models.

Information Retrieval Models

In this section the various Information retrieval models viz., Exact Match models,vector space models Probabilistic models, Google Page Rank Model and Language models are discussed.

- **Exact Match Models:**
    - Boolean model [Frakes and Baeza-Yates 1992].
    - Extended Boolean model.
- Vector Space Model [Salton And McGill 1983].
- Probabilistic Model [Robertson 1977].
- Google Page Rank Model [Brin And Page, 1998].
- Language Model [Ponte And Croft 1998],[Hiemstra And Kraaij 1998].

In each model the document representation method, query expansion process and matching process differs.

Exact Match Models

Boolean Model

This model is based on set theory and Boolean algebra. As mentioned earlier any model has a method of representing the document, the query and a method for ranking. In the Boolean model the documents are represented as set of terms. The queries are expressed as Boolean expressions of terms connected using Boolean operators and, or and not. A document is predicted or considered to be relevant if the document terms match exactly with the query expression terms.

It is mostly adopted in many systems like library OPAC's, dialog systems and few search engines.

Example

The rows represent the documents and the columns represent the terms. If the row column intersection has a 1 it indicates the presence of a term in a document and a '0' indicates the absence of a term in a document.

Let us assume that there are five documents related to the missile launches made by DRDO.

The information in the five documents after preprocessing (which include removal of less important stop words, Reduction of words to root words) four significant terms are identified. The identified terms are DRDO, MISSILE, MISSION and LAUNCH. The information of the five missile launches available in the four documents are represented in the following DOCUMENT TERM Matrix(Table 1)

Now let us see how the retrieval process is done using Boolean model.

Suppose a query expression is given as

(DRDO**AND**MISSION) **OR** ((**NOT** MISSION) **AND** (MISSILE**OR**LAUNCH))

Document 3, Document 4 and Document 2 are retrieved.

Table 1. Document Term Matrix

	drdo	missile	mission	launch
Document1	1	0	0	0
Document 2	1	0	0	1
Document 3	1	1	0	0
Document 4	1	0	1	0
Document 5	0	0	0	0

Christopher manning et al. uses a incidence matrix to store the information of term occurrences in the documents. In the incidence matrix rows represent the term vectors and columns referred as document vectors. Usually this matrix stores Boolean values representing the presence or absence of terms in the documents. Later researchers use the integer values to show the frequency count of each term in the documents.

Index Construction and Posting Lists

Indexing is a process which maps the terms to the documents. The index terms are kept in the memory and there are pointers to the posting lists which are stored in the secondary storage. The posting list has the document identifiers (an unique identifier assigned to each document) which contains the term. The terms occurring in the documents are sorted alphabetically and with each term an inverted list or posting list is associated. Sometimes along with term, the frequency count, position of the term occurrence in the document is also stored.

Advantages of Boolean Model

1. Simple model based on set theory and hence easy to implement and understand.
2. Results are predictable, relatively easy to explain.
3. Efficient processing since many documents can be eliminated from search

Disadvantages of Boolean Model

1. Equal weightage is given to all the terms in the query.
2. The ranking of the documents is not possible. It is nor suitable for complex queries.

3. The size of the incidence matrix becomes too big and unmanageable as it depends on the size of the documents (number of words (terms) in the document) and the number of documents in the collection.
4. Sometimes no documents are retrieved.
5. Uncertainty is not handled.
6. The and operator is too strict and or is too broad and hence have an effect on the retrieval results.
7. Ambiguity in using the and/or operators. The users sometimes get confused with the semantics of logical and/or and English words 'and/or' and hence retrieval results may not be effective.

Smart Boolean Model

A variation of the Boolean model[Marcus 1991][Marcus 1994] which supports the user by formulating the queries using the Boolean operators for the natural language query submitted by the user. The synonyms of the terms in the NLP query, relationship among the terms of the query and proximity factors are taken into consideration for automatically formulating the query. It takes the feedback from the user and reformulates the query and returns better retrieval results.

Advantages

1. No need for Boolean operators. The user need not be aware or have the burden of understanding the Boolean operators in formulating queries.
2. User interaction or feedback facilitates improved retrieval results.
3. Stemming, conceptual relationship considerations for formulation of query.

Disadvantages

1. Lack of visual interface in early models and users have the burden of navigating through the suggestions to support the query reformulation process.
2. Structural relevance feedback.

Extended Boolean Model

The Boolean model was extended to address the following two issues.

1. The Boolean operators semantics were redefined to reduce the strictness of the Boolean operators.

2. This model facilitates ranking the retrieved documents.

The terms of the query and documents were assigned weights which aided the ranking process.

Fox[1983] developed a p-norm method to allow the ranking of the documents. The frequency statistics of term occurrences were used as weighting method to distinguish most relevant to less relevant documents. If the term is strictly needed the p coefficient proposed by fox has to be kept as infinity and 1 if it is less strictly important.

Fuzzy set theory is the method used to handle uncertainty. In IR domain, the users are not expected to be precise to express their information need precisely. Hence the fuzzy set concepts are used to determine the relevancy of the document to the query posed by the user. The degree of membership of an element to a set is of varied nature than the traditional binary membership of a set. The degree of membership of fuzzy set theory was used to assign the weights to an index term. Fox and Sharat [1986] proposed the "mixed min and max" model to leverage the strictness of the Boolean operators. The OR operator was used to defined "max" and AND operator to define "min". The model helped to determine the query document similarity and helped to rank the documents.

Advantages

- The strictness of Boolean operators was softened.
- A ranking model was provided which was lacking in boolean model.

VECTOR SPACE MODEL

In vector space model the documents and queries are modeled as m dimensional vectors where m is the number of terms [Pablo Castellset. Al. 2007] . The index terms are weighted using non binary weights. The query vector is matched with the document vector to retrieve the relevant documents and the retrieved documents are sorted in the decreasing order of relevance. The documents are normalized and the term inverse document frequency is used to calculate the similarity score of the document. Usually cosine similarity is used to measure the similarity of document and the query vector.

TF-IDF Weighting Scheme

The term frequency and inverse document frequency is used to determine the relevance of the document to the query. For term frequency and inverse document frequency is calculated for the query and the document. Basically the importance of term is determined by computing the frequency of the term in the document and in the documents in the collection.

The term frequency is calculated using the following formula

$$tf\left(ti\right) = \sum ti \,/\, \sum twi$$

Where tf of ti is the term frequency ti and twi refers to total number of words in the documents.

Example

Assume let document 1 contains 1000 words(/∑twi) and it contains the term "god" 500 times(∑ ti) then the term frequency tf("god") = 500/1000 = 0.5.

Inverse Document Frequency

Is it enough to calculate term frequency to determine the importance of the term? We all know in a document the words like "is","of","but", occur many times in comparision to other words. But it do not help in identifying the significant terms. Hence the inverse document frequency is calculated. Inverse document frequeny decreases the weights of the frequent terms and increases the weight of the rare terms and hence helps in identifying the significant and important words.

The inverse document frequency is computed as given below.

$$IDF\left(ti\right) = \log\_e\left(\frac{tdi}{ndti}\right)$$

where tdi is the total number of documents in the collection and ndti refers to the number of documents which has the word in it.

Example

Let the total number of documents in the collection is 2,00,000. Let us assume the word "god" occurs in 1000 documents. Then the idf (ti) is 2,00,000/10000= 20. Now the tf.idf is product of .5*20 = 10.

The ranking of the document is done based on this tf-idf method. The tfidf of each query term has to be calculated and then summed up to compute the query document similarity.

Probabilistic Models

In this model the probability that the document is relevant to the query is calculated. The ranking of the documents is based on the probability scores of the document. The Bayes rule is used to calculate the probability of the document whether it is relevant to the query or not is measured. Here also the term weightage is taken into consideration as in vector space model for ranking the documents. The basic assumption is this model is the terms are considered as independent terms. A probabilistic retrieval model ranks documents in decreasing order of probability of relevance to the information need: p(r l q,di).the probability of relevance is evaluated based on occurrence of terms in query and documents. An initial estimate is required which refined through feedback. The similarity of a query to the document is computed by a similarity function which is a ratio of the probability of relevance to probability of non relevance.

The probabilistic retrieval model is based on the probability ranking principle, which states that an information retrieval system is supposed to rank the documents based on their probability of relevance to the query, given all the evidence available [Belkin and croft 1992]. The principle takes into account that there is uncertainty in the representation of the information need and the documents. There can be a variety of sources of evidence that are used by the probabilistic retrieval methods, and the most common one is the statistical distribution of the terms in both the relevant and non-relevant documents.

We will now describe the state-of-art system developed by turtle and croft (1991) that uses Bayesian inference networks to rank documents by using multiple sources of evidence to compute the conditional probability(info needl document) that an information need is satisfied by a given document. The dictionary or the vocabulary index terms is used to construct a document network and the information need is also constructed as a query network. The inference network refers to the document network and the query network. The initial values are instantiated and propagated through the inference network and for each node the probability scores are derived. These probability scores are used to rank the documents.

The uncertainty problem is addressed using this probability model. But it requires prior knowledge to compute the probabilities. Though the statistical property of the documents is taken into consideration for ranking the documents there is no way to consider the linguistic features.

So far we had an overview of the information retrieval models. Now let us see how these models concepts are realized in search engines.

Search Engines and Information Retrieval

With the evolution of web information retrieval models have gained momentum. The search engines are practical applications of information retrieval techniques to huge collections of texts. The search engines mentioned may be commercial or open source search engines used for research purposes. Few open source search engines are lucene,lemur/indri and galago.

Though the process involved in traditional information retrieval systems and search engines remains same the challenges of search engines are

1. **Efficient Indexing and Faster Searching Mechanism is Required:** The design of the indexing technique plays a crucial role in search engines. The response time should be reduced, the indexing technique should be faster and effectiveness should be improved through better query throughput.
2. **Coverage of New Data:** The indices updation should dynamic and how recently the indices are updated becomes important to have a better coverage of data. The recent updations provide freshness of data.
3. **Scalability:** Should not compromise on the performance like response time when the number of users and data increases tremendously. Parallel and distributed algorithms need to be employed to provide scalability.
4. Adaptability required for fresh and new applications.

Architecture of Search Engine

The search engines are architected to provide effectiveness and efficiency. The quality of the search results (retrieval results) determines the effectiveness and the time within which the search results are produced and the throughput.

The major processes in the search engine are

- Storage of documents in a document store. This process is called text acquisition.
- Identification of index terms and features for the documents in the document store (text transformation).

- Creation of indexing structures for faster searching. It is similar to the posting lists reported in information retrieval system.
- **Ranking:** Based on the query the documents are ordered and displayed to the user.
- **Evaluation:** The effectiveness and the efficiency of the search engines are measured and on reviewing the effectiveness and efficiency the new techniques are employed to improve the same.
- **User interaction:** Suggests and supports query refinement.

Text Acquisition

Basically, the text acquisition process is carried out by crawlers in search engines. Crawlers are programs which crawl the websites to read the WebPages of the websites for creating the search engine indices. A crawler is otherwise called as spider or bots. A crawler program uses links to find documents. The other source of documents is through the RSS (rich site summary or RDF site store) feeds. Usually weblogs, news and online publishers feed their data through RSS. Then these documents are converted into a consistent xml format. The text could be encoded using UTF8 to support different languages. The metadata of the documents like links, content type, creation time and anchor text.

Text Transformation

The documents are processed by a parser to generate text tokens which includes headings, titles and links of the document. The tokenizer identifies the tokens for the parser and processes characters like comma, apostrophe, hyphens, and delimiters etc., the tags of the documents are used by the parser to identify the structural elements of the document. The pre-processing tasks of the information retrieval systems stop word removal and stemming are used. The stop word removal removes common words or stop words like "the", "in" etc., the stemming process to identify the common root stem word to group words originating from a root word. Page rank algorithms analyses the links and anchor text in the web pages to identify the popularity and community information. Information like name of people, names of locations company name dates are extracted by information extraction techniques. The name of people, names of locations company name dates are referred to as named entities the text classification algorithms Sambyal et al (2016) are used to classify the topics, sentiment, genre of the documents.

Creation of Indices

The index terms count and their positions are computed to gather the document statistical information. The weighting method mentioned in vector space model is adapted for ranking the documents. As the websites is populated with lot of Web-Pages the features or the index terms required to represent the entire collection is huge. In this context distributed and parallel techniques are used to distribute the index terms, documents across sites and computers to increase the search efficiency.

Compression of Index Terms

Some search engines store n grams as index terms. This increases the disk and memory space. Hence compression methods are used to store indices. The compression ratio should be good and the decompressing process should be easy. Various encoding methods are used for compression of index terms and document numbers. Delta encoding, bit align code and elias-γ code are commonly used for compression.

Expression of Information Need Using Query Languages

The user should be provided with an interface and a way of expressing the information need. The famous query languages like indri queries, Boolean queries and galago queries are used to describe complex users information need. The search engine should have parser to parse the queries expressed in different query languages. The search engine also allows query reformulation, query suggestions, spelling corrections in the queries. For query expansion thesauri or dictionaries are used.

Lemur Project: Open Source Search Engines for Research and Development

The lemur project was started in 2000 by the center for intelligent information retrieval (CIIR) at the University of Massachusetts, Amherst, and the language technologies Institute (LTI) at Carnegie Mellon University.

Researchers from both University Of Massachusetts, Amherst, and the language technologies institute (LTI) at Carnegie Mellon University have developed and designed software tools and search engines which is based on the language models for IR tasks..

Few of the significant contributions are

- Indri search engine.
- The lemur query log toolbar for capture of user interaction data.
- Toolbars for browsers.
- Text mining software.
- The clueweb09 dataset for research on web search.
- Galago query engine.

In the following sections let us discuss few of the contributions of lemur research group.

Indri Search Engine [Trevor Strohman et. Al.,2005]

Indri search engine retrieval process is information retrieval model which is based on language model (Metzler et al. 2004a) and probabilistic model (Turtle and croft 1991). The queries are evaluated using the language modeling estimates instead of the statistical estimates (tf-idf estimates). The indri query language supports the operators used by inquery and also allows complex operators. The indexing mechanism used in indri is concurrent and hence allows retrieval of information from large collections of the order of terabytes or more. For larger collection sizes the indri is designed efficiently to process the queries using clusters of servers. The indri system allows all the complex operators that inquery as well as new operators. The indri parser is capable of handling all kinds of documents like plain text,html,xml,pdf and Unicode text. The pre-processing tasks are also included in indri to remove stop words and do stemming. The disk input output time is minimized by storing the index in main memory. The i/o writes are done in the background thread. Query optimization is done to improve query processing time. . Indri is written in C++ and java API's are available for processing the queries.

Galago Retrieval Model

The first binary version (3.14159) of galago was released in dec 2011. Subsequent releases are made twice per year in June and December. The lemur project extends the galago search engine for research purposes. As such, many components have been significantly modified to support further extensions and experimentation.

As galago is designed for experimentation purposes the user has the facility to control the different functionalities of the system by changing the parameters. The behavior of the system is changeable as the system allows choosing and changing the functionalities of the system.

The existing classes can be modified by the users and developers and the modified classes can be plugged into the system.

Galago includes tupleflow, which is a distributed computation framework like mapreduce or dryad. Tupleflow serialization of data, sorts the data and supports distributing processing. Data structures similar to inverted lists storing key value pairs are stored and managed by the indexreader and indexwriter classes

These classes help the users to build their own indexing mechanisms and data structures to improve the information retrieval task. This also supports other operators used in the indri language. There is flexibility to add new operators. The new operator should be put in the classpath and reference for processing the queries.

The galago system provides many simple functions to allow accessing the index data structures. Expalining all the operators in beyond the scope of this chapter and hence the basic categories of functions alone are outlined here. Basically there are three categories of functions supported by galago:

- Indexing functions like build, build-background, build-partial-index etc.,
- Retrieval functions like doc-name, discount, batch-search, search, xcount etc.,
- Index dump functions like dump-connection, dump-corpus, dump-doc-terms, Dump-index etc.

Processing Models

The processing model for testing against a test data set could be chosen and galago facilitates it. The behavior of the retrieval process is defined and controlled by the processing models. The processing model defines the method of processing the query through the execute function. The org.lemurproject.galago.core.retrieval.processing.processingmodel interface should be extended to define the processing model to be used to process a query.The user has to choose the processing model and set that as the value for the processing model parameter. The value of this parameter indicates the class that will be used for retrieval.

The most important existing processing models are the following:

Ranked Document Model

This processing model is to perform straightforward document-at-a-time (daat) processing model.

Ranked Passage Model

Passage level retrieval scoring is carried out in this model.

Maxscore Document Model

Assumes the use of delta functions for scoring, then prunes using maxscore that speeds up the processing time.

Two Pass Document Passage Model

This model does retrieval at two levels. At the first level document level retrieval is done and further the passage level retrieval scoring is done at the second level.

Working Set Document Model

The retrieval model is performed on a collection of documents which is referred to as working set.

Stemmer Used in Galago

Both stemmed and non-stemmed terms are used for indexing in galago. The krovetz stemmer is used for stemming process. Sometimes porter stemmer is also used. The user can also specify whether to include non stemmed words or stemmed words should be used for query processing.

Galago Query Language

Galago views document is as a sequence of text which contain arbitrary tags . When the document is processed by the galago engine for each of the unique tags of the document a single context is generated. An extent is seen as a sequence of text that are within a single begin/end tag pair of the same type as the context. The galago query language was developed and is seen as an extension of indri query language. The Indri query operators are supported by galago and slightly the syntax of the query language differs from the indri query language. Despite the change in the syntax of the query language, the functionality of the query operators of indri query language is preserved in the galago query language.

The query in galago is represented as a query tree. The nodes in the query tree are operators. The operator is named and has a set of parameters used to define the functionality of the operator. The model chosen by the user make use of the operators functionality defined and based on which the documents score is computed for all the documents in the collection. Few parameters used to define the functionality of the operators are static and hence not dependent on the document being scored. Few other operators' parameters depend on the document.

One important feature of the galago query language is the presence of traversals. A traversal transforms a query tree from one form into another. Traversals are used internally to annotate or transform query nodes with additional information that can be extracted from the retrieval object. Traversals are also used to make the query more efficient to process

Evaluation

The evaluation is key issue in evaluating the effectiveness and efficiency of the search engines. The evaluation of search engines is carried out either as a controlled experiment or can be tested online. The search engine efficiency and effectiveness is related to the system configuration being used and depending on which the costliness varies.

The following evaluation corpus is usually used for evaluation.

CACM, GOV2, AP, TREC collections.

Each evaluation corpus is characterized by number of documents,average length of the documents, average length of the queries and average number of relevant documents /query.

Performance metrics in Information retrieval systems

- **Precision:** What percentage of the retrieved documents are relevant to the query.
- **Recall:** What percentage of the documents relevant to the querywere retrieved.

Role of Relevance Feedback and Query Logs

User's relevance feedback would improve the query reformulation and query suggestion process. The log data and user click information would improve the search effectiveness.

The relevance feedback collection for all the documents is a tedious task and expensive one. TREC uses a pooling method which takes into consideration the top 50-200 results from the ranking lists of various search engines are merged as a pool. The duplicate results are removed.

Another method for improving effectiveness and efficiency is by using the query logs. It also assists the search engine in query reformulation. The query terms, click history, the user information are some of the information kept track in the query logs.

Similarity Measures

In all of these models the similarity measures play a key role in identifying the relevant documents.

Matching Process and Similarity Measures

The similarity measures are used in the matching the queries and the documents. Semantic similarity is defined as a measure assigned to a set of terms of an information source based on the likeliness in semantic content of the terms. The human ability to assess similarity is based on the amount of knowledge the human beings possess in a particular domain. Russell and norvig define semantic similarity as a measure which quantifies the common intrinsic features shared by the two concepts (Russell and Norvig 2003).

There are various classification of similarity measures[k.sarualdha,2011]

1. Path length based measures.
2. Information content based measures.
3. Hybrid measure.
4. Feature based measures.
5. Ontology based measures.

Role of Ontologies in Information Retrieval

Ontologies are explicit shared conceptual vocabulary of a domain. This aid in the query expansion process. The query terms are matched with the concepts of the ontologies and the concepts are used for expanding the queries. The ontologies could also be used for learning the retrieval results. Personalized information systems are supported by user profile ontologies and for the same query terms different retrieval results would be returned according to the personal interests of the user.

Ontology Mapping and IR Systems

The ontology mapping is a process of finding correspondences among different concepts of the ontologies and this would generate alignments which list the concepts of the ontology1 and ontology2 along with the similarity measure. These correspondences could help in the query rewriting process. The automatically rewritten queries could broaden the search and help to fetch the relevant documents.

Another direction of research is designing ontologies to formalize the concept relationships and detect associations between the concepts. A lot of work has been reported in the literature to develop ontologies for cause of diseases Alkhammash et al(2016).

Cross Lingual Information Retrieval Systems

Cross-lingual information retrieval (CLIR)[Jian-Yun Nie,2010] refers to the retrieval of documents that are in a language different from the one in which the query is expressed. This allows users to search document collections in multiple languages and retrieve relevant information in a form that is useful to them, even when they have little or no linguistic competence in the target languages. Cross lingual information retrieval is important for countries like India where very large fraction of people are not conversant with English and thus don't have access to the vast store of information on the web.

CLIR became an active area of research in the mid 1990's. NIST encouraged conducting CLIR experiments IN TREC-6 conference in the year 1997. TREC 4 and TREC 5 CLIR experiments on translating English queries to Spanish queries. In TREC 7 CLIR experiments were conducted with European languages like English, German, French, Italian, and Dutch and so on. In 2000, Cross language experiment forum conducted experiments with English, German, Dutch documents with queries expressed in English, Dutch, German, French, Italian, and Swedish. In CLEF (Cross language evaluation Forum) 2007, Indian languages like Hindi, Telugu and Marathi were studied.NII(National Institute of Informatics) of Japan focused on Asian languages IR. FIRE (Forum for information retrieval Evaluation) was started in the year 2008 for indian languages. All these forums contributed a lot to the CLIR research.

Three approaches are followed for CLIR

1. **Query Translation Approach:** Many methods are used for query translation. Few of the approaches reported in literature is discussed here.
2. **Dictionary Based Approach [JianfengGao et. Al., 2001]:** The main task in CLIR systems is finding accurate and equivalent words of one language in another language. This is usually achieved by making use of bilingual dictionaries. This approach is found to be simple but suffers from the following disadvantages.
    a. The coverage of the dictionary is poor.
    b. Selection of the correct translation of words given in the dictionary. This problem is referred to as translation ambiguity.

Jianfenggao et. al., 2001 proposes a method to overcome the disadvantages of dictionary based approach. They have attempted to translate English language words to chinese words. Using a statistical method the noun phrases are identified and the probabilities of the translated phrases in the chinese language is determined. Apart from these noun phrases the other words are translated as words itself. This method tries to identify the best translation of the words and contributes to solve the translation ambiguity.

3. **Document Translation Approach:** This approach takes into consideration the contexts and the availability of efficient Machine translation Systems. Lot of researchers have studied and compared the efficiency of query translation approach and document translation approach. Experimental studies of Franz et al.(1999) using the IBM machine translation system did not show any clear advantage of one approach over the other. Mccarley(1999) experimental results revealed that the effectiveness of the translation depends on the translation direction. He reported in his studies that French to English translation outperformed the English to French translation. The limitations of this approach are:
    a. The target language to which the document to be translated should be known in advance.
    b. All the translated versions of the document should be stored and storing all the translation documents in different languages becomes impracticable though a multilingual translation platform should support it.
4. **Pivot Language or Interlingua Approach:** As discussed previously the limitations of translation resources and the translation ambiguity it makes the direct translation between the two languages impossible. Hence a new approach where a pivot language is used translates the document or query to the pivot language. After the translation to the pivot language then it is translated to the target language. If the document and query are both translated to the pivot language the approach is called the Interlingua approach.

Webcrawlers and Search Engines

A webcrawler is a program which downloads and stores webpages for a web search engine. The downloaded webpages are further used for various retrieval tasks. There are two types of web crawling strategies viz., breadth first search and best first search.

There are four classes of web crawlers:

- **Focused Web Crawler:**
    - Uses the best first web crawling strategy
    - Fetches webpages which are only relevant to the topic searched
- **Incremental Crawler:** A traditional crawler, in order to refresh its collection, periodically replaces the old documents with the newly downloaded

documents. On the contrary, an incremental crawler incrementally refreshes the existing collection of pages by visiting them frequently based upon the estimate as to how often pages change

- **Parallel Web Crawler:** Multiple crawlers are often run in parallel, which are referred as Parallel crawlers [24]. A parallel crawler consists of multiple crawling Processes called as C-procs which can run on network of workstations .
- **Distributed Web Crawler:** Distributed web crawling is a distributed computing technique. Many crawlers are working to distribute in the process of web crawling, in order to have the most coverage of the web.

TOOLS AND LANGUAGES USED FOR IR RESEARCH

- Wordnet thesaurus developed by princeton.
- Universal networking language(unl) for clir.
- JWNL(java wordnet library).
- Jena library.
- Porter stemmer.
- Postagger.
- Lucene indexer.

The other perspectives of information retrieval are cross lingual IR, distributed and parallel IR.

FUTURE RESEARCH DIRECTIONS IN IR

Nowadays the paradigm has shifted from text based retrieval to content based retrieval, non textual retrieval Hemalatha et.al(2017), Wang et.al.(2016) using image queries. A lot of retrieval results for different query sets could be analyzed using parallel information retrieval approaches. Similarity measures used in IR systems is used for web services composition and recommendations. Improving the indexing methods for faster retrieval is another interesting research topic. Further usage mining and opinion mining Baumgarten et al(2013) are recent research areas in information retrieval. The IR techniques is used for recommender systems, linking heterogeneous data, to profile and provide personalized search results to the users. The usage mining techniques are used to help learn the browsing patterns of the users which in turn would help retrieval effectiveness. Document clustering techniques also adapt the preprocessing tasks used in the information retrieval domain and use corpora of MEDLINE for optimizing mining tasks Wahiba Ben Abdessalem Karaa et. al(2016), Noreen Kausar et. al(2016)

Opinion mining using IR techniques help in summarizing reviews and lot of opinion summarization systems have been recently reported in the literature. The role of ontology matching systems also aids semantic web based retrieval.

CONCLUSION

This chapter provides an overview of the information retrieval process, various information retrieval models. It also discusses in depth the representation of the documents and the information needs. The information retrieval models reported in the literature have been discussed in detail. The open source tools available for performing various IR tasks are also mentioned. This chapter has also provides a trail of information retrieval models have gained significant importance with the invention of WWW and how they have been adapted in current search engines like google.

REFERENCES

Alkhammash. (2016). *Designing Ontology for Association between Water Quality and Kidney Diseases for Medical Decision Support System.* VI International Conference Industrial Engineering and Environmental Protection 2016 (IIZS 2016), Zrenjanin, Serbia.

Ashour, Sassi, Roy, Kausar, & Dey. (2016). MEDLINE Text Mining: An Enhancement Genetic Algorithm Based Approach for Document Clustering. In Applications of Intelligent Optimization in Biology and Medicine (pp. 267–287). Springer International Publishing.

Baumgarten, M., Mulvenna, M. D., Rooney, N., & Reid, J. (2013, April). Keyword-Based Sentiment Mining using Twitter. *International Journal of Ambient Computing and Intelligence*, *5*(2), 56–69. doi:10.4018/jaci.2013040104

Castells, P., Farnandez, M., & Vallet, D. (2007, February). An Adaptation of the Vector Space model for Ontology based Information Retrieval. *IEEE Transactions on Knowledge and Data Engineering*, *18*(2), 261–271. doi:10.1109/TKDE.2007.22

Croft, B., Metzler, D., & Strohman, T. (2010). *Search Engines: Information Retrieval in Practice*. Pearson Education.

Croft & Callan. (2016). *Lemur Project*. Retrieved http://www.lemurproject.org/

Hemalatha, et al. (n.d.). *A Computational Model for Texture Analysis in Images with Fractional Differential Filter for Texture Detection*. IGI Global.

Kausar, N., Palaniappan, S., Samir, B. B., Abdullah, A., & Dey, N. (2016). Systematic Analysis of Applied Data Mining Based Optimization Algorithms in Clinical Attribute Extraction and Classification for Diagnosis of Cardiac Patients, Applications of Intelligent Optimization in Biology and Medicine Volume 96 of the series Intelligent Systems. *The Reference Librarian*, 217–231.

Koubarakis, M., Skiadopoulos, S., & Tryfonopoulos, C. (2006, December). Logic And Computational Complexity For Boolean Information Retrieval. *IEEE Transactions on Knowledge and Data Engineering*, *18*(12), 1659–1665. doi:10.1109/TKDE.2006.193

Manning, Raghavan, & Schütze. (2008). Introduction to Information Retrieval. Cambridge University Press.

Nie. (2010). *Cross-Language Information Retrieval*. Morgan & Claypool Publishers.

Russell, S. J., & Norvig, P. (2016). *Artificial Intelligence – A Modern Approach*. PHI.

Salton & McGill. (1986). Introduction to Modern Information Retrieval. McGraw-Hill, Inc.

Sambyal, , & Abrol, P. (2016). Feature based Text Extraction System using Connected Component Method. *International Journal of Synthetic Emotions*, *7*(1), 41–57. doi:10.4018/IJSE.2016010104

Strohman, T., Metzler, D., Turtle, H., & Bruce Croft, W. (2005). *Indri: A language model based search engine for complex queries* (extended version). Technical Report IR-407. CIIR, CS Dept., U. of Mass. Amherst.

Wang, , He, T., Li, Z., Cao, L., Dey, N., Ashour, A. S., & Shi, F. et al. (2016, October). Image Features based Affective Retrieval employing Improved Parameter and Structure Identification of Adaptive Neuro Fuzzy Inference System. *Neural Computing & Applications*. doi:10.1007/s00521-016-2512-4

Wiberg, . (2012). *Interaction Per Se: Understanding "The Ambience of Interaction" as Manifested and Situated in Everyday & Ubiquitous IT-Use*. IGI Global. doi:10.4018/978-1-4666-0038-6.ch007

Yates & Neto. (1999). *Modern Information Retrieval*. ACM.

KEY TERMS AND DEFINITIONS

Crawler: Crawlers are programs which crawl the websites to read the webpages of the websites for creating the search engine indices.

Data Retrieval: Data retrieval is the process of identifying and extracting data from a database, based on a query provided by the user or application.

F-Measure: It is defined as harmonic mean of precision and recall.

Information Retrieval: Information retrieval is essentially a matter of deciding which documents in a collection should be retrieved to satisfy a user's need for information.

MAP: Mean average precision is the mean average precision over all queries.

Precision: In the field of information retrieval, precision is the fraction of retrieved documents that are relevant to the query.

Preprocessing: Preprocessing is an important task and critical step in text mining, natural language processing and information retrieval. In the area of text mining, data preprocessing used for extracting interesting and non-trivial and knowledge from unstructured text data.

Recall: Recall in information retrieval is the fraction of the documents that are relevant to the query that are successfully retrieved.

Search Engine: A program that searches for and identifies items in a database that correspond to keywords or characters specified by the user, used especially for finding particular sites on the World Wide Web.

Stemming: Stemming is the process of reducing inflected (or sometimes derived) words to their word stem, base or root form—generally a written word form.

Chapter 3
A Study on Models and Methods of Information Retrieval System

Manisha Malhotra
Chandigarh University, India

Aarti Singh
Guru Nanak Girls College, Yamuna Nagar, India

ABSTRACT

Information Retrieval (IR) is the action of getting the information applicable to a data need from a pool of information resources. Searching can be depends on text indexing. Whenever a client enters an inquiry into the system, an automated information retrieval process becomes starts. Inquiries are formal statements which is required for getting an input (Rijsbergen, 1997). It is not necessary that the given query provides the relevance information. That query matches the result of required information from the database. It doesn't mean it gives the precise and unique result likewise in SQL queries (Rocchio, 2010). Its results are based on the ranking of information retrieved from server. This ranking based technique is the fundamental contrast from database query. It depends on user application the required object can be an image, audio or video. Although these objects are not saved in the IR system, but they can be in the form of metadata. An IR system computes a numeric value of query and then matches it with the ranking of similar objects.

DOI: 10.4018/978-1-5225-2483-0.ch003

INTRODUCTION

Information retrieval (IR) is the action of getting the information applicable to a data need from a pool of information resources. Searching only depend on text indexing. Whenever a client enters an inquiry into the system, an automated information retrieval process becomes activated. Inquiries are formal statements which is required for getting an input (Rijsbergen, 1997). It is not necessary that the given query provides the relevant information. That query matches the result of required information from the database. It doesn't mean it gives the precise and unique result likewise in SQL queries (Rocchio, 2010). Its results are based on the ranking of information retrieved from server. This ranking based technique is the fundamental contrast from database query. It depends on user application, the required object can be an image, audio or video. Although these objects are not saved in the IR system, but they can be in the form of metadata. An IR system computes a numeric value of query and then matches it with the ranking of similar objects. However user appears the result having top rank object/ article/ text as shown in Figure 1.

The above figure reflects all results of *information retrieval* in the form of Wikipedia, pdf, ppt etc. This query provides approximate fifty lakh results. But the user can change the query according to requirements. For example user can ask for *information retrieval pdf* as shown in Figure 2. As it is reduce the number of results. Now it shows eighteen lakh results.

Figure 1. Query on Web Search Engine

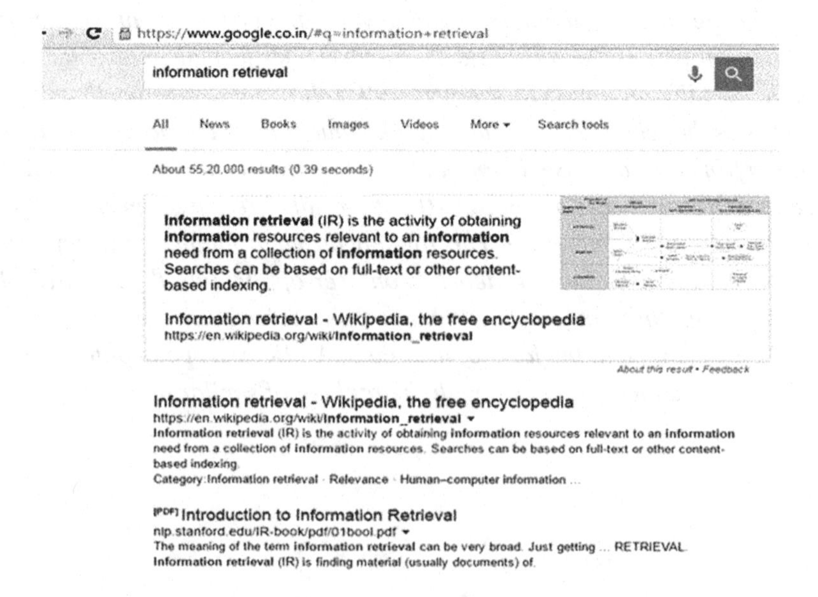

Figure 2. Refined Query on Web Search Engine

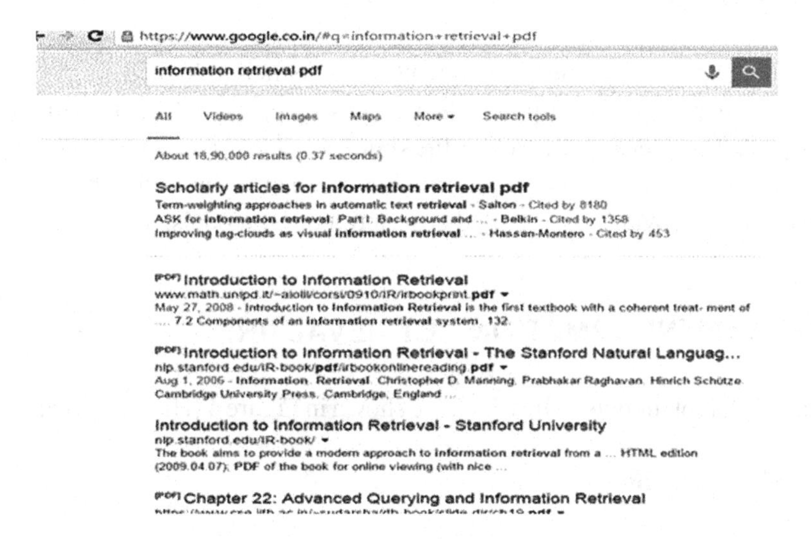

All IR system works on general concept of retrieval. Whenever a query is forwarded to web server, searching will start in the pool of resources present in database. After searching, an indexing will take place and provides similar kind of objects. All the retrieved document or objects will display on user screen in ranked way. Basic IR architecture is explained in below Figure 3.

Next section depicts on background of IR which throws some light on work which already been done in this field.

Figure 3. IR Architecture

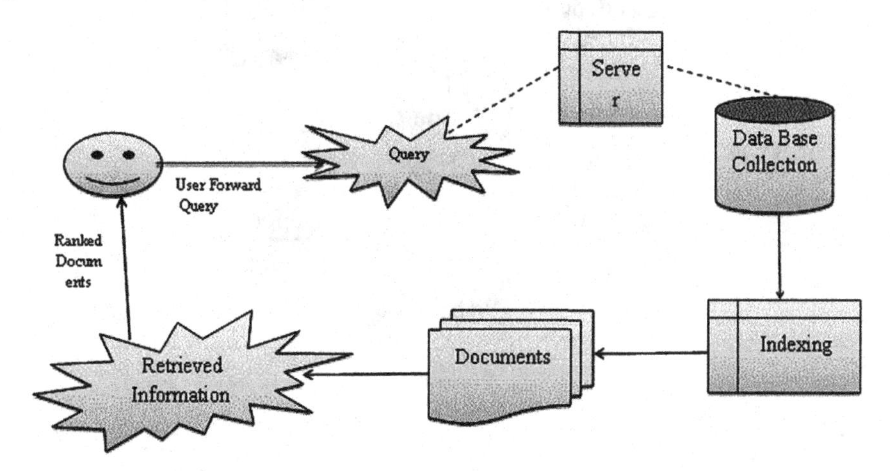

BACKGROUND

This section explains literature by eminent researchers in this field.

Santofimia et al. (2012) explains the rule based approach for automatic service composition. They discussed that how the system can be improved by amalgamation of automatic service composition with reasoning capability for a distributed system.

Next section provides the detailed descriptionof IR models.

MODELS OF INFORMATION RETRIEVAL (IR)

There are different models of IR which are shown in Figure 4 (Hiemstra et al., 2000).

Basic Model of IR

It is basically divided into four main components shown in Figure 5.

- **Query:** It is entered by user and formulate the query $q \to (N, L)$, where N is the information asked by user and L is the length of information.

Figure 4. Models of Information Retrieval

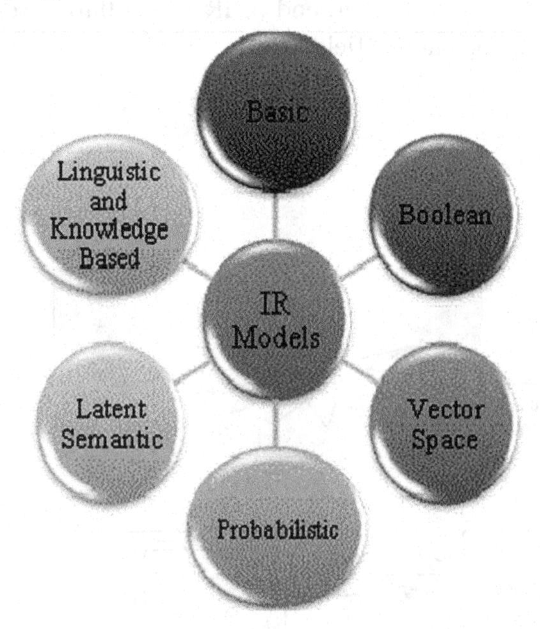

Figure 5. Basic Model of IR System

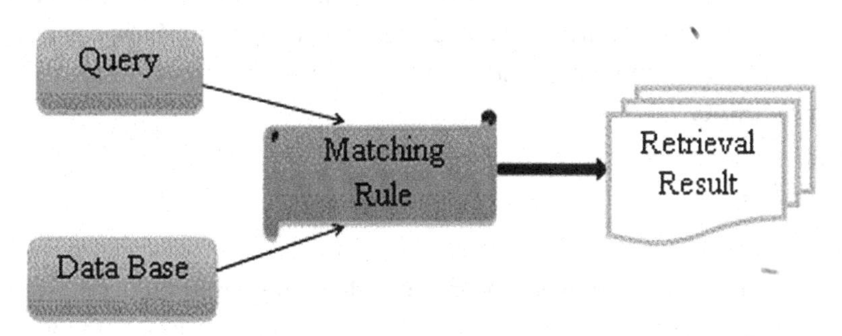

- **Database:** It is used for storing the data on web server and make an index file (I).
- **Matching Rule:** It consists of (N, I) after comparing the required information received from query and indexing from database by applying a matching algorithm.
- **Retrieval Result:** It acquires the relevant document which is shown to the user on display screen.

Boolean Model

It is a conventional model of IR which is based on standard Boolean algebra and set theory. It formulates the query based on pure Boolean logic. Here documents are set of terms and query is in Boolean terms. A Boolean expression (Christos et al., 1997) consists of index terms and operators AND (^), OR ($\vee$) and NOT ($\neg$). The resultant predicted if and only if it satisfies query expressions. The main disadvantage of this model is that it is purely for professional. User can write a query in natural language and the meaning of AND, OR, NOT becomes totally different. Another disadvantage of this model is that it is based on exact match. There is no space for partial matching even no ranking. All retrieved documents are not in ranked order. Hence it is very complicated for a simple user.

Vector Space Model

It represents the documents and queries in vector form. For example:

$$\vec{d} = \sum_{j=1}^{t} w_{ij} \qquad (1)$$

Here d is the document and w_{ij} is the weight of term j in document i. For finding similar object, it compare the cosine angle between them. Suppose q is query passed to find the document d, then vector space model firstly finds the *cosine similarity measure.*

$$\cos\theta = S(d_i, q) \tag{2}$$

All results in terms of ranked documents which are based on decreasing value of $\cos\theta$. It can defines as

$$\begin{cases} S(d,q) = 0 & when\, d = q \\ S(d,q) = 1 & when\, d \neq q \end{cases} \tag{3}$$

Probabilistic Model

It is an uncertain model which used different statistical approaches like probability theory, fuzzy logic and theory of evidence (Hiemstra et al., 2009). There is a mismatch problem between the query term and index term because information is stored in query term and document is in index term. Whenever a query is generated, the result is based on ranked documents in decreasing order of probability value of related objects or images.

Latent Semantic Indexing Model

A few factual and AI methods have been utilized as a part of relationship with area semantics to extend the vector space model to beat a portion of the recovery issues described above, for example vocabulary issue. One such strategy is Latent Semantic Indexing (LSI). In LSI the relationship among terms and archives are computed and misused in the recovery procedure (Hiemstra et al., 2009). The suspicion is that there is some “inactive” structure in the example of word utilization crosswise over reports and that factual system can be utilized to gauge this inert structure. Leverage of this methodology is that questions can recover records regardless of the fact that they have no words in like manner. The LSI system catches further cooperative structure than straightforward term-to-term relationships and is totally programmed. The main contrast amongst LSI and vector space strategies is that LSI speaks to terms and reports in a diminished dimensional space of the determined indexing measurements. Similarly as with the vector space technique, differential term weighting and significance criticism can enhance LSI execution generously.

Linguistic and Knowledge-Based Approaches

In the least difficult type of programmed information retrieval, clients enter a series of keywords that are utilized to seek the rearranged lists of the record catchphrases. This methodology recovers archives construct exclusively with respect to the nearness or nonattendance of careful single word strings as indicated by the coherent representation of the inquiry. Obviously this methodology will miss numerous pertinent records since it doesn't catch the complete or profound importance of the client's question. Phonetic and information based methodologies have likewise been created to address this issue by playing out a morphological, syntactic and semantic examination to recover archives all the more viably. In a morphological investigation, roots and attaches are broken down to decide the grammatical form (thing, verb, descriptor and so on.) of the words (Hiemstra et al., 2000). Next complete expressions must be parsed utilizing some type of syntactic investigation. At last, the phonetic techniques need to determine word ambiguities and/or create significant equivalent words or semi equivalent words taking into account the semantic connections between words. The advancement of a refined etymological recovery framework is troublesome and it requires complex learning bases of semantic data and recovery heuristics. Subsequently these frameworks frequently require strategies that are generally alluded to as artificial intelligence techniques.

Inference Reference Model

This model works on an inference process under inference network. Most procedures utilized by IR systems can be actualized under this model. In the least complex execution of this model, a record instantiates a term with a specific quality, and the credit from various terms is gathered given a question to register what might as well be called a numeric score for the archive. From an operational point of view, the quality of instantiation of a term for an archive can be considered as the heaviness of the term in the record, and report positioning in the least difficult type of this model gets to be distinctly like positioning in the vector space show and the probabilistic models depicted previously. The quality of instantiation of a term for an archive is not characterized by the model, and any definition can be utilized.

All the IR models have their own pros and cons. So it depends on user which kind of result he wants and further it depends on requirement and situation. Next section describes the various methods of information retrieval.

CAPABILITIES OF IR

Following are the capabilities of the information retrieval are:

Search Capability

The goal of the search capability is to take into consideration a mapping between a client's predefined requisite and the things in the data database that will reply that need. The pursuit question explanation is the implies that the client utilizes to impart a depiction of the required data to the framework. It can comprise of common dialect message in arrangement style as well as inquiry terms (alluded to as terms in this book) with Boolean rationale markers between them. How the framework makes an interpretation of the hunt question into preparing ventures to locate the potential pertinent things is depicted in later parts. One idea that has at times been executed in business frameworks (e.g., Retrieval Ware), and holds critical potential for helping with the area and positioning of significant things, is the "weighting" of pursuit terms. This would permit a client to show the significance of hunt terms in either a Boolean or regular dialect interface. The inquiry articulation may apply to the total thing or contain extra parameters restricting it to a coherent division of the thing (i.e., to a zone). Finding a name in a Book reference does not really mean the thing is about that individual. Later investigate has demonstrated that for longer things, limiting a question proclamation to be fulfilled inside a touching subset of tile report (entry looking) gives enhanced accuracy. As opposed to permitting the inquiry explanation to be fulfilled anyplace inside a report it might be required to be fulfilled inside a 100 words of the thing. Based upon the calculations utilized as a part of a framework a wide range of capacities are connected with the framework's understanding the hunt articulation. The capacities characterize the connections between the terms in the hunt explanation (e.g., Boolean, Normal Language, Proximity, Contiguous Word Phrases, and Fuzzy Searches) and the understanding of a specific word (e.g., Term Masking, Numeric and Date Extend, Contiguous Word Phrases, and Concept/Thesaurus development). As opposed to proceeding with the utilization of the term preparing token to speak to the searchable units separated from a thing, the phrasing "word" or "term" is likewise utilized as a part of a few settings as a guess that is instinctively more significant to the peruser.

Boolean Logic

Boolean rationale permits a client to coherently which relate various ideas together to characterize what data is required. Normally the Boolean capacities apply to handling tokens recognized anyplace inside a thing. The run of the mill Boolean administrators are AND, OR, and NOT. These operations are actualized utilizing set crossing point, set union and set distinction techniques. A couple of frameworks presented the idea of "elite or" yet it is proportional to a marginally more intricate inquiry utilizing alternate administrators and is not for the most part valuable to clients since most clients do not comprehend it. Putting bits of the hunt explanation in enclosures are utilized to obviously indicate the request of Boolean operations (i.e., settling capacity). On the off chance that enclosures are not utilized, the framework takes after a default priority requesting of operations (e.g., regularly NOT then AND then OR). In the cases of impacts of Boolean administrators, no priority request is given to the administrators and questions are handled Left to Right unless brackets are incorporated. Most business frameworks don't permit weighting of Boolean questions. An uncommon kind of Boolean inquiry is called "M of N" rationale.

Proximity

Proximity is utilized to confine the separation permitted inside a thing between two inquiry terms. The semantic idea is that the nearer two terms are found in content. Nearness is utilized to build the exactness of an inquiry. In the event that the terms PC and DESIGN are found inside a couple expressions of each other then the thing will probably be talking about the outline of PCs than if the words are sections separated. The commonplace arrangement for closeness is:

TERM1 inside "m . . . . units" of TERM2

The separation administrator "m" is a whole number and units are in Characters, Words, Sentences, or Paragraphs. Certain things may have other semantic units that would demonstrate helpful in indicating the proximity operation. For extremely organized things, removes in characters demonstrate valuable. For containing imbedded pictures (e.g., computerized photos), message between the pictures could help in accuracy when the goal is in finding a specific picture. Now and then the closeness relationship contains a heading administrator showing the course (before or after) that the second term must be found inside the quantity of units indicated. The default is either heading. An extraordinary instance of the Proximity administrator is the Adjacent (ADJ) administrator that regularly has a separation administrator of one and a forward just course (i.e., in WAIS). Another exceptional case is the place the separation is set to zero significance inside the same semantic unit.

Contiguous Word Phrases

Contiguous Word Phrase (CWP) is both for determining a question term and an uncommon inquiry administrator. A Contiguous Word Phrase is at least two words that are dealt with as a solitary semantic unit. It has four words that indicate a pursuit term speaking to a solitary particular semantic idea (a nation) that can be utilized with any of the administrators talked about above. Hence a question could indicate "producing" AND "Joined States of America" which gives back anything that contains the word "producing" and the adjacent words "Joined States of America."

A contiguous word state additionally acts like an uncommon pursuit administrator that is like the closeness (Adjacency) administrator yet takes into consideration extra specificity. In the event there are two terms are determined, the touching word state and the vicinity administrator utilizing directional single word parameters or the Adjacent administrator are indistinguishable. For adjacent word expressions of more than two terms the main method for making an equal inquiry explanation utilizing vicinity and Boolean administrators is by means of settled Adjacencies which are not found in most business frameworks. This is on the grounds that Vicinity and Boolean administrators are paired administrators yet coterminous word phrases are a "N"ary administrator where "N" is the quantity of words in the CWP. Contiguous Word Phrases are also called Literal Strings in WAIS.

Fuzzy Searches

Fuzzy Searches give the capacity to find spellings of words that are like the entered seek term. This capacity is essentially used to adjust for mistakes in spelling of words. It builds review to the detriment of diminishing accuracy (i.e., it can incorrectly distinguish terms as the hunt term). In the way toward extending a question term fluffy looking incorporates different terms that have comparative spellings, giving more weight (in frameworks that rank outpu0 to words in the database that have comparative word lengths and position of the characters as the entered term. A Fuzzy Search on the expression "PC" would consequently incorporate the accompanying words from the data database: "PC," "compiter," "conputer," "computter," "figure." An extra improvement may query the proposed elective spelling and on the off chance that it is a legitimate word with a distinctive significance, incorporate it in the inquiry with a low positioning or exclude it at all (e.g., "suburbanite"). Frameworks permit the particular of the most extreme number of new terms that the extension incorporates into the inquiry. For this situation the substitute spellings that are "nearest" to the inquiry term is incorporated. "Nearest" is a heuristic work that is framework particular. It has its most extreme use in systems that acknowledge things that have been Optical Character Read (OCR). In the OCR procedure a printed copy thing is examined into a twofold picture (for the most part at a determination of 300 dabs for every inch or more). The OCR procedure is an example acknowledgment handle that sections the filtered in picture into significant sub regions, regularly considering a fragment the zone characterizing a solitary character. The OCR procedure will then decides the character what's more, make an interpretation of it to an inner PC encoding

Term Masking

Term masking is the capacity to extend an inquiry term by veiling a segment of the term and tolerating as legitimate any handling token that maps to the unmasked bit of the term. The estimation of term covering is much higher in frameworks that do not perform stemming or just give an extremely basic stemming calculation. There are two sorts of hunt term concealing: settled length and variable length. Settled length concealing is a solitary position veil. It covers out any image in a specific position or the absence of that position in a word. It not just permits any character in the veiled position, additionally acknowledges words where the position does not exist. Settled length term concealing is not as often as possible utilized and normally not basic to a system. Variable length "don't cares" permits concealing of any number of characters inside a preparing token. The concealing might be in the front, toward the end, at both front and end, or imbedded. The initial three of these cases are called postfix look, prefix seek and imbedded character string look, individually. The utilization of an imbedded variable length couldn't care less is from time to time utilized. In the event that "*" speaks to a variable length couldn't care less then the accompanying are cases of its utilization:

"*COMPUTER" Addition Search

"COMPUTER*" Prefix Search

COMPUTER" Imbedded String Search

Numeric and Data Range

Term concealing is helpful when connected to words, however does not work for discovering scopes of numbers or numeric dates. To discover numbers bigger than "125," utilizing a term "125"" won't locate any number aside from those that start with the digits "125." Systems, as a component of their standardization procedure, portray words as numbers or dates. This takes into consideration particular numeric or date extend preparing against those words. A client could enter comprehensive (e.g., "125-425" or "4/2/93- 5/2/95" for numbers and dates) to limitless extents (">125," "<=233," speaking to "More prominent than" or "Not exactly or Equal") as a major aspect of a question.

Natural Language Query

As opposed to having the client enter a particular Boolean inquiry by determining look terms and the rationale between them, Natural Language Queries permit a client to enter a composition proclamation that portrays the data that the client needs to discover. The more drawn out the writing, the more precise record comes about returned. The most troublesome rationale case connected with Natural Language Queries is the capacity to determine refutation in the pursuit articulation and have the system remember it as nullification.. The strategies for finding things like the inquiry explanation are suited for discovering things like different things yet don't have natural procedures to avoid things that resemble a specific bit of the hunt articulation. For some clients, this kind of an interface gives a characteristic expansion to inquiring somebody to play out a hunt.

Browse Capability

Once the inquiry is finished, Browse abilities furnish the client with the capacity to figure out which things are of intrigue and select those to be shown. There are two methods for showing a rundown of the things that are connected with a question: line thing status and information perception. From these rundown shows, the client can choose the particular things mid zones inside the things for show. The framework additionally considers simple transitioning between pass on outline shows and survey of particular things. On the off chance that hunts brought about high exactness, then the significance of the peruse capacities would be reduced. Since query return numerous things that are not applicable to the client's data require, peruse capacities can help the client in concentrating on things that have the most elevated probability in addressing his need.

Ranking

Under Boolean systems, the status show is a tally of the quantity of things found by the question. Each one of the things meet all parts of the Boolean question. The reasons why a thing was chosen can without much of a stretch be followed to and shown (e.g., through highlighting) in the recovered things. Hits are recovered in either a sorted arrange (e.g., sort by Title) or in time arrange from the freshest to the most established thing. With the presentation of positioning based upon anticipated importance values, the status synopsis shows the significance score connected with the thing alongside a brief descriptor of the thing (typically both fit on one show screen line). The significance score is a gauge of the pursuit system on how nearly the thing fulfills the seek articulation. This permits the client to decide at what indicate quit investigating things in light of decreased probability of pertinence. Hypothetically everything in the framework could be returned however large portions of the things will have a significance estimation of 0.0 (not applicable). For all intents and purposes, frameworks have a default least esteem which the client can adjust that quits returning things that have a significance esteem underneath the predetermined esteem. Since one line is normally committed per thing in an outline show, part of a zone truncated by designated space on the show is normally shown with the importance weight of the thing. This zone is as often as possible the Title and gives the client with extra data with the importance weight to abstain from selecting non relevant things for survey. For example, a few systems make pertinence classes and demonstrate, by showing things in various hues, which classification a thing has a place with. Different frameworks utilizes a classification, for example, High, Medium High, Medium, Low, and Non-important. The shading procedure expels the requirement for composed sign of a thing's importance, accordingly giving extra positions in a line to show a greater amount of the title yet causes issues with clients that experience the ill effects of incomplete or aggregate partial blindness. As opposed to restricting the quantity of things that can be evaluated by the number of lines on a screen, other graphical perception methods demonstrating the significance connections of the hit things can be utilized. For instance, an a few dimensional diagram can be shown where focuses on the chart speak to things and the area of the focuses speak to their relative relationship between each other what's more, the client's question. Sometimes shading is additionally utilized as a part of this representation. This procedure permits a client to see the grouping of things by subjects and peruse through a bunch or move to another topical group. This has a similarity of moving through the stacks at a library. In a solitary picture the client can see the impacts of his seek articulation instead of showing a couple of things at once.

Zoning

At the point when the client shows a specific thing, the goal of minimization of overhead still applies. The client needs to see the base data expected to figure out whether the thing is important. Once the assurance is made a thing is conceivably important, the client needs to show the total thing for nitty gritty audit. Restricted show screen sizes require selectability of what parts of a thing a client necessities to see to make the importance assurance. For instance, show of the Title and Abstract might be adequate data for a client to foresee the potential pertinence of a thing. Restricting the show of every thing to these two zones permits numerous things to be shown on a solitary show screen. This makes most extreme utilization of tile speed of the client's intellectual procedure in examining the single picture and understanding the potential pertinence of the numerous things on the screen.

Highlighting

Another show help means that why a thing was chosen. Diverse qualities of highlighting demonstrate how emphatically the highlighted word took an interest in the choice of the thing. Another ability, which is increasing solid acknowledgment, is for the system to decide the entry in the archive most important to the question and position the peruse to begin at that entry. Highlighting has dependably been helpful in Boolean frameworks to demonstrate the reason for the recovery. This is a direct result of the immediate mapping between the terms in the hunt and the terms in the thing. Utilizing Natural Language Processing, programmed development of terms by means of thesauri, and the comparability positioning calculations examined in detail later in this book, highlighting loses some of its esteem The terms being highlighted that brought about a specific thing to be returned might not have immediate or evident mapping to any of the pursuit terms entered. This causes disappointment by the client attempting to think about why a specific thing was recovered and how to utilize that data in reformulating the inquiry proclamation to make it more correct. In a positioning framework distinctive terms can add to various degrees to the choice to recover a thing. The highlighting may fluctuate by presenting hues and powers to demonstrate the relative significance of a specific word in the thing in the choice to recover the thing. Data representation gives off an impression of being a superior show procedure to help with helping the client detail his question than highlights in things.

Miscellaneous Capabilities

There are numerous extra capacities that encourage the client's capacity to input inquiries, lessening the time it takes to produce the questions, and diminishing a priori the likelihood of entering a poor inquiry. Vocabulary peruses gives information on the preparing tokens accessible in the searchable database and their circulation as far as things inside the database. Iterative looking and pursuit history logs condense past hunt exercises by the client permitting access to past outcomes from the present client session. Canned inquiries permit access to questions produced and spared in past client sessions.

METHODS OF INFORMATION RETRIEVAL

This section discusses mainly two methods of IR:

- Text Based Information Retrieval (TBIR).
- Content Based Information Retrieval (CBIR).

Text Based Information Retrieval (TBIR)

It is based on annotations entered by user manually against a query (Alhenshiri, 2010). It can be a keyword and any description of information which retrieved the relevant information in the account of query. Keywords can be a word or phrase which depicts the required content. It is used as a metadata for the description of text, images or any related document (Gobeill et al., 2007). All the result retrieved in TBIR system are generally based on ranking methods of vector space model. To retrieve the desired results (Sagayam et al., 2012), it follows number of steps as shown in Figure 6.

The detailed description of above mentioned steps are as follows in Table 1.

TBIR has some limitations also:

- The retrieved information is extremely subjective.
- It given the large data in the form of results, further it can be irrelevant in respect to the required information.
- Few of the words have multiple meaning so the retrieved information is not accurate.
- It receives inconsistent data because it depends upon user query. It might be different for generated query.
- This method is highly time consuming as well as required more efforts.

Figure 6. Steps of Text Based given Information Retrieval

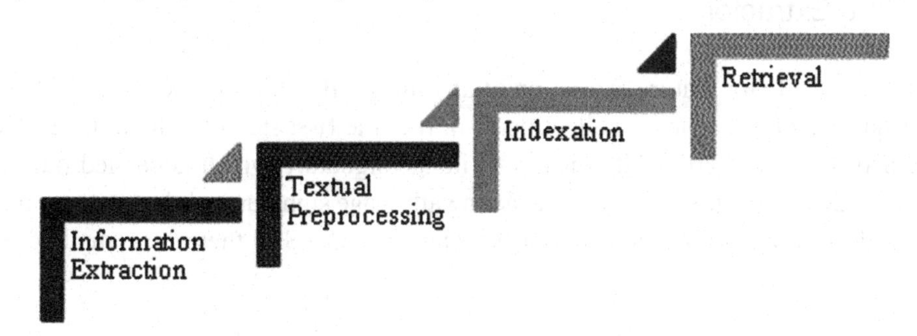

Table 1. Description of TBIR steps

Steps	Step Name	Description
Step-I	Information Extraction	In this step, textual information is selects in any language like English, Hindi, French etc.
Step-II	Textual Preprocessing	It processes the retrieved text by eliminating punctuation marks, semantic empty words and derived words from their stem.
Step-III	Indexation	Using white space analyzer, it indexed the data and differentiates the tokens.
Step-IV	Search	Final information is retrieved in this step after applying ranking.

Content Based Information Retrieval (CBIR)

The problem occurred in TBIR has been resolved in CBIR. In this system, the generated query is content based which is results in consistent data and provides more accurate and efficient results (Gudivada & Raghavan, 1995). Content based query can be classified into two categories: one is text based query and another one is image based query. In text based query user has to put an exact query or description for accurate results. Again it is a time consuming task. In case of image based query, there are number of components which depend on similar kind of image extraction like image feature, color and texture. So basically it is more appropriate for image extraction. The CBIR architecture is shown in Figure 7:

CBIR Working

Basically CBIR system consists of two main components (see figure 8):

- Feature Extractor.
- Similarity Engine.

Feature Extractor

It is responsible for feature extraction of any image. It applies on both ends i.e. on user query and on database collection also. It is the first step of content based IR (Remco & Tanase, 2000). It consists of image signature which is carried out by color, structure and texture. After extracting all image signatures and take it as input for analysis which performed similarity or annotations. Still there is no method or

Figure 7. CBIR Architecture

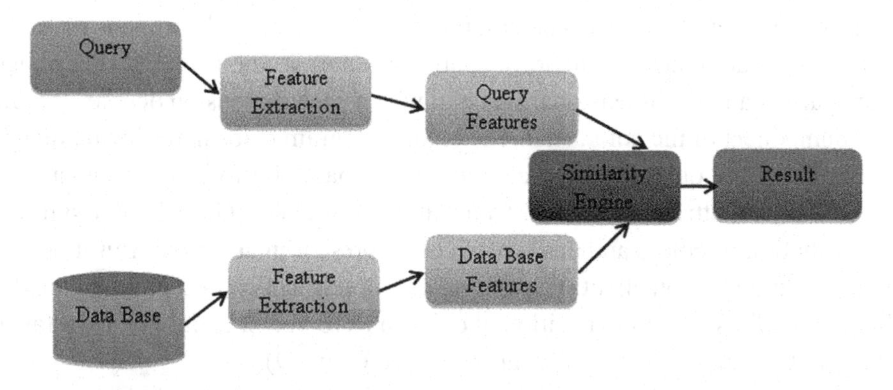

Figure 8. Components of CBIR System

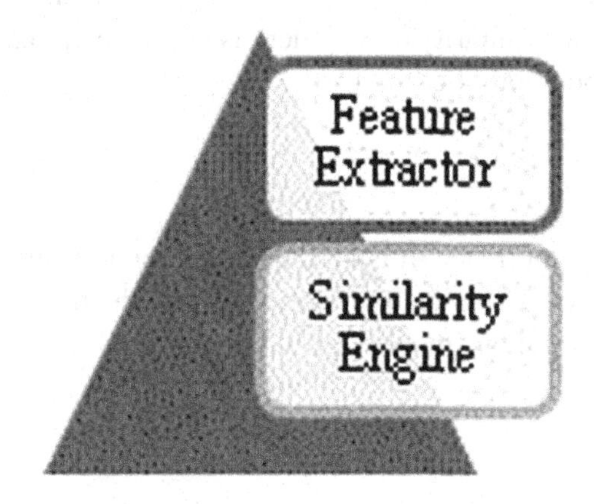

technique has been developed which is used only one feature and provides the accurate result. Combination of all features (Color, Structure and Texture) is required to find out the suitable result. The workings of all these features are detailed as below:

Color

Color is considered as the most directed feature for viewing images. It is mainly used for retrieving similar images. Here, color image can be represented by color space. However RGB space denotes the sum of red, green and grey level intensities. Retrieval system can easily use color moments especially when an image contains the object. Effective and efficient color distribution of the image can be proved by three order diversions i.e. first order for mean, second order for variance and third order for skewness. A color histogram describes the amount of colors present in an image (Ruiet et al., 1999). The color structure descriptor determines the color distribution of an image and its local spatial structure in the form of other image. Color space is a multidimensional space in which each dimension denotes the different component of the color. Also, the color histogram helps in retrieving images by visualizing the quantity of pixels within an image. Further color signature is divided into two attributes: Global Color and Local Color. Global color signifies the distribution of colors and amount of colors present in an image. But it doesn't contain the information about the position of color. Local color represents the distribution of colors as well as position of color in RGB vector form. For an instance, let us take two images having similar color (see Figure 9).

Now compare these two images on the basis of global and local color.

- **Global Color:** Similar images due to same color quantity.
- **Local Color:** No similarity due to there is no overlapping. Henceforth it also considers the position of color also.

Structure

It represents the shape of image. It is defined as the feature surface of an object i.e. as an outline or contour. This feature alone has the identity to make objects recognized and also the similar images can be retrieved on their content basis. Here

Figure 9.

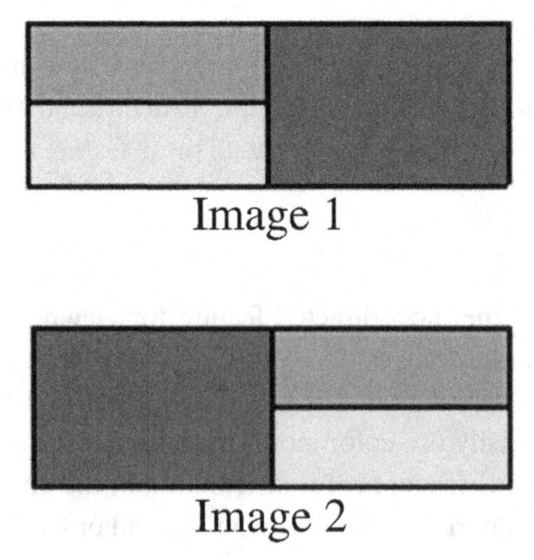

a query can be sent to retrieve an image of similar look. As a result, an image will be shown whose features will closely matches with that query image. This shape feature is closely defined into two ways: global features and local feature. Global feature defines the aspect ratio, circular and moment in variant whereas local feature defines group of consecutive boundary. For example image 1 and image 2 are similar because both have same structure.

Texture

It plays a vital role to separate regions. Various texture representations have been visualized in recognition of pattern and computer vision (Ruiet et al., 1999). Commonly known texture properties are contrast, coarse, directional, regularity and roughness. Texture of two objects can be similar like in fabric and wood. Now see in the next section that how all these signatures will help to find the results in similarity engine.

Similarity Engine

It uses the similarity measure for evaluating the value of query image and collection of images. First of all it calculates the mean of signatures of query image and database images extracted from feature extraction and then it searches the all nearest values images. If the image signatures are matched with in the feature extraction, then it considers only those images in the retrieval system (Nastar et al., 1998). Although, it does not give the exact match but all similar images present in the data base against the query image (Eakins et al., 1998). It represents the result on the basis of visualization. As a result, it gives number of similar image that are ranked.

Detailed view of CBIR is shown in Figure 10.

From the above discussion it has been observed that the problems occurred in the text based information retrieval system have been removed in content based information retrieval system (Frankel et al., 1997). CBIR is the best approach to find the content from web search engine because of many features like semantic gap. It handles all kind of queries whether it is on text based, image based or any other kind of objects. It can also handle the video queries (Chang et al., 1997). In case of query image, it gives efficient results, which will be forwarded to server. It is now very much familiar and applicable in the medical field, forensic science, face recognition, engineering design etc.

Figure 10. Detailed View of CBIR

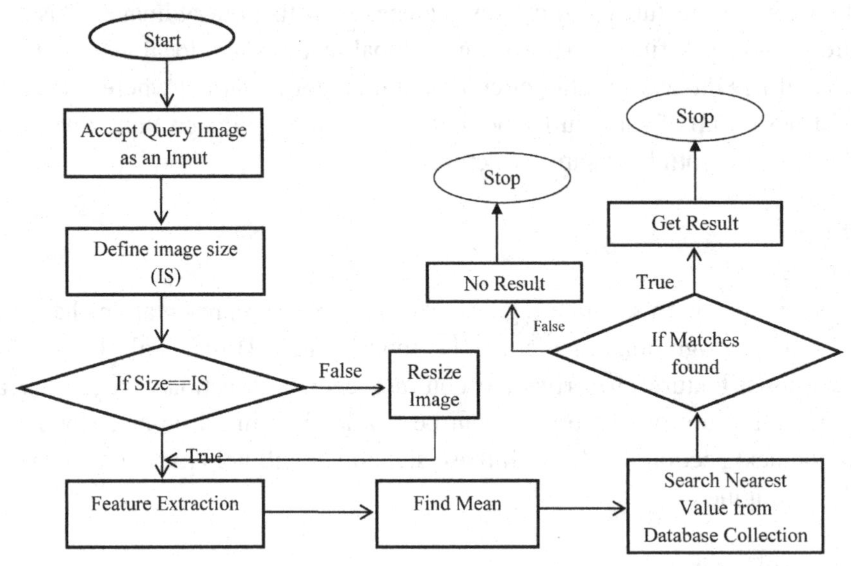

EVALUATION OF IR

To evaluate the effectiveness of information retrieval, there is a standard way of test collection which comprises of mainly three things:

- Documents Collection.
- Query.
- Judgment.

The standard way to deal with information retrieval assessment rotates around the idea of relevant and non-relevant documents. As for a client data require, an archive in the test accumulation is given a double characterization as either important or not. This choice is alluded to as the highest quality level or ground truth judgment of pertinence. The test archive gathering and suite of data needs must be of a sensible size: you have to normal execution over genuinely expansive test sets, as results are exceptionally factor over various reports and data needs. As a dependable guideline, fifty information needs has as a rule been observed to be an adequate least.

Significance is evaluated with respect to a query. For instance, an information may be as:

Information on whether drinking red wine is more viable at diminishing your danger of heart attacks than white wine. This may be converted into an inquiry, for example, wine and red and white and heart and assault and attack.

A record is important on the off chance that it addresses the expressed data require, not on account of it simply happens to contain every one of the words in the question. This qualification is regularly misjudged practically speaking, on the grounds that the information need is not clear. In the event that a client sorts python into a web index, they may need to know where they can buy a pet python. Then again they may need information on the programming language Python. From a single word inquiry, it is exceptionally troublesome for a context to comprehend that what the information need is. However, the client has one, and can judge the returned comes about on the premise of their pertinence to it. To assess a system, we require a basic articulation of an information need, which can be utilized for judging returned records as relevant or nonrelevant.

Numerous systems contain different weights (frequently known as parameters) that can be changed in accordance with tune system execution. It isn't right to report comes about on a test accumulation which were gotten by tuning these parameters to expand execution on that gathering. That is on account of such tuning exaggerates the normal execution of the system, in light of the fact that the weights will be set to boost execution on one specific arrangement of questions as opposed to for an irregular specimen of inquiries. In such cases, the right technique is to have at least one improvement test accumulations, and to tune the parameters on the advancement test gathering. The analyzer then runs the system with those weights on the test gathering and reports the outcomes on that accumulation as an impartial measure of execution.

EVALUATION OF UNRANKED RETRIEVAL SETS

The most standard practice to measure the effectiveness of information retrieval are precision and recall. Precision defined as the ratio between significant documents retrieved to the total document retrieved.

Precision (P) = Significant Documents retrieved / Total Retrieved Documents
Recall is the ration between significant documents retrieved to the total significant documents.
Recall (R)= Significant Documents retrieved / Total Significant Documents

Let us take an example to clear the notions of precision and recall.

Table 2. Notions of Precision and Recall

	Significant	Non Signifcant
Retrieved Documents	True (SRD)	False (NSRD)
Non Retrieved Documents	True (SNRD)	False (NSNRD)

In this case Precision is
P = SRD / (SRD+ NSRD)
R = SRD / (SRD + SNRD)

There is a justifiable reason motivation behind why exactness is not a fitting measure for data recovery issues. In all conditions, the information is to a great degree skewed: typically more than 99.9% of the reports are in the nonrelevant classification. A framework tuned to expand precision can seem to perform well by basically esteeming all archives nonrelevant to all questions. Regardless of the possibility that the framework is very great, attempting to mark a few archives as significant will quite often prompt to a high rate of false positives. Be that as it may, naming all archives as nonrelevant is totally unacceptable to a data recovery framework client. Clients are continually going to need to see a few archives, and can be accepted to have a specific resistance for seeing some false positives giving that they get some helpful data. The measures of exactness and review focus the assessment on the arrival of genuine positives, soliciting what rate from the applicable reports have been found and what number of false positives have likewise been returned.

The benefit of having the two numbers for exactness and review is that one is more critical than the other much of the time. Run of the mill web surfers might want each outcome on the primary page to be pertinent (high exactness) however have not the smallest enthusiasm for knowing not to mention taking a gander at each report that is significant. Interestingly, different expert searchers, for example, paralegals and knowledge examiners are extremely worried with attempting to get as high review as could reasonably be expected, and will endure genuinely low accuracy brings about request to get it. People looking their hard circles are additionally frequently inspired by high review seeks. All things considered, the two amounts plainly exchange off against each other: you can simply get a review of 1 (however low exactness) by recovering all archives for all inquiries! Review is a non-diminishing capacity of the quantity of records recovered. Then again, in a decent framework, exactness normally diminishes as the quantity of records recovered is expanded. When all is said in done we need to get some measure of review while enduring just a specific rate of false positives.

EVALUATION OF RANKED RETRIEVAL RESULTS

Precision and recall are basic methods for evaluation. Moreover they applied on unordered data. Now we have the requirements to evaluate the ranked retrieval system, so it is necessary to extend these measures. In case of ranked retrieval context, suitable set of retrieved documents are listed as first k retrieved documents. Precision and recall curve appears like distinctive curve whenever the (k+1)th retrieved document is non relevant, then recall is same but precision has dropped. If it becomes relevant, then precision and recall increase.

CONCLUSION

This chapter illustrates the study of existing models and methods of information retrieval. Various models (like basic model, Boolean model, vector space model, latent semantic, probabilistic model etc.) have been used to define the query. All have their own pros and cons. It depends what kind of information user wants and at what extent. Professionals are generally using Boolean model to find out exact match. It also discusses the capabilities of IR along with two major methods that have been used for extracting the information. It mainly discusses the text based and content based information retrieval methods. Along with their working, it has been observed that CBIR is more efficient and effective than TBIR and also meets to find out accurate result. Last but not least it exemplifies the evaluation of ranked and unranked retrieval result which retrieved after a query.

REFERENCES

Alhenshiri, A. (2010). Web Information Retrieval and Search Engines Techniques. *Al-Satil Journal*, 55-92.

Anand, D., & Niranjan, D. U. C. (1998). Watermarking Medical Images With Patient Information.*Proceedings of the 20th Annual International Conference of the IEEE Engineering in Medicine and Biology Society*, 703–706.

Balas, V. E., Dey, N., Ashour, A. D., & Pistolla, S. (2016). Image Fusion Incorporating Parameter Estimation Optimized Gaussian Mixture Model And Fuzzy Weighted Evaluation System: A Case Study In Time-Series Plantar Pressure Dataset. IEEE Sensors Journal, 1-15.

Chang, S., Smith, J., Beigi, M., & Benitez, A. (1997). Visual information retrieval from largedistributed online repositories. *Communications of the ACM*, *40*(12), 63–71. doi:10.1145/265563.265573

Christos, F., & Douglas, W. (1995). *A Survey of Information Retrieval and Filtering Methods*. CS-TR-3514.

Dey, N., Samanta, S., Chakraborty, S., Das, A., Chaudhuri, S., & Suri, J. (2014). Firefly Algorithm for Optimization of Scaling Factors during Embedding of Manifold Medical Information: An Application in Ophthalmology Imaging. *Journal of Medical Imaging and Health Informatics*, *4*(3), 384–394. doi:10.1166/jmihi.2014.1265

Eakins, J. P., B, J. M., & Graham, M. E. (1998). Similarity retrieval of trademark images. *IEEE Multimedia Magazine*, 53–63.

Frankel, C., Swain, M., & Athitsos, V. (1996). *WebSeer: An image search engine for the world-wide web*. Technical Report 94-14, Computer Science Department, University of Chicago.

Gobeill, J., Müller, H., & Ruch, P. (2007). Translation by Text Categorization: Medical Image Retrieval. Lecture Notes in Computer Science, 4730, 706-710.

Goker, A., & Davies, J. (2009). Information Retrieval: Searching in the 21st Century. John Wiley and Sons, Ltd.

Gudivada, V. N., & Raghavan, V. V. (1995). Content-based image retrieval systems. *IEEE Computer*, *28*(9), 18–31. doi:10.1109/2.410145

Hiemstra, D., Arjen, P., & Vries, D. (2000). Relating the new languagemodels of information retrieval to the traditional retrieval models. CTIT technical report TR-CTIT.

Kodi, T., Kumari, G. R. N., & Perumal, S. M. (2016). Review of CBIR Related with Low Level and High Level Features. *International Journal of Synthetic Emotions*, *7*(1), 27–40. doi:10.4018/IJSE.2016010103

Le, D. N., Dey, N., & Nguyen, G. N. (2017). Machine Learning In Medical Imaging And Health Informatics. *Journal of Medical Imaging and Health Informatics*.

Meier, R., & Lee, D. (2009). Context-Aware Services for Ambient Environments (2009). *International Journal of Ambient Computing and Intelligence*, *1*(1), 1–14. doi:10.4018/jaci.2009010101

Michael, S. L., Huijsmans, D. P., & Denteneer, D. (1996). *Content based image retrieval: KLT, projections, or templates*. Amsterdam University Press.

Mokhtar, S. B., Raverrdy, P. G., Urbieta, A., & Cardoso, R. S. (2008). Interoperable Semantic and Syntactic Service for Ambient Computing Environment. Proceeding of Adhoc AMC.

Mukherjea, S., Hirata, K., & Hara, Y. (1997). Towards a multimedia world-wide web information retrieval engine. *Proceedings of the 6th International World-Wide Web Conference*, 177-188. doi:10.1016/S0169-7552(97)00046-9

Nastar, C., Mitschke, M., Meilhac, C., & Boujemaa, N. (1998). A flexible content-based image retrieval system. Proceedings of the ACM International Multimedia Conference, 339–344.

Odella, F. (2016). Technology Studies and the Sociological Debate on Monitoring of Social Interactions. *International Journal of Ambient Computing and Intelligence*, *7*(1), 411–423. doi:10.4018/IJACI.2016010101

Remco, C. V., & Tanase, M. (2000). *Content-based image retrieval systems: A survey.* Technical Report UU-CS-2000-34, Utrecht University, Department of Computer Science.

Rijsbergen, C. V. (1979). *Information Retrieval.* London: Butterworths.

Rocchio, J. J. (2010). *Relevance feedback in information.* The SMART Retrieval System, Experiments in Automatic Document Processing.

Rui, Y., Thomas, S. H., & Shih, F. C. (1999). Image retrieval: Currenttechniques, promising directions and open issues. *Journal of Visual Communication and Image Representation*, *10*(1), 1–23. doi:10.1006/jvci.1999.0413

Sagayam, R., Srinivasan, S., & Roshni, S. (2012). A Survey of Text Mining:Retrieval, Extraction and Indexing Techniques. *IJCER*, *2*(5), 1443–1444.

Salton, G., & Buckley, C. (1998). Term weighting approaches in automatic text retrieval. *Information Processing & Management*, *24*(5), 513–523. doi:10.1016/0306-4573(88)90021-0

Salton, G., & McGill, M. (1983). *Introduction to Modern Information Retrieval.* McGraw-Hill.

Santofimia, M., Toro, X., & Villanueva, F. (2012). A Rule-Based Approach to Automatic Service Composition. *International Journal of Ambient Computing and Intelligence*, *4*(1), 16–28. doi:10.4018/jaci.2012010102

Sosnin, P. (n.d.). Precedent-Oriented Approach to Conceptually Experimental Activity in Designing the Software Intensive Systems. *A Computational Model for Texture Analysis in Images with Fractional Differential Filter for Texture Detection*, *7*(1), 69-93.

Section 2
Associating Semantics With Information

Chapter 4
Technique for Transformation of Data From RDB to XML Then to RDF

Kaleem Razzaq Malik
University of Engineering and Technology Lahore, Pakistan

Tauqir Ahmad
University of Engineering and Technology Lahore, Pakistan

ABSTRACT

This chapter will clearly show the need for better mapping techniques for Relational Database (RDB) all the way to Resource Description Framework (RDF). This includes coverage of each data model limitations and benefits for getting better results. Here, each form of data being transform has its own importance in the field of data science. As RDB is well known back end storage for information used to many kinds of applications; especially the web, desktop, remote, embedded, and network-based applications. Whereas, EXtensible Markup Language (XML) in the well-known standard for data for transferring among all computer related resources regardless of their type, shape, place, capability and capacity due to its form is in application understandable form. Finally, semantically enriched and simple of available in Semantic Web is RDF. This comes handy when with the use of linked data to get intelligent inference better and efficient. Multiple Algorithms are built to support this system experiments and proving its true nature of the study.

DOI: 10.4018/978-1-5225-2483-0.ch004

INTRODUCTION

Transformation of data depends on data models along with their limitations and dependencies. Data modeling plays the most crucial part for all what we see around us even in business, government, economics, social and daily life entities for analyzing facts and producing results. Data models like hierarchal, network and relational have their own importance and long history. But above all others relational data model gained its importance due to its record keeping capabilities along with maintaining the data integrity. Due to which majority of data found in the world are kept and stored in Relational Database (RDB). A relation in RDB is build-up on a combination of rows and columns where each cell represents a single piece of information titled under a field. A field represents a column and a row represents an instance of record concerning current relation in a table. Data model of RDB is a combination of the datatype, constraint, and functional dependency on data (Codd, 1970). Information concerning each element of data against a relation is kept in the form of the schema (structure defined for data to be stored in a relation) and data values (actual literals stored in table cells). In web, RDB is used at backend for storage of data. Inventions like the internet in networking imposed the need of intermediate language which can make data supported among all systems attached nearby. Which also brought the creation of XML as an intermediate language. Having said so, it became most common language after 0's and 1's bits, which actually are close to machine with high-level understanding and interpretation, used as machine-processable language. Support of data types among RDB, XML, and RDF during mapping play necessary role when trying to transforming one's data model into another. Customization of data types are possible in XML Schema (XMLS) (Biron, Malhotra, & Consortium, 2004).

When it comes to importance, XML as a standard for the data transformation is commonly and majorly used among applications, devices, operating systems and computers. For the Web as HTML rules are built in XML and XML is a language freely customizable by other to support their data in any other electrical network supported device. Which makes it more and more useful all over where remote access to data comes. Now almost all smart devices support XML. This is the reason that's why XML became most famed and well-known standard for data-based communication all around the World. Whereas, a web page is less organized and semi-structured while making searching of data complicated and more inaccurate (Rusu et al., 2013). In web, for searching and accessing resources like people, videos, audios, and images etc. search engines are used as a tool on the web (Hepp, Leymann, Domingue, Wahler, & Fensel, 2005). Despite gradual improvement introduced in these search engines, a dramatic increase in the volume of web contents produces loss of technological improvements. To resolve this issue, representation of web contents are required to be transformed into machine processable format. Semantic

Web (SW) has introduced machine processable form with the help of Resource Description Framework (RDF) (Antoniou & Van Harmelen, 2004).

SW has gained a large fame due to its capability of enhanced methods and intelligent data seeking mechanisms which made it a great innovation in next generation of the web. Different transformation models and techniques are introduced to transform web contents mapped up into SW (Pham Thi Thu Thuy, Lee, & Lee, 2009; Pham Thu Thi Thuy, Lee, Lee, & Jeong, 2007, 2008; Van Deursen, Poppe, Martens, Mannens, & Walle, 2008). RDF is a language to show data in the form of triples; subject, predicate and object forming a statement in SW (Manola, Miller, & McBride, 2004). Furthermore, different graph representations are introduced for SW based data. SW have a big impact on data in producing hierarchal relationship by mapping resources used in graph-based representation. This SW graph based data representation formats for RDF include JSON, Turtle, RDF/XML, RDFa, and TriG (Manola et al., 2004). Whereas, RDF/XML is the most commonly used representation due to its capability to exchange data among computers, operating systems, and applications. RDF/XML is built upon on XML as its name also suggests. Whereas, RDF/XML as built-up on XML is complex than JSON, Turtle, and N-Triple data representatives but commonly adaptive due to it's adaptive and compatible nature due to XML (Manola et al., 2004). Improvements in RDF did lead us to OWL language which was actually inclusion of constraints and inference elements in RDF. This made language somewhat complex and less compatible and more specialized for machine learning purposes only. This was not the actual cause or only cause of its existence. So, new and hot research concepts like Big-Data did make use of Semantic Web data model but at the basic level which is RDF due to its less complex nature of data representation.

For data to move from one paradigm to another basing on different data models requires a careful transforming mechanism. To do so it becomes necessary to transform one data form into another. This transformation process starts with mapping each data model similar and variant features. Making it necessarily to overcome any deficiencies found on either side of at the process of transformation. This is why change made by various transformation methods and tools neglect backing each other at their maximum level for data to be compatible for use among RDB, XML, and RDF. It's essential to investigate diverse abilities of information sorts bolstered by XML either by DTD or XMLS alongside their constraints. In this study, data models of RDB and RDF are being transformed by the use of mapping each other's capabilities and limitations (Pham Thi Thu Thuy et al., 2009; Pham Thu Thi Thuy et al., 2007, 2008; Van Deursen et al., 2008). Whereas, data and meta-data both are needed to keep track of each data model limitations and capabilities.

BACKGROUND

The main part of information and data found on the Web are majorly being recovered and stored with the use of Relational Database Management System (RDBMS). Relational database is composed of relational data model (Codd, 1970). A data model is defined by its structure, constraints and functional support. Constraints like primary key and foreign key for defining data uniqueness and relationship among supporting contents of a relation. Transforming relational data model into semantic web based data model requires careful mapping to both models. Many methods and tools have been presented to help by providing the ways to explore relational data transformation to become compatible to Semantic Web based systems (Ravindra & Anyanwu, 2014). Whereas, transformation process attempts to map two different data models to come to an agreement. Some of the state of art techniques introduced for transformation include Direct Mapping, R2O, eD2R, Relational.OWL, D2RQ, Triplify, R2RML, and R3M (Sahoo et al., 2009). Yet, there exist problems in clearly gaining results with high performance and compatibility (Hert, Reif, & Gall, 2011; Sahoo et al., 2009; Spanos, Stavrou, & Mitrou, 2012). Different researchers have attempted different approaches to achieve the required outcome of reaching to a next generation web that is the Semantic Web. Diverse data analysts have worked with distinctive ways; to overcome the difficulties, and to satisfy the required results, through the use of cutting edge web technology that is Semantic Web.

Generally, in Web applications data is stored in the form of Relational Database (RDB). When same data is transformed from RDB to Semantic Web (SW) based system then compatibility issues arise. It requires looking into the weaknesses generated during the transformation process from RDB into the SW. For evolving data keeping changes intact is hard and difficult to sustain. To achieve this, data mapping can be used to understand their differences at the level of data types. Then mapping is done using Extensible Markup Language (XML) based data structure as their intermediate data presenter. The main focus of this study is to map up common features found in both data models of RDB and SW based schema using either form of XML like Document Type Definition (DTD) or Extensible Markup Language Schema (XMLS) as an intermediate which will help in improving transformation results. These data mappings can further help in gaining better compatibility options for data transformation.

The study on Semantic Web data model using RDF shows that efforts done for collaboration with different fields extended its use beyond the Web (Hepp et al., 2005). The standard which is known as XML gives labels as tags to the web. However, XML documents are composed using schema as rules created utilizing either XMLS or DTD. This intermediate form of data is used for changing relational data composition into RDF schema and RDF based data. We need to do it mostly as relational data transformed into XML and after that XML schema and data transformed further into RDF. Mapping can be done from RDB to RDF either by direct or indirect methods. Indirect methods like RDB to RDF Mapping Language (R2RML) involves table mapping from RDB to RDF without intermediate utilization of XML. Other indirect methods are about transforming schema from RDB to RDF using XML. XML schema can be either in the DTD or XML (Hert et al., 2011; Sahoo et al., 2009; Spanos et al., 2012). Which is focusing on indirect methods based mapping. Transformation of data and schema from RDB to RDF found in form of either direct or indirect mode. In direct techniques like R2RML includes table mapping from RDB to RDF without using XML as intermediate for transformation process. Other strategies based on indirect transformation are about changing mapping from RDB to RDF utilizing XML. This study is concentrates on different methods for transformation along with our proposed model. Improved methods, algorithms and newly introduced tools being acquainted with help of the approaches to investigate relational data in enabling systems to work with Semantic Web (Ravindra & Anyanwu, 2014). Yet, there exist issues in obviously picking up results with better compatibility and performance when transforming data from RDB to RDF (Hert et al., 2011; Sahoo et al., 2009; Spanos et al., 2012).

For transforming a database schema into the Document Type Definition (DTD) and then into Resource Description Framework Schema (RDFS) either partially or completely can give less opportunities for data analysis. DTDs at the end of XML document have limited possibilities for the web data structure to be transformed and then mapped into RDF schema. Whereas, the well-known standard which is XMLS provides highly customization to XML based document's tags for the web. Where semi-structured and user defined, and predefine tags are stored. Though, the XML document is written either using XML schema or DTD (Biron et al., 2004). So, for transforming a relational schema into RDF schema, we have to do it partially as relational schema into XML schema and then XML schema into RDF schema or relational into DTD and then DTD into RDF schema. After that transforming it back into its original form of relational schema. By looking into tags available in the XML document to pick better suitable tags for the satisfying role as class or property (Pham Thu Thi Thuy et al., 2007). On the other hand, XML documents can be updated to gain capability of being interpreted as RDF. It would be better if the XML's original structure remains unchanged and transformation process better results and coverage of the developed technique (Bohannon, Fan, Flaster, & Narayan, 2005; Martens, Neven, Schwentick, & Bex, 2006; Shah, Adeniyi, & Al Tuwairqi, 2005; Pham Thu Thi Thuy et al., 2008).

There have been endeavors made for changing a database composition into the Document Type Definition (DTD) and afterward into Resource Description Framework Schema (RDFS) either incompletely or totally. DTDs toward the end of XML record for the web can be changed and mapped into RDF pattern. By investigating labels accessible in XML archive to pick better suitable labels for the wonderful part as class or property. Then again, XML records can be upgraded to pick up ability of being deciphered as RDF. It would be better if XML's unique structure stays unaltered and change prepare better results and scope of the created strategy. Inside and out, assets connecting among database, DTD and RDF is by utilizing questions without changing setting and importance of online information to frame its semantic presence. These methodologies can be caught to get a solitary side change approach. Other than these distinctions the significant one is that every asset in RDF are allotted a novel URI for distinguishing proof. Along these lines, data in both of these semantic based expressions is given a state of triples.

There have been attempts made for transforming a database schema into the Document Type Definition (DTD) and then into Resource Description Framework Schema (RDFS) either partially or completely. DTDs at the end of XML document for the web can be transformed and mapped into RDF schema. The standard which is known as XML document provides tags for the web. Where semi-structured and user defined, and predefine tags are stored. Though, the XML document is written either using XML schema or DTD (Biron et al., 2004). So, for transforming a relational schema into RDF schema, we have to do it partially as relational schema into XML schema and then XML schema into RDF schema or relational into DTD and then DTD into RDF schema. After that transforming it back into its original form of relational schema. By looking into tags available in the XML document to pick better suitable tags for the satisfying role as class or property (Pham Thu Thi Thuy et al., 2007). On the other hand, XML documents can be updated to gain capability of being interpreted as RDF. It would be better if the XML's original structure remains unchanged and transformation process better results and coverage of the developed technique (Bohannon et al., 2005; Martens et al., 2006; Shah et al., 2005; Pham Thu Thi Thuy et al., 2008).

This study can help to reduce complexity and compatibility issues for the process of transformation. As complexity and compatibility issues arise due to database schemas and ontologies are evolving at a constant speed to map with application and user requirements. Therefore, instead of mapping being redefined from scratch it should evolve on top (Spanos et al., 2012). The update statement concerning RDF stores is still under progress and its semantics are not yet well defined, and uncertainty remains concerned about the transformation of few SPARQL (SPARQL Protocol and RDF Query Language) Update statements. Only elementary (attribute-to-property & relation-to-class) mappings have been studied up to now. The problem of modifying relational data using SPARQL Update is the same as to view update problem the classic database (Grobe, 2009; Spanos et al., 2012; Zaveri, Maurino, & Equille, 2014).

It is thought that one cause for the delay in the recognition of the Semantic Web is the deficiency of application and tools showing benefits of semantic web technology. The success depends of large amount of data concerning semantic web of these tools. Because relational databases are considered as highly used medium for storage of data on web. The solution was to automatic manage mass of data in SW form as RDF. We have studied the transformation model from relational DB to RDF and currently used storage mechanism of RDF stores in RDB. It is important to map existing relational representation among relational schema, DTD, XML schema, and RDFS (Biron et al., 2004; Decker et al., 2000; Fallside & Walmsley, 2004). Proposed study of above mentioned problem situation is possible through mapping of differences at schema level, enriching the DB contents on web based mapping results and identifying grey areas.

We have considered the change model from social DB to RDF and as of now utilized stockpiling instrument of RDF stores in RDB. It is critical to delineate social representation among social diagram, DTD, XML composition, and RDFS. Proposed study for aforementioned issue circumstance is conceivable through mapping of contrasts at pattern level, enhancing the DB substance on electronic mapping comes about and distinguishing hazy areas.

TRANSFORMATION TECHNIQUE

Web has been used as a common medium for applications to run regardless of Operating System and type of device. Structure of a web page is followed using w3c rules built in XML. XML has capability of introducing customized tags readable by machine for further utilization in any sort of application. XML is now used as a standard and common language when transforming data from one entity to another in the field of computer science. This entity can be a device, application, embedded software and web based sources and services. XML based data can be taken from Relational DB. Whereas, relational DB is a collection of relations (tables) built up on the relational data model. Transformation of data from one data model of Relational Database (RDB) into another data model of Semantic Web (SW) has rare chances of covering every aspect. For this reason, a careful mapping of data models is required to support systems using data, passed through transformation process, to keep on working as they are intended. Now, consider this transformation to be bidirectional. Bidirectional transformation process will come with high complexity level as of covering both end of data models. This required keep track of each and every feature required during the process of bidirectional transformation. Tracking information as metadata for data being transformed will require to induce new mechanism to achieve better outcomes.

Transformation technique proposed in this study starts with introducing a model to show stepwise coverage of data transformation from one data model into another comes with its limitations. Then mapping between different data models are compared and represented with their alternatives. Then the process of transformation using XMLS is given with the use of algorithms. A control experiment presented to show that how transformation works and on the bases of that results are given.

Transformation Model

At the point when attempting to be more in control change (as appeared in Figure 1) is required then RDB Schema to XML Schema and afterward into XML Schema will work fine as these accompany rich interface to change up to the need. Among semi-organized information which has wealthier methodology is better because of as being enhanced to increase better results and future needs.

At that point in Figure 2 is a complete procedure of how transformation is being performed through indicating info through flow chart for our experiment work. Through connection string, connection with database is established. Then a query is executed to read metadata of database that include names of all tables defined within relational database. The table name list is stored within array list for future use. Now second phase of transformation is to read data / tuples / values from database tables and write it in XML file according to World Wide Web Consortium (W3C) defined rules. This transformation also contains two sub task that are reading from database and write records in XML file.

Important steps in the process of transformation from one data form into another.

Step 1: Developed a container data model before starting a transformation.
Step 2: Understand all possible constraints which are required to be captured.

Figure 1. Looking at the nature of Transformation by following DTD or XMLS

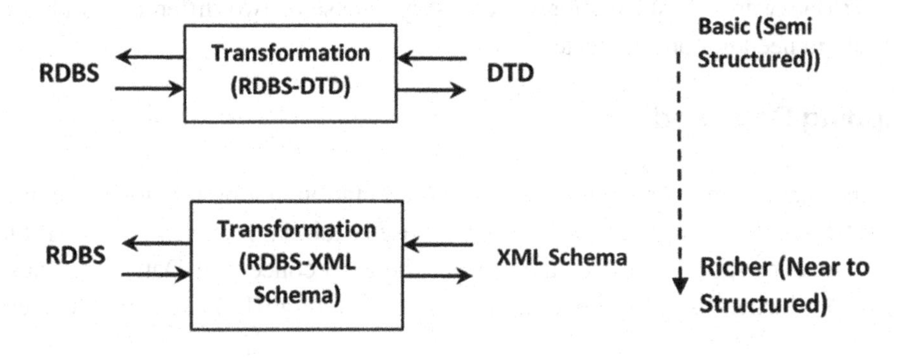

Figure 2. Complete Process of Transformation

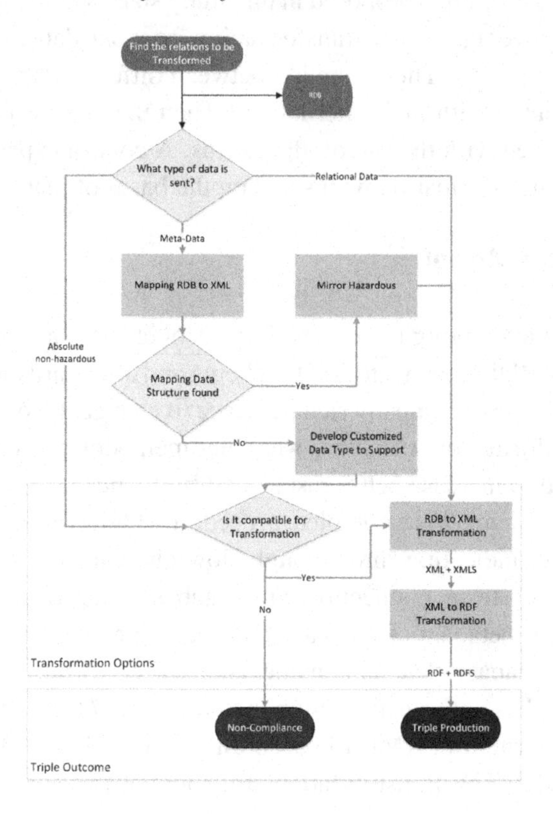

Step 3: Build up a plan of how to integrate two different platforms e.g. DB and XML or XML and RDF.

Step 4: Devise resolutions to the issues arising due to compatibilities and limitations.

a. Create your own solution to overcome such an issue.

Step 5: Each transformation needs to be validated

Step 6: Take care of results by becoming able to fu.rther process according to the suggested model.

Step 7: Backward transformation is necessary in case of two different paradigms are in need to communicate.

Mapping Data Models

It is important to map existing relational representation among relational schema, DTD, XML Schema, and RDFS. So, we have used a tabular representation in Table 1 to show corresponding Schema entity for the each concept of Database. These entities are further used for proper transformation among RDB and semantic web.

Table 1. Syntax and Semantic Comparison

Term	Relational Schema	XML Schema	RDFS
Table	Table_Name	Complex type element	Class
Field	Field_Name	Element	Rdf:Property
Cardinality	Field(>=0)	Restriction(Pattern)	owl:restriction
Cardinality	Field(>0)	Restriction(Pattern)	owl:restriction
Referencing	Field	Simple type element Ref xs:keyref	domain (Property)
Primary Key	Field	xs:key	Range (Property)
Composite key		xs:key	Rdfs:subPropertyOf
Data type	Field	Type	Type

The major difference which is not visible in the table is that each resource in RDF are assigned a unique URI for identification. So, information in both of these semantic based expressions is given a shape of triples.

For our research to work accurately only those documents which have followed mapping table and implementation rules through given cases will be able to give results of bidirectional transformation from RDBS to RDFS. Whereas Table 2 shows what features a technology being used can support us in our work along with their limitations.

Table 2. Showing capabilities of data models used in transformation process

Features	RDBS	XML Schema	RDFS
Referential Resource Identifier	✓	✓	✓
Unique Identifier	✓	✓	✓
Composite Unique Identifiers	✓	✓	✓
Enclosed Lists	✓	✓	
Formal Semantics			✓
Inheritance			✓
Datatypes	✓	✓	✓
Constraints	✓	✓	
Cardinality constrains	✓	✓	

Cases Involved

Following cases discussed in two phases are concerned with the logic of transforming from RDB to XML Schema/DTD and then XML Schema/DTD to RDFS whereas each case is focusing on the symbols or keywords within mapping of elements and when if they appear then what they would mean during implementation phase of this research work.

Phase I (Transforming from RDB to XML)

RDB Schema to XML Schema

Case 1: Attribute in XML Schema can be used to represent primary key of the table for RDB forcing uniqueness through use="required".

Case 2: Simple element having ref as reference to another element is representing a refrence key of a relation.

Case 3: Sequence in complex element represents different attributes of RDB table whereas table is represented by the element itself.

Case 4: If elements are placed within the parenthesis, can be more than one separated by comma, means are sub child of the parent node element.

Case 5: But type for example xs="string" in XML Schema is representing the data type of the field which in this case can only be varChar without showing the length of that field in RDB (which can be solved using pattern defined for related element type).

Phase II (Transforming from XML to Web Semantic)

XML Schema to RDF Schema

Case 1: As table belongs to a database file so it can become a class for DB.

Case 2: Property of a class shows an attribute of a relation being declared as an instance instead of schema due to its nature of change along with the scenario but table remains the same.

Now we can move toward the implementation section as the needed information related to technologies being used are being introduced up-to needed level of detail.

Algorithms

Phases represented in the form of cases are being implemented in the form of two algorithms. One working with process of transformation to tackle changing RDB data form into XML and XMLS form. And the other algorithm is covering transformation process of XML based data into RDF and RDFS form. Each of these algorithms can further be divided into two portions one mapping of data models and other is the transforming data into the required format. Here, data and meta-data both are transform with careful caring for any data and information loss. To see its capability and resourcefulness in chapter a case study on NLP based DB is done. This shows that this techniques and methodology can be a fruitful resource to reform any kind of data found in RDB form. Let's begin with the Algorithm 1 and its implementation.

Given Algorithm 1 represents an effective method to resolve transformation from RDBS into XMLS. Initially, this algorithm take input from given DB and scans for available relations and meta-data on relations. Beginning from taking input from RDB computation starts and eventually continues by producing resulting schema for XML to be built on. The transition from relations to tags keeps on happening depending on input.

After then, a loop is executed that will execute until we read names of all tables in it. Within this loop, we are getting some basic information about table that include minimum and maximum occurrences in said table along with information of key elements that include information about primary key / composite key of the table and foreign key constraints. This information is also forwarded to a list of string type. After reading basic information of table names. A loop is started that pick names of table one by one from the list. A query is executed to fetch record set of table (all tuples in this table) along with some basic information regarding column names and their data type. We introduce one more loop within that to read fetched information of column of focused table. If value is of integer type then it is type casted to store as string. All this information is also stored in ArrayList for future use to write XML file. This information is also forwarded to a list of string type.

Typically, by incorporation from W3C rules for XML based tagging along with mapping rules defined in this study output is reform from each tuple. Algorithm can be divided into following sections:

- Undertaking of RDB relation.
- Defining element tag for each relation.
- Grabbing and keeping track of each information of all tuples concerning.
- Tracking keys and reference key used for uniqueness identification information in a relation and then recoding them in separate tags.

Algorithm 1. Transformation from RDBS to XML Schema

```
Input: RDBS Document
Output: XSD Document (XML Schema)
Begin
Build Tag <?xml version="1.0" encoding="UTF-8" ?>
Build Tag <xs:schema xmlns= http://www.w3.org/2001/XMLSchema elementFormDefault="qualified" attributeFormDefault="unquali
fied">
Select RDBS from the document
Make XML Document.name as RDBS.name
Suppose RDBS has total n table's schemas in it
Loop For i = 1 to n do
Select table_i.name from RDBS
Make table_i.name as elementi.name under XML document
Build Tag <xs:element name="table_i.name">
Suppose table_i.name has total m fields in it
Build Tag <xs:complextype>
Build Tag <xs:sequence>
Build Variable string pArray[] and int pCount = 0 //for primary [composite] key and counting
Build Variable string fArray[] and int fCount = 0 //for foreign keys and counting
Inner Loop For j = 1 to m do
Select field_j of table_i
/*under [] brackets written properties are optional, use if needed*/
Build Tag <xs:element name="field_j.name" [nillable="true" minOccurs="0" maxOccurs="unbounded"] >

Build Tag <xs:simpleType>
/* xs:xmltype can be either equal to xs:int, xs:string, and xs:dateTime etc.*/
Make field_j equal to base property mapped to xml type xs:xmltype equally mapped to field_j.datatype
Build Tag <xs:restriction base="xs:xmltype" >
/* Following conditions are for testing data type constraints*/
Condition IF xs:xmltype is xs:dateTime
Build Tag <xs:minInclusive value="0100-01-01T00:00:00">
Build Tag <xs:maxInclusive value="9999-12-31T23:59:59">
Build Tag <xs:pattern value="\p{Nd}{4}-\p{Nd}{2}-\p{Nd}{2}T\p{Nd}{2}:\p{Nd}{2}:\p{Nd}{2}"/>
Condition Else
/*here temporary variables minLen, maxLen, minValue and maxValue are representative of minimum and maximum value contained for
corresponding data type constraint */
/*under [] brackets written restrictions are optional, use if needed*/
[Build Tag <xs:minInclusive value=minValue>]
[Build Tag <xs:maxInclusive value=maxValue>]
[Build Tag <xs:minLength value=minLen>]
[Build Tag <xs:maxLength value=maxLen>]
End IF

/* Following conditions are for testing primary [composite] key and foreign keys*/
Condition IF field_j is primary key
/*save value of field_j.name in pCount iteration of pArray array variable*/
Assign Array Value pArray[pCount] = field_j.name
Add one to pCount
Condition Else IF field_j is foreign key
/*save value of field_j.tableName, foreign key own table name to whom it is primary key, in fCount iteration of fArray array variable*/
Assign Array Value fArray[fCount] = field_j.tableName
Add one to fCount
End IF
End Inner Loop
Inner Loop For k = 1 to fCount-1
Build Tag <xs: element ref= fArray[k] minOccurs="0" maxOccurs="unbounded"/>
End Inner Loop
Build Tag </xs:sequence>
Build Tag </xs:complextype>
Inner Loop For k = 1 to pCount
Build Tag <xs:key name=table_i.name+"_PrimaryKey_"+k>
Build Tag <xs:selector xpath="."/>
Build Tag <xs:field xpath= pArray[k] />
Build Tag </xs:key>
End Inner Loop
Condition IF pCount == 1
Inner Loop For k = 1 to fCount
Build Tag <xs:keyref name= fArray[k-1] +"_ForeignKey_"+k refer= table_i.name+"_PrimaryKey_"+1 >
Build Tag <xs:selector xpath= fArray[k-1] />
Build Tag <xs:field xpath= pArray[0] />
Build Tag </xs:key>
End Inner Loop
End IF
End Loop
Build Tag </xs:schema>
End
```

In Algorithm 2 while reading information of XSD, we introduce three loops used to traverse XML schema. Two inner loops are used. One is used for reading columns and constraints of a table while second is used to find out keys in this table.

Hence, after executing this nested loop, at end we are able to have all information regarding our defined elements, their defined attributes along with constraints applied on these.

CASE STUDY

There are several NLP techniques in use. Different tools in the market have built-in natural language processing techniques either for developing XML, RDFs and making semantic clouds. Artificial Intelligence is also being applied to easily process natural language. Considerations in this study will be to decrease the computational efforts in terms of natural language processing. Our developed service / program will take natural language as an input and convert it in Lexicons with the help of WordNet Synsets. It will automatically be converted to XML and RDF through the use of multi-agents. Agents are able to communicate with each other and act as collaborative agents. XML and RDF are according to standards defined by W3Cand end results obtained will be in the form of triples comprised of Subject, Object, and Predicate. As shown in Table 3 comparison of elements like central component, user, linkage and vocabulary between simple Web and Semantic Web.

For implementation of case study, Java[1] NetBeans[2] 8.2 is used having JDK 7. WordNet packages is imported in NetBeans to use services of WordNet to get Synsets. Java based technologies are selected due to its strong features of object oriented language, portability, multi-platform support, secure and of course freely available to use. Some famous relational database management systems (RDBMSs) are Microsoft SQL Server, Oracle, Sybase, IBM DB2, Informix, PostgreSQL and MySQL. For this case study RDB used is MySQL[3].

First phase of transformation is started with user input that is actually a string. When system receives an input, this is converted into tags / Synsets considered as very first transformation task. Meanwhile, system of WordNet is activated to get their respective tag / lexicon, then its core responsibility of function is to save these lexicons in their respective table of relational database named as "mydb". Second phase of transformation is to read data / tuples / values from database tables and write it in XML file using implementation following Algorithm 1 defined in previous section. Third and last but important phase of transformation of thesis study is to transform XSD and XML into Resource Description Framework (RDF) schema and RDF file using Algorithm 2. Extension of RDF schema and RDF file is same as *.RDF.

Algorithm 2. Transformation from XML Schema to RDFS

Input: XML Document (XML Schema)
Output: RDFS Triples
Begin
Select XML Document.name from the document
Build Triple XML Document.name rdfs:Class rdf:resource
/* here dot symbol shows property of the document selected*/
Suppose XML Document has total n complex elements in it
Loop For i = 1 to n do
Select $element_i$ **from XML Document**
Selected Tag <xs:$element_i$ *name=” $element_i$.name”*>
/*i-th element of complex type*/
Make Triple XML Document.name rdf:Type rdfs:Class
Make Triple $element_i$*.name* **rdf:Type rdfs:Class**
Make Triple $element_i$*.name* **rdf:subClassOf XML Document.name**
Suppose $element_i$ **has total m sub elements in its sequence tag**
Inner Loop For j = 1 to m do
Select $sub\text{-}element_j$ **of** $element_i$
Make Triple $element_i$*.name* **rdf:Property** $sub\text{-}element_j$*.name*
Make Triple $sub\text{-}element_j$*.name* **rdfs:domain** $element_i$*.name*
Make Triple $sub\text{-}element_j$*.name* **rdfs:range rdfs:Literal**
Make Triple $sub\text{-}element_j$*.name* **rdfs:DataType** $sub\text{-}element_j$*.type*
Suppose $sub\text{-}element_j$ **has q tags under** ***xs:restriction*** **tag**
Inner Loop For l = 1 to q do
/* tag represents inner tag depending on what element *xs:restriction* contains among *xs:minInclusive, xs:maxInclusive, xs:minLength* and *xs:maxLength/**
Switch tag_l
Case: *xs:minInclusive*
Make Triple $sub\text{-}element_j$*.name* **owl:minCardinality** tag_l*.value*
Make Triple $sub\text{-}element_j$*.name* **rdfs:comment “xs:minInclusive”**
Case: *xs:maxInclusive*
Make Triple $sub\text{-}element_j$*.name* **owl:maxCardinality** tag_l*.value*
Make Triple $sub\text{-}element_j$*.name* **rdfs:comment “xs:maxInclusive”**
Case: *xs:minLength*
Make Triple $sub\text{-}element_j$*.name* **owl:minCardinality** tag_l*.value*
Make Triple $sub\text{-}element_j$*.name* **rdfs:comment “xs:minLength”**
Case: *xs:maxLength*
Make Triple $sub\text{-}element_j$*.name* **owl:maxCardinality** tag_l*.value*
Make Triple $sub\text{-}element_j$*.name* **rdfs:comment “xs:maxLength”**
End Inner Loop
Suppose $element_i$ **has total p *xs:key* and** $xs{:}keyref_k$ **in it**
Inner Loop For k = 1 to p do
Condition IF $xs{:}key_k$.
/*equivalent to the tag <xs:key name=*$table_i$.name*+”_PrimaryKey_”+count>*/
Make Triple $xs{:}key_k$*.field.xpath* **rdfs:isDefinedBy** $element_i$*.name*
Make Triple $xs{:}key_k$*.field.xpath* **rdfs:subPropertyOf** $element_i$*.name*
Condition Else IF $xs{:}keyref_k$
/*equivalent to the tag <xs:keyref name= *fArray[k-1]* +”_ForeignKey_”+count refer= *$table_i$.name*+”_PrimaryKey_”+1 >*/
Make Triple $xs{:}keyref_k$*.field.xpath* **rdfs:isDefinedBy** $element_i$*.name*
Make Triple $xs{:}keyref_k$*.field.xpath* **rdfs:subPropertyOf** $xs{:}keyref_k$*.selector.xpath*
End IF
End Inner Loop
End Loop
End

Table 3. Comparison between Simple Web and Semantic Web

Elements	Simple Web	Semantic Web
Central Component	Semi-structured	Related data components
User	Humans	Machine
Linkage	Location based	Location and Semantic-based
Vocabulary	Formatting	Meaning and Logics

Transformation of DB into XML involves two major steps that are reading relational database tuples in the form of record sets that are from tables (One record set for one table) and second is writing of XML file on the basis of information read from database. This whole process is pictorially shown by a flow chart diagram in Figure 3 provided below;

An abstract level representation of transformation process is shown in Figure 4 that explains a process of transformation from XSD to RDF. When mapping techniques are used to transform ER diagram into relational schema, the resultant schema obtained for mydb database is provided in Figure 5.

Figure 3. Transformation process flow chart from DB tuples to XML

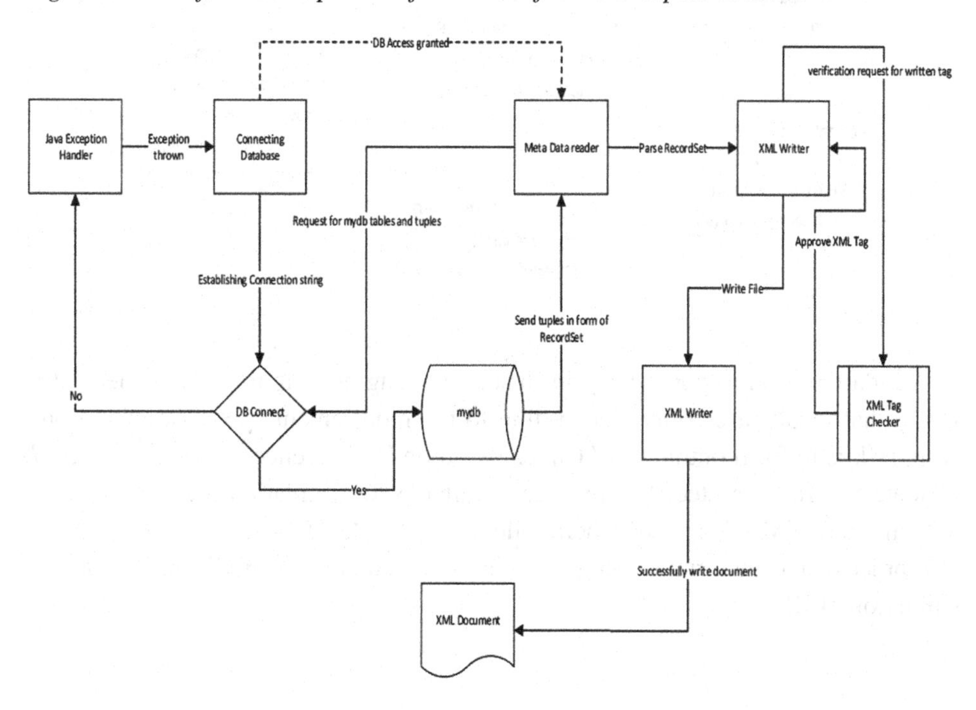

Figure 4. Transformation process of XSD to RDF Schema

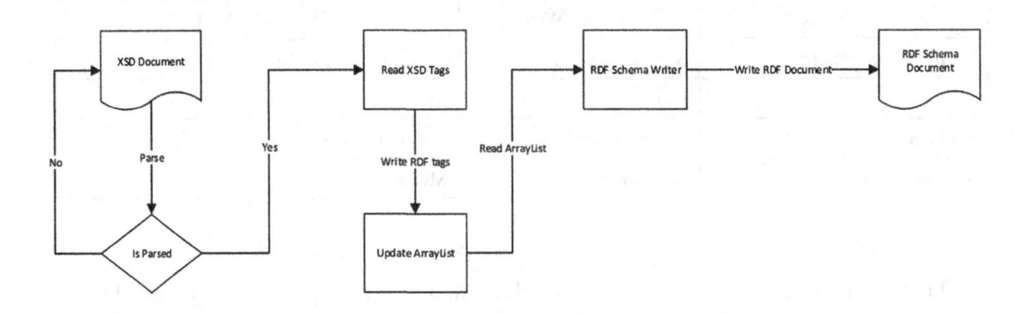

Figure 5. Relational Schema obtained for mydb after transforming its ERD

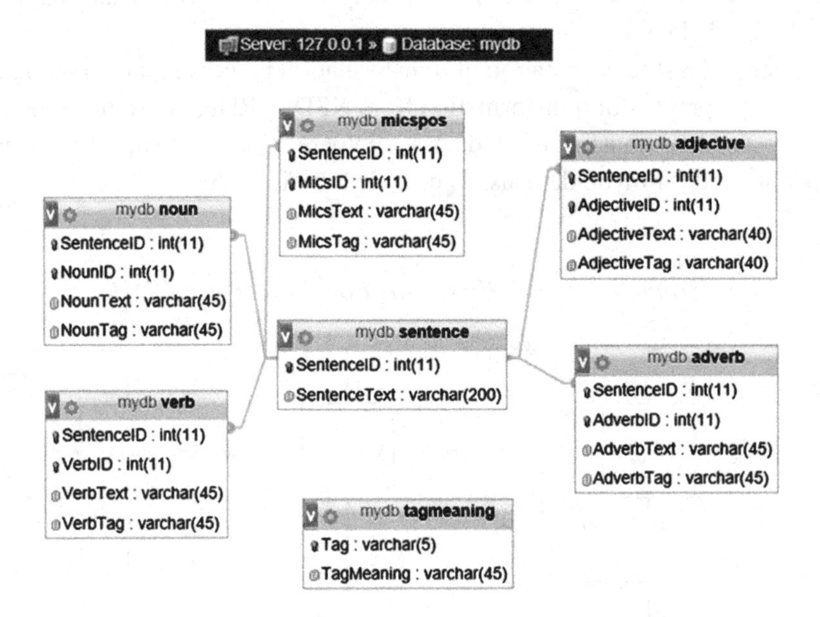

Validation is an important aspect in software engineering to test the check and verify that results are coming according to the requirement specification. In our case, task is to form ontologies / triples based on RDF. Hence we have to verify / validate the files created. So, the files available for validation are XSD (XML Schema file), XML file, RDF schema file and RDF file. Hence, we divided validation process into two major categories that are validation of XML and second is validation of RDF.

RESULTS AND DISCUSSION

Traditional systems, majorly build upon on a relational data model, and latest technologies like Big-Data, Cloud Computing, and other hot research areas are using the RDF data model for semantical improvements, enhancing the need to have better cooperation and communication mechanism on bases of data compatibility. To make the data useable at both types of systems we need to improve data transformation mechanism. It would be better to introduce a bidirectional transformation to resolve issues concerning data for compatibility. This transformation will be conducted between Relational Database Schema (RDBS) to Resource Description Framework Schema (RDFS). This study is to produce a model based on transformation to recover better outcomes from both types of schema levels. Furthermore, to observe lacking of other tools and techniques like D2R, D2O, R3M, R2ML and Triplify, working on similar nature of transformation, can be used to prove our method accuracy. After mapping results gained through R3M, R2ML and our proposed technique Figure 6 shows the outcome. Outcome represents the rich features are covered in our proposed method of transformation then others.

For the cases like training samples on image detection based on agents are using XML tagging. Which further can be reformed into linked data by using RDF data model.

FUTURE RESEARCH CONCERNS

One feature of big data is to work with a variety of data, which can be in any form coming into or going out of the system. This data can be semantically rich data,

Figure 6. Mapping R2M, R3M with proposed transformation technique

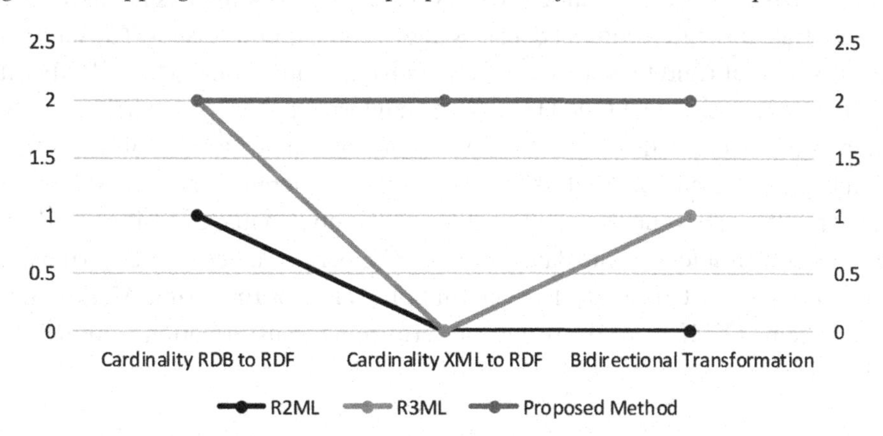

relational data, hierarchal data or other form of data. Therefore, data found in the shape of RDF, RDB or XML needs to be capable to transform in any direction. Which is yet in the form of maturing as a problem which needs to be addressed and sorted out. Our study main focus is on bidirectional transformation of heterogeneous data into RDF and then back. As a special case we have focused on RDB and RDF based on bidirectional transformation.

Afterwards, we have also a bidirectional transformation to work with our generalized proposed model of big data using agents as domain experts capable of translating each data category into XML form. Then by passing through bidirectional transformation algorithms, resulting in becoming more capable of further production of analytical analysis after being processed.

Implementation of XML.

- (XML data model in OOP) Develop a class that can contain all features of an element.
  - This class will also contain an ArrayList as self-contained to build other elements.
  - Should create class diagram and object diagram to show how this will work.

Current need to provide most simplified form of RDF for better utilization of data linkage without facing complexity issues embedded due to constraints.

CONCLUSION

In Web applications, generally data is stored in the form of Relational Database (RDB) or Resource Description Framework (RDF). When these data sets needs to transform from RDB to Semantic Web (SW) based system, there is no known way to do this transformation without data loss due to compatibility issues. The literature describes several rigid techniques that do transformation from RDB to RDF with limited customization, but failed to present an intermediate way that helps to avoid compatibility issue. In this paper we are introducing a new idea that allow us to do data mapping that can be used to understand their differences at the level of data types. This mapping is done using Extensible Markup Language (XML) based data structure as their intermediate data presenter. We performed control experiment to investigate whether Document Type Definition (DTD) or Extensible Markup Language Schema (XMLS) works better for performing transformation from RDB to

RDF, and shows XMLS give better mapping results for process of transformation. This approach will allow data transformation from RDB to RDF without data loss and compatibility issue and as a result traditional systems can easily be transformed to Semantic Web based system. This study suggestion in regard of improvements like simplified data form when data retrieval and storage is required by system at either end of RDB and RDF. It's been observed during the implementation phase, by the use of the proposed model, data can be translated into any of these three data models which are RDB, XML and RDF. These data models are playing a key role among majority of work done in data science. This requires careful selection of mapping between different features and capabilities of each data model. Whereas, each data model has its own constraints and limitations. Keeping all that in consideration this study still gives better results to support our model. Gaining a high level of control for customization is the most desired form needed by scientists of this era. The outcome of this study can further be used to achieve the nearest form of maximized customization when transforming one data model to another.

REFERENCES

Antoniou, G., & Van Harmelen, F. (2004). *A semantic web primer*. MIT press.

Biron, P., Malhotra, A., & Consortium, W. W. W. (2004). XML schema part 2: Datatypes. *World Wide Web Consortium Recommendation REC-xmlschema-2-20041028*.

Bohannon, P., Fan, W., Flaster, M., & Narayan, P. (2005). Information preserving XML schema embedding.*Proceedings of the 31st international conference on Very large data bases*.

Codd, E. F. (1970). A relational model of data for large shared data banks. *Communications of the ACM*, *13*(6), 377–387. doi:10.1145/362384.362685

Decker, S., Melnik, S., Van Harmelen, F., Fensel, D., Klein, M., Broekstra, J., & Horrocks, I. et al. (2000). The semantic web: The roles of XML and RDF. *IEEE Internet Computing*, *4*(5), 63–73. doi:10.1109/4236.877487

Fallside, D. C., & Walmsley, P. (2004). XML schema part 0: primer second edition. W3C recommendation, 16.

Grobe, M. (2009). Rdf, jena, sparql and the 'semantic web'.*Proceedings of the 37th annual ACM SIGUCCS fall conference*.

Hepp, M., Leymann, F., Domingue, J., Wahler, A., & Fensel, D. (2005). *Semantic business process management: A vision towards using semantic web services for business process management.* Paper presented at the e-Business Engineering, 2005. ICEBE 2005. IEEE International Conference on. doi:10.1109/ICEBE.2005.110

Hert, M., Reif, G., & Gall, H. C. (2011). A comparison of RDB-to-RDF mapping languages.*Proceedings of the 7th International Conference on Semantic Systems.*

Manola, F., Miller, E., & McBride, B. (2004). RDF primer. *W3C Recommendation, 10*, 1-107.

Martens, W., Neven, F., Schwentick, T., & Bex, G. J. (2006). Expressiveness and complexity of XML Schema. *ACM Transactions on Database Systems, 31*(3), 770–813. doi:10.1145/1166074.1166076

Ravindra, P., & Anyanwu, K. (2014). Nesting Strategies for Enabling Nimble MapReduce Dataflows for Large RDF Data. *International Journal on Semantic Web and Information Systems, 10*(1), 1–26. doi:10.4018/ijswis.2014010101

Rusu, O., Halcu, I., Grigoriu, O., Neculoiu, G., Sandulescu, V., Marinescu, M., & Marinescu, V. (2013). *Converting unstructured and semi-structured data into knowledge.* Paper presented at the Roedunet International Conference (RoEduNet), 2013 11th. doi:10.1109/RoEduNet.2013.6511736

Sahoo, S. S., Halb, W., Hellmann, S., Idehen, K., Thibodeau Jr, T., Auer, S., . . . Ezzat, A. (2009). *A survey of current approaches for mapping of relational databases to rdf.* W3C RDB2RDF Incubator Group Report.

Shah, A., Adeniyi, J., & Al Tuwairqi, T. (2005). *An Algorithm for Transforming XML Documents Schema into Relational Database Schema. In Transformation of knowledge, information and data: theory and applications* (pp. 171–189). Idea Group Publishing. doi:10.4018/978-1-59140-527-6.ch008

Spaniol, M. (2014). *A Framework for Temporal Web Analytics*. Université de Caen.

Spanos, D.-E., Stavrou, P., & Mitrou, N. (2012). Bringing relational databases into the semantic web: A survey. *Semantic Web, 3*(2), 169–209.

Strohbach, M., Ziekow, H., Gazis, V., & Akiva, N. (2015). *Towards a Big Data Analytics Framework for IoT and Smart City Applications. In Modeling and Processing for Next-Generation Big-Data Technologies* (pp. 257–282). Springer.

Thuy, P. T. T., Lee, Y.-K., & Lee, S. (2009). DTD2OWL: automatic transforming XML documents into OWL ontology.*Proceedings of the 2nd International Conference on Interaction Sciences: Information Technology, Culture and Human*. doi:10.1145/1655925.1655949

Thuy, P. T. T., Lee, Y.-K., Lee, S., & Jeong, B.-S. (2007). *Transforming valid XML documents into RDF via RDF schema.* Paper presented at the Next Generation Web Services Practices, 2007. NWeSP 2007. Third International Conference on. doi:10.1109/NWESP.2007.23

Thuy, P. T. T., Lee, Y.-K., Lee, S., & Jeong, B.-S. (2008). *Exploiting XML schema for interpreting XML documents as RDF.* Paper presented at the Services Computing, 2008. SCC'08. IEEE International Conference on. doi:10.1109/SCC.2008.93

Van Deursen, D., Poppe, C., Martens, G., Mannens, E., & Walle, R. (2008). *XML to RDF conversion: a generic approach.* Paper presented at the Automated solutions for Cross Media Content and Multi-channel Distribution, 2008. AXMEDIS'08. International Conference on. doi:10.1109/AXMEDIS.2008.17

Zaveri, A., Maurino, A., & Equille, L.-B. (2014). Web Data Quality: Current State and New Challenges. *International Journal on Semantic Web and Information Systems*, *10*(2), 1–6. doi:10.4018/ijswis.2014040101

ENDNOTES

1 JDK Java Development Kit http://www.oracle.com/technetwork/java/javase/downloads/index.html

2 IDE NetBeans https://netbeans.org/downloads/

3 MySQL https://www.mysql.com/downloads/

Chapter 5
Conversion of Higher into Lower Language Using Machine Translation

Raghvendra Kumar
Lakshmi Narain College of Technology, India

Prasant Kumar Pattnaik
KIIT University, India

Priyanka Pandey
Lakshmi Narain College of Technology, India

ABSTRACT

This chapter addresses an exclusive approach to expand a machine translation system beginning higher language to lower language. Since we all know that population of India is 1.27 billion moreover there are more than 30 language and 2000 dialects used for communication of Indian people. India has 18 official recognized languages similar to Assamese, Bengali, English, Gujarati, Hindi, Kannada, Kashmiri, Konkani, Malayalam, Manipuri, Marathi, Nepali, Oriya, Punjabi, Sanskrit, Tamil, Telugu, and Urdu. Hindi is taken as regional language and is used for all types of official work in central government offices. Commencing such a vast number of people 80% of people know Hindi. Though Hindi is also regional language of Jabalpur, MP, India, still a lot of people of Jabalpur are unable to speak in Hindi. So for production those people unswerving to know Hindi language we expand a machine translation system. For growth of such a machine translation system, used apertium platform as it is free/open source. Using apertium platform a lot of language pairs more specifically Indian language pairs have already been developed. In this chapter, develop a machine translation system for strongly related language pair i.e Hindi to Jabalpuriya language (Jabalpur, MP, India).

DOI: 10.4018/978-1-5225-2483-0.ch005

INTRODUCTION

Natural Language Processing

Natural language is an integral part of our day today lives. Language is the most common and most ancient way to exchange information among human beings. people communicate and record information.NLP is a field of computer science and artificial intelligence; here natural language means the language used by human being for communication among themselves. NLP is a form of human-to-computer interaction. ie the nlp basically implies making human to machine interaction easy and in human language .

One of the major problems encountered by any nlp system is lexical ambiguity here the term lexical ambiguity means the particular word having more than one meaning lexical ambiguity in simple words can better be stated as presence of homonymy and polysemy. Ambiguity is further of two types syntactic and semantic. Syntactic ambiguity means when sentence can be parsed in more than one manner. The word's syntactic ambiguity can be resolved in language processing by part-of-speech taggers with very high level of accuracy. Semantic ambguty The problem of resolving semantic ambiguity is generally known as word sense disambiguation (WSD) and has been proved to be more difficult than syntactic disambiguation.

Word Sense Disambiguation

Any natural language known to human beings there exists that can have more than one possible meaning, for example a bat can be a small creature or a cricket equipment and a bank can mean river 's bank or a money bank (the financial institution one) . since if the other meaning than the intended one is used in particular context it can cause a huge translation hazard Given these complications, it is important for a computer to correctly determine the meaning in which a word is used. hence it is very clear to s that Ambiguity is natural phenomena in to human language and it constitutes one of the most important problem for computational applications in of Natural Language Processing (NLP). Ideally, systems should be able to deal with ambiguity in order to increase performance in nlp applications such as Text Summarization and Information Retrieval. The process of assigning the correct sense of ambiguous words Words can have different senses. Some words have multiple meanings. This is called Polysemy. For example: bank can be a financial institute or a river shore. Sometimes two completely different word are spelled the same.

For example: Can, can be used as model verb: You can do it, or as container: She brought a can of soda. This is called Homonymy. Distinction between polysemy and homonymy is not always clear. Word sense disambiguation (WSD) is the problem of determining in which sense a word having a number of distinct senses is used in a given sentence. Take another example; consider the word "bass", with two distinct senses:

1. A type of fish.
2. Tones of low frequency.

And the sentences "The bass part of the song is very moving" and "I went fishing for some sea bass". To a human it is obvious the first sentence is using the word "bass" in sense 2 above, and in the second sentence it is being used in sense 1. But although this seems obvious to a human, developing algorithms to replicate this human ability is a difficult task.

Words can have one or more than one meaning based on the context of the word usage in a sentence. The term Word Sense Disambiguation (WSD) is to identify the meaning of words in context in a computational manner.

HISTORY OF WSD

The task of WSD is a historical one in the field of Natural Language Processing (NLP).WSD was first formulated as a distinct computational task during the early days of machine translation in the 1940s, making it one of the oldest problems in computational linguistics. Warren Weaver in 1949 first introduced WSD problem in a computational context. In the 1970s, WSD was a subtask of semantic interpretation systems developed within the field of artificial intelligence, but since WSD systems were largely rule-based and hand-coded they were prone to a knowledge acquisition bottleneck. In the 1990s, the statistical revolution swept through computational linguistics, and WSD became a paradigm problem on which to apply supervised machine reach a plateau in accuracy, and so attention has shifted to semi-supervised, unsupervised corpus-based systems and combinations of different methods. Still, supervised systems continue to perform best. Word Sense Disambiguation (WSD) is one of the major problems faced during Machine Translation (MT). Several attempts have been made to handle WSD. WSD rules when developed manually demands hard work and are quite time consuming. and to increase complexity of situation if the rules are developed for bilingual WSD, they may get very specific for particular language pair. If the rules are monolingual, it is difficult to decide the granularity for different senses. While the statistical method may be helpful in handling the languages involved in MT.

Word Sense Disambiguation is needed in Machine Translation, Information Retrieval, and Information Extraction etc. WSD is typically configured as an intermediate task, either as a stand-alone module or properly integrated into an application (thus performing disambiguation implicitly).

Approaches in Wordsense Disambiguation

Two Main approaches in word sense disambiguation are deep approach and shallow approach .

- **Deep Approach:** Deep approaches assume that we have body of outer world Knowledge, such as "in case of word bass meaning both fish as well as a musical instrument depending upon the context in which it in used. in deep approach we can judge the correct meaning by comparing the scenario with our outer word knowledge. These approaches are not very successful in practice, mainly because such a body of knowledge does not exist in a computer-readable format.
- **Shallow Approach:** Shallow approaches don't try to understand the text. They just consider the surrounding words, using information such as in context of word bass which mean a fish as well as a musical instrument depending upon the context where it is used "if *bass* has words *sea* or *fishing* nearby, it probably is in the fish sense; if *bass* has the words *music* or *song* nearby, it is probably in the music sense." These rules can be automatically derived by the computer, using a training corpus of words tagged with their word senses. This approach, while theoretically not as powerful as deep approaches, gives superior results in practice, due to the computer's limited world knowledge. However, it can be confused by sentences like *The dogs bark at the tree* which contains the word *bark* near both *tree* and *dogs*.

There are four conventional approaches to WSD:

1. **Dictionary and Knowledge-Based Methods:** These rely primarily on dictionaries, and lexical knowledge bases, without using any corpus evidence.
2. **Supervised Methods:** These make use of sense-annotated corpora to train from.
3. **Semi-Supervised or Minimally Supervised Methods:** These make use of a secondary source of knowledge such as a small annotated corpus as seed data in a bootstrapping process, or a word-aligned bilingual corpus.
4. **Unsupervised Methods:** These eschew (almost) completely external information and work directly from raw un annotated corpora. These methods are also known under the name of word sense discrimination.

Dictionary and Knowledge-Based Methods

The Lesk method (Lesk 1986) is the seminal dictionary-based method. It is based on the hypothesis that words used together in text are related to each other and that the relation can be observed in the definitions of the words and their senses. Two (or more) words are disambiguated by finding the pair of dictionary senses with the greatest word overlap in their dictionary definitions. For example, when disambiguating the words in *pine cone*, the definitions of the appropriate senses both include the words *evergreen* and *tree* (at least in one dictionary)

In this style of approach the dictionary provides both the means of constructing a sense tagger and target senses to be used. An attempt to perform large scale disambiguation has lead to the use of Machine Readable Dictionaries (MRD). In this approach, all the senses of a word to be disambiguated are retrieved from the dictionary. Each of these senses is then compared to the dictionary definitions of all the remaining words in context. The sense with highest overlap with these context words is chosen as the correct sense. For example: consider the phrase pine cone for selecting the correct sense of word cone and following definitions for pine and cone:

Pine:

1. Kinds of evergreen tree with needle-shaped leaves.
2. Waste away through sorrow or illness.

Cone:

1. Solid body which narrows to a point.
2. Something of this shapes whether solid or hollow.
3. Fruit of certain evergreen trees.

In this example, Lesk's method would select **cone**^{3} as the correct sense since two of the words in its entry, evergreen and tree, overlap with words in the entry for pine. A major drawback of Dictionary based approaches is the problem of scale

Supervised Methods

Supervised methods are based on the assumption that the context can provide enough evidence on its own to disambiguate words (hence, world knowledge and reasoning are deemed unnecessary). Probably every machine learning algorithm going has been applied to WSD, including associated techniques such as feature selection, and learning. memory-based learning have been shown to be the most successful approaches, to date, probably because they can cope with the high-dimensionality of the feature space. However, these supervised methods are subject to a new knowledge acquisition bottleneck since they rely on substantial amounts of manually sense-tagged corpora for training, which are laborious and expensive to create.

Semi-Supervised Methods

The bootstrapping approach starts from a small amount of seed data for each word: either manually-tagged training examples or a small number of surefire decision rules (e.g.,*play* in the context of *bass* almost always indicates the musical instrument). The seeds are used to train an initial classifier, using any supervised method. This classifier is then used on the untagged portion of the corpus to extract a larger training set, in which only the most confident classifications are included. The process repeats, each new classifier being trained on a successively larger training corpus, until the whole corpus is consumed, or until a given maximum number of iterations is reached.

Other semi-supervised techniques use large quantities of untagged corpora to provide co-occurrence information that supplements the tagged corpora. These techniques have the potential to help in the adaptation of supervised models to different domains.

Also, an ambiguous word in one language is often translated into different words in a second language depending on the sense of the word. Word-aligned bilingual corpora have been used to infer cross-lingual sense distinctions, a kind of semi-supervised system.

Unsupervised Methods

Unsupervised learning is the greatest challenge for WSD researchers. The underlying assumption is that similar senses occur in similar contexts, and thus senses can be induced from text by clustering word occurrences using some measure of similarity of context. Then, new occurrences of the word can be classified into the closest induced clusters/senses.

Performance has been lower than other methods, above, but comparisons are difficult since senses induced must be mapped to a known dictionary of word senses. It is hoped that unsupervised learning will overcome the knowledge acquisition bottleneck because they are not dependent on manual effort.

ANUSAARAKA

- **Purpose:** The main purpose of this paper is to suggest an approach that does not keep all the load of translation on machine .it incorporates human efforts and thus the translation process become more effective because of the presence of outer world knowledge. it ses more interactive web based wsd so that user may also contribute in developing wsd rules

Description

Anusaaraka is the language assessor cum machine translation system. Ausaaraka works on paninian grammar.

Unique Features of Anusaaraka

The system has the following unique features.

Faithful representation: The system tries to give more correct translation rather than giving a meaningful translation. The user can infer the correct meaning from the various layers of translation output.

No loss of information: All the information available on the source language side is made available explicitly in the successive layers of translation.

Graceful degradation (Robust fall back mechanism): The system ensures a safety net by providing a "pad sutra layer", which is a word to word translation represented in special formula tic form, representing various senses of the source language word.

Goals of Anusaaraka System

The major goals of the Anusaaraka system are to:

1. Reduce the language barrier by facilitating access from one language to another
2. Demonstrating the practical usability of the Indian traditional grammatical system in the modern context.
3. Enabling users to become contributors in the development of the system. Providing a free and open source machine translation platform for Indian languages.

Figure 1. Architectre Of Anusaarka System

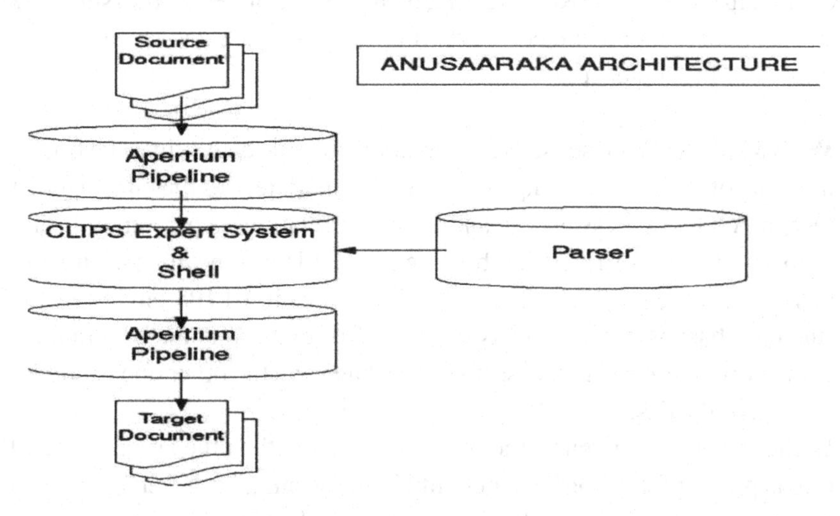

THE SURVEY OF CLIPS EXPERT SYSTEM

CLIPS: Is a public domain software tool for building expert systems. The name is an acronym for "C Language Integrated Production System. The first versions of CLIPS were developed by NASA. Like other expert system languages, CLIPS deals with rules and facts. Various facts can make a rule applicable.

CLIPS expert shell consists of different modules. Each module loads a set of initial facts and generates a set of new facts which is again given as input to the other modules. Below is the description of different modules and its functionalities.

1. **Category Consistency:** This module checks the consistency in determining the part of speech tag of a word using the parser output and POS-tagger output and some heuristic rules. More preference is given to the parser output in determining the final POS tag.
2. **Local Word Grouper:** Local word grouping is done for the finite verb phrases in the sentence. This module takes the input of chunker and parser relation as input facts and and groups all the finite verb groups along with its

TAM\footnote{Tense, Aspect and Modality} present in the sentence .

3. Aninian relations Painian relations are a kind of dependency relations based on the Paninian grammar formalism. These are binary relations which represent "Father-Son" kind of relation between two words.

Example: In the sentence Ram is eating mangoes one of the relation subject-kriya 1 3 represents the relation subject as word in the position 1 and kriya as the word in position 3 of the sentence.

4. **WSD Module:** Word sense disambiguation module determines the final Hindi meaning of a ambiguous English word. This module uses the information from morph Analyser, POS tagger and Paninian relations, position and semantic property of the word to disambiguate to final Hindi meanings. This module consists of thousands of manually written rules in CLIPS environment. The rule data-base is made up of two types of rules. One is the generalized rule comes with the Anusaaraka software package and the other one is provisional (user given) rules.
5. Higher priority is given to the provisional rules, than the system rules. If no rule is present for a word, the default Hindi meaning is chosen from the bilingual dictionary. Multi words are also translated with the help of a multi word dictionary.
6. The rules are in CLIPS language, which can be written directly in CLIPS or through a web interface available over Internet for the users to contribute towards enriching the WSD rule database:
    a. **Pada Formation:** Pada is a group of word similar to English constituent phrases. There are basically two types of Padas sbanta: means pada having a single or a group of word having the head word in nominal form and tinganta pada where the head word is in verbal form.
    b. **GNP Agreement:** Gender, number and person information agreement is done between various pada groups in Hindi. The algorithm for agreement of the verb group is given in the figure. Intra-pada agreement is already done in the pada formation module.
7. **Hindi Word Ordering:** Hindi constituent (pada) is the mirror image of English pada order. The default Hindi order is as follows: Sentence opener, subject, object or subject samAnAXikarana[2], kriyA mula, kriyA niReXaka, verb (kriyA). In the case of modifier-modified relation, modifier is done in the pada formation module.
8. **Generation:** From the CLIPS expert shell the final output is given in the form of analyzed Hindi constituents (Padas), with all its attributes (e.g gender, number, person, tense, case markers etc.). This information is given as input to the Apertium pipeline which uses the FST based generator for final Hindi sentence generation. The deformatter module is used for restoring the source text form (e.g. html, xml, doc, rtf, txt). Finally the translated Hindi sentence is presented in a specialy designed user interface.

WSD USING CLIPS EXPERT SYSTEM

WSD Rule

To begin forming WSD rules with the help of CLIPS, we will take a small example sentence.

Word: Chair

- **Sentence1:** This is an old chair.
- **Sentence2:** The President chaired the session.

In the above two sentences the word "chair" have different Hindi meanings "KURSI" and "ADHYKSTA KARNA" respectively. These two different Hindi meanings are coming due to the different POS (Part of Speech) category of the word "chair" -- noun and verb respectively. Hence the rule will be:

```
RULE NO 1:
defrule chair0(declare (salience 4000))
(id-root ?id chair)
?mng <-(meaning_to_be_decided? id)
(Id-cat coarse? id noun)
=>
(retract? mng)
(assert (id-wsd_root_mng ?id kursI))
(if ?*debug_flag* then
(printout wsd_fp "(rule_name-id-wsd_root_mng chair0 " ?id "
kursI)" crlf))
)
Rule no 2.
(Defrule chair1
(declare (salience 4000))(id-root?id chair)
?mng <-(meaning_to_be_decided?id)
(Id-cat_coarse?id verb)
=>(retract ?mng)(assert (id-wsd_root_mng ?id aXyakRawA_kara))
(if ?*debug_flag* then))
(printout wsd_fp "(rule_name-id-wsd_root_mng chair1 " ?id "
aXyakRawA_kara)"))
```

We can divide each of the above CLIPS rules into two parts -- condition part and action part. In the condition part we will give all the required conditions for pattern matching. If all the conditions are matched, then the required action is defined in the action part.

Now we will try to understand each line in the above CLIPS rules.

(defrule chair0): This line gives a unique rule id "chair0" to the given rule. For ease of identification we are adding a number after the word.

declare (salience 4000)): Here we are giving the saliency (priority) to the rule. Priority is controlled with the help of range of numbers. The need of giving priority to a rule is required, for the reason, if there are multiple rules for a single word, we can set the order in which these rules will be fired by the CLIPS inference engine.

The following rule of thumb may help you to fix the saliency of a 'sense'. The 'default' sense (which is the most general sense and is usually listed as the first meaning in the dictionary) has the least number of constraints stated in the rule. The saliency of the default sense would be 'very low'. As the constraints become more and more complex and specific for a sense, the saliency goes higher. In the event of there being an extremely specific condition for a sense, the saliency would be 'very high'.

(id-root?id chair): The syntax of the above statement is like "son-father Ram Dasarath". The relation is between two entities separated by a hyphen. For e.g. "**id-root**" . The relation is between **id** and **root.** In a sentence we are assigning a serial id to each word on the basis of its position. This helps giving a unique id to each word in a sentence irrespective of its repetition. For e.g. 'The farmer took two months to produce the grains but he took much longer to find a market for his produce'. The word 'produce' has been used twice but for each occurrence of the word it has to be assigned a distinct id.

?mng <-(meaning_to_be_decided?i: This fact is a dummy fact to control the firing of rules . If the given rule is matched then in the action part we will retract(remove) this fact. Hence it will check the inference engine from firing further rules. For e.g., given above are two rules for chair. If first rule "chair0" is fired then this dummy fact will be retracted, hence the next rule "chair1" will never be matched.

(id-cat_coarse ?id noun) This is like the previous fact "(id-root ?id chair)". Here the relation is "id-cat_coarse". Hence the first entity is "id" and the second entity is its coarse category.=>

This defines the end of the "Condition part" and start of the "action part".

(retract ?mng): As described this statement removes the fact "?mng <-(meaning_to_be_decided ?id) " once all the conditions in the conditions part is matched.

WSD of TO Infinitive Into Hindi: An Information Based Approach by Akshar Bharati and R. Vaishnavi Rao

Purpose: in this paper the two most commonly used approaches of wsd, information based and rule based are described and the example of TO infinitive's wsd into Hindi using information based approach is described.

Description: Wsd is one of the most complicated tasks of nlp. Majorly two approaches are used for wsd rule based and information based. Rule based WSD, works with t he synt ax of a sentence and i s hence surface st ructure dependent. Rule based wsd in technology dependent as it changes with new advent of technology. Information based approach on other hand is semantic approach deeper approach which would enlighten us about where the information about the language phenomenon is available would be of greater advantage. The results of such analysis can be always used along with further development in technology as the analysis is independent of technological constrains.

The TO infinitive marker in English can be used differently in different context let's take few example.

E: I would love to live in New York.
H: maiM New York meM rahanA pasaMda karUMgI.
E: He tried to leave quietly.
H: usane chupachApa jAne kA prayatna kiya.
E: I am going there to see my sister.
H: maiM apanI bahana ko dekhane ke liye vahA.N jA rahI hU.N.
E: She refused to accept that there was a problem.
H: usane mAnane se inakAra kara diyA ki koI samasyA thI.
E: She is the next person to speak.
H: vaha hai agali bolane vAlI vyakti.

From above sentences it is clear that in English there is one infinitive marker, a single 'to', whereas Hindi requires a marker 'nA' optionally followed by nominal suffixes (vibhaktis) such as kA, ke_liye, se, vAlI, etc . Here we see that the major difference between Hindi and English is that the Hindi require an explicit vibhakti marker with "na" in order to know the appropriate sense in which it is used. to- infinitive can be translated into Hindi as 'nA *' where '*' stands for the parasargas (post-positions) such as '0', 'kA', 'ke liye' etc. thus it is quite clear that English language and Hindi language quite huge structural difference. This information may used for further translation of TO_ infinitive to Hindi. Using panian grammar rules we can further formulate the rules based on the semantics of the to infinitive, which is to be otherwise inferred from the context in which it is used. To put it explicitly, in the effort to get the information about the contexts in which Hindi takes a particular vibhakti for the otherwise inexpressive to infinitive, we get to know as to what are the various meanings of the to infinitive. The various senses of the to infinitive can be broadly classified into the following categories –

1. To infinitive semantically connected to another verb.
2. To infinitive semantically connected to a noun or an adjective.
3. ECM constructions.
4. To infinitive forming part of a verb group, as in 'have to go'.
5. Exception of translation of to infinitive into nA*.

These categories are explained in more detail in the following paragraphs:

1. To infinitive semantically connected to another verb.
    a. To infinitive denoting the purpose as in

E: I am going there to see my sister.
H: maiM apanI bahana ko dekhane ke liye vahA.N jA rahI hU.N.

Hindi uses 'ke_liye' to indicate the purpose, and hence in such cases, to-Infinitives is to be translated as 'nA~ke_liye'.

    b. To infinitive as a modifier of the main verb meaning 'desire'

E: I would love to live in New York.

Here the object of the main verb 'love' is another action itself; in this case 'Living in New York '. Here, the nonfinite verb indicates only action (bhAva). Hindi uses 'nA' to indicate the bhAva and hence in such cases, to- infinitive is to be translated as 'nA'.

H: maiM New York meM rahanA pasaMda karUMgI.

2. To infinitive semantically connected to noun or adjective.

E: It is time to go home.
H: yaha ghara jAne kA samaya hai.

Here the infinitive describes the 'time' and literally acts as an adjective to it. In Hindi the relation between an adjective and its corresponding noun is indicated by shhashhThI vibhakti with the parasarga 'k [AI]', as in case of 'safeda raMga kI chAdara'. Hence, the infinitive takes shhashhThI vibhakti here.

b. To infinitive modifying the nouns such as 'ability', 'tendency', 'Opportunity' etc.

E: I have a tendency to tease.
H: mujhe chheDane kA svabhAva hai.

The phenomenon explained in (2a) applies here also. This instance is covered by the Paninian rule.

c. To infinitive related with adjectives such as 'afraid' etc.:

E: I was afraid to go home.
H: maiM ghara jAne se bhayabhIta thI.

3. ECM constructions: Certain verbs, such as 'want', exhibit a special behavior in English. For Example, in the sentence -

E: I want him to go.

'He' which is in the subject position of the verb 'go' gets case assigned by the verb 'want'. Here the kartA of the verb 'want' is 'I' and the kartA of the verb 'go' is 'he'. However, in Hindi, as in Sanskrit, the verbs denoting desire share their agents with the infinitive. We can notice that English also allows sentences with the main verb denoting 'desire' sharing its agent with the infinitive, as in -

E: I want a pen to write.

The translation for this follows from rule (1a) and hence the translation for this Sentence would be:

H: maiM likhane ke liye kalama chAhatI hU.N.

4. To infinitive forming part of a verb group. These are to be treated case by case. Hindi equivalents of each of t h e tam group's e.g.have_to_0, ought_to_0, etc. need to be given separately.

E: I have to go home.
H: mujhe ghara Jana hai.
E: That child ought to be in bed.
H: usa bachche ko bistara meM honA chAhiye.

5. Exception of translation of to infinitive into nA *: There are a few cases which are exceptions to the default rule that to infinitive is 'nA *'. To- infinitive related to adjectives such as 'glad', 'sorry' etc.:

E: I am glad to hear that news.
H: maiM vaha khabara sunakara khush huI.

When these WSD rules are implemented in anusaaraka mt system all the rules have found accuracy ranges between 60 to 100%.

CONCLUSION

Word Sense Disambiguation (WSD) is a hard task as it deals with the full complexities of language. WSD is the ability to identify the meaning of words in context in a computational manner and it heavily relies on knowledge .A rich variety of techniques have been researched such as knowledge based, supervised, unsupervised etc. Supervised methods undoubtedly perform better than other approaches. To obtain a high-accuracy wide-coverage disambiguation system, we probably need a corpus of about 3.2 million sense-tagged words. Comparing and evaluating different WSD systems is extremely difficult, because of the different test sets, sense inventories, and knowledge resources adopted .WSD is problematic in part because of the inherent difficulty of determining or even defining word sense, and this is not an issue that is likely to be solved in the near future. Machine translation is the original and most obvious application for WSD but disambiguation has been considered in almost every NLP application, and is becoming increasingly important in recent areas. now coming we comes to ansaaraka mt system. Word sense disambiguation module determines the final Hindi meaning of a ambiguous English word. This module uses the information from morph Analyser, POS tagger and Paninian relations, position and semantic property of the word to disambiguate to a final Hindi meanings. This module consists of thousands of manually written rules in CLIPS environment. The rule data-base is made up of two types of rules. One is the generalized rule comes with the Anusaaraka software package and the other one is provisional (user given) rules. Higher priority is given to the provisional rules, than the system rules. If no rule is present for a word, the default Hindi meaning is chosen from the bilingual dictionary. Multi words are also translated with the help of a multi word dictionary. The rules are in CLIPS language, which can be written directly in CLIPS or through a web interface available over Internet for the users to contribute towards enriching the WSD rule database. User has to fill up the forms using different facts available for the given word. These forms when saved, automatically converts the facts into CLIPS format rules.

Thus anusaaraka approach solves wsd in quite innovative manner.

REFERENCES

Anusaaraka: An Approach to Machine Translation. (n.d.). Retrieved from: http://sanskrit.uohyd.ac.in/faculty/amba/PUBLICATIONS/papers/hyd-anu-mt.pdf

Anusaarka. (n.d.). Retrieved from: http://www.anusaaraka.iiit.ac.in

Section 3

Extracting Knowledge From Information

Chapter 6
Knowledge Discovery From Massive Data Streams

Sushil Kumar Narang
SAS Institute of IT and Research, India

Sushil Kumar
IIT Roorkee, India

Vishal Verma
MLN College, India

ABSTRACT

T.S. Eliot once wrote some beautiful poetic lines including one "Where is the knowledge we have lost in information?". Can't say that T.S. Eliot could have anticipated today's scenario which is emerging from his poetic lines. Data in present scenario is a profuse resource in many circumstances and is piling-up and many technical leaders are finding themselves drowning in data. Through this big stream of data there is a vast flood of information coming out and seemingly crossing manageable boundaries. As Information is a necessary channel for educing and constructing knowledge, one can assume the importance of generating new and comprehensive knowledge discovery tools and techniques for digging this overflowing sea of information to create explicit knowledge. This chapter describes traditional as well as modern research techniques towards knowledge discovery from massive data streams. These techniques have been effectively applied not exclusively to completely structured but also to semi-structured and unstructured data. At the same time Semantic Web technologies in today's perspective require many of them to deal with all sorts of raw data.

DOI: 10.4018/978-1-5225-2483-0.ch006

1. INTRODUCTION TO KNOWLEDGE DISCOVERY

Knowledge Discovery (KD) is a concept which involves the developments of strategies and procedures for making sense out of massive data. In recent years, data have become increasingly available in substantial amounts (petabytes or zettabytes). It has numerous sources including automation of business activities (trading, mobile communication, airline reservation, or credit card usage), online activities (social media, social networking), scientific activities (experiments, simulations, and environmental sensors), biological databases (DNA/RNA/protein structures, gene expression profiles) etc. In addition, new application scenarios like weather forecasting, artificial intelligence, earth observation satellites and so forth produce terabytes of data every day. Clearly, the massive size of data ruled out any manual approach of analyzing (make sense of) collected data. If this massive data will have to be understood at all, it must be analyzed by the use of computers. Although, there are statistical procedures available for data analysis and interpretation, but this explosive growth of data requires new intelligent techniques which can astutely transform the useful data into knowledge. Knowledge discovery is the significant process of digging out meaningful patterns from huge data using automated (or semi-automated) computational tools and techniques (Devedzic, 2002; Piatetsky-Shapiro, 1996). The goals of knowledge discovery are usually identified by business domain. For instance

- Marketing agencies make use of knowledge discovery frameworks to find patterns in the way customers purchase retail items. Once they find that many individuals purchase item A along with item B, they can easily make an appropriate and potentially successful business or marketing announcement.
- Airline companies make use of knowledge discovery systems to find patterns in which their passengers fly (routes, return flights, frequency of flying to a specific destination and so forth). Based on the patterns discovered, they can give promotional offers to frequent travelers, thus attract more customers to the company.
- Banks make use of knowledge discovery frameworks to explore the database of their credits and loans. Based on the patterns discovered, they can more successfully predict the risk of approving loan to their clients, thus increasing the quality of their business decisions.

Of course, most of these goals were well existing even before knowledge discovery was conceptualized. They have been achieved by human expertise, numerical modeling and on the basis of database OLAP (online analytical processing). However, in Knowledge Discovery, these goals are achieved by applying automated (or semi-automated) computational tools and techniques to the huge amount of stored data.

Subsequently, knowledge discovery has turned out to be strategically important for big business units, government institutions, and research organizations. However, successfully producing knowledge from massive data sets is very challenging. A lot of research is going on in the area of knowledge discovery to establish stable and well-defined standards which are well understood throughout the community. These standards need to be formalized to make the process more translucent and repeatable.

2. KNOWLEDGE DISCOVERY PROCESS

The Knowledge Discovery Process (KDP) is a long process that not only limited to actual data analysis but includes methods for data collection and preparation; data reduction and projection; data analysis and interpretation, and finally evaluation and action based on the discovered knowledge. Since the 1990s, several KDP models have been proposed (Kurgan & Musilek, 2006; Mariscal, Marban, & Fernandez, 2010). The early models were proposed by academic researchers but quickly followed by some peculiar industry research. The first basic model of the knowledge discovery process was proposed by Fayyad, Piatetsky-Shapiro, and Smyth (1996a, 1996b) and later modified/enhanced by others. The KDP model suggested by Fayyad et al. comprises of nine steps as portrayed beneath:

1. **Learning and Understanding the Application Domain:** This is the initial preparatory step. This step incorporates learning the relevant and prior knowledge of the application domain and defining the goals for the end users of the discovered knowledge.
2. **Creating a Target Data Set:** Once the goals have defined, the input data for knowledge discovery should be determined. In this step, a subset of data (samples) and variables (attributes) is selected that will be utilized to perform discovery tasks. This step normally incorporates querying the existing data to choose the desired subset.
3. **Data Cleaning and Pre-Processing:** The purpose of this step is to enhance data reliability. This step incorporates fundamental operations like eliminating errors and outliers (if appropriate), handling missing attribute values, correcting inconsistencies in the data, and accounting for time sequence information.
4. **Data Reduction and Projection:** In this stage, data is prepared and developed for data mining. It incorporates techniques for data transformation like normalization, feature construction, aggregation, generalization, data reduction and so forth, which transform the original data set to the data representation that is more suitable for mining algorithms. It also incorporates methods for discovering the useful features to represent the data depending on the goal of

the task. This step is usually very project-specific and often crucial for the success of the entire KD project.

5. **Choosing the Data Mining Task:** Here the data miner decides the type of data mining to use, for example, predictive or descriptive. This mostly depends on the KD goals and on the previous steps. The purpose of predictive mining is mainly to construct a model that predict future outcome from current behavior. Whereas descriptive mining finds interesting patterns in the bulk of data and present them in a human-understandable form.
6. **Choosing the Data Mining Algorithm:** This stage includes selecting the specific method to be used for fitting models or searching patterns in the data such as classification algorithms, visualization techniques, regression analysis, association or link analysis etc. Two or more methods can also be combined depending upon the data models. It also decides the appropriate control parameters of the methods that may be used.
7. **Data Mining:** This step implements the data mining algorithm to find rules or patterns of interest in a particular representative form like classification rules, decision trees, regression models, association rules, etc. In this step, we might need to employ the algorithm several times by tuning the algorithm's control parameters until a satisfied result is obtained.
8. **Interpreting Mined Patterns:** In this step, the mined rules or patterns are interpreted and evaluated with respect to the goals defined in the first step. This step also involves the removal of redundant or non-predictive patterns and the conversion of useful ones into forms understandable by the users. It also concentrates on the comprehensibility, applicability, and usefulness of the mined rules or patterns.
9. **Consolidating Discovered Knowledge:** The last step comprises of documenting the discovered knowledge and integrating it into the system. This step may also check the new discovered knowledge for potential conflicts with previously believed knowledge.

The Fayyad et al. KDP model is interactive and iterative with many feedback loops between several of the steps which are usually executed if revisions are required. The model gives a point by point technical portrayal with respect to data analysis but lacks in business perspectives. Moreover, it does not provide the specific details of feedback loops. However, it has become a foundation for the later models. Some other models popular in real knowledge discovery projects includes eight-step model proposed by Anand and Buchner (1998), six-step model proposed by Cios, Teresinska, Konieczna, Potocka, and Sharma (2000), five-step model proposed by Cabena, Hadjinian, Stadler, Verhees, and Zanasi (1998) and six-step CRISP-DM model (Shearer, 2000; Wirth & Hipp, 2000). Table 1 compares the steps of these models.

All KDP models in Table 1 comprise of multiple steps which are executed in the defined order. Every ensuing step is started upon successful culmination of the past step, and requires the outcome produced by the past step as its input. In addition, all these process models accentuate on iterative nature in terms of many feedback loops that are executed by a revision process. In spite of the fact that these models generally emphasize independence from specific application domain, yet they can be largely categorized into academic and industrial models. Fayyad's nine-step model is typically geared towards academic model which for the most part is not concerned with several important business issues. On the other hand, the CRISP-DM model is exceptionally industry-oriented. However, the academic models can be used generally in the industrial setting with ease and vice versa. The remaining three models occupy the middle ground, blending both academic and industrial issues. In literature, apart from the above discussed KDP models, several other models are also proposed (Alnoukari & El Sheikh, 2011; Berry & Linoff, 1997; Furletti, 2009; Edelstein, 2000; Haglin, Roiger, Hakkila, & Giblin, 2005; Han, Kamber, & Pei, 2012b; Klösgen & Zytkow, 2002; Rennolls & Al-Shawabkeh, 2008). The fundamental difference among the various models is in the proposed number of steps and scope of their specific steps. The various steps of all proposed models includes the range of activities which stretches from the task of learning the ap-

Table 1. Comparison of popular knowledge discovery process models

<table>
<tr><th>Model</th><th>Fayyad et al.</th><th>Anand & Buchner</th><th>Cios et al.</th><th>Cabena et al.</th><th>CRISP-DM</th></tr>
<tr><td rowspan="10">Steps</td><td rowspan="2">Learning and understanding the application domain</td><td>Human resource identification</td><td rowspan="2">Understanding the problem domain</td><td rowspan="2">Business objectives determination</td><td rowspan="2">Business understanding</td></tr>
<tr><td>Problem specification</td></tr>
<tr><td>Creating a target data set</td><td>Data prospecting</td><td rowspan="2">Understanding the data</td><td rowspan="5">Data preparation</td><td rowspan="2">Data understanding</td></tr>
<tr><td>Data cleaning and pre-processing</td><td>Domain knowledge elicitation</td></tr>
<tr><td>Data reduction and projection</td><td>Methodology identification</td><td rowspan="3">Preparation of data</td><td rowspan="3">Data preparation</td></tr>
<tr><td>Choosing the data mining task</td><td rowspan="2">Data pre-processing</td></tr>
<tr><td>Choosing the data mining algorithm</td></tr>
<tr><td>Data mining</td><td>Pattern discovery</td><td>Data mining</td><td>Data mining</td><td>Modeling</td></tr>
<tr><td>Interpreting mined patterns</td><td rowspan="2">Knowledge post-processing</td><td>Evaluation of the discovered knowledge</td><td>Domain knowledge elicitation</td><td>Evaluation</td></tr>
<tr><td>Consolidating discovered knowledge</td><td>Using the discovered knowledge</td><td>Assimilation of knowledge</td><td>Deployment</td></tr>
</table>

plication domain, through data preparation and mining, to evaluation, understanding and application of the extracted knowledge. In general, we can divide the various activities of the KD process in three main phases: Data Pre-processing, Data Processing (also called Data Mining) and Data Post-processing. Data pre-processing includes methods (like cleaning, integration, transformation, reduction, etc.) that help to prepare the input data into a representation that is more efficient for mining algorithms. Data mining includes methods (like classification, regression, association, clustering, etc.) to search for interesting patterns and knowledge in the data. And data post-processing includes methods (like pruning, summarization, visualization, etc.) that aimed at refining and validating the knowledge discovered by the mining process. Among these, the data pre-processing phase is considered to be the most time-consuming phase of the KD process. The general structure of knowledge discovery process with feedback loops is shown in Figure 1.

3. DATA PRE-PROCESSING

Data pre-processing (or data preparation) is the initial preliminary stride of knowledge discovery process. It is required since many real-world datasets are usually noisy (containing errors/outliers), incomplete (have missing attribute values), and inconsistent (containing discrepancies in the data). There may be various reasons for this low quality of practical real-world datasets including faulty data collection instruments, errors in data entry, errors in data transmission, huge data size, multiple heterogeneous sources of data, and so forth. Mining low-quality data will lead to low-quality extracted patterns or models. Thus, data pre-processing techniques can be applied before mining to enhance the quality of the collected data and to transform the data into a representation that is appropriate for mining. The major tasks of data pre-processing include data cleaning, integration, normalization, transformation, dimensionality reduction etc. (Han et al., 2012b). These are not mutually exclusive tasks; they may progress together. For instance, data cleaning may also involve

Figure 1. General structure of knowledge discovery process

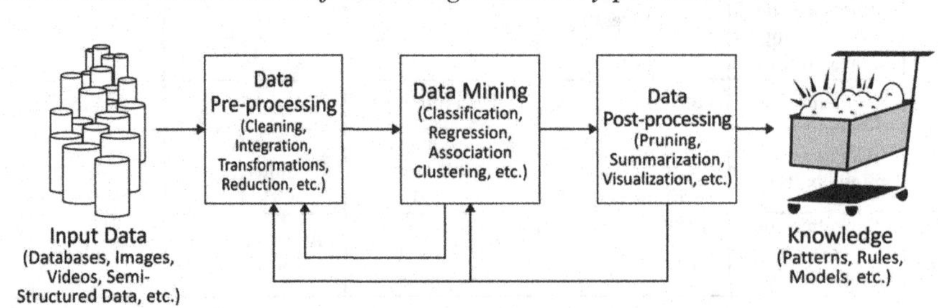

data transformation to fix inappropriate data, such as transforming all differently formatted *date/time* type values to a common format.

3.1 Data Cleaning

Data cleaning attempts to clean the data by filling in missing values, removing noise from data, correcting inconsistencies in data, and identifying or removing outliers. This considerably improves the overall quality of the data and/or reduces the time required for the actual mining. Commercial tools like data scrubbing tools, data auditing tools etc. may be used to aid the data cleaning step. Data cleaning can involve the following:

- **Handling Missing Values:** It might be possible that many tuples have no recorded value for some attributes. This may be due to equipment malfunction, attribute values may not be considered important at the time of entry, values inconsistent with the other recorded data and hence deleted, and so forth. These missing values can be handled as follows:
    - Ignore the tuples that have blank attribute values. However, it is an inefficient method.
    - Fill in the missing values by manually finding the most suitable value for it. However, it is very time consuming and not practical for large data sets containing several missing values.
    - Use a global constant (like NULL, unknown etc.) to fill in all the missing values. Despite of being simple, this method is inefficient.
    - Use the attribute mean for all tuples (or tuples belonging to the same class as the given tuple) to fill in all the missing values for that attribute.
    - Use the most probable value to fill in the missing value. It may need to use methods such as Bayesian classification or decision trees to automatically infer missing attribute values. This is the most popular method of predicting the missing values.
- **Handling Noisy Data:** Noise is a random error or variance in an attribute value. Noisy data may be due to faulty data collection instruments, data entry errors, data transmission errors, and so forth. Data smoothing and outlier removal methods are generally used to eliminate noise in data. Some of these methods are as follows:
    - Regression can be used for data smoothing. It helps to smooth out the noise by fitting the numerical data to a function.
    - Binning can also be used for numerical data smoothing. The method first sorts the data values and then these sorted values are divided into several equal-width bins (or buckets). Thereafter, smoothing of data can

be done by using methods like smoothing by bin means, smoothing by bin medians, or smoothing by bin boundaries.
  - Clustering can be used to detect and remove outliers. An outlier is a data value which is very much different from the remaining data. Most data mining algorithms discard outliers as noise. However, in the applications like fraud detection, medical analysis etc., outliers are the data of interest.
  - Outliers may also be identified by combined computer and human inspection. In this method, computer first detects the suspicious values (possible outliers) which are then checked by humans.
- **Correcting Inconsistencies:** Inconsistencies are discrepancies in the collected data. These discrepancies may come from several reasons like human error in data entry, many formats for input fields (e.g., *date/time*), updating some but not all data occurrences, inconsistent use of codes, data integration (e.g., where a given attribute can have different names in different databases) and so forth. Some inconsistencies may be corrected manually using domain knowledge and expert decision. There are a number of commercial tools available in the market that can also be used to correct inconsistencies in data.

3.2 Data Integration

Data integration is a pre-processing task which involves merging of data from different heterogeneous sources (such as multiple databases, flat files, data cubes etc.) and consequently creating a coherent data store (such as a data warehouse). Data migration and ETL (extraction/transformation/loading) tools can be used to assist the data integration step. During the data integration, one has to consider many issues as discussed below:

- **Schema Integration:** While integrating data from many autonomous data sources, we must assume that they do not conform to the same schema. For example, *employee_id* in one database schema may be *emp_id* in a different database schema. Therefore, the data analysts must resolve the schema heterogeneity and create a unified schema for data. Databases typically have metadata containing description about each attribute including the name, meaning, data type, domain, and constraints. Such metadata can be used to identify the semantically equivalent schema elements for schema integration.
- **Redundancy:** Integration of data from multiple sources may produce attribute redundancies in the resulting data set. An attribute is redundant if it is a copy of another attribute (direct redundancy), or if it can be derived from another attribute or set of attributes (indirect redundancy). For example, the

data set after integration may include the attributes *sex* and *gender* (direct redundancy), or *date_of_birth* and *age* (indirect redundancy, as *age* can be derived from the *date_of_birth*). Redundancy (if uncontrolled) can also lead to inconsistency in the database. Popular techniques for detecting attribute redundancy are correlation analysis (for numeric data), and chi-square method (for categorical data).

- **Data Value Conflicts:** Data value conflicts occur due to differences in representation scheme, scaling, or encoding of attribute values in different data sources. For example, a weight attribute of an item entity may be stored in different units in different data sources. Similarly, the data codes for *gender* attribute of an employee entity in one database may be *M* (for male) and *F* (for female), while *1* (for male) and *2* (for female) in another database. Data value conflicts are usually resolved by data analysis techniques.

3.3 Data Transformation

Data transformation involves transforming the original data set to the data representation that is more appropriate for some specific data mining technique. ETL tools can be used to assist the data transformation step. However, these tools typically support only a confined set of transformations, therefore, to perform some customized transformations, the data analysts may also choose to write custom scripts for this step. Several techniques are available for data transformations as discussed below:

- **Normalization:** It scales the attribute values so that they fall within a small specified range, such as between 0 and 1. The data mining algorithms like neural networks, nearest neighbor classification, and clustering provide better results if the data to be analyzed have been normalized. Most commonly used normalization methods are min-max normalization, z-score normalization, and decimal scaling normalization.
- **Attribute Construction (or Feature Construction):** It involves construction of new attributes from the set of existing attributes to help the data mining process. For example, a *density* attribute constructed from the *mass* and *volume* attributes (i.e., *density* = *mass* / *volume*), can be used directly to accurately classify the materials like wood, clay, bronze, gold etc.
- **Aggregation:** It produces summarization of underlying data using aggregation operations like sum, avg, min, max etc. For example, the sales data of four quarters of a year may be aggregated to produce annual sales. Aggregation is typically used in constructing data cubes which store multidimensional aggregated information. Data cubes provide fast access to pre-computed and summarized data, thus benefiting data mining process.

- **Generalization:** It replaces the low-level (or primitive/raw) concepts by higher-level concepts using concept hierarchies. For example, the numerical values for *age* attribute in an employee entity may be mapped to define higher-level concepts, like *youth* (18-30), *middle_aged* (31-50), and *senior* (51-60).

3.4 Data Reduction

Data reduction helps in obtaining a reduced representation of the available large data set. Complex data analysis/mining process may take a long time to run on complete data set. However, the mining on the reduced data set is much more efficient yet produce the same (or almost the same) analytical results. Most commonly used data reduction techniques are:

- **Dimensionality Reduction:** It is the process of reducing the effective number of attributes or variables under consideration. Attribute subset selection is one of the most commonly used technique of dimensionality reduction in which irrelevant, less relevant, or redundant attributes (or dimensions) are detected and removed.
- **Data Compression:** It is the process of obtaining a reduced or compressed representation of the original data using data compression techniques. Wavelet transform and principal components analysis are most common techniques of data compression which transform or project the original data onto a smaller space (T. Li, Q. Li, Zhu, & Ogihara, 2002; Walia & Verma, 2014).
- **Data Cube Aggregation:** Data cube aggregation is the process in which data is expressed in summary form in a data cube in multidimensional form. This approach results in a data set which is smaller in volume but still maintains all the information necessary for the analysis task.
- **Numerosity Reduction:** Numerosity reduction techniques reduce the data volume by choosing alternative smaller data representations. These representations may be parametric or non-parametric. For parametric representations, a model is used to estimate the data, therefore only the data parameters (and sometimes outliers) are stored instead of the actual data. Examples of such techniques are regression and log-linear models. Non-parametric methods are used to store data in reduced forms such as histograms, clustering, sampling, and so forth.

4. DATA MINING

Data mining is the main phase of knowledge discovery process. It is the process of discovering interesting rules and patterns from huge amount and variety of data by applying automated (or semi-automated) techniques. The data sources can include traditional databases (like relational databases, transactional databases, object-oriented databases, etc.), data warehouses, unstructured and semi-structured repositories (like World Wide Web), and advanced databases (like spatial databases, multimedia databases, time-series databases, etc.). A large number of data mining algorithms from the fields of statistics, machine learning, pattern recognition, and databases have been described in the literature (Han et al., 2012b; Kantardzic, 2011). These algorithms can be broadly categorized into two classes: verification-oriented and discovery-oriented data mining techniques. Figure 2 displays this taxonomy. The verification-oriented data mining techniques verify the pre-specified patterns (i.e., user's hypothesis) against the available data, whereas the discovery-oriented data mining techniques find new rules and patterns autonomously from the available data. The verification-oriented techniques include the most widely recognized methods of traditional statistics like goodness of fit test, tests of hypotheses (e.g. t-test of means), ANOVA (analysis of variance), and so forth. These methods are less associated with data mining than their discovery-oriented counterparts, since in most real world situations we are concerned with discovering new patterns in large amounts of available data rather than testing the known ones.

Figure 2. Data Mining Taxonomy

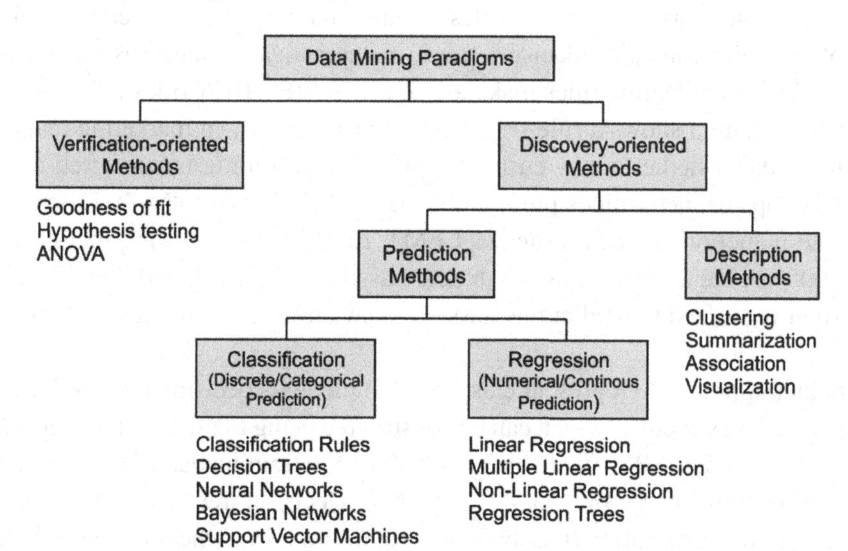

On the other hand, discovery-oriented data mining methods involve fitting models to or determining patterns from underlying huge data. The models can be utilized to predict the future data values, while the patterns describe the relationships among available data values. A discovered model or pattern of interest in a particular representational form like classification rules, decision trees, regression models, clustering models, etc. can be treated as knowledge. Discovery-oriented data mining methods can be classified into two categories: prediction methods and description methods. Prediction methods attempt to find the relationship between input attributes (also referred to as independent variables) and a target attribute (also called a dependent variable) using training data. The discovered relationship is expressed in a structure known as a model. The model describes the hidden phenomena in the dataset and can be utilized for predicting the value of target attribute knowing the values of input attributes. Description methods, on the contrary, characterize the general properties of the available data to find patterns in a human-understandable form. The goals of prediction and description methods can be achieved using following data mining methods:

- **Classification:** Classification is the process of finding a model (or function or classifier) that maps (classifies) a data item into one of few pre-defined classes. For instance, in the bank loan approval, classification techniques can be used to construct a model that classifies a customer (loan applicant) as risky or safe. The general approach to classification is a two-step process. In the first step, a model is derived based on the analysis of a set of training data (i.e. datasets for which the class labels are known). In the second step, the model is utilized to predict the class label of datasets for which class labels are unknown. Typically, a classification model is represented in the form of classification rules, decision trees, mathematical formulae or neural networks. Classification rules make use of a set of IF-THEN rules for classification. Figure 3 shows a rule-based classifier that assists a marketing manager to predict whether a new customer with a given profile is interested to buy a laptop (i.e. determines pre-defined class label "Yes" or "No"). First, using rule-induction algorithm such as LEM1, LEM2, AQ, etc. (Grzymala-Busse, 2005) on the training data rule-based classifier is defined, and then this classifier is utilized to predict the class of a new customer with a given profile.

Another approach to represent classification model is decision tree. A decision tree is a tree like structure, which can be constructed using tree-induction algorithm such as ID3, C4.5, CART, etc. (Murthy, 1998) on the training data. Thereafter, this tree is utilized to foresee the class of new data. Decision trees can also be easily converted into classification rules by following the path from the root node to every

Figure 3. Classification using classification rules (a) building classification rules for training data (b) using classification rules on new data

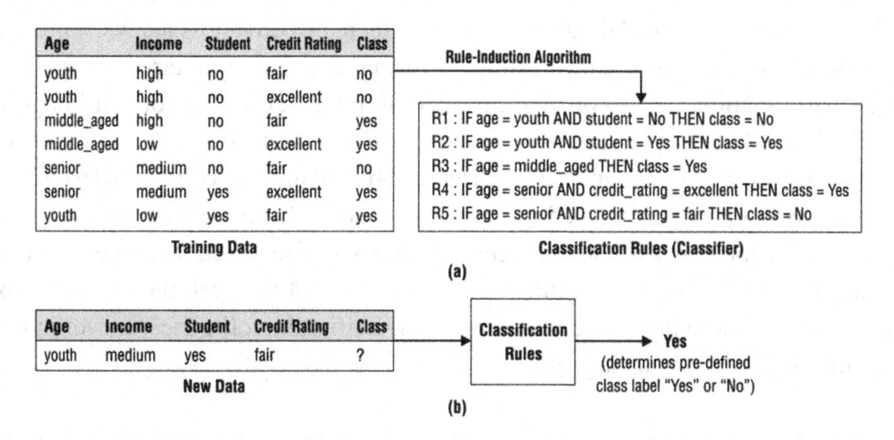

leaf node in the tree. Neural network is another well-known classification approach which can be utilized to model complex relationships between input and target attributes. A neural network is a scientific or mathematical classifier that comprises of a set of neuron-like processing elements with weighted connections amongst input and output parameters. During the training phase, the network learns by adjusting the weights in order to predict the correct class label of the new datasets. In literature, several neural networks (like Feedforward Neural Networks, Hopfield Neural Networks, Kohonen's Self-organizing Maps etc.) and neural network algorithms (like backpropagation) are available (Zhang, 2009). The neural network algorithms are inherently parallel; therefore, parallelization techniques can be utilized to accelerate the computation process. However, neural networks have been criticized for their poor interpretability; because it is difficult for humans to interpret the meaning behind the learned weights in the network. This factor has motivated research to build up a few strategies for rule extraction from trained neural networks which help to improve the interpretability of the learned network.

In addition to the above methods, various advanced methods for building classification models such as Bayesian classification, support vector machines, nearest neighbor classification, etc. also exist (Han, Kamber, & Pei, 2012a). Bayesian classifiers are statistical in nature which can predict class membership probabilities (i.e. the probability that a given dataset belongs to a particular class). Support vector machines are binary classifiers that divide the data into two classes utilizing essential training datasets called support vectors. Nearest-neighbor classifiers simply store the training datasets (rather than doing any model construction from them) and wait for the new dataset. Thus, in nearest-neighbor classifiers the process of training is very fast. When new dataset is given, the classifier identifies its category based on its similarity to the stored training datasets. Classification techniques have applications in numerous domains, including fraud detection (e.g. loan approval, credit card transactions), medical diagnosis (e.g. treatment effectiveness analysis, protein structure classification), spam filtering, performance prediction, target marketing, image classification, and so on. For instance, in image classification, an image is classified based upon its visual contents (like texture, shape, color etc.) into one of few pre-defined classes (Tomar & Agarwal, 2014; Walia & Verma, 2016). Classification techniques can be used to construct a model from a collection of classified images, which classify new images on the basis of its visual contents (Seetha, Muralikrishna, Deekshatulu, Malleswari, & Hegde, 2008). Such models have applications in the domains like computer vision, artificial intelligence, surveillance, medicine, weather forecasting, etc.

- **Regression:** Regression is the process of finding a model (or function or classifier) that often maps a data item to a numerical value. For instance, a regressor can predict the demand of a new product given its characteristics. The difference between classification and regression is that classification manages discrete/categorical target attributes, whereas regression deals with numerical/continuous target attributes. In other words, if the target attribute contains continuous values, then a regression technique is required. Linear regression is the most common form of regression, in which a line that best fits the data (having two attributes, one target attribute and one input attribute) is calculated (i.e., the line that minimizes the average distance of all the points from the line). This line represents a predictive model. When the value of the target attribute is not known; its value is predicted by the point on the line that corresponds to the value of the input attribute. Multiple linear regression is an extension of linear regression, where one target attribute and more than one input attributes are involved and the data are fit to a multidimensional surface. Further, if the data does not show a linear dependence, non-linear regression (like polynomial regression) can be utilized to get a more accurate model. In addition to linear and non-linear regression data models, numerous other regression-based models like log-linear models, generalized linear models, and regression trees also exist (Han & Kamber, 2006). Regression techniques have applications in domains like sales forecasting, biomedical and drug response modeling, environmental modeling, business planning, social media modeling, and so on. For instance, Facebook uses regression model to predict the future engagements for a user based on the factors like the amount of personal information shared, friend requests accepted or initiated, number of photos tagged, likes, comments, etc.

- **Clustering:** Clustering is the process of dividing a large data set into categorical classes (or groups or clusters) such that data inside a cluster have high similarity in comparison with the data in other clusters. Thus, it represents the large data set by few clusters and subsequently presents the data in a simplified form which is more understandable to the user. Cluster analysis has been broadly utilized in numerous applications, including market or customer segmentation, biological studies (e.g., to find genes or proteins having similar functionality), astronomy (e.g., aggregation of stars, galaxies, or super galaxies), spatial data analysis (e.g., to find group of spatial locations prone to earth quakes), pattern recognition, web document classification, and many others. For instance, in marketing, clustering can be used to discover distinct groups of their customers and use this knowledge to develop targeted marketing programs. Figure 4 shows a 2D plot of customer data regarding their locations in a city and three clusters of customers for possible targeted marketing.

Unlike classification in which the classes are pre-defined, the classes in clustering must be determined from the data set. In spite of the fact that classification is an effective means for finding classes of data, at the same time it requires costly collection and labeling of training data, which the classifier uses for model construction. For large data sets, clustering is often more desirable which first partitions the

Figure 4. 2D plot of customer data regarding their locations in a city and three clusters of customers for possible targeted marketing

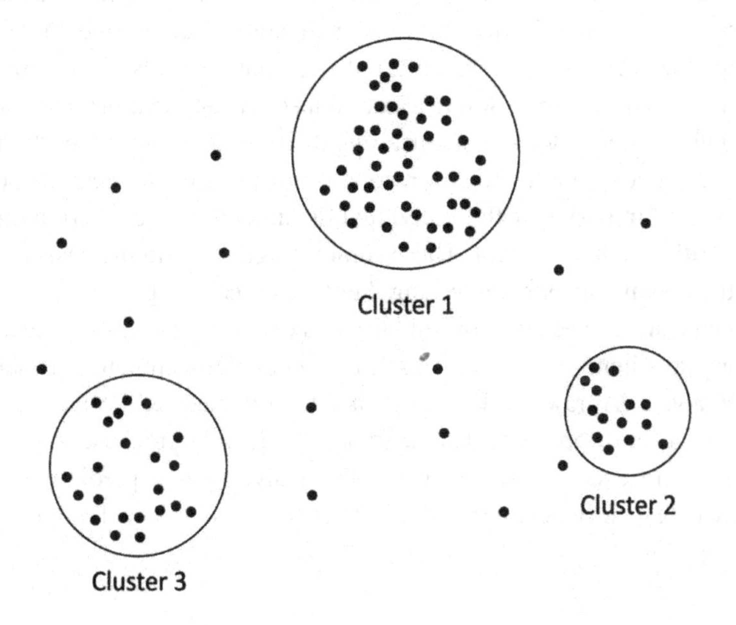

data set into groups based on data similarity (using clustering methods), and afterward assigns labels to the relatively small number of groups. More importantly such a clustering-based process is adaptable to changes and can discover valuable features that distinguish different groups. Numerous well-known clustering methods including agglomerative algorithm, divisive algorithm, k-means method, PAM, CLARA, DBSCAN, OPTICS, STING, etc. exist in the literature (Berkhin, 2006; Han et al., 2012b). These methods determine clusters by finding natural groupings of data items based upon similarity metrics or probability density models. Clustering can also be used during pre-processing step of other algorithms to get insight into data distribution prior to mining.

- **Summarization:** Summarization is the process of mapping data into subsets with simple descriptions. The summarized dataset gives general overview of the data with aggregated information. Simple summarization methods are based on statistical measures such as mean, standard deviation and variance of data fields. For example, the call data of a customer can be summarized into total call minutes, total spending, total calls etc. instead of detailed calls. Such information can be presented to sales manager for analysis of his customer and business. Summarization can scale up to various levels of abstraction and can be seen from different angles. For example, the call data can further be summarized into domestic calls and international calls. Generally, summarization techniques are applied for exploratory data analysis, data visualization, and automated report generation where the actual data is huge (Alfred, 2008). For instance, using summarization techniques (like data cube, histogram etc.) intelligently within visualization systems, one could not only reduce the size and dimensionality of large data, but also highlight relevant and important features. Summarization also has applications in domains including automatic document clustering, text mining, Internet portal management, help-desk automation for responses to customer queries, and so on. For instance, summaries of the individual documents in a collection can reveal similarities in their content. These summaries then form the basis for clustering the documents or categorizing them into specified groups.
- **Association:** Association or link analysis discovers interesting relationships among data items in a huge dataset. It is a popular technique for market basket analysis (Agrawal, Mannila, Srikant, Toivonen, & Verkamo, 1996) to identify a set of products that customers frequently purchase together. Such findings are exceptionally valuable for analyzing and predicting customer behavior. For instance, retailers might utilize this type of data mining to re-

veal that customers always buy crisps when they buy beers, and, therefore, they can put beers and crisps next to each other to save time for customer and increase sales. Moreover, this is the type of data mining that drives the Amazon recommendation system and Netflix movie recommendations. Typically, association rules are used to uncover relationships between apparently unrelated data in a transaction-oriented database, relational database or other information repository. The general approach of association rule mining can be viewed as a two-steps process (Han et al., 2012b; Hipp, Güntzer, & Nakhaeizadeh, 2000). In the first step, all frequent itemsets (a set of items, such as crisps and beer, which appear frequently together in a dataset) are determined using algorithms like Apriori, FP-growth, Eclat etc. Then in the second step, association rules are generated from the frequent itemsets. Association analysis also plays a vital role in applications like marketing promotions (targeting coupons/deals or advertising), product clustering, store layout and catalog designing, web mining, medical diagnosis, scientific & biological data analysis, and so forth. For instance, in the analysis of Earth science data, the association patterns may reveal some interesting connections among the land, ocean, and atmospheric processes. Such information may help the Earth scientists to understand how the different elements of the Earth system interact with each other.

- **Visualization:** Visualization is the process of presenting the large data in a graphical format that allows the user to gain insight into the data, interact directly with the data, and identify new patterns. Visualization has been proved effective in application domains like information retrieval, astronomy, biological data analysis, geographic data analysis, web visualization, text visualization, business data visualization and analysis, sports data visualization and analysis, and so on (S. Liu, Cui, Wu, & M. Liu, 2014). For instance, digital map applications like google maps, HERE maps etc. provide a powerful visual representation for geographic data (e.g., streets, parks, rivers, etc.) along with textual information. Such representation can be used to get details about the local places, driving directions, and so forth. Several well-known and proven visualization techniques including histograms, scatter-plot matrices, treemaps, parallel coordinates, spatial visualization, 2D and 3D graphs, stick figures, perspective wall, and so forth (Keim, 2002) have been suggested in the literature. These techniques can be utilized during the different stages of the KD process so as to explore the data prior to mining, to help in the data mining process to extract interesting rules or patterns, and to understand and explore the discovered rules or patterns.

5. DATA POST-PROCESSING

Data post-processing is a significant phase after data mining in knowledge discovery process. In this phase the knowledge discovered by data mining algorithms will undergo some kind of refinement, interpretation, and evaluation before presenting it to the users (Bruha & Famili, 2000). The goal of this phase is to convert the discovered knowledge into useful, comprehensible, and applicable knowledge desired by the end users. Most commonly used post-processing procedures are pruning, summarization, and visualization (Baesens, Viaene, & Vanthienen. 2000). These procedures are not mutually exclusive and may work together in any post-processing attempt.

- **Pruning:** The knowledge discovered by data mining algorithms usually have huge structure containing many non-predictive and redundant components. These superfluous or non-predictive components in discovered knowledge may be due to noise in training data, incorrect sampling size of training data, unknown probability distribution of collected data, stochastic nature of the sampling process, and so forth. It is necessary to remove these superfluous components from discovered knowledge before presenting it to the users. These superfluous components in discovered knowledge may be removed using the process called pruning. By removing superfluous parts, pruning mechanisms not only reduce the size of the discovered knowledge, but also improve its efficiency and accuracy. There are many techniques proposed to filter and prune discovered knowledge. For instance, Toivonen, Klemettinen, Ronkainen, Hätönen, and Mannila (1995) proposed rule covers to prone discovered rules; Liu, Sun, and Zhang (2009) presented a technique for rule reduction using closed set; Baralis and Chiusano (2004) proposed essential rule set to yield a minimal rule set without information loss for the classification knowledge available in a classification rule set; Li, Han, and Pei (2001) proposed CMAR algorithm for long rule pruning and redundant rule pruning; and many more.
- **Summarization:** Although pruning significantly reduces the size of discovered knowledge, however, it may still be substantially large. Summarization is the process of representing the discovered knowledge (usually after pruning) with a small subset without losing much information. Such summarized knowledge is easier to understand and interpret by the users. Lent, Swami, and Widom (1997) proposed to summarize the learned association rules by clustering. Liu, Hsu, and Ma (1999) proposed a technique for pruning and summarizing discovered associations by first removing insignificant associations and then creating direction setting (DS) rules, a summary of the discovered associations. Pasquier (2009) presented a technique for filtering and

summarizing discovered associations. The technique first filters irrelevant and useless association rules and then summarizes a reduced set of association based on condensed representations.

- **Visualization:** Visualization is an effective way to aid in understanding and exploring discovered knowledge. A large number of techniques have been proposed for visualizing the extracted knowledge. For instance, Yamamoto, de Oliveira, and Rezende (2009) proposed the visualization techniques to assist the generation and exploration of association rules. Kohavi and Tesler (2001) proposed 3D visualization of decision trees to assist the tree exploration. Chen and Liu (2004) proposed an approach for visual cluster analysis. In addition, several commercial visualization tools like DBMiner, Spotfire, WinViz, etc. (Tomar & Agarwal, 2014) are also available to extract, explore and evaluate the knowledge from underlying large volumes of data.

6. KNOWLEDGE DISCOVERY IN WEB (AND SEMANTIC WEB)

The World Wide Web (or Web) is rapidly emerging as the huge and dynamic collection of data related to nearly every aspect of society including commerce, science, politics and government, health, and so on. This web data is stored in one or more web servers. Web mining (or knowledge discovery from Web) is the application of data mining techniques to discover potentially useful information or patterns or knowledge from the web data. But web data is generally not structured like databases; rather it is semi-structured data such as HTML documents or unstructured data such as text, graphs, images and video. Therefore, the extraction of information and interesting patterns out of the Web is a complex task. However, there have been increasing efforts in the research community to realize the next generation Web called the Semantic Web (Berners-Lee, Hendler, & Lassila, 2001). The current Web has huge amount of unstructured data that can only be understood by humans; machine understandability is limited. The Semantic Web is not a separate Web but an extension of the current one, which have the basic idea to enrich the web pages with machine-understandable data (e.g. for software agents, sophisticated search engines, and web services). The key technology of Semantic Web architecture is Ontologies (Staab & Studer, 2013) that represents the web page data in a well-defined and structured manner which can be processed by automated tools as well as manually by users. Semantic web is innovative in trying to combine the domain knowledge (expressed in ontologies) and the process of knowledge discovery. The domain knowledge helps to filter out the redundant or inconsistent data in the pre-processing phase. During the searching and pattern generating process, domain knowledge helps to reduce the search space and guide the search path. Furthermore, in the post-processing step, discovered patterns can be cleaned out with the help of domain knowledge. It seems therefore to be valuable to perform web mining on information with a well-defined meaning to improve the knowledge discovery process.

6.1 Data on the Web and Semantic Web

The Web is a huge collection of data. HTML (HyperText Markup Language) is the standard language of publishing data on web in the form of HTML documents. However, these documents are not very machine friendly because computer programs do not know the meaning of the data while parsing the HTML tags. HTML tags only indicate how the data should be displayed. To overcome the problems of HTML, XML (eXtensible Markup Language) was developed. It provides the facility to describe data in web documents by defining tags and the structural relationship between them. Since there is no predefined tag set in XML, all the semantics of an XML document will be defined by the scripts or programs that process them. Moreover, XSD (XML Schema Document) is the XML schema language that can be used to validate the XML documents. It provides a means for defining the elements that can be used in the documents and the set of constraints for the contents of the elements in the documents. Thus, XML and XSD allow users to create dynamic structures in documents but say nothing about their meaning, the exact meaning of the tags lies with the programmer (the writer of the script or program).

The Semantic Web is an extension of the Web which promotes the idea to add semantics to web documents. RDF (Resource Description Framework) (Manola, Miller, & McBride, 2004) is the data model of the Semantic Web developed to provide the required structural constraints to represent semantics. It expresses any web resource in terms of RDF statements. RDF statement is defined as a triple (s, p, o) having a subject (s), a predicate (p), and an object (o). The subject represents any resource described in terms of properties (i.e., predicates) and property values (i.e., objects). Consider the following statements about a web document:

- Vishal is the architect of the Document1.
- The architect of the Document1 is Vishal.

These statements convey the same meaning. RDF attempts to provide an unambiguous method of expressing semantics by extracting the RDF terms. For instance, Document1 as subject, architect as predicate, and Vishal as object can be extracted from above statements to form the triplet (Document1, architect, Vishal). RDF graph is a representation of the document triple as directed labeled graph. Subject (draws as oval) and object (draws as rectangle) represent nodes of the graph and the predicate (draws as arc) is the directed link from subject to object. Figure 5 shows a RDF

Figure 5. RDF Graph

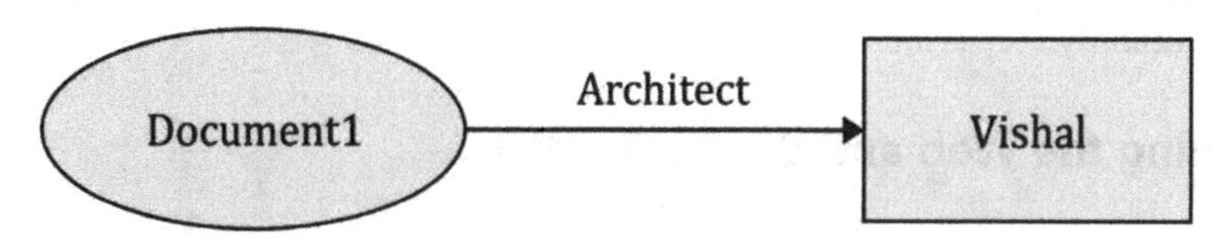

graph of a triplet described above. RDF was originally designed to add metadata like author, creation date/time, modification date/time, language, etc. to the web documents, but later used for storing any type of data. RDF/XML is an application of XML that can be used to represent RDF graphs in web documents. RDF Schema (RDFS) is an extension of RDF which includes facilities for representing subclass/superclass relationships as well as the options to impose constraints on the statements specified in the documents conforming to the schema. Thus, RDFS is more expressive than RDF. RDF (or RDFS) documents are being used for situations in which data needs to be processed by applications, rather than just presented to humans. For instance, they have applications in domains like resource discovery (to provide improved search engine capabilities), cataloging (for describing the contents and relationships between web documents that are available at a particular Web site or digital Library), software agents (to facilitate knowledge-sharing and exchange), content rating (to evaluate collection of web pages which represent a single logical document), describing property rights of web pages, privacy preferences of a user, privacy policies of a web site, etc.

The Web Ontology Language (OWL) (Antoniou & Van Harmelen, 2004) is an ontology-based language for Semantic Web built on top of RDF and RDFS. The term ontology is from philosophy and is co-opted by computer science. In computer science, it defines the base concepts and relationship structures used to describe and represent a knowledge domain. The basic elements of the OWL ontology are classes, properties, instances of classes, and relationships between these instances which can be represented using XML based syntax. It also includes elements from description logics and provides many constructs for the specification of semantics (including conjunction and disjunction, existentially and universally quantified variables and property inversion). Using these constructs, a reasoning module can make logical inferences and derive knowledge that was previously only implicit in the data. Thus, OWL has much higher level of expressive power and logical reasoning/inferencing capabilities than RDF/RDFS. However, the expressiveness of OWL comes at the cost of increased complexity. Therefore, OWL provides three increasingly expressive sub-languages designed for use by specific communities of implementers and users: OWL-Lite, OWL-DL, and OWL-Full. These languages are extensions of each other (OWL-Lite $\subseteq$ OWL-DL $\subseteq$ OWL-Full) both syntactically and semantically.

6.2 Mining the Web and Semantic Web

The Web has made an enormous amount of data electronically accessible. The purpose of Web mining is to develop methods and systems for discovering models or patterns from the data on the Web and for web-based systems. Usually, web mining can be classified into three broad categories (B. Singh & H. K. Singh, 2010), according to the types of data to be mined:

- Web content mining, which operates on the contents of web documents (that may consist of text, images, audio, video etc.) to extract useful information and patterns. The techniques for web content mining are the extension of basic data mining methods (like classification, clustering, summarization etc.) for the web data. For instance, the goal of web document classification is to construct a classifier from a collection of classified documents, which can classify new web documents on the basis of its contents. Application of such techniques is in spam filters, which scan the text contents of email messages to classify them as spam or regular email (Androutsopoulos, Koutsias, Chandrinos, Paliouras, & Spyropoulos, 2000). Similarly, the purpose of web document clustering is to divide the large numbers of web documents into groups of similar documents based of their contents. This is usually an intermediate process for optimizing search or retrieval of web documents. Moreover, summarization techniques are used to reduce the length of web documents by analyzing their semantics. With the rapid growth of the web documents, there are increasing applications of web content mining techniques in the domains like information extraction, topic identification and tracking, concept discovery, focused crawling, content-based personalization, intelligent search tools, text mining, image mining, and so forth (Singh, Sharma, & Dey, 2015).
- Web structure mining, which makes use of the hyperlink structure of web documents as an additional informational source for mining. The techniques for web structure mining utilize the link structure of the Web along with data mining methods to discover useful information and patterns. For instance, popular search engines like Google, Bing, Clever etc. use algorithms (such as PageRank, Weighted PageRank and HITS) based on link structure of the Web for document retrieval and ranking (da Costa & Gong, 2005; O'Neill & Curran, 2011). Link prediction is also an active research area in data mining for social network analysis and the discovery of web communities. Link-

based classification and clustering are the most recent upgrade of a classic data mining tasks to linked domains (Getoor, 2003).

- Web usage mining, which analyzes web usage data to construct a model that predicts the user's behavior. The techniques for web usage mining utilize the data mining methods on usage data such as web servers access logs, browser logs, user profiles, user queries, bookmark data etc. to analyze the user's access pattern and try to predict the user's behavior. For instance, in e-commerce applications, recommender systems extend the use of mining techniques like clustering, classification, and association rules to web usage data to predict and make recommendations to the users (Sumathi, Valli, & Santhanam, 2010). Good quality recommendation system not only helps in satisfying the customer preferences, but also aids in improving sales and attracting new customers. Web usage mining techniques also have applications in the domains like user and customer behavior modeling, web-site optimization, web marketing, targeted advertising, and so on (Srivastava, Cooley, Deshpande, & Tan, 2000).

Semantic Web enhances the current Web with formally encoded semantics in the form of ontologies (or RDF/RDFS). This promises to enrich web mining and eventually the knowledge discovery process. Rather, the fields of Semantic Web and web mining combine to produce a new research field called Semantic web mining (Stumme, Hotho, & Berendt, 2006). In literature, several ontology-based web mining and knowledge discovery tasks have been proposed (Dou, Wang, & Liu, 2015). For instance, knowledge in the form of ontologies can be used to infer additional information about documents, potentially providing a better foundation for web document classification and clustering (Bloehdorn & Hotho, 2004; Hotho, Staab, & Stumme, 2003). Aljandal, Bahirwani, Caragea, and Hsu, (2009) presented a link prediction framework for online social networks (like Twitter, Facebook, Google+, etc.) with ontology enriched numerical graph features. The latest advancements in Semantic web are indications of a future which is already perceptible. The most successful future digital ventures will be the ones that realize today to capture, analyze, and visualize data in the semantic web, and utilize that information to predict the needs of their users even before they know themselves.

7. OTHER APPLICATION AREAS OF KNOWLEDGE DISCOVERY

Knowledge discovery techniques have extensively been applied in various scientific and business application domains and the results were found extremely helpful as those were convincingly used as input for efficient decision making. Some of the target applications have been described below:

7.1 Scientific Applications

Astronomy, space science, planetary science, weather forecasting, biological data analysis, etc. (Fayyad, Haussler, & Stolorz, 1996) are some of the scientific processes which have been benefitted and bettered using knowledge discovery techniques as discussed below:

- **Sky Objects Cataloging:** The Second Palomar Observatory Sky Survey (Reid et al., 1991) was a major undertaking of astronomy and space science which produced a multi-terabyte of image data containing billions of sky objects. The basic objective of this survey was to classify the sky objects based on their attributes into various classes (star, galaxy etc.). The attributes and classes for sky objects have been defined by the astronomers. Once the classification done, astronomers could be able to conduct all sorts of scientific analysis such as studying the evolution of galaxies, evaluation of large structures in the universe, formation of astrological structure from star/galaxy counts, etc. However, massive size of database ruled out to undergo image classification manually. For analyzing large-scale sky surveys, Fayyad, Weir, and Djorgovski (1993) developed an automated system called SKICAT (SKy Image Cataloging and Analysis Tool) by integrating the techniques from image processing, data classification and knowledge discovery. SKICAT system classifies the sky objects with high accuracy, the majority of which being too faint for visual recognition by astronomers.
- **Automated Detection of Volcanoes on Planet Venus:** NASA's Magellan spacecraft orbited the planet Venus for over five years (1990-1994) and produced a dataset consisting of over 30,000 high-resolution images of the planet Venus. This dataset was uniquely valuable for planetary science because of its completeness and similarity of Venus with Earth in size. However, the huge size of the dataset prevented planetary geologists from effectively exploiting its contents. To help the geologists, JARtool (JPL Adaptive Recognition Tool) (Burl, Fayyad, Perona, Smyth, & Burl, 1994) was developed to analyze this dataset. The idea behind this system was to automate the search for volcanoes on Venus (an important feature of study) by training the system via examples. The geologists initially label the volcanoes on a few images, the system then automatically constructs a classifier that would proceed to scan the rest of the image database and attempt to locate and measure the estimated 1 million small volcanoes.

- **Biological Data Analysis:** During the last few decades, rapid growth has been observed in both the volume and the complexity of biological data (DNA/RNA/protein structures, gene expression profiles etc.). Analyzing these huge databases is a challenging task not only because of their complexity and multiple correlated factors but also because of the continuous evolution of many understandings about the biological systems. Classical approaches of biological data analysis are no longer efficient as these produce only a very limited amount of productive information. This led to the development of biological knowledge discovery techniques (Elloumi & Zomaya, 2013) that take into account both the characteristics of the biological data and the general requirements of the knowledge discovery process. These techniques have been found very useful in applications like DNA/protein sequencing and linkage analysis, disease pattern classification, and so forth.
- **Geological and Geophysical Applications:** Knowledge discovery applications in geology and geophysics include weather prediction, earthquake prediction, land use analysis etc. These applications have gigabytes of datasets collected from satellite and remote sensing devices. One of the early successful and proven knowledge discovery system for atmospheric data analysis was CONQUEST (CONcurrent QUErying in Space and Time) (Stolorz et al., 1995). This system was designed to handle queries concerning the presence, duration, and strength of cyclones and tornadoes in the atmosphere via spatio-temporal mining. Stolorz and Dean (1996) introduced an automatic application Quakefinder as an extension to CONQUEST, which detects and measures tectonic activities in the Earth's crust during earthquakes using satellite imagery data of a fault-laden area. Similar approaches are nowadays being applied to a number of applications related to land use analysis, global climate change, mineral prospecting, ecological modeling etc.

7.2 Business Applications

Knowledge Discovery has altogether changed what actually business was used to be in the past. Almost all varieties of business domains including marketing, finance, manufacturing, telecommunications, and many others are utilizing knowledge discovery methodologies to deal with correct prediction, fraud detection, optimization of business processes and adaptability to different dynamic environments. Some important domains are described below:

- **Marketing and Sales:** Most applications of data mining and knowledge discovery in the marketing and sales domain comes under the broad area called Database Marketing. This type of marketing relies on analysis of customer database to identify different customer groups and predict their behavior. For instance, one such popular application is market-basket analysis (Agrawal et al., 1996), which looks at possible combination of products frequently bought by the customers. Here the association or link analysis techniques analyze the transaction oriented database to find the frequent patterns such as "If customer buys item A, he/she is also likely to buy item B and item C". Such patterns may be used by retailers for taking decisions about different marketing activities like product placement, promotional pricing, and continuous flow process for materials etc. Other applications are more descriptive, focusing on discovering patterns that help market analysts to make adaptability to different dynamic environments. For example, CoverStory and Spotlight (Brachman, Khabaza, Kloesgen, Piatetsky-Shapiro, & Simoudis, 1996) were among the first few commercial systems developed and deployed to analyze supermarket sales data. They produced reports that identify the significant differences in regional sales across time and geographic regions, and provide reasonable explanations for these differences using natural language and business graphics tools. Other knowledge discovery systems for large business databases are EXPLORA and KDW (Knowledge Discovery Workbench) (Fan & Li, 1998). They were designed to support analysts in extracting new knowledge about a business domain using data clustering, summarization, classification, and change detection techniques.

- **Investment:** Many popular financial investment and management companies such as LBS Capital Management, Morgan Stanley and Co., Daiwa Securities and NEC Corp., Fidelity, etc. are employing neural networks and other advanced data mining techniques for tasks like portfolio creation and management, trading model creation, and many more (Hall, Mani, & Barr, 1996; Krishnaswamy, Gilbert, & Pashley, 2000). These portfolio management and investment tools analyze a large number of stocks and investments and thereafter select an optimal portfolio based upon the estimated stock risk and expected rate of return. However, to establish a competitive advantage over others, the users and developers of such application tools rarely publicize their precise details and achieved effectiveness.
- **Fraud Detection:** Fraud detection aims at revealing fraudulent user behavior from analysis of underlying domain data. Many systems were developed for fraud detection using knowledge discovery techniques in the field of telecommunications, credit card operations, finance, and insurance. For instance, AT&T developed a system to detect fraudulent international calls using change detection techniques (Eick & Fyock, 1996). The FALCON fraud assessment system was developed by HNC Inc. using neural networks and is used by many retail banking institutions to detect suspicious credit card trans-

actions. The Financial Crimes Enforcement Network AI System (FAIS) uses knowledge discovery techniques to identify possible money laundering activity within large financial transactions (Senator et al., 1995). The ASPeCT (Advanced Security for Personal Communications Technologies) European research group used unsupervised clustering to detect fraud in mobile phone networks (Burge et al. 1997). Fraudulent behavior is suspected with marked differences between user history and current usage.

- **Other Areas:** The knowledge discovery techniques are also very useful in the areas of manufacturing and production, telecommunications, healthcare etc. In manufacturing and production, KD techniques are used to ensure the quality of end products. For example, CASSIOPEE troubleshooting system was developed by General Electric and SNECMA to diagnose and predict the malfunctions of Boeing aircraft engines using clustering methods. Telecommunication companies use knowledge discovery methodologies to improve marketing tactics, detection of fraud, and better management of telecommunication networks. For instance, TASA (Telecommunication Network Alarm Sequence Analyzer) (Hatonen, Klemettinen, Mannila, Ronkainen, & Toivonen, 1996) was a knowledge discovery system developed for predicting faults in a communication network from a database of telecommunication network alarms using rule induction. In the area of healthcare, Health-KEFIR (KEy FIndings Reporter) (Matheus, Piatetsky-Shapiro, & Mc- Neill, 1996) was a knowledge discovery system developed to perform an automatic drill-down analysis through healthcare data to find the most interesting deviations of specific quantitative measures using deviation detection techniques. It also generates explanations for most interesting and frequent deviations and may even generate recommendations for necessary actions.

8. CONCLUSION

Knowledge Discovery is a process that finds new knowledge about an application domain from underlying large volumes of data and uses that knowledge for making decisions and strategies in related application areas. It is a growing field which combines techniques from domains like machine learning, artificial intelligence, pattern recognition, databases, statistics etc. There is no question that earlier tools and techniques (based on statistical and numerical modeling) bestow value to organizations that collect and analyze their data. More is expected from knowledge discovery tools than simply creating models as in areas like machine learning and pattern recognition. One can actually accomplish the automated (or semi-automated) computational tools and techniques by focusing on the cognitive factors that make the resulting models coherent, realistic, reliable, easy to use, and easy to communicate to other. The knowledge discovery has applications in numerous scientific and business domains; however the World Wide Web is one of the most fertile areas for data mining and knowledge discovery research because it contains huge amount of information. Web mining is the application of data mining techniques to discover and analyze potentially useful information from Web data. These techniques also utilized for the analysis of social media data, behavior of individual users, access patterns of pages or sites, properties of collections of documents and so forth. With Semantic Web, ontologies can be used to encode the domain knowledge and provides a good support for the various web mining tasks and eventuality the knowledge discovery process. While knowledge discovery techniques hold the promise to unlock the knowledge lying in huge databases, they suffer some shortcomings such as problems in incremental rule generation when database is expanded, representing multiple interrelated relations in databases and finally consistency and accuracy of the generated rules. However, the ability of knowledge discovery techniques to process huge volumes of data in various potential applications makes it a necessity. The truth is that Knowledge Discovery is a prerequisite for innovation. As new types of data, new applications, and new analysis demands continue to emerge, there is no doubt that more and more novel data mining and knowledge discovery tasks will appear in the future. The future seems to be dazzling for knowledge discovery. Increasing computational power and continuous creative solutions will certainly revolutionize the way the data is mined and information is processed.

REFERENCES

Agrawal, R., Mannila, H., Srikant, R., Toivonen, H., & Verkamo, A. I. (1996). Fast discovery of association rules. *Advances in Knowledge Discovery and Data Mining, 12*(1), 307-328.

Alfred, R. (2008). *A Data Summarisation Approach to Knowledge Discovery*. University of York.

Aljandal, W., Bahirwani, V., Caragea, D., & Hsu, W. H. (2009). Ontology-Aware Classification and Association Rule Mining for Interest and Link Prediction in Social Networks. In *AAAI Spring Symposium: Social Semantic Web: Where Web 2.0 Meets Web 3.0* (pp. 3-8).

Alnoukari, M., & El Sheikh, A. (2011). Knowledge Discovery Process Models: From Traditional to Agile Modeling. *Business Intelligence and Agile Methodologies for Knowledge-Based Organizations: Cross-Disciplinary Applications*, 72-100.

Anand, S. S., & Büchner, A. G. (1998). Decision support using data mining. *Financial Times Management.*

Androutsopoulos, I., Koutsias, J., Chandrinos, K. V., Paliouras, G., & Spyropoulos, C. D. (2000). An evaluation of naive bayesian anti-spam filtering.*Proceedings of the workshop on Machine Learning in the New Information Age*.

Antoniou, G., & Van Harmelen, F. (2004). Web ontology language: Owl. In *Handbook on ontologies* (pp. 67–92). Springer Berlin Heidelberg. doi:10.1007/978-3-540-24750-0_4

Baesens, B., Viaene, S., & Vanthienen, J. (2000). Post-processing of association rules.*The Sixth ACM SIGKDD International Conference on Knowledge Discovery and Data Mining (KDD'2000)*, 2-8.

Baralis, E., & Chiusano, S. (2004). Essential classification rule sets. *ACM Transactions on Database Systems*, *29*(4), 635–674. doi:10.1145/1042046.1042048

Berkhin, P. (2006). A survey of clustering data mining techniques. In *Grouping multidimensional data* (pp. 25–71). Springer Berlin Heidelberg. doi:10.1007/3-540-28349-8_2

Berners-Lee, T., Hendler, J., & Lassila, O. (2001). The semantic web. *Scientific American*, *284*(5), 28–37. doi:10.1038/scientificamerican0501-34 PMID:11341160

Berry, M. J., & Linoff, G. (1997). *Data mining techniques: for marketing, sales, and customer support*. John Wiley & Sons, Inc.

Bloehdorn, S., & Hotho, A. (2004, August). Boosting for text classification with semantic features. In *International Workshop on Knowledge Discovery on the Web* (pp. 149-166). Springer Berlin Heidelberg.

Brachman, R. J., Khabaza, T., Kloesgen, W., Piatetsky-Shapiro, G., & Simoudis, E. (1996). Mining business databases. *Communications of the ACM*, *39*(11), 42–48. doi:10.1145/240455.240468

Bruha, I., & Famili, A. (2000). Postprocessing in machine learning and data mining. *ACM SIGKDD Explorations Newsletter*, *2*(2), 110–114. doi:10.1145/380995.381059

Burge, P., Shawe-Taylor, J., Cooke, C., Moreau, Y., Preneel, B., & Stoermann, C. (1997, April). Fraud detection and management in mobile telecommunications networks. In *Security and Detection, 1997. ECOS 97., European Conference on* (pp. 91-96). IET. doi:10.1049/cp:19970429

Burl, M. C., Fayyad, U. M., Perona, P., Smyth, P., & Burl, M. P. (1994, June). Automating the hunt for volcanoes on Venus. In *Computer Vision and Pattern Recognition, 1994. Proceedings CVPR'94., 1994 IEEE Computer Society Conference on* (pp. 302-309). IEEE. doi:10.1109/CVPR.1994.323844

Cabena, P., Hadjinian, P., Stadler, R., Verhees, J., & Zanasi, A. (1998). *Discovering data mining: from concept to implementation*. Prentice-Hall, Inc.

Chen, K., & Liu, L. (2004). VISTA: Validating and refining clusters via visualization. *Information Visualization, 3*(4), 257–270. doi:10.1057/palgrave.ivs.9500076

Cios, K. J., Teresinska, A., Konieczna, S., Potocka, J., & Sharma, S. (2000). Diagnosing myocardial perfusion from PECT bulls-eye maps-A knowledge discovery approach. *IEEE Engineering in Medicine and Biology Magazine, 19*(4), 17–25. doi:10.1109/51.853478 PMID:10916729

da Costa, M. G., & Gong, Z. (2005, July). Web structure mining: an introduction. In *2005 IEEE International Conference on Information Acquisition*. IEEE.

Devedzic, V. (2002). Knowledge discovery and data mining in databases.Handbook of Software Engineering and Knowledge Engineering Vol. 1-Fundamentals, 615-637.

Dou, D., Wang, H., & Liu, H. (2015, February). Semantic data mining: A survey of ontology-based approaches. In *Semantic Computing (ICSC), 2015 IEEE International Conference on* (pp. 244-251). IEEE. doi:10.1109/ICOSC.2015.7050814

Edelstein, H. (2000). Building profitable customer relationships with data mining. In Customer Relationship Management (pp. 339-351). Vieweg+ Teubner Verlag.

Eick, S. G., & Fyock, D. E. (1996). Visualizing corporate data. *AT&T Technical Journal, 75*(1), 74-86.

Elloumi, M., & Zomaya, A. Y. (2013). *Biological Knowledge Discovery Handbook: Preprocessing, Mining and Postprocessing of Biological Data* (Vol. 23). John Wiley & Sons. doi:10.1002/9781118617151

Fan, J., & Li, D. (1998). An overview of data mining and knowledge discovery. *Journal of Computer Science and Technology, 13*(4), 348–368. doi:10.1007/BF02946624

Fayyad, U. M., Haussler, D., & Stolorz, P. E. (1996, August). KDD for Science Data Analysis: Issues and Examples. In *Proceedings of the 2nd International Conference on Knowledge Discovery and Data Mining*, (pp. 50-56).

Fayyad, U. M., Piatetsky-Shapiro, G., & Smyth, P. (1996a, August). Knowledge discovery and data mining: towards a unifying framework. In KDD (Vol. 96, pp. 82-88).

Fayyad, U. M., Piatetsky-Shapiro, G., & Smyth, P. (1996b). The KDD process for extracting useful knowledge from volumes of data. *Communications of the ACM, 39*(11), 27–34. doi:10.1145/240455.240464

Fayyad, U. M., Weir, N., & Djorgovski, S. (1993). SKICAT: A Machine Learning System for Automated Cataloging of Large Scale Sky Surveys. In *Proc. Tenth Intl. Conf. on Machine Learning* (pp. 112-119). doi:10.1016/B978-1-55860-307-3.50021-6

Furletti, B. (2009). *Ontology-driven knowledge discovery* (PhD Thesis). IMT Institute for Advanced Studies, Lucca, Italy.

Getoor, L. (2003). Link mining: A new data mining challenge. *ACM SIGKDD Explorations Newsletter, 5*(1), 84–89. doi:10.1145/959242.959253

Grzymala-Busse, J. W. (2005). Rule induction. In Data Mining and Knowledge Discovery Handbook (pp. 277-294). Springer US. doi:10.1007/0-387-25465-X_13

Haglin, D., Roiger, R., Hakkila, J., & Giblin, T. (2005). A tool for public analysis of scientific data. *Data Science Journal, 4*, 39–53. doi:10.2481/dsj.4.39

Hall, J., Mani, G., & Barr, D. (1996). Applying computational intelligence to the investment process.*Proceedings of CIFER-96: Computational Intelligence in Financial Engineering*. Washington, DC: IEEE Computer Society.

Han, J., & Kamber, M. (2006). Classification and Prediction. In *Data mining: concepts and techniques* (2nd ed.; pp. 285–382). Elsevier.

Han, J., Kamber, M., & Pei, J. (2012a). Classification: Advanced methods. In Data mining: concepts and techniques. Elsevier.

Han, J., Kamber, M., & Pei, J. (2012b). *Data mining: concepts and techniques* (3rd ed.). Elsevier. doi:10.1007/978-1-4419-1428-6_3752

Hatonen, K., Klemettinen, M., Mannila, H., Ronkainen, P., & Toivonen, H. (1996, February). Knowledge discovery from telecommunication network alarm databases. In *Data Engineering, 1996.Proceedings of the Twelfth International Conference on* (pp. 115-122). IEEE. doi:10.1109/ICDE.1996.492095

Hipp, J., Güntzer, U., & Nakhaeizadeh, G. (2000). Algorithms for association rule mining—a general survey and comparison. *ACM SIGKDD Explorations Newsletter, 2*(1), 58-64.

Hotho, A., Staab, S., & Stumme, G. (2003, November). Ontologies improve text document clustering. In *Data Mining, 2003. ICDM 2003. Third IEEE International Conference on* (pp. 541-544). IEEE. doi:10.1109/ICDM.2003.1250972

Kantardzic, M. (2011). *Data mining: concepts, models, methods, and algorithms.* John Wiley & Sons. doi:10.1002/9781118029145

Keim, D. A. (2002). Information visualization and visual data mining. *IEEE Transactions on Visualization and Computer Graphics, 8*(1), 1–8. doi:10.1109/2945.981847

Klösgen, W., & Zytkow, J. M. (2002). *Handbook of data mining and knowledge discovery.* Oxford University Press, Inc.

Kohavi, R., & Tesler, J. D. (2001). *Method, system, and computer program product for visualizing a decision-tree classifier.* U.S. Patent No. 6,278,464. Washington, DC: U.S. Patent and Trademark Office.

Krishnaswamy, C. R., Gilbert, E. W., & Pashley, M. M. (2000). Neural network applications in finance: A practical introduction. *Financial Practice and Education, 10,* 75–84.

Kurgan, L. A., & Musilek, P. (2006). A survey of Knowledge Discovery and Data Mining process models. *The Knowledge Engineering Review, 21*(01), 1–24. doi:10.1017/S0269888906000737

Lent, B., Swami, A., & Widom, J. (1997, April). Clustering association rules. In *Data Engineering, 1997. Proceedings. 13th International Conference on* (pp. 220-231). IEEE. doi:10.1109/ICDE.1997.581756

Li, T., Li, Q., Zhu, S., & Ogihara, M. (2002). A survey on wavelet applications in data mining. *ACM SIGKDD Explorations Newsletter, 4*(2), 49–68. doi:10.1145/772862.772870

Li, W., Han, J., & Pei, J. (2001). CMAR: Accurate and efficient classification based on multiple class-association rules. In Data Mining, 2001. *ICDM 2001,Proceedings IEEE International Conference on* (pp. 369-376). IEEE.

Liu, B., Hsu, W., & Ma, Y. (1999, August). Pruning and summarizing the discovered associations. In *Proceedings of the fifth ACM SIGKDD international conference on Knowledge discovery and data mining* (pp. 125-134). ACM. doi:10.1145/312129.312216

Liu, H., Sun, J., & Zhang, H. (2009). Post-processing for rule reduction using closed set. *Post-Mining of Association Rules: Techniques for Effective Knowledge Extraction*, 81-99.

Liu, S., Cui, W., Wu, Y., & Liu, M. (2014). A survey on information visualization: Recent advances and challenges. *The Visual Computer, 30*(12), 1373–1393. doi:10.1007/s00371-013-0892-3

Manola, F., Miller, E., & McBride, B. (2004). RDF primer. *W3C recommendation, 10*(1-107), 6.

Mariscal, G., Marban, O., & Fernandez, C. (2010). A survey of data mining and knowledge discovery process models and methodologies. *The Knowledge Engineering Review, 25*(02), 137–166. doi:10.1017/S0269888910000032

Matheus, C., Piatetsky-Shapiro, G., & McNeill, D. (1996). Selecting and Reporting What is Interesting: The KEFIR Application to Healthcare Data. In *AKDDM*. Cambridge, MA: AAAI/MIT Press.

Murthy, S. K. (1998). Automatic construction of decision trees from data: A multi-disciplinary survey. *Data Mining and Knowledge Discovery, 2*(4), 345–389. doi:10.1023/A:1009744630224

ONeill, S., & Curran, K. (2011). The core aspects of search engine optimisation necessary to move up the ranking. *International Journal of Ambient Computing and Intelligence, 3*(4), 62–70. doi:10.4018/jaci.2011100105

Pasquier, N. (2009). Frequent closed itemsets based condensed representations for association rules. *Post-Mining of Association Rules: Techniques for Effective Knowledge Extraction*, 246-271.

Piatetsky-Shapiro, G. (1996). *Advances in knowledge discovery and data mining* (U. M. Fayyad, P. Smyth, & R. Uthurusamy, Eds.). Menlo Park, CA: AAAI press.

Reid, I. N., Brewer, C., Brucato, R. J., McKinley, W. R., Maury, A., Mendenhall, D., & Sargent, W. L. W. et al. (1991). The second palomar sky survey. *Publications of the Astronomical Society of the Pacific, 103*(665), 661. doi:10.1086/132866

Rennolls, K., & Al-Shawabkeh, A. (2008). Formal structures for data mining, knowledge discovery and communication in a knowledge management environment. *Intelligent Data Analysis, 12*(2), 147–163.

Seetha, M., Muralikrishna, I. V., Deekshatulu, B. L., Malleswari, B. L., & Hegde, P. (2008). Artificial neural networks and other methods of image classification. *Journal of Theoretical & Applied Information Technology, 4*(11).

Senator, T. E., Goldberg, H. G., Wooton, J., Cottini, M. A., Khan, A. U., Klinger, C. D., & Wong, R. W. et al. (1995). Financial Crimes Enforcement Network AI System (FAIS) Identifying Potential Money Laundering from Reports of Large Cash Transactions. *AI Magazine*, *16*(4), 21.

Shearer, C. (2000). The CRISP-DM model: The new blueprint for data mining. *Journal of Data Warehousing*, *5*(4), 13–22.

Singh, A., Sharma, A., & Dey, N. (2015). Semantics and Agents Oriented Web Personalization: State of the Art. *International Journal of Service Science, Management, Engineering, and Technology*, *6*(2), 35–49. doi:10.4018/ijssmet.2015040103

Singh, B., & Singh, H. K. (2010, December). Web data mining research: a survey. In *Computational Intelligence and Computing Research (ICCIC), 2010 IEEE International Conference on* (pp. 1-10). IEEE. doi:10.1109/ICCIC.2010.5705856

Srivastava, J., Cooley, R., Deshpande, M., & Tan, P. N. (2000). Web usage mining: Discovery and applications of usage patterns from web data. *ACM SIGKDD Explorations Newsletter*, *1*(2), 12–23. doi:10.1145/846183.846188

Staab, S., & Studer, R. (Eds.). (2013). *Handbook on ontologies*. Springer Science & Business Media.

Stolorz, P. E., & Dean, C. (1996, August). Quakefinder: A Scalable Data Mining System for Detecting Earthquakes from Space. In KDD (pp. 208-213).

Stolorz, P. E., Nakamura, H., Mesrobian, E., Muntz, R. R., Shek, E. C., Santos, J. R., . . . Farrara, J. D. (1995, August). Fast Spatio-Temporal Data Mining of Large Geophysical Datasets. In KDD (pp. 300-305).

Stumme, G., Hotho, A., & Berendt, B. (2006). Semantic web mining: State of the art and future directions. *Web Semantics: Science, Services, and Agents on the World Wide Web*, *4*(2), 124–143. doi:10.1016/j.websem.2006.02.001

Sumathi, C. P., Valli, R. P., & Santhanam, T. (2010). Automatic recommendation of web pages in web usage mining. *International Journal on Computer Science and Engineering*, *2*(09), 3046–3052.

Toivonen, H., Klemettinen, M., Ronkainen, P., Hätönen, K., & Mannila, H. (1995). Pruning and grouping discovered association rules. *MLnet Workshop on Statistics, Machine Learning, and Discovery in Databases*, 47-52.

Tomar, D., & Agarwal, S. (2014). A survey on pre-processing and post-processing techniques in data mining. *International Journal of Database Theory & Application*, *7*(4), 99–128. doi:10.14257/ijdta.2014.7.4.09

Walia, E., & Verma, V. (2014, July). Wavelet-based Warping Technique for Mobile Devices.*Proceedings of the Third International Conference on Digital Image Processing and Vision (ICDIPV 2014)*, 27-34.

Walia, E., & Verma, V. (2016). Boosting local texture descriptors with Log-Gabor filters response for improved image retrieval. *International Journal of Multimedia Information Retrieval*, 1-12.

Wirth, R., & Hipp, J. (2000, April). CRISP-DM: Towards a standard process model for data mining. In *Proceedings of the 4th international conference on the practical applications of knowledge discovery and data mining* (pp. 29-39).

Yamamoto, C. H., de Oliveira, M. C. F., & Rezende, S. O. (2009). Visualization to assist the generation and exploration of association rules. *Post-Mining of Association Rules: Techniques for Effective Knowledge Extraction*, 224-245.

Zhang, G. P. (2009). Neural networks for data mining. In Data mining and knowledge discovery handbook (pp. 419-444). Springer US. doi:10.1007/978-0-387-09823-4_21

Chapter 7
Knowledge Discovery and Big Data Analytics: Issues, Challenges, and Opportunities

Vinoth Kumar Jambulingam
VIT University, India

V. Santhi
VIT University, India

ABSTRACT

The era of big data has come with the ability to process massive datasets from heterogeneous sources in real-time. But the conventional analytics can't be able to manage such a large amount of varied data. The main issue that is being asked is how to design a high-performance computing platform to effectively carry out analytics on big data and how to develop a right mining scheme to get useful insights from voluminous big data. Hence this chapter elaborates these challenges with a brief introduction on traditional data analytics followed by mining algorithms that are suitable for emerging big data analytics. Subsequently, other issues and future scope are also presented to enhance capabilities of big data.

DOI: 10.4018/978-1-5225-2483-0.ch007

INTRODUCTION

As the era of data communication and expertise reaches across several fields quickly, most of the information has its origin in digital communication in addition internet nowadays. Lyman, P. and Varian, H. (2002) showed in a study that the new knowledge present in digital devices have crossed already over ninety percent all through the 21st millennium, whereas the scale of that new knowledge was additionally over hundreds of petabytes. In fact, the issues of analyzing the massive information did not rise abruptly, however, are there for many years as it has been that the data creation is felt easier than finding hidden knowledge or useful patterns from that information. Albeit personal computers nowadays are loT more quickly than those in the early 1960's, the massive size of information is a pitfall to perform research on the data we've got nowadays. As an answer to the issues of analyzing high volume data, Xu, R. & Wunsch, D (2009) proposed some effective techniques like sampling, density-dependent methods, data condensation, grid-dependent methods, divide and conquer, progressive learning, and distributed computing, are being offered. Obviously, these ways are perpetually accustomed to enhance the efficiency of the mechanisms of data analysis method (Lyman, P. et al., 2002).

The outcomes of those techniques show that with the effective techniques at our disposal, we tend to be able to perform better and larger data analysis in an exceedingly affordable time. Ding, C. & He, X (2004) presented a dimension based technique say PCA could be a classical example that's geared toward minimizing the input file size to speed up the method of knowledge discovery. Kollios, G., Gunopulos, D., Koudas, N., & Berchtold, S. (2003) presented another reduction scheme that minimizes the computations on accumulated data is sampling, which might even be accustomed to accelerate the computation time involved in knowledge discovery process. Even though the improvements in personal computers and web technologies have gone through the phenomenal rise of computing hardware obeying Moore's law since 1970's, the bottlenecks of handling the high-volume information are there though we are getting into the time of big data analytics. Fisher, D., DeLine, R., Czerwinski, M., & Drucker, S (2012) identified that large-scale data refers to the inability of the present information systems to manage and process load them in simpler machines. Also, present data mining algorithms and centralization of analytics won't work in the context of big data directly. Laney D (2001) given a popular definition in addition to the problems of the size of data also known as 3V's to clarify about big data namely volume, variety, and velocity. The terminology of 3Vs shows that the information size is massive, the information is made quickly, and also the information is existed in multiple varieties and taken from heterogeneous sources, correspondingly. Further studies Laney, D. (2001)

identified that the terminology of 3Vs is inadequate to clarify, hence now we have gone to add multiple V's namely validity, venue, value, variability, vagueness and vocabulary to complement clarification of big data by Laney, D. (2001). The study of IDC by press G (2013) shows that the promoting of big data is totaling to a staggering $18.1 billion in 2015. Another study of IDC estimates that it'll extend to $40 billion by 2017. The study of Taft, DK. (2013) identified that the promoting of big data can be $48 billion by 2020. Kelly, J., Vellante, D., & Floyer, D., (2014) shown even the promotion projection values in these study are different; these estimates sometimes show that the scope of big data will exponentially grow in the coming days. Chen, H., Chiang, R.H.L., & Storey, V.C., (2012) and Kitchin, R., (2014) in their study shown in addition to promoting, from the results of sickness management and interference decision making in business intelligence and urban planning via smart city that big data is of significant importance all over. Several scientists and researchers are thus specializing in creating efficient technologies to research and arrive at solutions. To debate in depth the issues of big data analytics, this chapter offers a scientific description of older analytics with differences between older and newer big data analytics. Though many information analytics and frameworks are given in recent years, with their merits and demerits being mentioned in numerous reports, an entire dialogue from the view of excavating and a pattern extracting in data though is required. As an end result, this chapter is focussed toward delivering a short report for the examiners on information excavating and scattered calculating to possess an undeveloped plan to create knowledge analytics for big data. The chapter is systematized as trails. Information analytics starts with a quick briefing to the traditional information analytics, and Big data analytics can communicate the dialogue of huge knowledge analytics still as an older know analytics procedures and backgrounds. The exposed problems are mentioned in challenges whereas the deductions and impending directions are presented in Conclusions.

DATA ANALYTICS

Knowledge discovery in databases can be made clear through the summarization of KDD into some operations such as data selection, data pre-processing, data transformation, mining and evaluation. Then, it is possible to construct a data analytics arrangement to collect information and then choose information from data and output the patterns to the consumer. To make a precise discussion three parts are taken consideration such as input, analytics and result and six operators such as collection, choice, alteration, pre-processing, mining and visualization.

DATA INPUT

As it has been shown in Figure 1, collection, selection, transformation, and pre-processing operations forms three input part of our system. Selection chooses which data must be selected for data analysis. This information is then collected from different sources and integrated. Pre-processing cleans and filters the data to make them useful ones. After this, the transformation is required to convert some other secondary data. It also makes use of dimension reduction, coding and sampling to scale down the data. These operators can be together called as pre-processing operators. It helps us extract useful data from raw or primary data after eliminating noise, inconsistent and incomplete data. Too complex data are reduced to increase the accuracy of analytics and it has its impact on results.

DATA ANALYSIS

As revealed in figure numbered 1 KDD is can find the buried rules or patterns from information, mining is the term used to refine raw data into knowledge. Data mining techniques are not restricted to information precise procedures (Han, J. 2005). Other methods such as machine learning are also used to perform analytics in the past. Statistical methods can be used to arrive at useful knowledge for tv program rating or opinion poll. Agrawal, R., Imieliński, T., & Swami, A., (1993) proposed some popular field particular procedures are established later such as an apriori algorithm for mining association rules. Cannataro, M., l

Figure 1. Knowledge Discovery in Databases

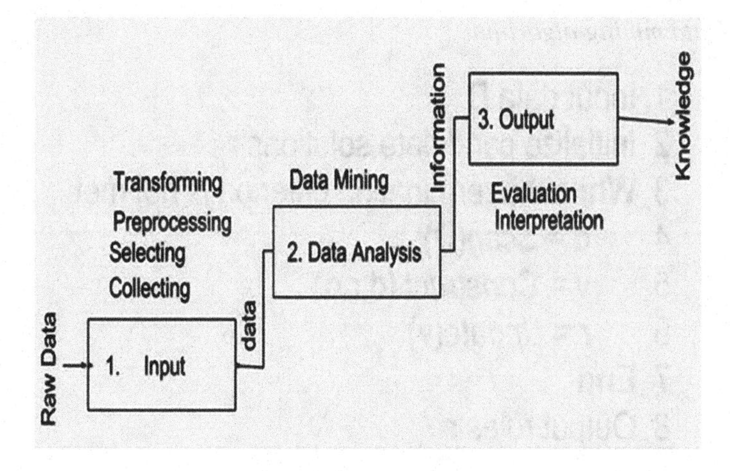

Congiusta, A., Pugliese, A., Talia, D., & Trunfio, P, (2004) proposed to solve data mining problem and in order to reduce the computation cost involved machine learning, metaheuristic procedures and scattered computing either unaided or mutual with information excavating techniques are employed. Krishna, K., & Murty, MN, (1999) provided a genetic algorithm along with k-means is adopted to acquire healthier output than k-means individually.

Usually, a data mining algorithm consists of initialization, input, scan, rule generation, rule update and output. In Figure 2, D refers to raw data, d refers to scan operation, r refers to rules or patterns extracted, v refers to candidate set and o predefined values.

Till termination criteria are achieved, scanning, construction, and updating are carried out repeatedly. Scanning is optional operation as its application depends on the design of mining method. So, basically, the mining procedure runs on a database of transactions and extracts a useful set of rules also called patterns which help in arriving at better business decision making. The algorithm shown in Figure 2 is the same for clustering, classification, association rule ming and sequential mining. Jain, A.K., Murty, M.N., & Flynn, P.J, (1999) delivered a clustering technique which can be used to group different kinds of input data. Classification is a method of grouping records based on a set of labels. McCallum, A., & Nigam K., (1998) delivered some popular classification methods namely naive bayesian, support vector machine and decision tree method. Sequential pattern mining and association rule mining are used to establish a relationship between input data, unlike clustering and classification. The main idea behind association rule algorithm is to determine relationships between input data. Kaya, M., Alhajj, R., (2005) revealed as apriori is expensive in computational cost, other methods like genetic algorithms are employed. Srikant, R., Agrawal, R., (1996) proposed in totaling to the relationship

Figure 2. Data mining algorithm

```
1 Input data D
2 Initialize candidate solutions r
3 While the termination criterion is not met
4     d = Scan(D)
5     v = Construct (d,r,o)
6     r = Update(v)
7 End
8 Output rules r
```

between input information if time or sequence series is obtained then it is sequential pattern mining.

OUTPUT THE OUTCOME

Result interpretation and evaluation are twofold important output operatives. Evaluation is simple the finds how to measure results. It can be one of the operations for excavating, such as the sum of squared errors that is deployed in the genetic algorithm as selection operative for a clustering solution. Jain, A.K., et al., (1999). For classifying the input data, two objectives are important namely cohesion which is the space between each information and sum of its group or gathering must as insignificant as it can and combination which is the space between information of altered collections begin as large as conceivable. Sum of squared errors (SSE) can be defined by the following equation as

$$SSE = \sum_{i=1}^{k} \sum_{j=1}^{ni} D\,(X_{ij} - C_i)$$

Where k is the amount of groups, n_i is the figure of information in the ith group, X_{ij} jth data in the ith group, C_i is an average of the ith cluster and n is the amount of information. Another distance measure called Euclidean distance depends on two locations Pi and Pj of two different datasets. Other distance measures include Manhattan, Minkowski, and cosine similarity. The Measure of correctness is the proportion of an amount of cases classified appropriately to the total amount of test cases.

$$ACC = \frac{Quantity\ of\ cases\ categorized\ rightly}{Total\ quantity\ of\ Cases}$$

To assess organization outcomes F-measure, exactness and recall can be used. It measures how many data does not form part of group A are wrongly grouped into set A and how many information that are part of set A are not grouped into set A.

A confusion matrix is the best way which can cover all the classification outcomes. Below is a table consisting of some efficient data mining methods that are listed.

Inequality may be wont to cut back the computation value of a clump algorithmic rule. Some new technologies can even be wont to cut back the computation time of information analysis methodology. Additionally to the well-known improved ways for these analysis ways like distributed computing an oversized proportion of stud-

Table 1. Effective data analytics procedures for information mining

Problem	Method
Clustering	BIRCH DBCAN TKM
Classification	FastNN GPU SVM
Association Rule mining	FP-Tree FAST
Sequential Mining	SPADE SPAM

ies designed their economical ways supported the characteristics of mining algorithms or downside itself, which may be seen. This type of improved methodology usually was designed for resolution the disadvantage of the mining algorithms or exploitation other ways to unravel the mining downside. These things may be found in most association rules and successive patterns issues as a result of the first assumption of those issues are for the analysis of the large-scale dataset. Since the frequent pattern algorithmic rule must scan the entire dataset persistently that is computationally terribly expensive? The way to cut back the amount of times the entire dataset is scanned so on save the computation value is one among the foremost vital things in all the frequent pattern studies. The similar state of affairs conjointly exists in knowledge clump and classification studies as a result of the planning conception of earlier algorithms, like mining the patterns on-the-fly, mining partial patterns at totally different stages and reducing the amount of times the entire dataset is scanned area unit so bestowed to reinforce the performance of those mining algorithms. Since a number of the information mining issues area unit NP-hard or the answer area is extremely massive, many recent studies have tried to use metaheuristic algorithmic rule because the mining algorithmic rule to induce the approximate answer among an affordable time. Plethoric analysis results of information analysis show doable solutions for managing the dilemmas of information mining algorithms. It means the open problems with knowledge analysis from the literature sometimes will facilitate us simply realize the doable solutions. For example, the clump result's very sensitive to the initial means that, which may be eased by exploitation multiple sets of initial means that. In step with our observation, most knowledge analysis ways have limitations for giant knowledge. There are three main problems with traditional data analytics which are scalability a decentralization problem, static and uniform data structure. Scalability is where most of the mining methods are not suitable for the complex and large dataset. The design of those algorithms is such that they can't be scaled up to accommodate larger datasets. They are capable of running in a single machine hence can handle a larger volume of data. Static schemes mean most methods are not dynamic referring they can't analysis data on the fly. For an instance, classifiers are predetermined initially. Laskov, P., Gehl, C., Kruger, S., & Müller K.R., (2006) presented in an incremental learning, classifiers can be modified after it is being started. The uniform data structure is where mining methods fix that the formats of data are same. Hence they can't be able to work on different formats with inconsistent and incomplete. But big data can solve this as it structures support. Static information sets square measure datasets wherever most ancient data analysis ways can't be dynamically adjusted for various things, that means that they are doing not analyze the input file on-the-fly. As an example, the classifiers square measure sometimes mounted that can't be mechanically modified. The progressive learning could be a promising analysis trend as a result of it will dynamically modify the classifiers on the coaching method with restricted resources. As a result, the performance of ancient information analytics might not be helpful to the drawback of rate problem of huge information. The constant arrangement is information wherever most of the info mining issues assume that the format of the input file is constant. Therefore, the standard data processing algorithms might not be ready to trot out the matter that the formats totally different input file could also be different and a few of the info could also be incomplete. a way to build the input information from completely different sources constant format are a potential answer to the range drawback of huge data.

BIG DATA ANALYTICS

According to Russom, P., (2011), Big data comprises of very large heterogeneous sources of data including streaming data. Unique features of big data are more dimensional, complex, incomplete, unstructured and noisy which cannot be handled properly by statistical and older data analytics approaches. Also, the large volume of information does not translate into more useful information. For an example, a user can use more than one account or a single version could be managed by multiple operators that can affect the mining results accurateness. Boyd, D., Crawford, K.(2012) presented New issues such as storage, privacy, fault tolerance quality and security have come up for data analytics. Big data is generated from the social network, IoT, handheld devices, multimedia and other applications.

BIG DATA INPUT

Handling massive datasets is age old problem with instances such as marketing, weather forecast, astronomy analysis, and gene molecule analysis. This applied to big data where we tend to pre-process the input to make it adaptable for the mining algorithm, platform, and computer. Older data analytics uses sampling, feature selection, and compression to pre-process the input data which can be extended to big data. Zhang, H., (2013) in reports show that domain knowledge can be leveraged for pre-processing input employed divide and conquer to sifter log's unwanted material for internet log analytics. Compression and sampling can be used as data reduction procedures in big data analytics to reduce the data size to make computation faster and less expensive. Satyanarayana, A, (2014) showed the performance of sampling may be affected by the issue of how many occurrences can be particular for information mining. Xue, Z, Shen, G., Li, J., Xu, Q., Zhang, Y., & Shao, J. (2012) presented a compression method can be used to reduce input data size by clustering that input into several different categories of input data.

BIG DATA ANALYTICS PLATFORMS AND FRAMEWORKS

Some prominent solutions presented for big data analytics are divided into three groups like processing Hadoop, Nvidia CUDA, storage HDFS analytics Mahout. The problem with big data is that it cannot be analyzed within a single machine as it needs several clusters of nodes running the tasks parallel.

RESEARCHES IN PLATFORMS AND FRAMEWORKS

Several tools and platforms have been developed by the popular organization for big data analytics. Cloud technologies can also be used to fulfill the demands of storage and computing power. KDD in big data could be relocated to cloud providers to increase the memory available and response evoked. Since the functions for managing the big data have been created slowly now focus of researchers have been turning towards how to find useful information from huge data stacks as they are not concerned about data gathering to data analysis. This duty is comparable finding a needle in a haystack.

From the viewpoint of performance, has indicated that most traditional analytics systems use the concept scale up or simply replacing the smaller system with the larger ones but big data wants to scale out which is raising the numbers of computers to hundreds or even thousand in cluster formation for performing distributed computing. Huai, Y., Lee, R., Zhang, S., Xia, C.H., Zhang, X. (2011) presented a scalable big data model where a matrix method involving three matrices for data-set D, parallel procedures O, and information changes T was known as DOT .the system is split into M sets each one is administered and analysed by single node in a way that completely sets are analysed parallel and results from nodes are gathered to one common node. By this way, the framework is comprised of more than one DOT blocks. If there is a need for more computation, new DOT blocks can be added. Another big data system is known as generalized linear distributed system. It is multilevel tree based system consisting of nodes of either worker or coordinator type. Experimental results show GLDS provides more performance than Hadoop system (Cheng, Y., Qin, C., Rusu, F., 2012). In Hadoop, there is only one master and it needs more storage and processing for data duplication. Essa, Y.M, Attiya, G., El-Sayed, A., (2013) provided agent based framework known as map reduce agent mobility system to solve above problems. In this, each agent can send its data and code to another agent. So, even if one agent fails the whole system won't fail. As this uses of both java and map-reduce its load time is lower than Hadoop. Wonner, J., Grosjean, J., Capobianco, A, Bechmann, D., (2012) presented an auto-improving analytics developed over Hadoop for data analytics. In this system, user doesn't have the need to modify Hadoop as the system itself adjusts needs of the system. A novel architecture for big data framework consisting of security, data structure, and infrastructure and data life cycle has been presented. From the viewpoint of result oriented, Fisher, D., et al., (2012) presented a pipeline model for big data to mine knowledge comprising of gathered data and reflecting works. Ye, F., Wang, Z.J., Zhou, F.C., Wang, Y.P., Zhou, Y.C. (2013) From the viewpoint of statistical mining provided an architecture that combines R programming interface termed as cloud-based analytics. it consists of four layers namely services, dataset, virtualization and infrastructure layer. This system has shown in simulation the performance is more satisfactory than Hadoop alone systems. One more study where a protocol called HACE is proposed where useful relationships can be extracted from large heterogeneous sources. They also provided a framework where data accessing and computing layer, privacy layer and domain layer and mining layer. Privacy has become an important issue recently.

COMPARISON BETWEEN PLATFORMS OF BIG DATA

A study offered architecture of big data as distributed data storage, big data collecting and inter big data analyzing. Zhang, J., Huang, M.L., (2013) provided a 5w model that refers to why a specific data, what kind it is, where it came from, who to get it last and when analysis was done over it. Chandarana, P., Vijayalakshmi,

M., (2014) presented a recent study which uses parameters like workload, owner, latency and complexity to differentiate Hadoop, storm, and drill. Sagiroglu, S., Sinanc, D., (2013) made a comparative study between Hadoop and high-performance computing cluster and arrived at the concept of multivariate and multi-key indexing on distributed computing.

BIG DATA ANALYSIS ALGORITHMS

Big data and big information excavating were first introduced in early 2000's Sagiroglu, S., et al (2013). The goal is to find or extract useful information from vast data that is accessible by analysts. Data mining and searching algorithms play a vital role in analyzing those data. So in the following sections, some specific algorithms are discussed in the context of big data analytics.

In the case of Clustering algorithms, the main requirement of clustering is that it needs same format data in a single machine. This poses a lot of challenges in big data. Shirkhorshidi, A., S., Aghabozorgi, S., R., Teh Y.W., Herawan, T., (2014) categorized clustering into two single machines based clustering and multiple machine based clustering. Xu, H., Li, Z., Guo, S., Chen, K., (2012) presented a cloud vista tool used a cloud-based platform for clustering in parallel mode. Feldman, D., Schmidt, M., Sohler, C., (2013) used a tree construction method for creating co-related sets in a parallel way under merge and reduce them. In the case of Classification algorithms to cope with the requirement of big data, classification techniques need to be modified. Tekin, C., van der Schaar, M., (2013) proposed a novel method involving heterogeneous learners to process distributed data is proposed. The method is classified or sends it to another learner. Reberstrost proposed a quantum based SVM for classification which had a low time complexity of O (log NM) where m is the number of the tuple in training set and n is the number of attributes. In Frequent pattern mining, there is two algorithms namely association rule mining and sequential mining. These two can be utilized for analysis a large dataset says, for example, shopping mall transactions running into tens of thousands of records. One such real implementation came in the form FP-tree where a tree has been used to minimize the time taken for finding associations. Also, Lin MY, Lee PY, Hsueh SC (2012) presented a map-reduce solution was given for FP-tree algorithm. In Machine learning algorithms for big data, some literature has exposed the abilities of machine learning in the perspective of big data. Unlike data mining algorithms, machine learning methods are not specific for mining problem. They are suitable for different purposes than a single specified purpose. If data analysis is termed into optimization problem then machine learning could be adopted to catch an estimated solution. For an instance, the genetic algorithm can applicable for both clustering and frequent pattern mining. Not only data analysis being performed instead feature selection of input can also be enhanced by machine learning. One of the problems in using machine learning is that like traditional mining they are designed for centralized computing. So, the obvious solution is that modified them to work in parallel computing model. Lin MY, Lee PY, Hsueh SC (2012) made a parallel version of genetic algorithm has been developed. In this new GA, the population is divided into subsets of the population so that each one can be assigned separately to an individual node for parallel execution. They indicated communication will be a hindrance in this framework along with difficulty in aggregating information from different computer nodes. Older map-reduce models do not assist iteration operations which impact time complexity. Hassan et al used cloud base resources to create multiple backpropagation and auto creating a map for classification. This in the simulation has shown it runs thrice as much as fast than earlier methods. Ku Mahamud K.R., (2013) report used ant colony algorithm for distributed big data computing. In this, some improvement has modified the original ant - based algorithm for clustering where each every ant is placed randomly on the grid. Machine learning trends can be divided into two. One deal with parallel programming models such as mahout and radio while the other focuses on neural network and ant-based algorithm by Ku Mahamud K.R., (2013). Though these works well as seen in the simulation they need to address high computation cost involved.

OUTPUT THE RESULTS OF BIG DATA

To evaluate the cloud and big data performances, several benchmarks have developed. Some of them are PigMix (2015), Terasort, TPC-H. Ghazal et al proposed a benchmark called big bench where metrics such as a spell for loading, spell for meting out queries are used. Computation spell is the main metric to compare the big data analytics. This metric has been used by Cheptsov A. (2014) to understand the ability to scale up by comparing it with HPC and cloud systems. Yuan, L.Y., Wu, L., You, J.H., Chi, Y., (2014) given a metric can be throughput which is a number of operations of per unit second and memory access latency. In another study, Zhao, J.M., Wang, W.S., Liu, X., Chen Y, F. (2014) et al found that the size of jobs, and data as vital metrics to depict the big data performance. Saletore, V., Krishnan, K., Viswanathan, V., Tolentino, M., (2014) study revealed evaluation can be done via execution and concurrency time of map and reduce. In addition to response time and computation time, factors like hardware, power, cost and bandwidth can also be taken for performance analysis. Zhang, L., Stoffel, A., Behrisch, M., Mittelstadt, S., Schreck, T., Pompl, R., Weber, S., Last, H., Keim, D., (2012) indicated visual analytics tasking can categorize into exploration, reporting, dashboards, alerting.

Also, Thusoo, A., Sarma, J.S., Jain, N., Shao, Z., Chakka, P., Anthony, S., Liu, H., Wyckoff, P., Murthy, R.(2009) presented the user interface in cloud systems can be an important research area where the idea is to explain extracted knowledge to users and to handle analytics at another hand . So a proper UI is required for taking out hidden information through all extracted by big data are not useful information. This syndrome is called as output the result. Statistical techniques could be hired to analysis flu condition for all affected area, information experts want other techniques to extract more relevant patterns and to prove their prediction. Hence UI can be adjusted to output more patterns which are immediately required.

This discussion of massive information analytics during this section was divided into the input, analysis, and output for mapping the info analysis method of KDD. For the input and output of massive information, many strategies and solutions planned before the massive information age may also use for large information analytics in most cases. However, there still exist some new problems with the input and output that the info scientists have to be compelled to confront. A representative

Table 2. List of framework and mining algorithms in big data analytics

Framework or Mining Algorithm Name	Description
DOT	Add more resources if required
Starfish	Self-tuning analytics system
MRAM	Agent-based technology
BDAF	Data-centric approach
HACE	Data mining based
Hadoop	Parallel computing
CUDA	Cloud-based data analytics
Storm	Parallel programming model
Mahout	Machine learning pack
MLPACK	Scalable MLib pack
Radoop	Relational Hadoop
PKM	MR-based clustering
Cloudvista	Cloud-based clustering
BDCAC	Ant algorithm-based computing model
Corest	Tree-based parallel computing
CoS	Parallel model based classification
SVM GA	GA based dimensionality reduction
Quantum computing based SVM	Quantum computing for classification
SFC and DPC	Map-reduce based frequent item mining

example we tend to mentioned in huge information input is that the bottleneck won't solely on the detector or input devices. It should additionally seem in different places of knowledge analytics. Though we are able to use ancient compression and sampling technologies to upset this downside, they'll solely mitigate the issues rather than resolution the issues fully. Similar things additionally exist within the output half. though many measurements will be wont to appraise the performance of the frameworks, platforms, and even data processing algorithms, there still exist many new problems within the huge information age, like data fusion from totally completely different data sources or data accumulation from different times. Many studies tried to gift AN economical or effective resolution from the angle of system or formula level. a straightforward comparison of those huge information analysis technologies from totally different views is delineated in the table given on top of, to convey a quick introduction to the present studies and trends of knowledge analysis technologies for the massive data. The primary column of this table explains that the study is targeted on the framework or formula level; the second column offers the more goal of the study and additionally the also abbreviated names of the strategies or platform. From the analysis framework perspective, this table shows that huge information framework, platform, and machine learning square measure the present analysis trends in huge information analytics system. For the mining formula perspective, the bunch, classification, and frequent pattern mining problems play the important role of those researchers as a result of many information analysis issues will be mapped to those essential problems.

OPEN CHALLENGES

Though data analytics nowadays could be ineffective for large-scale data due to the setting, devices, platforms, systems, and issues that are completely different from mining issues, as a result of much individuality of big data occur within the older analytics. Many exposed problems initiated by new age big data are self-addressed as a framework and information processing views during this segment to clarify what predicaments we tend to challenge due to big data.

FRAMEWORK AND PLATFORM CONTEXT

In Platform I/O ratio, Studies reveal that fertile outcomes of big data can hint us to a different sphere of the world where anything is conceivable. Hence big data is said to be omnipresent and omnipotent in the discipline. From the user viewpoint, big data analytics help us useful insights and possibilities which in turn get us "useful things". The scenario in the majority of the studies is that outcomes of big data analytics are highly appreciated but the commercial methods of several big data analytics are incomplete. In reality, assume that we have an unlimited computing resource of analytics which itself is not feasible to plan, I/O ratio or simply profits are required to be taken into consideration before creating a big data center by an organization. In System Intercommunication, as most of the big data systems can be developed on parallel computing model and they need to work with other systems communication across the entire system will affect the knowledge discovery process performance out rightly. Foremost issue in these communication criteria is the cost of communication incurred across arrangements of big data analytics. Scientists work on how to minimize this cost incurred can be the critical issue. Another issue can be how your big data analytics systems communicate among themselves does. Then the issue of inter-operability between different modules and systems of vendors which play an important in determining the consistency of the systems. As communication within big data analytics systems occurs often these two issues of communication cost and communication method and their impact on reliability and overall system cost is said to be most vital. In Hindrances on data analytics system because of the change in situations, schemes, and data source which are dissimilar from traditional analytics, there can be many hindrances in different areas of big data analytics. As in big data, the large scale data can surpass the limits of traditional systems storage, quickly which in turn rise the computational burden of the exploration system. This presents us a dilemma where a water torrent makes contact with a mountain in which how to separate or regulate input can be some important issues of interest. One solution to that bottleneck can be to put up more resources into computing resource pool while the second option is to separate it onto across several computational clusters of nodes. Hence a whole consideration of data analytics for all hindrances or bottlenecks is required for big data. In Security Concerns as there is more human and environmental behavior is involved in big data analytics, how to secure them can also be a problem since, without secure methods to access, analyze the accumulated information, big data could not become consistent and robust. Before big data can accumulate massive data for analytics we still don't have studies discussing security aspects in big data. We observe security issues of big data into four major categories namely input, analysis, output, and communication. In the case of input, which is data collection related to sensors, digital devices and IoT devices and Internet-based devices. An important issue in sensors related IoT is that they must be protected against possible adversaries. These kinds of active attacks can compromise the entire system performance. In the case of loT communication, security issues arise in the announcement between data analytics and supplementary systems such as cloud-based systems and search engines etc. these problems are termed as latent ones of big data analytics.

DATA MINING CONTEXT

Map-reduce based data mining methods as discussed earlier, the majority of the information mining procedures are not suitable for parallel computing model. Hence they can't apply and are useful for big data based mining. Some latest studies have indicated and shown that modifications to data mining schemes for Hadoop-based platforms are done. As long as there is a need to port the data mining technique to the Hadoop exists, making a modification to data mining algorithm so that it works on map-reduce architecture is a foremost important issue. Also, there not many studies exist that combine soft computing approaches with data mining algorithms on map reduce model because different computing environments are required to design and create such algorithms. For example, researchers need to have knowledge in both the Hadoop map-reduce model and expertise in data mining procedures. Other important concern is that maximum of the mining methods are designed keeping in mind unified computing which is they exertion on all the information at the similar time in a single location. Thus, making them execute on multiple systems parallel sharing the data and other computing resources is very difficult. Some recent studies revealed that few prominent data mining algorithms are modified to work in map-reduce architecture [145]. According to our study, there are no reports of soft computing and data mining algorithms being used together for big data analytics. hence this can be important issues. Partial and uneven data' though big data is a new age information, quite a few clarifications make use of traditional ways to perform analytics the issues of past haunt big data as well. Classical issues such as Noisy data, incomplete inconsistent data, and outliers in older data mining algorithms exist in big data systems as well. Because of data being generated from varied sensors and other systems, possibilities for the rise of incomplete and inconsistent data is more than reality. Also, their impact on big data analytics is quite high compared to traditional analytics. Hence these things along with their mitigation strategies can be issues of paramount interest. Hindrances on data mining algorithms include mining in big data must be designed such way that they obey parallel computing model. Though the modification is being done on mining algorithm to suit parallel programming, still the communication's message passing can inflict hindrances on the analytics system. One among them is the job synchronization across multiple parties as different mining algorithm instances may begin and end their execution at different points in time on the same set of datasets. Hence some instances have to wait for others to supply the updated data for their job execution. This arises because loading time of computing nodes can be different or speeds of convergence can change for a different instance of data mining algorithms.

Confidentiality issue can lead people to think that their personal information is not secure and feel not comfortable, particularly when systems fail to deliver some warranty that that information cannot be edited by further people and organizations. Privacy is different from the security as it requires that system to assure that nobody can extract any particular information from outcomes of big data through the input information to the system is anonymous. Confidentiality has become a vital problem as mining algorithm used in big data after analysis can reveal results which can expose certain individuals personal information. For an instance, though the data collected for shopping behavior of persons are anonymous because data gathered from different systems data mining method can reveal who purchased this diabetes medicine. For these motives, any confidential information needs to secure cautiously. Use of anonymization, encryption can provide privacy to big data analytics but the parameters of how they can be used, when they can be used on gathered data needs to be addressed.

CONCLUSION

In this chapter, a study on the transition of information analytics to latest big data analytics is carried out. Using the knowledge discovery in data process as a framework a study involving three elements namely input, decision analytics, and outcome have been done. From the context of big data, performance and result-oriented issues are discussed. From the viewpoint off mining, big data mining algorithms such as frequent pattern mining, classification and clustering are discussed. To get changes due to big data properly data analysis of knowledge discovery in data from platform to mining is focused. Certain issues of privacy, security, outcome quality and computational problems are elaborated. To reduce the computation time, parallel computing is suggested as a future trend to create analytics work for big data, and thus the tools of cloud computing, map-reduce or Hadoop will show the significant parts for the big data analytics. Also, to manage the computation resources of the cloud platform and to complete the task of information analysis as quicker, the scheduling process is suggested as future trends. Hence, for beginners in the field of emerging big data computing, this chapter serves as starters guide to understanding the issues and challenge's and past works along with future directions can be reached.

REFERENCES

Agrawal, R., Imieliński, T., & Swami, A. (1993). Mining association rules between sets of items in large databases.*ACM SIGMOD Int Conf Manag Data*, *22*(2), 207–16. doi:10.1145/170035.170072

Big data and analytics—an IDC four pillar research area, IDC, Technical Report. (n.d.). Retrieved November 1, 2016, from http://www.idc. com/prodserv/FourPillars/bigData/index.jsp

Boyd, D., & Crawford, K. (2012). Critical questions for big data. *Information Communication and Society*, *15*(5), 662–679. doi:10.1080/1369118X.2012.678878

Cannataro, M., Congiusta, A., Pugliese, A., Talia, D., & Trunfio, P. (2004). Distributed data mining on grids: Services, tools, and applications. *IEEE Transactions on System Man Cyber Part B Cyber.*, *34*(6), 51–65. PMID:15619945

Chandarana, P., & Vijayalakshmi, M. (2014). Big data analytics frameworks. *International Conference on Circuits, Systems, Communication and Information Technology Applications*, 430–434.

Chen, H., Chiang, R. H. L., & Storey, V. C. (2012). Business intelligence and analytics: From big data to big impact. *Management Information Systems Quarterly*, *36*(4), 1165–1171.

Cheng, Y., Qin, C., & Rusu, F. (2012). GLADE: big data analytics made easy.*ACM SIGMOD International Conference on Management of Data*, 697–700.

Cheptsov, A. (2014). Hpc in big data age: An evaluation report for java-based data-intensive applications implemented with Hadoop and OpenMP. *European MPI Users' Group Meeting*, 175-180.

Essa, Y. M., Attiya, G., & El-Sayed, A. (2013). Mobile agent based new framework for improving big data analysis.*International Conference on Cloud Computing and Big Data*, 381–386. doi:10.1109/CLOUDCOM-ASIA.2013.75

Feldman, D., Schmidt, M., & Sohler, C. (2013). Turning big data into tiny data: Constant-size coresets for k-means, PCA and projective clustering.*ACM-SIAM Symposium on Discrete Algorithms*, 1434–1453. doi:10.1137/1.9781611973105.103

Fisher, D., DeLine, R., Czerwinski, M., & Drucker, S. (2012). Interactions with big data analytics. *Interaction*, *19*(3), 50–59. doi:10.1145/2168931.2168943

Han, J. (2005). *Data mining: concepts and techniques*. San Francisco: Morgan Kaufmann Publishers Inc.

Huai, Y., Lee, R., Zhang, S., Xia, C. H., & Zhang, X. (2011) DOT: a matrix model for analyzing, optimizing and deploying software for big data analytics in distributed systems.*ACM Symposium on Cloud Computing*, 1-14. doi:10.1145/2038916.2038920

Jain, A. K., Murty, M. N., & Flynn, P. J. (1999). Data clustering: A review. *ACM Computing Surveys*, *31*(3), 264–323. doi:10.1145/331499.331504

Kaya, M., & Alhajj, R. (2005). Genetic algorithm based framework for mining fuzzy association rules. *Fuzzy Sets and Systems*, *152*(3), 587–601. doi:10.1016/j.fss.2004.09.014

Kelly, J., Vellante, D., & Floyer, D. (2014). *Big data market size and vendor revenues, Wikibon, Technical Report*. Retrieved November 1, 2016, from http://wikibon.org/wiki/v/Big_Data_Market_Size_and_Vendor_Revenues

Kitchin, R. (2014). The real-time city? Big data and smart urbanism. *GeoJournal*, *79*(1), 1–14. doi:10.1007/s10708-013-9516-8

Kollios, G., Gunopulos, D., Koudas, N., & Berchtold, S. (2003). Efficient biased sampling for approximate clustering and outlier detection in large data sets. *IEEE Transactions on Knowledge and Data Engineering*, *15*(5), 70–87. doi:10.1109/TKDE.2003.1232271

Krishna, K., & Murty, M. N. (1999). Genetic k-means algorithm. *IEEE Transactions on Systems, Man, and Cybernetics. Part B, Cybernetics*, *29*(3), 433–441. doi:10.1109/3477.764879 PMID:18252317

Ku Mahamud, K. R. (2013). Big data clustering using grid computing and ant-based algorithm.*International Conference on Computing and Informatics*, 6–14.

Laney, D. (2001). *3D data management: controlling data volume, velocity, and variety, META Group, Technical Report*. Retrieved November 1, 2016, from http://blogs.gartner.com/doug-laney/files/2012/01/ad949-3D-Data-Management-Controlling-Data-Volume-Velocity-and-Variety.pdf

Laskov, P., Gehl, C., Kruger, S., & Müller, K. R. (2006). Incremental support vector learning: Analysis, implementation and applications. *Journal of Machine Learning Research*, *7*, 19–36.

Lin, M. Y., Lee, P. Y., & Hsueh, S. C. (2012). Apriori-based frequent item set mining algorithms on map reduce.*International Conference on Ubiquitous Information Management and Communication*, 76:1–76:8.

Lyman, P., & Varian, H. (2002). *How much information 2003?* Technical Report. Retrieved November 1, 2016, from http://www2.sims.berkeley.edu/research/projects/how-much-info-2003/printable_report.pdf

McCallum, A., & Nigam, K. (1998). A comparison of event models for naive Bayes text classification.*National Conference on Artificial Intelligence*, 41–48.

PigMix. (2015). Retrieved November 1st 2016 from https://cwiki.apache.org/confluence/display/PIG/PigMix

Press, G. (2013). *$16.1 billion big data market: 2015 predictions from IDC and IIA, Forbes, Technical Report*. Retrieved November 1, 2016, from http://www.forbes.com/sites/ gilpress/2013/12/12/16-1-billion-big-data-market-2015-predictions-from-idc-and-iia/

Russom, P. (2011). *Big data analytics*. TDWI: Technical Report.

Sagiroglu, S., & Sinanc, D. (2013). Big data: a review.*International Conference on Collaboration Technologies and Systems*, 42–47.

Saletore, V., Krishnan, K., Viswanathan, V., & Tolentino, M. (2014). *HcBench: Methodology, development, and full-system char- termination of a customer usage representative big data Hadoop benchmark*. Advancing Big Data Benchmarks.

Satyanarayana, A. (2014) Intelligent sampling for big data using bootstrap sampling and Chebyshev inequality.*IEEE Canadian Conference on Electrical and Computer Engineering*, 1–6. doi:10.1109/CCECE.2014.6901029

Shirkhorshidi, A. S., Aghabozorgi, S. R., Teh, Y. W., & Herawan, T. (2014). Big data clustering: a review.*International Conference on Computational Science and Its Applications*, 707–720.

Srikant, R., & Agrawal, R. (1996). Mining sequential patterns: generalizations and performance improvements.*International Conference on Extending Database Technology: Advances in Database Technology*, 3–17. doi:10.1007/BFb0014140

Taft, D. K. (2013). *Big data market to reach $40 billion by 2018, EWEEK, Technical Report*. Retrieved November 1, 2016, from http://www.eweek.com/database/big-data-market-to-reach-40-billion-by-2018.html

Tekin, C., & van der Schaar, M. (2013). Distributed online big data classification using context information.*Allerton Conference on Communication, Control, and Computing*, 1435–1442. doi:10.1109/Allerton.2013.6736696

Thusoo, A., Sarma, J. S., Jain, N., Shao, Z., Chakka, P., Anthony, S., & Murthy, R. et al. (2009). Hive: A warehousing solution over a map-reduce framework. *VLDB Endowment*, *2*(2), 172–179.

Wonner, J., Grosjean, J., Capobianco, A., & Bechmann, D. (2012). Starfish: a selection technique for dense virtual environments.*ACM Symposium on Virtual Reality Software and Technology*, 101–104. doi:10.1145/2407336.2407356

Xu, R., & Wunsch, D. (2009). *Clustering. Hoboken: Wiley-IEEE Press. Ding, C. & He, X (2004). K-means clustering via principal component analysis*. Paper presented at 21st International Conference on Machine Learning, Canada.

Xu, H., Li, Z., Guo, S., & Chen, K. (2012). Cloudvista: Interactive and economical visual cluster analysis for big data in the cloud. *VLDB Endowment, 5*(12).

Xue, Z., Shen, G., Li, J., Xu, Q., Zhang, Y., & Shao, J. (2012). Compression-aware I/O performance analysis for big data clustering.*International Workshop on Big Data, Streams and Heterogeneous Source Mining Algorithms, Systems, Programming Models, and Applications*, 45–52. doi:10.1145/2351316.2351323

Ye, F., Wang, Z. J., Zhou, F. C., Wang, Y. P., & Zhou, Y. C. (2013). Cloud-based big data mining and analyzing services platform integrating.*Proceedings of the International Conference on Advanced Cloud and Big Data*, 147–151. doi:10.1109/CBD.2013.13

Yuan, L. Y., Wu, L., You, J. H., & Chi, Y. (2014). Rubato DB: A highly scalable staged grid database system for OLTP and big data applications.*ACM International Conference on Conference on Information and Knowledge Management*, 1–10. doi:10.1145/2661829.2661879

Zhang, H. (2013), *A novel data pre-processing solution for large scale digital forensics investigation on big data* (Master's thesis). Norway.

Zhang, J., & Huang, M. L. (2013). 5Ws model for big data analysis and visualization. *International Conference on Computational Science and Engineering*, 1021–1028. doi:10.1109/CSE.2013.149

Zhang, L., Stoffel, A., Behrisch, M., Mittelstadt, S., Schreck, T., Pompl, R., & Keim, D. et al. (2012). Visual analytics for the big data era—a comparative review of state-of-the-art commercial systems.*IEEE Conference on Visual Analytics Science and Technology*, 173–182. doi:10.1109/VAST.2012.6400554

Zhao, J. M., Wang, W. S., Liu, X., & Chen, Y. F. (2014). *Big data benchmark - big DS*. Presented at Advancing Big Data Benchmarks.

Section 4
Suggested Reading:
Applicability of Semantics-Driven Contents

Chapter 8
Web Semantics for Personalized Information Retrieval

Aarti Singh
Guru Nanak Girls College, Yamuna Nagar, India

Anu Sharma
ICAR-IASRI New Delhi, India

ABSTRACT

This chapter explores the synergy between Semantic Web (SW) technologies and Web Personalization (WP) for demonstrating an intelligent interface for Personalized Information Retrieval (PIR) on web. Benefits of adding semantics to WP through ontologies and Software Agents (SA) has already been realized. These approaches are expected to prove useful in handling the information overload problem encountered in web search. A brief introduction to PIR process is given, followed by description of SW, ontologies and SA. A comprehensive review of existing web technologies for PIR has been presented. Although, a huge contribution by various researchers has been seen and analyzed but still there exist some gap areas where the benefits of these technologies are still to be realized in future personalized web search.

DOI: 10.4018/978-1-5225-2483-0.ch008

INTRODUCTION

Current proliferation and innovations in web technologies has changed the face of web from information dissemination medium to knowledge provider. The web has become an important hub for providing information on almost all the aspects of human life from the most basic needs to highly specialized ones. Although, it has fascinated the masses but this abundance of information has led to many bottlenecks in accessing the right information at any point of time. This issue could be resolved by applying technologies like Data Mining (DM), Text Mining(TM) and Web Mining (WM). But, the present scenario has demanded the personalized face of web for an individual user to satisfy his information needs. This change has led to the development of a new area of research named as Web Personalization (WP).

WP can be defined as the ability of the system to provide a customized view of web by performing various actions for a single or group of users (Anand & Mobasher, 2005). It can deliver a wide variety of facilities to the users in the form of greetings, bookmarking, granting personalized rights, modifying web site structure, tailored offers & services and adapted web search results. Search engines are an important mode of retrieving desired information from the web. Currently available search engines however do not consider the preferences of the user in account while displaying Web Search Results (WSR). So, it is evident that the current search engines are not able to resolve ambiguous queries and are unable to identify the user preference automatically. So, there is need to add personalized preferences and interest for web IR (Singh & Alhadidi, 2008).

Further, intelligent SW technologies namely ontology and SA (Wooldridge & Jennings, 1995) are found useful in the retrieval of useful knowledge oriented WSR. Intelligent SW technologies provides an important paradigm for use in internet applications (Ehlert, 2003). A number of agents works collaboratively to enable personalization by recognizing individual interests and then recommending the contents. Unification of SW with web IR will enhance the efficiency, scalability of PIR along with complete automation of tasks.

This chapter is organized into four sections. A brief overview of the topic is explained in this section. Section two describes the basic components of a PIR system and section three outlines the existing SW technologies. Section four provides a framework for using web semantics for PIR. Discussion and future research directions are presented in section five.

ANATOMY OF PERSONALIZED INFORMATION RETRIEVAL SYSTEM ON WEB

The main components of the system are personalized user query expansion, personalized techniques for user profiling and ranking of web search results followed by personalized filtering of search results based on long and short term interest. The anatomy of a web PIR system is shown in Figure 1.

These components are described in brief in next sub-sections.

Query Expansion Techniques

The most challenging issue to consider in web information retrieval is to resolve the ambiguity arising out of poorly defined queries. Information requirements may vary with the different search sessions. Query expansion techniques aims at reformulating the query to meet the user requirements. Mainly two types of techniques are available- global and local. Global methods utilizes the existing thesaurus / WorldNet, create thesaurus automatically or perform spell check. Local methods consist of recording the relevance, pseudo relevance and indirect relevance feedback. Relevance feedback is recorded either implicitly or explicitly. Implicit user feedback is calculated by observing their behavior on web. These methods are further divided into word co-occurrence, probabilistic methods, context and location based methods. Figure 2 represents schematically the classification of query expansion techniques.

Various methods for creating user profiles are given in next sub-section.

Figure 1. Anatomy of a Web PIR system

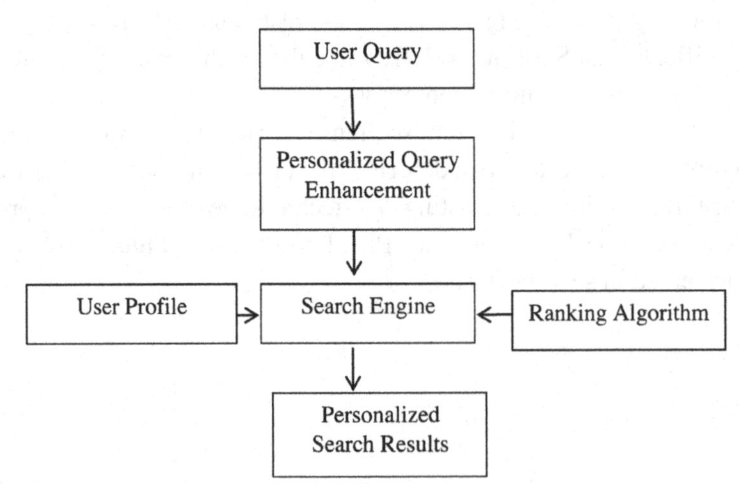

Figure 2. Various Types of Query Expansion Techniques

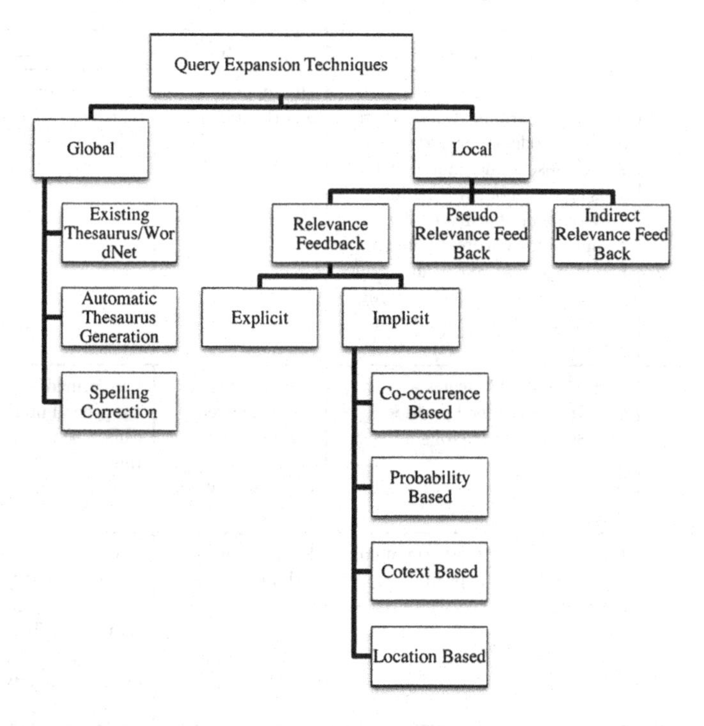

User Modelling

User Modelling (UM) is referred to as gathering and exploiting the information about preferences, interests and behavior of the individual user for creating user adaptive websites (Carmagnola et al., 2011). The prominent characteristics considered for user profiling are background information, interests, preferences, goals, emotional state and context. Main phases of UM are (i) information gathering, (ii) user profile representation and (iii) user profile construction. Information gathering is done by using explicit and implicit methods (Kelly & Teevan, 2003). Once the information has been collected user profile is constructed by using various representation techniques (Moukas, 1997; Chen et al. 1998; Minio and Tasso, 1996; Bloedorn, 1996) and there by leading to many ways of constructing user profiles. Some of important UM are shown in Table 1 along with their associated advantages and disadvantages.

Next component of PIR is to organize the WSR for a given query using ranking algorithms. These algorithms are described in next sub-section.

Table 1. UM Approaches with their Advantages and Disadvantages

UM Approach	Description	Benefits	Limitations
Overlay Modelling	This type of modelling was used in student learning system where the user model is represented as the subset of domain model. This type of modelling requires development of semantically complete and coherent domain knowledge base consisting of fine grained concepts. The knowledge model consists of concept-value pair.	Highly precise and flexible	Accurate domain modelling which is a very tedious task manually
Stereotype Modelling	This type of UM creates a set of predetermined profiles representing a group of similar users.	Comprehensive UM is created automatically with little knowledge about user	Pre-defined stereotypes are general in nature; they cannot be used to represent fine grained knowledge level
Keyword Based Profile	User profiles are most commonly represented as groups of keywords.	Simple and easy to build	Polysemy problem. This problem refers to different meanings assigned to same word. This results in inaccurate recommendation due to ambiguity in word sense.
Semantic Network Profile	Storing the profile in the form of a semantic network where each node represents a concept and is assigned a weight that reflect its importance	Solves polysemy problem	Complex to handle
Concept Based Profile	Network-based profile with nodes and arcs. But the nodes represent abstract topics considered interesting to the user, rather than specific words or sets of related words.	Tackles the problem of words sense ambiguity.	Requires developing reference taxonomy which is a difficult task.

Web Search Ranking Algorithms

Web search is used to retrieve information by using search engines, web directories and web browsing (Lawrence & Giles, 2000). Many algorithms have been suggested by researchers to rank the web pages obtained for a given query in a web search environment. The most popular of these is the PageRank algorithm (Brin et al., 1998) which considers the link structure of web pages but is not sensitive to the query topic. (Haveliwala, 2002) have proposed a modification to existing PageRank which gives more importance to the topic related to a given query in ranking.

HITS is a link analysis algorithm developed by Jon Klein berg, 1998 to rate Web pages and is sensitive to user query. SALSA uses important concepts from HITS and PageRank (Lempel & Moran, 2000).

Researchers continued their effort in this area with the objective of providing a user with a better web experience through the application of recent SW technologies. Next section gives a brief overview on these developments.

SEMANTIC WEB AS A BETTER APPROACH TOWARDS PERSONALIZED INFORMATION RETRIEVAL

Definition of SW according to (Shadbolt et al., 2006) is

The SW is a web of actionable information i.e. the information which is derived from data by operating it with semantic theory of interpreting symbols. The semantic theory provides an account of "meaning" in which the logical connection of terms establishes interoperability between systems.

Adoption of SW was constrained by the unavailability of software tools and methods at the time of its proposal (Lee et al., 2001). But gradually this became possible with the invention of new techniques. The main vision of SW is to make machines understand the meaning of web resources and thus making easier the exchange of information between them. It deploys semantic technologies like Resource Description Framework Schema (RDFS), ontology languages for describing concepts and relationships, query processing languages, rules description language and languages for marking up data inside Web pages.

Inherent distributed and uncertain nature of SW led researchers (Gerber et al., 2007; Shadbolt et al., 2006) to apply similar natured SA to realize it optimally. SA are capable of inferring new facts from distributed but conceptually related data (Tamma & Payne, 2008; Gladun, 2009). Evaluation of layers proposed by Tim Berner Lee was done by (Gerber et al., 2007) and a suggestion for improvement has been given. An analysis and evaluation of various SW architectures has been undertaken by (Singh et al., 2009). It was felt that full potential of SW can be realized by using SA.

SA may be defined as:

Autonomous agents are computational systems that inhabit some complex dynamic environment, sense and act autonomously in this environment and by doing so realize a set of goals or tasks for which they are designed (Buccafurri et al., 2006)

Agent technology has its origin from conventional object oriented and component based programming language paradigms. However, object oriented software has limited capacity to act autonomously with environment. On the other hand component based software products may be reused easily in other software without modification. The components which are autonomous and carry out some task are called SA. Wooldridge & Jennings (1995) defined an agent as a computer component that has been built with well design objectives for a particular environment, and is capable of operating independently. They have well defined states and properties and have complete control over their internal states and their behavior. They are capable of existing without intervention of other systems or humans. Figure 3 shows the various attributes of SA and Table 2 shows the various types of SA.

SA can also be categorized as Belief Desire Intention (BDI) agents (Sharma & Juneja, 2006), weak or strong agents (Whitman & Mattord, 2011), negotiation agents (Simon et al. 1998; Griffeth and Velthuijsen, 1993), distributed or MAS (Sycara, 1998) and even emotional agents (Nwana, 1996; Bates, 1994). Full potential of SA is realized when a number of agents works together in a system. In order to communicate with each other, a common language of understanding is required by SAs. Next section describes the ontology as a medium to enable agent communication.

Figure 3. Some Attributes of SA

Table 2. Types of SAs

Agent Type	Purpose
Table-Driven Agents	These agents use a lookup table. A lookup table is stored in the memory with the description of causes and actions.
Simple Reflex Agents	These are stateless components acting on the condition-action rules with no memory of past world states.
Agents with Memory	These agents store the historical data about its states.
Agents with Goals	These are a kind of pro-active agents which takes into consideration the possible occurrence of future events besides having the state information.
Utility-Based Agents	For a given goal, if there exist many solutions. Then utility based agent takes decision on the basis of efficiency of each solution.

Ontology

Ontology plays a significant role in increasing the effectiveness of a web based system. According to Gruber ontology may be defined as "*an explicit specification of a conceptualization*" (Gruber, 1993). Some other researcher has defined it in another way as "*Ontology is a formal description and specification of knowledge*".

It provides a communication pathway between SA and other system by stating the clear structure of the information. Reuse of constructed domain knowledge is another benefit of using ontology. It allows to separate domain knowledge from operational part of system.

Ontology development starts with the identification and description of entities which are nothing but any object of interest in real world. These entities are defined as a class in ontology. This step is followed by the identification of relationship between them. The identified relationships are used to arrange the classes in a hierarchy. It is followed by the specification of slots and allowable values for each slot. Ontologies are structured way of storing information.

Ontology is a widely accepted technology in multi-agent system because it allows all the participating agents in a system to agree on the use of shared understanding of the world. It also allows inferring new knowledge through semantic reasoner and this capability is moved from agent code to ontology. This facilitates reusing the knowledge across many applications. Further, standardization of communication language leads to clear understanding of items in a domain. It emergs as the most sought after technology for developing multi-agent systems.

Various languages have been developed for creating ontology. Some of the important languages are SHOE (Heflin, Hendler & Luke, 1999), OML, DAML (Coalition, 2002) and OWL (Heflin, 2016). OWL has emerged as the standard language for creating ontology. Ontologies in OWL are made up classes with relationships defined between them. Axioms impose various constraints on these classes and are utilized to infer the semantic associations between them. Various tools are available which allows developing OWL ontology easily. Some of these are WebOnto, OILEd, OntoEdit, Protege 2000 and WebODE for Java platform (Singh & Anand, 2013; Noy, Crubezy, Fergerson et al., 2003).

This section had outlined the basics of SW technology and it was observed that these technologies are going to provide better solutions to existing mechanisms deployed in PIR. Next section outlines the proposed synergy between PIR and web semantics

WEB SEMANTICS FOR PERSONALIZED INFORMATION RETRIEVAL

Benefits of applying SW technologies in the domain of web personalization has been studied by many researchers (Singh et al., 2015). Foremost challenges involved in effective PIR are personalized query expansion, user profile learning, modelling and personalized interaction. Intelligent techniques are required for generation of useful and actionable knowledge gained through reasoning from domain ontology for personalized user experience. This technology can provide solution to many existing issues like scalability, robustness, efficiency, privacy, and security and user profile generation in the area. A framework for synergy between SW and PIR is shown in Figure 4. SW interventions are found useful in various phases of PIR.

Following sub-sections describes the work done by researchers in each of the area specified in the framework.

Ontology and Agent Based Query Expansion

An approach for personalized query suggestion by extracting the concepts from the web-snippets of the search results returned from a query has been proposed by Leung et al. 2008. An approach for ontology driven conjunctive query expansion based on mining user logs has been proposed by Pahal et al. (2009). In this, the clustered indexed documents and information extracted from user log are mined. Also, the association rules and ontology have been used for inferring rules and for identifying the relationship between the concepts. Further, an algorithm has been proposed and the performance has been measured.

A query expansion model has been developed by Chen (2012) using an interest ontology. An algorithm for calculating the similarity between the query and concepts in the ontology is developed and is found to improve the precision and recall. An approach for understanding the query using SW technologies has been proposed

Figure 4. Framework for Web Semantics for Personalized Information Retrieval

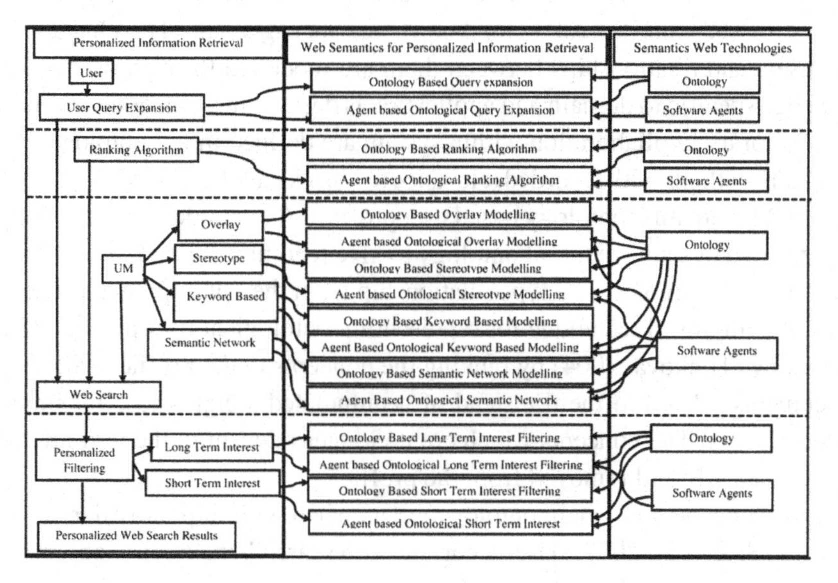

by Chauhan et al. (2013). Query expansion is done and the related information is retrieved from knowledge base. A multi-agent approach for semantic query expansion is proposed by Gao et al. (2013). Query is automatically expanded using ontology and is further improved by incorporating the user feedback. Another approach was proposed by Jianmin & Chang (2012) by combining the domain ontology and user's interest for expanding the query.

Web Semantics for User Profiling

Ontology (Singh et al., 2010) based user profiling using SW technologies and intelligent agents have been successfully applied to solve many problems inherent in UM. Ontology based user profiling is powerful representational medium and provides associated inference mechanism. They provide various mechanisms for inferencing and thus allow discovering the preferences which are otherwise not visible from direct user behavior.

An extensive study for identifying scope, applicability and state of art in applying semantics to WP is under-taken by (Singh et al., 2015). Semantically enhanced and ontological profiles are found (Sosnovsky & Dicheva, 2010; Middleton et al. 2004; Bhowmick et al. 2010) more appropriate for representing the user profile. A brief review of work on semantically enhanced and ontological dynamic user profiles is give below.

UM architecture based on ontology namely user, domain and log have been proposed by (Razmerita, 2003) for knowledge management. The characteristics of the users and relationships between them are modelled through user ontology. Knowledge specific to domain and application is defined through domain ontology. Semantics of user collaboration within system are defined in log ontology.

Implicit methods with recorded relevance feedback have been used by (Middleton et al. 2004) for creating ontology based user profiles. A methodology for solving the CSP is tackled by using external ontology to give recommendation to the new user. At present, only simplest is-a type relationship from the ontology is considered in the RS. An improved technique for representing ontological user profile has been proposed by (Trajkova, 2004) by ranking the concepts in the profiles with number of documents related to them instead of accumulated weights to offer improved profile accuracy. The concepts which are no longer relevant to the user are identified automatically and removed from the profile.

All the concepts in domain ontology are attached with implicitly derived interest scores (Sieg et al. 2007). User's current web search behaviour is observed and used to update the weightage assigned to each concept in profile by using spreading activation algorithm. Ontological user profiles to narrow down web search space returned by search engines had been utilized by (Sieg et al., 2007). In this approach Open Directory Project (ODP) is used as reference to build ontological user profile. User profile is represented as hierarchical concepts from ODP along with interest score. Interest scores are automatically updated with user's browsing behaviour. User's web search results are classified or clustered using ontological user profile. The limitation of this work is manual updating of ODP ontology to accommodate changes in the ontology. A solution to this has been proposed by (Safarkhani et al., 2009). They have proposed an approach for the generation of semantically enhanced clusters using Wikipedia as reference ontology. This approach overcomes the problem of manual creation and updating of domain knowledge along with coverage.

An off-line dynamic model has been proposed by (Aghabozorgi & Wah, 2009) using clustering on web usage data. The accuracy of user model is ensured by periodically adjusting the model to incorporate new transactions. A hybrid approach is adopted by (Bhowmick et al. 2010) by considering the features of static and dynamic user profiling techniques. Static user profile specifies the user's interest in a much focused manner and dynamic user profiling adds the feature of adaptability into it. But this approach is limited to the school curriculum related topics and also does not consider context and location while generating recommendations.

Users' behaviour and characterization of users' needs for context-aware applications had been analysed by (Skillen et al., 2012). Authors proposed a method for constructing a User Profile Ontology for a mobile based environment for developing personalized context-aware application. An approach for personalizing the web using user profile ontology has been proposed by (Vigneshwari & Aramudhan, 2012). These ontologies are created dynamically using the server log file through classification and clustering techniques. A global ontology is also created by identifying the word pairs that have occurred in most of the documents. A multi-dimensional model of user profile has been suggested by (Anil et al., 2013) by tracking the on-line and off-line activities of the user for personalized web search. But, this approach does not use SAs. In another work, Hoppe (2013) have proposed a framework for automatically constructing and populating profile ontology for each user identified by the system from heterogeneous resources in big data environment. This approach is useful for providing recommendations in real-time environment. (Chamiel & Pagnucco, 2009) have used existing ontology constructed with the help of experts to specify the user's preferences in an interactive and dynamic way.

Some other work on generating user profile dynamically is given by (Li et al. 2007; Hawalah & Fasli, 2011; Moawad et al., 2012; Woerndl and Groh, 2005). A strategy for maintaining the LTI and STI of the user through user topic tree and Page-History Buffer (PHB) had been proposed by (Li et al., 2007). A multi-agent approach has been proposed by (Hawalah and Fasli, 2011) for constructing a dynamic user profile which can automatically learn and adapt itself with changing user behaviour. But, it does not consider the contextual information in recommendations. An agent oriented approach for personalization of web search using dynamic user profile has been suggested by (Moawad et al., 2012). The user query is optimized by considering the preferences given in user profile and the query-related synonyms from the WordNet ontology. The search results obtained from a set of syntactic search engines are combined to produce the final personalized results. Another work (Woerndl & Groh, 2005) has proposed a framework for multi-agent based personalized context-aware information retrieval from distributed sources considering the privacy and access control. An agent based interface is proposed that optimize the user query using WordNet and user profile preferences and fetches the personalized search results from various search engines like Google, Yahoo etc.

A comparison of these techniques on the basis of six parameter namely

- Ontology Used(Y/N)
- STI(Y/N)
- LTI(Y/N)
- SA Used(Y/N)
- Context Included (Y/N)
- Dynamic(Y/N)

to assess the status of applying SW technologies for UM and with the possible improvement areas is given Table 3.

Table 3. Comparison of Various User Profiling Techniques

Reference	Dynamic	Ontology	LTI	STI	SA	Context
Razmerita, 2003	✓	✓	✓	✗	✗	✗
Middleton et al. 2004	✓	✓	✓	✗	✗	✗
Trajkova, 2004	✓	✓	✓	✗	✗	✗
Sieg et al. 2007	✓	✓	✓	✗	✗	✓
Aghabozorgi and Wah, 2009	✓	✗	✓	✓	✗	✗
Bhowmick et al. 2010	✓	✓	✓	✗	✗	✗
Sosnovsky and Dicheva, 2010	✓	✓	✓	✗	✓	✗
Skillen et al., 2012	✓	✓	✓	✓	✗	✓
Vigneshwari and Aramudhan, 2012	✓	✓	✓	✗	✗	✗
Li et al. 2007	✓	Taxonomy	✓	✓	✗	✓
Hawalah and Fasli, 2011	✓	✓	✓	✓	✗	✓
Moawad et al., 2012	✓	✓	✓	✗	✓	✗
Woerndl and Groh, 2005	✓	✓	✓	✓	✓	✓

Ontology and Agent Based Web Page Ranking

Although the web page ranking algorithms arrange the WSR on the basis on their popularity but still a lot of irrelevant and ambiguous information is displayed. So, there is need to add personalized preferences and interest for web IR. Personalization of WSR arranges the search results according to user context and preferences (Qiu & Cho, 2006). Most of the research efforts in this direction are directed towards (i) personalization of query by content analysis (ii) personalization by hyperlink analysis and (iii) by using users group. Content analysis based personalization approaches compare the search results with the profile of the user and re-ranking is done (Sugiyama et al. 2004). Link analysis based approaches uses the structure of web in ranking web pages. A revised version of PageRank algorithm has been proposed by (Brin et al., 1998) to re-rank the WSR for personalization. Another modification to PageRank is suggested by Richardson & Domingos (2002) by using a probabilistic model of the relevance of a page to a query. But this approach was computationally very time consuming and did not perform better with multiple word queries. Efficient execution of their algorithm at query time is made possible by precomputing at crawl time (and thus once for all queries) the necessary terms. An approach called Onto SQD-PageRank algorithm, that probabilistically combines a statistical relevance and a semantical relevance for computing the score of a web page was proposed by Djaanfar et al., (2012). Their model explores several ways in order to improve both PageRank and SQD-PageRank algorithm. Particularly, it exploits page content, link structure and domain ontology. It overcomes the problem of dependence between query terms when the words are highly dependent. User group based approaches use the profile of similar users to improve the search results.

A better approach combining the keyword based IR methods is enhanced with conceptual and ontological methods by Chahal et al. (2013). A New Integrated Case and Relation Based Page Rank Algorithm have been proposed by Preethi and Devi (2013) to rank the results of a search system based on a user's topic or query. Relation based page ranking algorithm produce more accurate results. The CARE algorithm is using Textual Case Based Reasoning (TCBR) [7] and Relation-based Page Ranking algorithms. The textual case based reasoning is used to reduce the number of incorrect result pages during the search process. Textual case based reasoning uses previous knowledge of the search results by using this it fetches the result for the search query which are more relevant to the search query, afterwards the annotated page graphs for these result pages are generated. By this the search time can be reduced by avoiding the generation of annotated page graphs for irrelevant results.

Lee et al.(2009) have proposed a semantic association search methodology that consists of how to find relevant information for a given user's query in the ontology, that is, a semantic network of resources and properties. From this work, users can search the semantically associated resources with their query as valuable and important information.

DISCUSSION

This study has highlighted the applications of SW technologies for PIR in order to bridge the gap between these technologies for better personalization experience. Details of PIR process has been provided along with the detailed description of each of the constituting components. Contribution of researcher in applying web semantics to PIR has been discussed. Although, a lot of research efforts are seen in this area yet many research gaps still exist that might be taken up in future studies for making PIR more effective. Some open research issues are discussed below:

- **Task Division among Agents in PIR:** Many multi-agent system has been proposed in the literature but more efforts are needed to specify the mechanism and protocols for agent interaction, co-ordination and task allocation to each agent for further improving the efficiency of the system.
- **Construction of Generalized and Domain Specific Ontologies:** Availability of domain and generalized ontologies is essential for utilizing the knowledge bases and SA in personalized web search. At present, limited domain ontologies are available and no comprehensive generalized ontology is available. So, research efforts may be put forth in this area.
- **Handling Complex Relationships within Ontology:** Available techniques are able to exploit only *is-a* type of relationship present in the ontology. Algorithms must be developed to include more complex relationships in PIR process to improve its accuracy.
- **Understanding User's Context:** Information requirements are usually dependent upon the context with which user is searching the web. Web semantic approaches may be applied to incorporate this feature with better performance.

REFERENCES

Aghabozorgi, S. R., & Wah, T. Y. (2009). Dynamic modelling by usage data for personalization systems.*Proceedings of 13th International Conference on Information Visualization*, 450-455. doi doi:10.1109/iv.2009.111

Anand, S. S., & Mobasher, B. (2005). Intelligent techniques for web personalization.*Proceedings of the 2003 International Conference on Intelligent Techniques for Web Personalization*, 1–36.

Anil, N.K., Kurian, S.B., Abahai, T. A. & Varghese, S.M. (2013). Multidimensional user data model for web personalization. *International Journal of Computer Applications*, *69*(12), 32-37.

Bates, J. (1994). Role of emotions in believable agents. *Communications of the ACM*, *37*(7), 122–125. doi:10.1145/176789.176803

Bhowmick, P. K., Sarkar, S., & Basu, A. (2010). Ontology based user modelling for personalized information access. *International Journal of Computer Science and Applications*, *7*(1), 1–22.

Bloedorn, E., Mani, I., & MacMillan, T. R. (1996). Machine Learning of User Profiles: Representational Issues.*Proceedings of AAAI 96*,433-438.

Brin, S., Page, L., Motwani, R., & Winograd, T. (1998). *The Page Rank citation ranking: bringing order to the web.* Technical Report. Stanford University. Available on the Internet at http://dbpubs.stanford.edu:8090/pub/1999-66

Buccafurri, F., Lax, G., Rosaci, D., & Ursino, D. (2006). Dealing with semantic heterogeneity for improving web usage. *Data & Knowledge Engineering*, *58*(3), 436–465. doi:10.1016/j.datak.2005.06.002

Carmagnola, F., Cena, F., & Gena, C. (2011). User model interoperability: A survey. *User Modeling and User-Adapted Interaction*, *21*(3), 285–331. doi:10.1007/s11257-011-9097-5

Chahal, P., Singh, M., & Kumar, S. (2013). Ranking of web documents using semantic similarity. *Proceedings of International Conference on Information Systems and Computer Networks (ISCON)*. doi:10.1109/ICISCON.2013.6524191

Chamiel, G., & Pagnucco, M. (2009). Ontology guided dynamic preference elicitation.*Proceedings of 3rd ACM Conference on Recommender Systems & the Social Web,*41-48.

Chauhan, R., Goudar, R., Sharma, R. & Chauhan, A. (2013). *Domain Ontology based Semantic Search for Efficient Information Retrieval through Automatic Query Expansion*. Academic Press.

Chen, H., Du, X., Chen, X., & Xia, C. (2012). Query expansion model based on interest ontology.*Proceedings of International Conference on Information Management, Innovation Management and Industrial Engineering (ICIII)*.

Chen, L., & Sycara, K. (1998). WebMate: A Personal Agent for Browsing and Searching.*InProceedings of the 2nd International Conference on Autonomous Agents* (pp 132-139). ACM Press. doi:10.1145/280765.280789

Coalition, D. S. (2002). DAML-S: Web service description for the semantic web. *Proceedings of ISWC*.

Djaanfar, A. S., Frikh, B., & Ouhbi, B. (2012). A hybrid method for improving the SQD-PageRank algorithm.*Proceedings of Second International Conference on Innovative Computing Technology (INTECH)*, 231-238. doi:10.1109/INTECH.2012.6457747

Ehlert, P. (2003). *Intelligent User Interfaces: Introduction and Survey*. Research Report DKS03-01/ICE 01, Faculty of Information Technology and Systems, Delft University of Technology.

Gao, Q., & Cho, Y. I. (2013). A multi-agent personalized ontology profile based query refinement approach for information retrieval. *Proceedings of 13th International Conference on Control, Automation and Systems (ICCAS)*. doi:10.1109/ICCAS.2013.6703997

Gerber, A. J., Barnard, A., & Van Der Merwe, A. J. (2007). Towards a semantic web layered architecture. In *Proceedings of IASTED International Conference on Software Engineering (SE2007)* (pp. 353-362). Innsbruck, Austria: IASTED.

Gladun, A., Rogushina, J., Sanchez, G. F., Bejar, M. R., & Breis, F. T. J. (2009). An application of intelligent techniques and semantic web technologies in E-Learning environments. *Expert Systems with Applications*, *36*(2), 1922–1931. doi:10.1016/j.eswa.2007.12.019

Griffeth, D. N., & Velthuijsen, H. (1993). Win/Win negotiation among autonomous agents.*Proceedings of the 12th International Workshop on Distributed Artificial Intelligence*, 187-202.

Gruber, R. T. (1993). Toward principles for the design of ontologies used for knowledge sharing. *International Journal of Human-Computer Studies*, *43*(5-6), 907–928. doi:10.1006/ijhc.1995.1081

Haveliwala, T. H. (2002). Topic-sensitive PageRank.*Proceedings of the 11th International Conference on World Wide Web,*517–526.

Hawalah, A., & Fasli, M. (2011). A multi-agent system using ontological user profiles for dynamic user modelling.*Proceedings of International Conferences on Web Intelligence and Intelligent Agent Technology*, 430-437. doi:10.1109/WI-IAT.2011.76

Heflin, J. (2016). *An Introduction to the OWL Web Ontology Language*. Lehigh University.

Heflin, J., Hendler, J., & Luke, S. (1999). *SHOE: A knowledge representation language for internet applications. Technical CS-TR-4078*. Institute for Advanced Computer Studies, University of Maryland.

Hoppe, A. (2013). Automatic ontology based user profile learning from heterogeneous web resources in a big data context.*Proceedings of the VLDB Endowment*, 6(12), 1428-1433. doi:10.14778/2536274.2536330

Jianmin, X., & Chang, L. (2012). Personalized Query Expansion Based on User Interest and Domain Knowledge. *Proceedings of Third Global Congress on Intelligent Systems (GCIS)*. doi:10.1109/GCIS.2012.70

Kelly, D., & Teevan, J. (2003). Implicit feedback for inferring user preference: a bibliography. *ACM SIGIR Forum, 37*(2), 18-28.

Lawrence, S., & Giles, C. L. (2000). Accessibility of information on the Web. *Intelligence, 11*(1), 32–39. doi:10.1145/333175.333181

Lee, M., & Kim, W. (2009). Semantic Association Search and Rank Method based on Spreading Activation for the Semantic Web. *Proceedings of the 2009 IEEE IEEM*, 1523-1527. doi:10.1109/IEEM.2009.5373086

Lempel, R., & Moran, S. (2000). The stochastic approach for link-structure analysis (SALSA) and the TKC Effect.*Proceedings of 9th International World Wide Web Conference*, 387-401. doi:10.1016/S1389-1286(00)00034-7

Leung, K. W., Ng, W., & Lee, D. L. (2008). Personalized concept-based clustering of search engine queries. *IEEE Transactions on Knowledge and Data Engineering, 20*(11), 1505–1518. doi:10.1109/TKDE.2008.84

Li, L., Yang, Z., Wang, B., & Kitsuregawa, M. (2007). Dynamic adaptation strategies for long-term and short-term user profile to personalize search. In G. Dong, X. Lin, W. Wang, Y. Yang, & J. X. Yu (Eds.), *Advances in Data and Web Management. Springer Berlin Heidelberg: LNCS 4505* (pp. 228–240). doi:10.1007/978-3-540-72524-4_26

Middleton, S. E., Shadbolt, N. R., & Roure, D. C. D. (2004). Ontological user profiling in recommender systems. *ACM Transactions on Information Systems, 22*(1), 54–88. doi:10.1145/963770.963773

Minio, M., & Tasso, C. (1996). User Modeling for Information Filtering on INTERNET Services: Exploiting an Extended Version of the UMT Shell.*Proceedings of UM96 Workshop on User Modeling for Information Filtering on the WWW.*

Moawad, I. F., Talha, H., Hosny, E., & Hashim, M. (2012). Agent-based web search personalization approach using dynamic user profile. *Egyptian Informatics Journal, 13*(3), 191–198. doi:10.1016/j.eij.2012.09.002

Moukas, A. (1997). Amalthaea: Information Discovery and Filtering Using a Multiagent Evolving Ecosystem. *Applied Artificial Intelligence, 11*(5), 437–457. doi:10.1080/088395197118127

Noy, N. F., Crubezy, M., & Fergerson, R. W. (2003). Protege-2000: an open-source ontology-development and knowledge-acquisition environment.*Proceedings of AMIA Annu. Symp.*, 953.

Nwana, H. S. (1996). Software agents: An overview. *The Knowledge Engineering Review, 11*(3), 1–40. doi:10.1017/S026988890000789X

Paha, I. N., Gulati, P., & Gupta, P. (2009). Ontology Driven Conjunctive Query Expansion based on Mining User Logs. *International Conference on Methods and Models in Computer Science*. doi:10.1109/ICM2CS.2009.5397960

Preethi, N., & Devi, T. (2013). New Integrated Case And Relation Based (CARE) Page Rank Algorithm. *International Conference on Computer Communication and Informatics (ICCCI)*. doi:10.1109/ICCCI.2013.6466260

Qiu, F., & Cho, J. (2006). Automatic identification of user interest for personalized search.*Proceedings of WWW*, 727-736. doi:10.1145/1135777.1135883

Razmerita, L., Angehrn, A., & Maedche, A. (2003). Ontology based user modeling for knowledge management systems. In *Proceedings of the 9th International Conference on User Modeling* (pp. 213–217). Springer-Verlag. doi:10.1007/3-540-44963-9_29

Richardson, M., & Domingos, P. (2002). Advances in Neural Information Processing Systems: Vol. 14. *The Intelligent Surfer: Probabilistic Combination of Link and Content Information in PageRank*. MIT Press.

Safarkhani, B., Mohsenzadeh, T. M., & Mojde, M. M. R. (2009). Deriving semantic sessions from semantic clusters. *Proceedings of International Conference on Information Management and Engineering*, 523-528. doi:10.1109/ICIME.2009.131

Shadbolt, N., Hall, W., & Lee, T. B. (2006). The semantic web revisited. *IEEE Intelligent Systems, 21*(3), 96–101. doi:10.1109/MIS.2006.62

Sharma, A. K., & Juneja, D. (2006). BDI-based architecture of intelligent agents. *Proceedings of National Seminar on Emerging Trends in Network Technologies held at Career Institute of Technology and Management*.

Sieg, A., Mobasher, B., & Burke, R. (2007). Learning ontology-based user profiles: A semantic approach to personalized web search. *IEEE Intelligent Informatics Bulletin, 8*(1), 7–18.

Sieg, A., Mobasher, B., & Burke, R. (2007). Ontological user profiles for personalized web search. American Association for Artificial Intelligence, 84-91.

Simon, P., Carles, S., & Nick, J. (1998). Agents that reason and negotiate by arguing. *J Logic Comput, 8*(3), 261–292. doi:10.1093/logcom/8.3.261

Singh, A., & Alhadidi, B. (2013, August23). Knowledge Oriented Personalized Search Engine: A Step towards Wisdom Web. *International Journal of Computers and Applications*, *76*(8), 1–9. doi:10.5120/13264-0744

Singh, A., & Anand, P. (2013). State of art in ontology development tools. *International Journal of Advances in Computer Science & Technology.*, *2*(7), 96–101.

Singh, A., Juneja, D. & Sharma, A.K. (2009). An extensive analysis of implementation issues in semantic web. *International Journal of Information Technology, 5*(4), 67-74.

Singh, A., Juneja, D., & Sharma, A. K. (2010). General design structure of ontological databases in semantic web. *International Journal of Engineering Science and Technology*, *2*(5), 1227–1232.

Singh, A., Sharma, A., & Dey, N. (2015). Semantics and agents oriented web personalization: State of the art. *International Journal of Service Science, Management, Engineering, and Technology*, *6*(2), 35–49. doi:10.4018/ijssmet.2015040103

Skillen, K. L., Chen, L., Nugent, C. D., Donnelly, M. P., Burns, W., & Solheim, I. (2012). Ontological user profile modeling for context-aware application personalization. In J. Bravo, D. López-de-Ipiña, & F. Moya (Eds.), *Ubiquitous Computing and Ambient Intelligence*. Springer Berlin Heidelberg. doi:10.1007/978-3-642-35377-2_36

Sosnovsky, S., & Dicheva, D. (2010). Ontological technologies for user modelling. *Int. J. Metadata. Semantics and Ontologies*, *5*(1), 32–71. doi:10.1504/IJMSO.2010.032649

Sugiyama, K., Hatano, K., & Yoshikawa, M. (2004). Adaptive web search based on user profile constructed without any effort from users.*Proceedings of 13th International World Wide Web Conference (WWW '04)*, 675-684. doi:10.1145/988672.988764

Sycara, K. P. (1998). Multi-agent systems. AI Magazine, 79-92.

Tamma, V., & Payne, T. R. (2008). Is a semantic web agent a knowledge-savy agent? *IEEE Intelligent Systems*, *23*(4), 82–85. doi:10.1109/MIS.2008.69

Trajkova, J., & Gauch, S. (2004). Improving ontology-based user profiles. In *Proceedings of RIAO 2004* (pp. 380-389). University of Avignon.

Vigneshwari, S., & Aramudhan, M. (2012). A novel approach for personalizing the web using user profiling ontologies. *Proceedings of IEEE- Fourth International Conference on Advanced Computing*. doi:10.1109/icoac.2012.6416815

Whitman, M. W., & Mattord, H. J. (2011). *Principles of information security* (International 4th Edition). Thompson Course Technology.

Woerndl, W., & Groh, G. (2005). A proposal for an agent-based architecture for context-aware personalization in the semantic web. In *Proceeding of IJCAI Workshop Multi-agent information retrieval and recommender systems*. Edinburg, UK: UK-IJCAI.

Wooldridge, M., & Jennings, N. (1995). Intelligent agents: Theory and practice. *The Knowledge Engineering Review*, *10*(2), 115–152. doi:10.1017/S0269888900008122

Chapter 9
Semantic Web-Based Framework for Scientific Workflows in E-Science

Singanamalla Vijayakumar
VIT University, India

Nagaraju Dasari
VIT University, India

Bharath Bhushan
VIT University, India

Rajasekhar Reddy
VIT University, India

ABSTRACT

In the future generation, computer science plays prominent role in the scientific research. The development in the field of computers will leads to the research benefits of scientific community for sharing data, service computing, building the frameworks and many more. E-Science is the active extending field in the world by the increase data and tools. The proposed work discusses the use of semantic web applications for identifying the components in the development of scientific workflows. The main objective of the proposed work is to develop the framework which assists the scientific community to test and deploy the scientific experiments with the help of ontologies, service repositories, web services and scientific workflows. The framework which aims to sustenance the scientific results and management of applications related to the specific domain. The overall goal of this research is to automate the use of semantic web services, generate the workflows, manage the search services, manage the ontologies by considering the web service composition.

DOI: 10.4018/978-1-5225-2483-0.ch009

INTRODUCTION

The massive data leads to increase in E-science activities in the business world. The activities pose a hazard challenges such as scheduling the jobs, and how to maintain the interoperability among the services and tools (N. Ravindran, et. al., 2010).

The real time issues will be addressed by workflow technologies in the e-science context by executing the experiments with massive data available in the repositories (E. Pignotti, et. al., 2008). The implementation of scientific workflows in the multidisciplinary is increasing with massive volume of data and services. The enormous tools help in executing the tasks in heterogeneous environment with significant improvement in execution time. The e-learning workflows by web service semantics makes the system not only reliable, scalable and computer processable but also computer interpretable. To improve the precision and recall, the search engine should point out relevant pages through machine processable information (G. Stumme, et. al., 2006).

The semantic search plays a crucial role in finding the exact resources on which the service and data is going to process. A workflow is a formal model in which the services or tasks are composed and coordinated to achieve the desired operation. The services are residing in different locations with various configurations are often very large by its workflow sequence.

The web service in semantic web service composition is a self-contained, loosely coupled process, deployed over standard middleware platform that can be described, published, discovered and invoked over a network (S. Bharath Bhushan, and Pradeep Reddy, CH, 2016).

The sematic web services in e-science have three key areas of concern which are service discovery, mediation and composition. In service discovery we have to find a service that matches with the given task from similar service repository. The composed service compatibility will be taken care in meditation phase. In order to satisfy the user, the group of service should compose to meet the business goal in the final phase of the workflow. The ontologies applied in workflows in which they achieved significant results are discussed in (Fensel, D., et. al., 2006, and OWL-S, 2006).

The semantic web is created by applying ontologies to the web, where it provides the knowledge base to develop the web service and workflows. The knowledge sharing and reuse can be achieved through ontologies (D. Fensel, et. al., 2001).

The personalization plays a crucial role in the e-learning system where the customer feedback is important criteria. The e-learning system will deliver the services according to their user preferences through continuous feedback.

To enable the e-science in service computing, we have two notable technologies by processing web services. They are International Virtual Observatory Alliance

(IVOA) and National Virtual Observatory (NVO) and few other technologies also exist. This protocol helps in maintaining the compatibilities between w-science web services in composed workflow. One more standardization committee to develop protocols such as Web Coverage Service (WCS), the Web Feature Service (WFS) and the Web Map Service (WMS) is Open Geospatial Consortium (OGC). The discussed protocols are widely adopted by various applications in e-science platforms.

LITERATURE REVIEW

The Voss A, et. al., 2008, author proposed an e-research model in which the resources are provided as services through dashboards with all operations that are essential. The end user can invoke the services through interface by submitting job.

The various scientific workflow management systems help in processing data, computing resources and as well as variety of applications. The popular workflow systems such as Kepler (Ludäscher B, et. al. 2005), Taverna (Oinn T, et. al., 2004), Triana (Taylor I, et. al., 2004), Pegasus (Deelman E, et. al., 2007), ASKALON (Fahringer T, et. al., 2005), SWIFT (Zhao Y, et. al., 2007) and Pipeline Pilot (Yang X, et. al., 2010). These work flow systems perform better in terms of usability, automation, efficiency and reproducibility.

In e-science, the scientific workflow is a vital component for delivering seamless services to end users. The few applications are illustrated for successful composition of workflows. To share and integrate the clinical, public health data, the Taverna is deployed on caGrid platform. In south California earthquake centre the Pegasus is engaged as a workflow engine and to compute probabilistic hazard curve they have used a cybershake workflow. The composer science is a work flow management system to implement workflows by enabling semantics of generated services and which finds optimal services for each workflow task (TAVERNA, 2010).

Learning through social networking sites is trending, but the huge amount of data is to be processed in the repositories. The sematic search helps in processing relevant pages with good precision and recall. To build a sematic search engine, the developer should focus on providing a common syntax and vocabularies with logical language (Cisco, 2008). The development of ontologies on e-learning repositories is to perform domain standardization. These ontologies are then used to write metadata for describing the resources which can then be referred to extracting most relevant and accurate information from the problem specific domain. The cisco proposed a reusable learning object system to match the semantics of specific explanation of the curriculum and activities.

Most e-learning units that teach new skills follow the lecture model: Present quite a lot of information or video and then give a quiz or test. The internet improves on in-class lectures in that students take lessons on their own time, and quizzes are graded right away. But few online programs require the density of active participation needed for efficient learning.

The e-learning presents the lecture content in the form of videos and then they assess by conducting online quiz or test. The learning through internet enhances the flexibilities of both facilitator as well as students, and tests are graded precisely without errors.

The (Bentley, R., et. al., 2005) authors developed a virtual observatory software application on group of network computers to access the resources from different repositories. It can handle various resources such as data, software, document and images.

The service monitoring is an important aspect of e-science to ensure the quality of workflow services and the features of underlying technologies. The author proposed a mechanism to monitor the workflow services at service level agreement stage (Yang, X., 2011). The e-science is evolved from grid to cloud by varying the approaching styles in business models, computing models and programming models.

The new scientific platform is established by "e-science 2.0", where the scientist can share raw experimental results, workflows, nascent theories, claims of discovery, and draft papers by forming a dynamic community on the Web to collectively conduct the research. The experimental results are distributed openly to the public. The IC Cloud is developed on e-science 2.0, which provide all types of services to end users with flexible interfaces. The virtualization shows a significant impact on e-science by providing simulated execution environment on top of the raw infrastructure (Duan Q, et. al., 2012). The virtual machines which act as a test bed for running e-science services with different workloads. To store e-science related data (Mell, P., Grance, T., 2009), the virtualized cloud storage plays a crucial role in storing, retrieving and computing terms. The disadvantage is various users are not showing interest in sharing the research data with cloud providers and even those data will be distributed across the world. And even the trust, legal and financial issues also backstabbing the user to store their data in cloud.

ONTOLOGY IN E-SCIENCE

The technology development changes the methods and way of performing the scientific research. Consistently large amount of data is being stored and management by the computational equipment. No single research group or institutes have all the required knowledge base and computational power to manage or process the data. E-Science activities are growing with more data and tools; it gives us more challenges like understanding and organizing of resources and interoperability with large set of data and tools. Ontologies are important building blocks of semantic web and essential for its success.

"E-Science is a universal collaboration in the major areas of science and next generation infrastructure that will enable it" – John Taylor (UK-e-science). E-Science domains are heterogeneous semi structured data. Powerful ontology holds the basic benefits of:

1. Localized tools, applications and users management.
2. Extraction of accurate sub portions of main ontologies is called as sub-ontologies from primary or main ontology.
3. Maintains Interoperability among heterogeneous ontology sources and applications.
4. Highly effective customization and usage of sub portions of ontologies.

In common, the ontology is referred as a specification of conceptualization, where conceptualization is a process of perceiving things and analyzing and understanding the relationships among them. Ontologies can be maintained in multiple simplified ways, it should be considered as a knowledge base of artificial intelligence rather than a collection of words and concepts. Few interesting characteristics of ontology is high-level compatibility and consistency among various domains and sub-domains and, representation of generic vs. specific ontologies. In e-science it is denoted as generic and upper; and specific or lower ontologies.

It has wide benefits for Scientists, service providers, research communities, laboratory groups. For example, Scientists need low level of information for validity checking to check with novel approaches to interpret the results. Along with them, debugging and updating of data sets is required to identify where exactly the changes happened with respect to changes. The semantics can be specified in two levels: classes of resources linked each other and shared relation as output and resources might bed_item and service_call, and second is the required vocabulary.

Scientific Advantages on Ontologies

Three main factors resulting the great advantage and gives good benefits:

1. Resource quantity improvement.
2. Representation quality.
3. Communication improvement.

Brief description of these factors are gives a great improvement to the scientific computing.

Resource Quantity Improvement: The result of improvement is get maximized when large quantity of resources or online services integrated as one, such as distributed computing is running a large set of data or e-resources.

Representation Quality: The quality of representation in scientific knowledge is more complex. The representation is clean and more number of scientists can utilize for their scientific investic investigation.

Communication Improvement: Increase in the exchange of ideas by connecting to online science environments. Ontologies are helping by annotating content of the scientific databases, illuminate scientific reasoning and provide virtual communities. These improvements show impact on the scientific data and methods.

Challenges

Three major challenges in the view of scientific semantic web in terms of capture, design and usage.

Capture: Ontology deriving from knowledge bases and even creating is more complex with existing automated and semi automated techniques.

Design: Ontology design is more challenging due to its little complex design guidelines, patterns and construction methods on ontologies. It needs to provide uniformity at upper level of generic methods like model, method, experiment.

Use: e-science is main thrust area for current researchers and it requires collaboration of human and computing system. Coordination in all aspects and work flow over distributed computing is a considerable challenge including the user interface.

Types and Components of Ontologies

The ontology is required to achieve a major goal in the science, such as, documentation of experiment analysis, annotation and sharing of results Few ontologies have been developed to achieve this goal is MGED Ontology (MO), it is developed to provide minimum information about aq micro array experiment and EXPO are examples.

Ontology is a vocabulary of concepts to express knowledge without semantic ambiguity. These are highly capable of solving when heterogeneous terminology identified. Few application areas like unable to access the information resources online and difficulty in knowledge sharing.

Different types of ontologies are useful for various activities in e-science and other related domains.

Top-Level Ontologies: Top level ontologies specify the independent to a specific domain and these are across many domains, such as events, time and space.
Domain Ontologies: These specific to a particular domain.
Application or Task Ontologies: These are very particular to a specific task.
Components: There are few components required to represent and access the ontologies. Such as classes, properties, instances, relations, restrictions, and rules.
Classes: classes are sets, collections and concepts.
Properties: Properties are attributes and characteristics representation and features.
Instances: Instances are individual objects.
Relations: It shows the bonding for classes and individuals.
Rules: Statements in the form of logical inference.

The basic characteristics of ontology must have minimum number or no ambiguities and should maintain internal consistency. It also has minimum or no coding bias with minimal commitment.

Advantages in science field are meaning should be explicit and human and computer readable. Data transfer should be possible without major meaning change. Helps to identify the errors is good advantage of ontology. Eliminates the redundancies in domain specific ontologies and provide reliable experimental methods and conclusions.

Ontology Libraries

In this section, the major ontologies are discussed in brief. BioPortal (Noy, N. F., *et al.,* 2009) is developed by national centre for bio medical ontology is a library for biomedical ontologies. OBO Foundry (Smith, B., *et al.,* 2007) is also similar to BioPortal but it has we documented and well defined and editors monitors the library and verifies it. OnGov (Hinkelmann, K., *et. al.,* 2010) is collection of ontologies for government and it depends on the blog system to publish ontologies. OntoSelect (Buitelaar, P., *et al.,* 2004) is library with advanced search mechanism and useful for natural language processing, facilitates annotation but searches restricted to particular language.

OntoSearch2 (Thomas, E., *et al.,* 2007) enables powerful query mechanism across many ontologies, and it provides simple keyword based search mechanism on all its ontologies. Schema-Cache[1] is developed for searching and browsing for RDF vocabularies. And TONES is a library for OWL ontologies useful for testing purposes, it is capable for sorting ontologies based on parameters and identifies its complexity.

WS-BPELOnto

The main purpose of WS-BPELOnto ontology is to provide a basis for conceptualization of the main components of a workflow based on a WS-BPEL model. The ontology was designed to facilitate and clarify the semantic description of the workflow model and connect the initial description of the workflow model with the WS-BPEL execution obtained at the end of the process.

The workflow management coalition (WfMC) is an organization that aims to expand workflow technology through the development of standards and common terminology. WS-BPELOnto ontology was developed based on technical definitions proposed by the WfMC (Shin, D., *et al.,* 2009), associated with the terminology related to the WS-BPEL workflow model.

Basic terms presented in the terminology proposed in (Shin, D., *et al.,* 2009), and used for the development of WS-BPELOnto, were adapted to the context of scientific workflows, considering that the proposal of (Sanchez F. G., *et al.,* 2009) is related mainly to the nomenclature used in the definition of business workflows. In addition to basic concepts, there are other concepts and connections that are related to these basic concepts. Thus, we used these other concepts for the development of WS- BPELOnto ontology in order to expand its expression power.

From the WS-BPEL model, basic concepts related to a workflow, expressed in this language and considered indispensable for a workflow description, were extracted. We also added concepts found in (Shin, D., *et al.,* 2009), relating them whenever possible. Basic concepts from the WS-BPEL used in WS_BPELOnto are Process, PartnerLink and Variable, shown in Figure. 1.

The Process class and its subclasses represent a WS-BPEL process. A workflow is represented in WS-BPEL by a Process. A WS-BPEL document contains an XML element that identifies the represented process <process>. This element involves logic processing and the definition of the process itself, including steps to interconnect Web services to make the process itself. Figure 2 shows the structure of the Process class. The ontological term 'Thing' is the root of the OWL hierarchy (it was defined by OWL creators), represented in Protege tool. Considering that a process in WS-BPEL is a workflow, we consider this semantic connection in the ontology structure. Thus, according to WS-BPELOnto ontology, a workflow can be a business workflow (BusinessWorkflow or BusinessProcess) or a scientific workflow (ScientificWorkflow or ScientificProcess). In the context of this work, we only consider the definition of scientific workflows. PartnerLink class represents a service. Considering a WS-BPEL workflow model, each task that composes a workflow or a process is represented by a PartnerLink. In WS-BPEL, each PartnerLink represents a Web service and thus a workflow is composed of several Web services. Figure 3 shows the PartnerLink class structure.

Considering that each PartnerLink corresponds to a task of a workflow, we can consider that a PartnerLink is an activity (<Activity>) or a task (<Task>) or a step (<Step>) of a workflow. Based on the terminology provided by (Sirin, E., 2004), an activity (Activity) can be automatic (AutomatedActivity) or manual (ManualActivity). An Automated activity may be a function (Function), an application that is invoked (InvokedApplication), a service (Service), or more specifically, a Web service (Web Service), which is the type of task that makes up a workflow in the context of E-Science. The Variable class represents a variable and an input or output of a service or workflow. Figure 4 shows the structure of the Variable class. A variable can be input (InputVariable) or may be an output/result (OutputVariable) of a service (InputPartnerLinkVariable). The scope of a variable can also access the full workflow.

SERVICES OF E-SCIENCE

The main intension of computational e-science is designed for the highly developed networking environments. And also, it may use immense data sets that can be manipulating with grid computing and including technologies to enable the distributed collaborations for accessing the grid. This is introduces by John Taylor in 1999 and is developed for the huge networking in the sense of science and technology. Actually, the E-science is interpreted more and more with computer applications that is to be under taking the new scientific development study, including the groundwork, analysis, dataset collection, simulation performance, and huge storage and accessibility of overall materials maintained by the scientific process. In 2014, IEEE series of E-science communication is defined as "the E-science novelty in modern technique analysis, simulation performance and data intensive research across all controls, throughout the research lifecycle" as single definition used by the authorized owners. However, it encompasses the "what is often referred to as big data, which has revolutionary since such as the large hadron collider at CERN – that generates large amounts of E-science data includes computational biology, bio-informatics, genomics" and the human digital footprint for the social sciences.

The basic E-science revolutionizes both scientific method and empirical research, especially through digital big data; and theoretical scientific analysis, especially for building the computer simulation. These models are described from the scientific techniques with help of White House Office in 2013. Many of the e-science products are aforementioned for preservation and access requirements under the memorandum's directive. This process of analysis could be performed by the following methods.

Semantic Search

The innovations in data intensive scientific application are towards significant role in the field of semantic e-science which is based on semantic technologies. The e-science applications gain a significant value in various fields such as life sciences, meteorology, oceanography, ecology and especially in solar related areas. The need of semantic based tools and technologies plays a vital role in e-science development. To enhance the research in traditional fields such as modeling, simulation and prediction is computed by the applications based on e-science. The researchers find the e-science as important as the theoretical and empirical techniques.

The domain ontologies and semantic web services are helpful in the semantic search of web services, as web services semantics are semantically annotated web services. As the domain ontologies are basis for semantic notations in semantic web service search process. The composed services through semantic search process are based on semantic description of the user selected workflows and as well as defined ontologies. The each atomic service in composed service is filtered from the semantic description database provided by the user. The description provided by the user is compared with the content synthesized from the OWLS of each atomic service.

In health care and life science communities the semantic web services plays a crucial role, such as World Wide Web Consortium (W3C) which was founded a semantic e science interest group on healthcare. The e-science ontology use is at present largely motivated by operational efficiency, with downstream impacts on scientific knowledge development minimized at present, and significantly below their potential.

The semantic infrastructure is a platform for semantic web to gather web semantic information by exploiting data management and artificial intelligence technologies. The e-science is applied in bioinformatics for silicon experiments through the use of computer based information databases by data analytics and visualization.

The e-science is leveraged towards cloud computing, by which the services are running on virtualized platforms and also massive cloud storage helps in processing the data. The disadvantage is various users are not showing interest in sharing the research data with cloud providers and even those data will be distributed across the world. And even the trust, legal and financial issues also backstabbing the user to store their data in cloud.

Service Composition

Most studies on the automatic composition of Web services create compositions considering only input and output of available services, without considering its semantics. Thus, results that are not relevant to the users work can be generated.

Moreover, processing complexity becomes very high as all possible combinations of available services are considered.

The framework proposed in this paper takes these problems into account and scientific workflows are created through the composition of semantic Web services. Several approaches have been proposed to address various aspects of Web services composition, such as composition languages, formalization of composition, systems to support composition. Among the languages for composition of Web services, WS-BPEL has distinguished itself as an XML-based language and specifically designed to support service composition. In terms of formalization, the basic objective is to use formal description techniques such as Petri Nets for the verification of composition properties. Finally, the mentioned systems consist of projects specifically designed to support composition. Composer-Science is a framework that supports the composition of Web services to specify scientific workflows.

As noted above, Petri Nets are mathematical formalisms that enable graphic representation, and they have methods for the formal analysis of a system. Nodes and transitions of Petri Nets are used to model logical views of the system. In this section we will describe how Petri Nets can be used in composition of Web services. The method consists of three steps: the first is the construction of a Petri Net topology consistent with the semantic specification of the user's defined workflow. The second step is the definition of semantically possible compositions with available services, and the latter step aims at the structural analysis of services and the generation of semantically and structurally possible compositions.

OWLS-X plan is a web service dataset and a service composition planner applied for emergency medical assistance. The OWLS-X plan converts the services into an equivalent domain description which are specified in the PDDL 2.1 (planning domain description language) and invoke an efficient AI planner X plan to generate a service composition plan which meets user preferences. The e-services are selected by an agent-based web service discovery framework, which satisfies client preferences through web service semantics.

TRADITIONAL SCIENCE VS. E-SCIENCE

The main intension of computational e-science is designed for the highly developed networking environments. And also, it may use immense data sets that can be manipulating with grid computing and including technologies to enable the distributed collaborations for accessing the grid. This is introduces by John Taylor in 1999 and is developed for the huge networking in the sense of science and technology. Actually, the E-science is interpreted more and more with computer applications that is to be under taking the new scientific development study, including the groundwork, analysis, dataset collection, simulation performance, and huge storage and accessibility of overall materials maintained by the scientific process. In 2014, IEEE series of e-science communication is defined as "the e-science novelty in modern technique analysis, simulation performance and data intensive research across all the science fields.

The traditional science is considering from two distinct philosophical traditions within the history of science. However, the e-science is argued by required paradigm shift and also sibling's of the sciences. The main idea is "to open the data is not modern aspect which indeed the history of study and philosophy of science". In 1660s, Robert Boyle is recognized with the concept of skepticism, transparency and reproducibility for independent verification of publishing the scholarly. After that, the scientific model was divided into two approaches, deductive and empirical approaches. In the scientific model of deductive approach is concerned for the theoretical analysis that should be creating a new branch. For this type of analysis Victoria is advised a computational approaches, which is performing for finalization of scientific researchers activities in all the computational aspects. From last 20 years this type of achievements for people tackling to handle changes in high performance computing and simulation. For this consideration the e-science can be combining both empirical and theoretical traditions*, while computer simulations can create synthetic data, and real-time big data can be used to analysis theoretical simulation models.

In order to revolves to developing new methods for support scientists in various scientific research aspects. With this aim to making new scientific ideas discovering by using the vast amount of data analysis over the web based usage with several computational resources. And moreover, the values discovered without easily analyzes by providing the computational tools for producing the pre-request results analysis. Rather than the results are to be needful with original, and creative aspect to achieve the nature that is not made by automatic. At that time, this has guide to various research topics that are defined by the properties of e-science objectives. In order to provide these objectives can be support a new paradigm of doing science, and new rules to get the required parameters preserving and they make to computational results which are available data analysis operations. For that, we have to reproducible in traceable, logical steps, as an essential requirement for producing the newly modern scientific developments/achievements. With this, we are able to perform an extenuation of the "Boyle's tradition in the computational age".

E-Science Modelling Processes

In this view, we perform a modern sciences discovery process instance serves a similar purpose to mathematical proof. This can be performed by the similar properties namely it allows the results should be deterministically reproduced when re-analyzed and that intermediate results can be viewed to aid examination.

CONCLUSION

In the context of e-science, computational resources are becoming increasingly important for the carrying out of scientific research, accompanied by a proliferation of data and tools. In this article, we presented a framework to help in the discovery and composition of semantic web services. Our contribution is the development of a framework that uses semantic resources such as ontologies and semantic Web services, together with Petri Nets and workflow languages to assist scientific workflow composition, thus making the process simpler and more effective. Specifically, the Composer-Science enables the storage and search for domain ontologies and semantic annotations of Web services as well as composition based on these semantic annotations and in Web services input and output. The WS-BPELOnto is an initial proposal and in its current version neither integration nor alignments with other ontologies have been considered. It is important to expand the scope of the work. Algorithms used for structural analysis must be improved too. Currently, we are working on mediation infrastructures to help in structural analysis improvement.

REFERENCES

Bentley, R., Bogart, R., Davis, A., Hurlburt, N., Mukherjee, J., Rezapkin, V., . . . Weiss, M. (2005). *A Framework for Space and Solar Physics Virtual Observatories*. Retrieved from hpde.gsfc.nasa.gov/VO_Framework_7_Jan_05.pdf

Bharath Bhushan, S., & Pradeep Reddy, C. H. (2016). A Four-Level Linear Discriminant Analysis Based Service Selection in The Cloud Environment. *International Journal of Technology.*, *7*(5), 530–541.

Buitelaar, P., Eigner, T., & OntoSelect, T. D. (2004). A Dynamic Ontology Library with Support for Ontology Selection. *Proc. of the Demo Session at the International Semantic Web Conference*.

Cisco. (2008). *Cisco reusable learning object strategy: designing and developing learning objects for multiple learning approaches*. Retrieved from http://business.cisco.com/

Deelman, E., Mehta, G., Singh, G., Su, M., & Vahi, K. (2007). Pegasus: mapping large-scale workflows to distributed resources. In I. Taylor, E. Deelman, D. Gannon, & M. Shields (Eds.), *Workflows for e-Science* (pp. 376–394). New York: Springer. doi:10.1007/978-1-84628-757-2_23

Duan, Q., Yan, Y., & Vasilakos, A. V. (2012). A Survey on Service-Oriented Network Virtualization Toward Convergence of Networking and Cloud Computing. Network and Service Management. *IEEE Transactions*, *9*(4), 373–392.

Fahringer, T., Jugravu, A., Pllana, S., Prodan, R., Seragiotto, C. Jr, & Truong, H. (2005). ASKALON: A tool set for cluster and Grid computing. *Concurr Comput Pract Exp*, *17*(2–4), 143–169. doi:10.1002/cpe.929

Fensel, D., Lausen, H., Polleres, A., De Bruijn, J., Stollberg, M., Roman, D., & Domingue, J. (2006). *Enabling Semantic Web Services: Web Service Modeling Ontology*. Springer.

Fensel, D., van Harmelen, F., Horrocks, I., McGuinness, D. L., & Patel-Schneider, P. F. (2001). OIL: An Ontology Infrastructure for the Semantic Web. *IEEE Intelligent Systems*, *16*(2), 38–45. doi:10.1109/5254.920598

Hinkelmann, K., Thönssen, B., & Wolff, D. (2010). Ontologies for E-government. In *Theory and applications of ontology: Computer applications* (pp. 429–462). Springer Netherlands. doi:10.1007/978-90-481-8847-5_19

Lemos, M. (2004). *Workflow para bioinformatica* (Ph.D. Thesis). Programa de Pos-Graduacao em Informatica, Pontificia Universidade Catolica do Rio deJaneiro, Rio de Janeiro, Brazil. (in Portuguese)

Ludäscher, B., Altintas, I., Berkley, C., Higgins, D., Jaeger, E., Jones, M., & Zhao, Y. et al. (2005). Scientific workflow management and the Kepler system. *Concurr Comput Pract Exp*, *18*(10), 1039–1065. doi:10.1002/cpe.994

Matos, E. E., Campos, F., Braga, R., & Palazzi, D. (2009). CelOWS: An ontology based framework for the provision of semantic web services related to biological models. *Journal of Biomedical Informatics*, *43*(1), 125–136. doi:10.1016/j.jbi.2009.08.008 PMID:19695346

Matthias, K., & Gerber, A. (2006). Fast composition planning of owl-s services and application. In *Web Services, ECOWS'06.4th European Conference on*. IEEE.

Mell, P., & Grance, T. (2009). *The NIST definition of cloud computing*. Retrieved from http://www.nist.gov/itl/cloud/upload/cloud-def-v15.pdf

Noy, N. F., Shah, N. H., Whetzel, P. L., Dai, B., Dorf, M., Griffith, N., & Musen, M. A. (2009). BioPortal: Ontologies and integrated data resources at the click of a mouse. *Nucleic Acids Research*, *37*(suppl 2), W170–W173. doi:10.1093/nar/gkp440 PMID:19483092

Oinn, T., Addis, M., Ferris, J., Marvin, D., Senger, M., Greenwood, M., & Li, P. et al. (2004). Taverna: A tool for the composition and enactment of bioinformatics workflows. *Bioinformatics (Oxford, England)*, *20*(17), 3045–3054. doi:10.1093/bioinformatics/bth361 PMID:15201187

OWL-S Working Group. (2006). *OWL-S 1.2 Pre-Release*. Retrieved from http://www.ai.sri.com/ daml/services/owl-s/1.2/

Parastatidis, S. (2009). A Platform for All That We Know: Creating a Knowledge-Driven Research Infrastructure. In The Fourth Paradigm: Data Intensive Scientific Discovery. Academic Press.

Pignotti, E., Edwards, P., Preece, A., Gotts, N., & Polhill, G. (2008). Enhancing workflow with a semantic description of scientific intent. *5th European Semantic Web Conference*, Tenerife, Spain. doi:10.1007/978-3-540-68234-9_47

Ravindran, N., Liang, Y., & Liang, X. (2010). A labeled-tree approach to semantic and structural data interoperability applied in hydrology domain. *Information Sciences*, *180*(24), 5008–5028. doi:10.1016/j.ins.2010.06.015

Schema-cache. (2010). Retrieved from http://schemacache.test.talis.com/

Shin, D., Lee, K., & Suba, T. (2009). Automated generation of composite Web services based on functional semantics. *Journal of Web Semantics*, *7*(4), 332–343. doi:10.1016/j.websem.2009.05.001

Sirin, E. (2004). *OWLSAPI*. Retrieved from http://www.mindswap.org/2004/owl-s/api/

Smith, B., Ashburner, M., Rosse, C., Bard, J., Bug, W., Ceusters, W., & Leontis, N. et al. (2007). The OBO Foundry: Coordinated evolution of ontologies to support biomedical data integration. *Nature Biotechnology*, *25*(11), 1251–1255. doi:10.1038/nbt1346 PMID:17989687

Stumme, G. (2006). Web Semantics: Science, Services and Agents on the World Wide Web 4. Semantic Web Mining State of the art and future directions, 124–143.

TAVERNA. (2010). *Taverna Workflow System*. Retrieved from http://www.taverna.org.uk/

Taylor, I., Shields, M., Wang, I., & Harrison, A. (2007). The Triana workflow environment: architecture and applications. In I. Taylor, E. Deelman, D. Gannon, & M. Shields (Eds.), *Workflows for e-Science* (pp. 320–339). New York: Springer. doi:10.1007/978-1-84628-757-2_20

Taylor, I. J., Deelman, E., Gannon, D. B., & Shields, M. (2006). *Workflows for e-Science, Scientific Workflows for Grids* (1st ed.). Springer.

Thomas, E., Pan, J. Z., & Sleeman, D. H. (2007, June). ONTOSEARCH2: Searching Ontologies Semantically. OWLED.

TONES Ontology Repository. (2010). Retrieved from http://owl.cs.manchester.ac.uk/repository/

VISTRAILS. (2010). Retrieved from http://www.vistrails.org/index.php/Main_Page

Voss, A., Meer, E. V., & Fergusson, D. (2008). *Research in a connected world*. Retrieved from http://www.lulu.com/product/ebook/research-in-a-connected-world/17375289

WfMC. (1999). *Workflow management coalition – Terminology and glossary*. Retrieved from http://www.wfmc.org/Download-document/WFMC-TC-1011-Ver-3-Terminology-and-Glossary-English.html

WS-BPEL. (2007). *Web Services Business Process Execution Language Version 2.0*. Retrieved from http://docs.oasis-open.org/wsbpel/2.0/OS/wsbpel-v2.0-OS.html

Yang, X. (2011). QoS-oriented service computing: bring SOA into cloud environment. In X. Liu & Y. Li (Eds.), *Advanced design approaches to emerging software systems: principles, methodology and tools*. IGI Global USA.

Yang, X., Bruin, R., & Dove, M. (2010). *Developing an end-to-end scientific workflow: a case study of using a reliable, lightweight, and comprehensive workflow platform in e-Science*. doi:.21110.1109/MCSE.2009

Zhao, Y., Hategan, M., Clifford, B., Foster, I., von, Laszewski, G., Nefedova, V., Raicu, I., Stef-Praun, T., & Wilde, M. (2007). Swift: fast, reliable, loosely coupled parallel computation. *Proceedings of 2007 IEEE congress on services (Services 2007)*, 199–206. doi:10.1109/SERVICES.2007.63

Chapter 10
State-of-the-Art Information Retrieval Tools for Biological Resources

Shashi Bhushan Lal
ICAR-Indian Agricultural Statistics Research Institute, India

Mohammad Samir Farooqi
ICAR-Indian Agricultural Statistics Research Institute, India

Anu Sharma
ICAR-Indian Agricultural Statistics Research Institute, India

Sanjeev Kumar
ICAR-Indian Agricultural Statistics Research Institute, India

Krishna Kumar Chaturvedi
ICAR-Indian Agricultural Statistics Research Institute, India

Dwijesh Chandra Mishra
ICAR-Indian Agricultural Statistics Research Institute, India

Mohit Jha
ICAR-Indian Agricultural Statistics Research Institute, India

ABSTRACT

With the advancements in sequencing technologies, there is an exponential growth in the availability of the biological databases. Biological databases consist of information and knowledge collected from scientific experiments, published literature and statistical analysis of text, numerical, image and video data. These databases are widely spread across the globe and are being maintained by many organizations. A number of tools have been developed to retrieve the information from these

DOI: 10.4018/978-1-5225-2483-0.ch010

databases. Most of these tools are available on web but are scattered. So, finding a relevant information is a very difficult, and tedious task for the researchers. Moreover, many of these databases use disparate storage formats but are linked to each other. So, an important issue concerning present biological resources is their availability and integration at single platform. This chapter provides an insight into existing biological resources with an aim to provide consolidated information at one place for ease of use and access by researchers, academicians and students.

INTRODUCTION

Sanger, way back in 1988, discovered successful methods for sequencing of proteins, Ribonucleic Acid (RNA) and Deoxyribonucleic Acid (DNA) which opened a new era in biological science (Sanger, 1998). In the world of biological sciences, when the advancement in sequencing technologies has made human genome sequenced to a great extent, one cannot imagine a world without nucleotide and protein sequences (Stretton, 2002). A very large number of researchers in life sciences have been working since then, which has generated an enormous amount of biological sequences and its derived data. SWISS-PROT database was developed in the year 1986 which had around seventy thousand protein sequences from five thousand different organisms.

After Sanger, emergence of further refined technologies for genome sequencing were discovered, namely Pacific Biosciences, Ion Torrent, 454/Roche, Illumina, SOLiD and so on. This technological advancements have led to the whole genome sequencing of a wide range of species across animals, insects, plants and human. Being the fastest growing area in biological science, there has been a remarkable increase in the volume of biological data. These data are sequences obtained from experiments, published literature and their computational and statistical analyses. The format of data obtained can be in the form of either text, numbers, videos, images or diagrams (Schaller, Mueller, & Sung, 2008). These data are available on the public domain for carrying out research in biological science.

Although a large number of these databases are available on open domain, yet their retrieval system has always been a challenge for the developers (Kamal et al., 2016; Singh, Sharma, & Dey, 2015). Many attempts have been made by researchers to integrate these databases and develop an efficient retrieval system. Information retrieval from these databases are maintained by various organizations to provide ease of access to the end users. But, due to the rapid growth in the biological data, requirement of computational resources for its storage and retrieval system always remain a challenge for computational experts to meet the growing needs.

In this chapter, a comprehensive compilation of existing biological databases have been provided at one place for easy accessibility of researchers, academicians and students. The organization of this chapter is as follows: first section deals with the nature of biological data and its organization, followed by types of biological databases. In the second section classification of biological databases, its detailed description with few examples are presented. Third section discusses about the means of interconnection between these databases followed by the drawbacks in the biological databases explained in the fifth section. In the sixth section, retrieval system of these biological databases have been discussed. Finally, conclusions are presented in the last section.

NATURE OF BIOLOGICAL DATA

Current century is facing a big challenge to store, manage and retrieve the variety of biological data generated from numerous genome sequencing projects. These projects generate a variety of the data. Two important types of data are:

1. Sequence: This is associated with the DNA of a tissue from various species and usually consists of strings containing set of DNA nucleotides bases namely Cytosine (C), Guanine (G), Adenine (A), or Thymine (T).
2. Structure: This deals with the three-dimensional structure of biological macromolecules such as proteins, RNA, and DNA.

Broadly, a biological database is classified into sequence and structure databases. Sequence database consists of DNA and protein sequences whereas structure databases are related to proteins. Due to huge volume of this kind of data, their storage needs, connecting technique among their various types (e.g. sequences, structure information and so on) and requirement of a quick and easy retrieval system, there was a need to develop biological databases.

A biological database is defined as a collection of data that is organized in a manner so that its contents can easily be accessed, managed, and updated (Attwood & Parry-Smith, 2002). The major functions of a biological database are to provide the computer readable form of biological data and make the data available to the scientists and researchers spread all over the world for further analysis.

The biological data, in general, are classified into three categories namely *primary, secondary* and *specialized* databases based on the source (primary or derived from the primary). This type of classification have been represented in a diagram showing the flow as shown in Figure 1.

Figure 1. Major Classification of Biological Databases

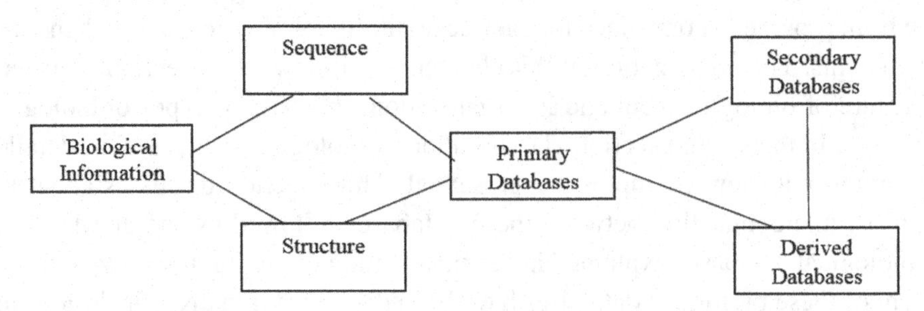

- **Primary Databases:** These databases are populated directly by researchers and are archival in nature. These data are experimentally derived data such as nucleotide sequence, protein sequence or macromolecular structure. Once this data is submitted online, an accession number is allocated which is unique for every submission, and then, the data in the primary database can never be changed (Brooksbank, 2006).
- **Secondary Databases:** These databases consist of the results obtained by literature research and interpretation, and analyzed information from the primary databases. It has the data about the family of proteins obtained by application of multiple sequence alignments. Many complex algorithms are applied on primary data, or combination of many computational tools are used to derive new knowledge.
- **Specialized Databases:** These databases are developed normally to serve a specific research community or to focus on specific organisms. This type of database contains sequences or some other types of information. There can be overlap of the sequences of this database with the primary database. It may also contain new sequences submitted by authors and later, curated by the team of experts. Majority of these databases are available in public domain for free access.

Therefore, it is observed that a large scale processing of heterogeneous data comes from diverse sources. These are primary databases such as GenBank of National Center for Biotechnology Information (NCBI), European Molecular Biology Laboratory (EMBL) of European Bioinformatics Institute (EBI), Protein Data Bank (PDB), DNA Data Bank of Japan (DDJB) and so on, or, secondary databases such as TrEMBL, UniProt and many other. The development of interface to allow access to these data sources is a complex job due to wide variation in the requirement of programming techniques for development of an efficient retrieval system (Sharma, Rai, & Lal, 2013).

More details about primary, secondary and specialized database are given in Biological database resources section later in this chapter. In the following section a detailed description of storage structure of the most popular primary biological databases available on open domain is presented.

STORAGE STRUCTURE OF BIOLOGICAL DATABASES

There are mainly three types of database formats – flat files, relational databases and object oriented databases. These types of databases are described below:

- **Flat Files (Text):** This is a large file containing texts with data separated by a special character such as tab, space, comma or dash. Therefore, searching in this kind of file for a particular piece of information is obviously an inefficient process. This is not manageable in case of big databases with complex data types. Searching through this kind of files is memory-intensive and can crash the entire computer system (Xiong, 2006).
- **Relational Databases:** The organization, access, and retrieval from the data, an efficient software is required, called database management systems (DBMS). The DBMS contains entries in the form of a relation (table) with defined relationships among the entities. The primary goal of designing a database is to establish a non-redundant database with quick, easy and fast information retrieval for the user's queries. In Relational DBMS (RDBMS) the data is stored in a number of tables called relational tables. Relationships are established among these tables using keys defined on these tables.
- **Object Oriented Databases:** In RDBMS, it is not possible to specify the relationship between data items. Object oriented databases are based on the concepts of object oriented programming (OOP) where data is in the form of objects. These objects contain data and code which is executable. The search system on these databases are implemented using these objects and their specified references.
- The biological databases available in public domain have generally flat file formats. The other formats are also found which are relational and object oriented. Flat file system databases are not very convenient for applying queries and getting the results faster as compared to relational databases. The reason for using mostly flat file databases can be the design steps involved in RDBMS which may not be convenient for biologists (Xiong, 2006).

Nucleotide sequences are the fundamental biological data for various organisms. These data provide the information to understand its structure and functions. Researchers submit their experimental data on the primary sequence databases namely NCBI, EMBL and DDBJ before publishing their findings in the research journals. These three organizations are in close collaboration since 1986-87 and share every submission by the researchers so that their primary databases have same set of data. This collaboration is called International Nucleotide Sequence Database (INSD). The formats of their databases are mostly similar with minor differences in its organization and meta data (Cochrane, G., Karsch-Mizrachi, & Nakamura, 2011).

The database structure of INSD organizations have a common feature table and annotation standards. This feature table helps to provide a convenient medium for carrying manipulations and operations. This also makes easier data exchange among them. These databases follow a tabular approach and consist of following items:

- **Feature Key**: A single word or abbreviation indicating functional group
- **Location**: Instructions for finding the feature
- **Qualifiers**: Auxiliary information about a feature

A sequence submission portal for biological database has also been developed, specifically, for the bioinformatics researchers in India for submitting their nucleotide sequences as an outcome of their experiments at ICAR-Indian Agricultural Statistics Research Institute (ICAR-IASRI), New Delhi. The database working behind this portal follows RDBMS concepts and has been designed keeping in view of the feature tables available at INSD collaborating institutes (Lal et al., 2013).

A summarized listing of various attributes of the sequence databases at NCBI, DDBJ and EMBL with their sub-fields, data types and their availability in these three databases have been presented in Table 1.

These three major databases record nucleotide sequences which are outcome of the experimental results by biologists worldwide. These records are stored in the fields and sub-fields as mentioned above. Most of the data in this database are contributed directly by authors. Generally, there are no annotation information in the primary databases. Primary databases contain raw nucleotide sequences that need to be processed for making it meaningful and extracting some biological knowledge. Secondary databases have computationally processed sequence information. The information stored in the secondary databases are translated sequences from DNA with related data pertaining to structures and functions. The computational processing needed for this may also vary depending on the algorithm applied on them.

Table 1. Details of fields and sub-fields in genomic databases under INSD Collaboration

Field Name	Sub Field	Data Format	NCBI	DDBJ	EMBL
LOCUS	Locus Name	Character	Y	Y	Y
	Sequence Length	Character	Y	Y	Y
	Molecular Type	Character	Y	Y	Y
	Topology	Character	Y	Y	Y
	Taxonomy Division	Character	Y	Y	Y
	Modification Date	Date	Y	Y	Y
	Sequence Version No	Character	N	N	Y
	Data class (Taxonomy Class)	Character	N	N	Y
DEFINITION	Scientific Name	Character	Y	Y	Y
	Gene Name	Character	Y	Y	Y
	Product Name	Character	Y	Y	Y
	Complete Coding Sequence (CDS)	Character	Y	Y	Y
SUBMISSION		Character	Y	Y	Y
VERSION		Character	Y	Y	N
KEYWORDS		Character	Y	Y	Y
SOURCE		Character	Y	Y	Y
ORGANISM		Character	Y	Y	Y
REFERENCE		Number	Y	Y	Y
AUTHORS	Last Name	Character	Y	Y	Y
	Middle Name	Character	Y	Y	Y
	First Name	Character	Y	Y	Y
TITLE		Character	Y	Y	Y
JOURNAL	Journal name	Character	Y	Y	Y
	Volume Number	Number	Y	Y	Y
	Issue Number	Number	Y	Y	Y
	Page Number	Number	Y	Y	Y
	Publication Year	Number	Y	Y	Y
COMMENT	Comments	Character	Y	Y	Y
FEATURES	Features	Location/Qualifiers	Y	Y	Y
	Source • Sequence Length • Organism Name • Organelle Name • Source Modifier • Molecular Type	 Number Character Character Character Character	 Y Y Y Y Y	 Y Y Y Y Y	 Y Y Y Y Y

continued on next page

Table 1. Continued

Field Name	Sub Field	Data Format	NCBI	DDBJ	EMBL
	Gene				
	• Sequence Length	Number	Y	Y	Y
	• Gene Name	Character	Y	Y	Y
	• Gene Allele	Character	Y	Y	Y
	• Gene Description	Character	Y	Y	Y
	CDS				
	• Sequence Length	Number	Y	Y	Y
	• Gene	Character	Y	Y	Y
	• Protein Name	Character	Y	Y	Y
	• Protein Description	Character	Y	Y	Y
	• EC Number	Number	Y	Y	Y
	• Translation	Character	Y	Y	Y
	Misc_Feature				
	• Sequence Length	Number	Y	Y	Y
	• Gene	Character	Y	Y	Y
	• Gene_Synonym	Character	Y	Y	Y
	• Note	Character	Y	Y	Y
BASE COUNT		Character	Y	Y	Y
ORIGIN		Character	Y	Y	Y

In the next section, primary, secondary and specialized biological database resources have been described. Few important databases selected according to their popularity have also been listed with their important functions.

BIOLOGICAL DATABASE RESOURCES

The most important online primary biological data repository are: SWISS-PROT and Protein Information Resources (PIR) for protein sequences, GenBank, DDBJ and EMBL for nucleotide sequences and PDB for protein structures. The huge volume of data are being maintained by these online database services which are equipped with quick, easy and user-friendly interfaces for the users involved in the submission of biological data. It also has facility of querying the already available data and carrying out analysis using numerous tools integrated on these web sites.

Primary Databases

Primary biological databases can further be classified into many categories such as genomics, proteomics, phylogenetics, metabolomics and microarray data. Genomics refers to the database of genome sequences, proteomics – database of proteomes including structural information, phylogenetics – database related evolutionary relationships among species, metabolomics – database about metabolic content of an organism and microarray database refers to microarray gene expression data.

A detailed classification of biological databases has been shown in Figure 2.

According to the above classification, few important names of databases are available in public domain. The brief description have been presented in Table 2.

Similarly many bioinformatics databases such as compound-Specific, comprehensive metabolomic, drug, RNA, SNP, microsatellites, literature, crystallographic, NMR spectra, carbohydrate structure, protein-protein interactions, signal transduction pathway, primer, taxonomic databases and so on, also fall in this category.

Secondary Databases

The primary biological databases have very limited information as they are merely raw sequences. To convert this into more sophisticated biological knowledge a rigorous post processing of sequence information is essentially needed. A secondary structure database contains entries of PDB based on their structures. Many taxonomic specific genome databases are covered under this category. Few secondary databases have been described below:

- **SWISS-PROT**: This database was developed by A. Bairoch in 1986. The contents of this database includes completely annotated protein sequences with structure, function and its family. The sequence data is curated by domain experts and derived from a database called TrEMBL – a database of translated nucleic acid sequences of EMBL. SWISS-PROT is considered to be a non-redundant database which is documented and cross referenced. Curator of this database work towards finding value added information from

Figure 2. Detailed Classification of Biological Databases

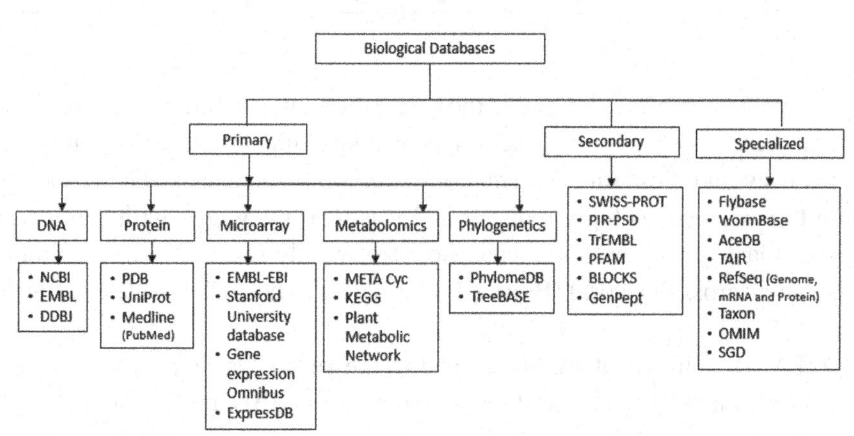

Table 2. Major Public Sequence Databases with their description

Name	Description
Primary Nucleotide Databases	
GenBank	Database of nucleotide sequences, literature and other genome resource available on public domain
DDBJ	Nucleotide sequences submitted by Japanese scientists mainly, but allows others too.
EMBL	Primary nucleotide sequence database in Europe
Primary Protein Databases	
Uniprot	Database of protein sequences and functional information
PDB	Annotations related to sequence, structure and function. Analysis and visualization with search facility
Metabolomics Databases	
META Cyc	Metabolic pathways database
Kyoto Encyclopedia of Genes and Genomes (KEGG)	Database resources for dealing with genomes, biological functions, pathways.
Plant Metabolic Network (PMN)	Pathways and their catalytic enzymes, organism-specific information on reactions and metabolites and genes
Phylogenetics Databases	
PhylomeDB	Complete database of gene (phylomes), phylogenetic tree visualization, history of genes (Huerta-Cepas, Capella-Gutiérrez, Pryszcz, Marcet-Houben, Gabaldón, 2007, 2008, 2011, 2014).
TreeBASE	Database of phylogenetic tree and related data for its generation (Anwar, & Hunt, 2009).
Microarray Database	
ArrayExpress- EMBL-EBI	Archive of high-throughput functional genomics experimental data. (Kolesnikov et al., 2015)
Gene expression Omnibus (GEO) (NLM)	Database for functional genomics data, MIAME compliant data support, download facility of gene expression profiles
ExpressDB- Harvard	RNA expression data for yeast and E. coli

scientific literatures. This adds the annotation information to each sequences which includes structure, function, post-translational modification, metabolic pathway and similarity information from other sequences. The redundancy in this database is higly reduced and it is well integrated with primary and secondary databases. This database have weekly releases and has about 50 servers across the world (Boutet, Lieberherr, Tognolli, Schneider, & Bairoch, 2007).

- **TrEMBL**: This database, developed in the year 1996, is a derived database from coding sequence translation database of EMBL. It is populated using a software which takes annotated EMBL coding sequences (CDS) as input. It is a complement to SWISS-PROT. It is to be noted that all known sequences of proteins can be obtained by adding sequences from SWISS-PROT and TrEMBL together (Bairoch, & Apweiler, 2000).

- **UniProt**: UniProt database is a union of SWISS-PROT, TrEMBL and PIR. This is the reason that size of this database is bigger than any one of them. However, it retains important features of SWISS-PROT such as zero or less redundancy, cross-referencing and quality of annotation (UniProt Consortium, 2008).
- **PFAM and BLOCKS**: These are secondary databases that provides information from classification of protein family on the basis of their structure and functions. It also has information about aligned proteins and derived motifs. This information is very useful for protein classification and functions. (Finn et al., 2014, Henikoff & Henikoff, 1996).

Protein Information Resources-Protein Sequence Database (PIR-PSD)

Protein Information Resource, MIPS (Munich Information Center for Protein Sequences) and JIPID (Japan International Protein Information Database) collaborated for development of this database. It contains information about classified and functionally annotated proteins.

It is more than 20 year old public database in the world containing protein sequences which is curated also. The sequences and annotation information in this database have also been incorporated in UniProt database. Cross-referencing in PIR-PSD and UniProt knowledge bases have provided easy connectivity and easy information retrieval from these databases. (Wu et al., 2003).

- **Genpept**: This database consists of gene products from GenBank of NCBI. These gene products are translated sequences of all CDS features and the qualifier of the translation.

There are many other protein databases such as G protein-coupled receptors (GPCRDB) (Munk et al., 2016), International ImMunoGeneTics information system (IMGT) (Lefranc, 2001), YPD (Yeast) (Payne & Garrels, 1997) etc.

Specialized Databases

Specialized databases normally focus on a specific organism for serving a particular research community or it focuses on specific organisms. This database contains either sequences or other types of information. There are chances of overlap of this database with primary databases. Taxonomic specific databases such as Flybase (A Database of Drosophila Genes & Genomes) (Drysdale, 2008), WormBase (Database on the genetics of C elegans and related nematodes) (Harris et al., 2003), AceDB (database for handling genome and bioinformatics data) (Stein & Thierry-Mieg, 1998), and The Arabidopsis Information Resource (TAIR) (Huala et al., 2001) fall under this category of databases.

Other Databases in Molecular Biology

The number of databases available on open domain are considerably large. Therefore, some of them have been selected and listed here along with their description in Table 3.

The biological databases available worldwide does not have same format and structure. This is the reason the interconnectivity between these database is an important point to be discussed. In the next section, some details about interconnectivity between biological databases have been presented.

INTERCONNECTIVITY BETWEEN BIOLOGICAL DATABASES

While accessing the information from secondary and specialized databases, there is a frequent need to connect to the primary databases because, all the necessary information may not be available in single database. Cross-referencing and linking of databases are essential for conveniently providing the appropriate and complete report to the user without letting him visit multiple database repository.

The idea of linking different biological databases faces barriers due to the presence of different formats of these databases. While linking these databases, the format incompatibility may intensify the complexity. It was stated earlier that most of the biological databases have flat file formats. But, at some places, other formats such as relational and object oriented also exist. This heterogeneity in the databases enhances the complexity while communicating between them. As a solution to this kind of problem, the following methods can be adopted.

- **Common Object Request Broker Architecture (COBRA):** It uses an "interface broker" for communication in a network using a specification language. They don't need to understand the structure of their databases.
- **eXtensible Markup Language (XML):** This is a protocol which helps in bridging the databases. In XML format, the records are broken down into small basic components. This also has tags similar to HTML tags but in this

Table 3. Other biological databases and their description

Database	Description
ArrayExpress	A data repository for storage of data generated from functional genomic experiments that can be queried and downloaded to guide reproducible research
Dali	Dali web server is based on distance alignment matrix method and used to compare three-dimensional protein structures.
DIP	Database of Interacting Proteins (DIP): Information combination from different sources to build a set of protein-protein interaction.
Hits	Hits is a database of protein domains. It also contains tools to discover the relationships amid protein sequences and motifs.
InterPro	InterPro is a protein signature database to functionally characterize proteins into families. It is used for annotation and large scale mapping of protein.
ConsensusPathDB	It integrates interaction information from different databases including protein, genetic & drug-target interactions in human.
PROSITE	A protein database containing collection of biologically significant signatures outlined as profile or patterns
Reactome	A database of pathways, biological processes and reactions.
SAGEmap	A data repository and tool for performing statistical tests on gene expression data for differential analyses.
Stanford Microarray Database	A data repository for storage of processed and raw data from microarray research, provides interface for retrieval, analysis and visualization of data.
TIGR Gene Indices	Multi organism gene indices that use a specialized protocol to analyze gene and EST sequences to detect and classify expressed transcripts.
TRANSFAC	A database containing data relevant for expression of genes at the transcriptional level.
UniGene	It divides sequences to form a non-redundant gene cluster. Every UniGene cluster represent a unique gene.

case there is a hierarchical nesting in XML. XML has evidenced distribution and exchange of data (such as complex sequence annotation) very convenient and efficient.

It has been noticed that the biological databases have certain drawbacks such as redundancy, reliability of sequence information, errors in the database and so on. In the following section it has been discussed in detail.

DRAWBACKS IN BIOLOGICAL DATABASES

The biological databases contain the sequence information and related annotations which are not reliable. Errors in the sequence databases are often ignored. Primary biological databases consist of data that may also have redundancies. Therefore, the annotation of genes may also be false or inappropriate sometimes. Most errors in the primary databases are caused by sequencing errors. Since, these primary databases are the initial source, these errors are propagated to other databases too.

These errors can also be a reason for frame shifts making identification of gene or other task very difficult. There are situations when sequences from cloning vectors contaminate the gene sequences. The considerable amount of duplicate information is contained in the biological databases due to diverse experiments by various research laboratories. The causes of redundancy in the database are many. It can be due to repeated submission of same or overlapping sequences by the same or other submitter, submission of revised annotations or many other types of submissions. As a result, size of some of the primary databases are unreasonably large making retrieval of information a cumbersome task. However, redundancy can be reduced to a great level if the database is designed properly by following the RDBMS concepts.

NCBI has taken a step towards reducing the redundancy and created a non-redundant database. This database is called RefSeq. RefSeq has merged multiple entries of the same organism or associated segments to a single entry. It also clearly linked derived protein sequences and marked them as a related entry. As mentioned earlier in this chapter, the SWISS-PROT database has very low redundancy as compared to other protein databases. UniGene (Wagner, & Agarwala, 2013) is a sequence-cluster database in which combined EST sequences, derived from same gene are stored. This has reduced a considerable amount of redundancy in the database.

Another problem found in these databases are errors in annotation. It is often noticed that unrelated genes with same name or same gene with different names are found in the database. Solving this kind of problem needs reannotation of genes and proteins using a controlled vocabulary. Another way to solve this problem can be to use gene ontology technique which can provide unambiguous naming system.

With advancement in the web technologies, the retrieval system working on these databases are supposed to be very fast and user-friendly. There are a number of retrieval systems available for biological data. In the following section these retrieval systems have been described.

RETRIEVAL SYSTEM FOR BIOLOGICAL DATABASES

A primary objective of biological database is to provide quick, easy, efficient and user-friendly access to the stored data. For example, Entrez is one of the popular retrieval system from biological databases. It provides access to multiple databases for retrieval of results for the user's queries. Boolean operators are commonly used to perform complex queries in these databases too. The commonly used Boolean operators are AND, OR and NOT. The keywords to be searched, can be joined using these operators. For grouping of words, parentheses () can also be used. As per rules of mathematical operators, the parentheses have highest precedence which applies to online database searches also (O'Neill, & Curran, 2013). This facility is inbuilt in most of the biological databases and web sites (Xiong, 2006).

Retrieval system for biological databases works through an interface which can access and navigate through all the relevant biological databases. These databases could be DNA and protein sequence, literature records or structural and mapping databases. Literature database such as PubMed may access the information about sequencing of genes available on GenBank. Similarly, protein database may have sequences which is derived or coded from nucleotide sequences available at Gen-Bank. In case the structure of protein is known, the structure database may contain the coordinates for the structure. Mapping database can provide region specific information if the gene is mapped to a chromosome. Therefore, it is essential to devise a method using which it can save a user from visiting multiple database web sites for getting the desired information (Baxevanis, 2001; Baxevanis, & Francis Ouellette, 2005).

Some of the popular interfaces available for information retrieval from biological databases are - Entrez system of NCBI, EMBL-EBI Web Services, Search and Analysis facility of DDBJ and so on. The retrieval system provided by the most of the biological databases are now web based (Cooper, Landrum, Mizrachi, & Weisemann, 2010).

GenBank - Entrez

As stated earlier, Entrez has integrated nucleotide and protein databases, protein structure information and abstracts from PubMed articles. It has also integrated sequence similarity search through BLAST program. NCBI has web based retrieval system with analysis services. It provides the facility of File Transfer Protocol (FTP) services and download Entrez and BLAST programs (Benson, 1998). The search option available on Entrez provides precise and managed results. It also has *Advanced search* facility that provides the option of customized search for providing the users more narrowed results. *Search History* option on Entrez stores the recent searches made by the user. The search results also include links to other databases which is integrated in Entrez. The interconnection of databases in Entrez facilitates the user to move around the other databases for getting quick and most relevant results (Geer, & Sayers, 2003). Entrez system has very strong molecular and literature database with frequent updates being carried out with new entries (Schuler, Epstein, Ohkawa, & Kans, 1996). An alphabetical list of the current databases with its description is given below (Table 4). All the databases in the list are available on web with appropriate as well as quick and easy to use search facilities. For more details NCBI-Entrez web site may be seen.

EMBL-EBI Web Services

The web services are a good source for providing web-enabled application programming interface for implementing in-depth searches on biological databases available worldwide. These web services are available for executing extensive searches on the databases at EMBL-EBI. The cross-referencing information available in the data helps to explore the data through the network of resources.

These web services have web methods that can extract the entered data in different file formats as well as access data from individual fields of the database. Tools available for analysis of data may also be called using these web services. Some of these tools are - FASTA and BLAST for sequence alignment and similarity search, CLUSTAL OMEGA for multiple sequence alignment, InterProScan for pairwise alignment and functional analysis and many more tools (Brooksbank, Cameron, & Thornton, 2010; McWilliam et al., 2013). Table 5 may be referred for viewing tools and databases available over EMBL-EBI with their brief description and their functions (Cook et al., 2015; McWilliam et al., 2013).

EB-eye is a web service from EMBL-EBI that helps in searching information over several databases using a single query (Valentin et al., 2010). It can also navigate through cross-reference links for extracting information from the same or other databases. The search facility allows refinement of searches using Boolean operators. Another distinctive facility of this web service also provides searching within the specific fields of the database. It uses indexes for execution of search query with the help of complementary services called *dbfetch* and *WSDbfetch* (Pillai et al., 2005).

Entry of data using these web services support many file formats such as UniProtKB flat file format, Fasta format, Generic Feature Format (GFF), UniProt XML format, SeqXML format etc. The names of web services available on EMBL-EBI with their performing activities are listed in Table 6 (Cook et al., 2015; McWilliam et al., 2013).

Table 4. The databases available on NCBI Entrez and their description

Database	Description
Assembly	The Assembly database contains information about the structure of assembled genomes.
BioProject	A collection of biological data associated to a specific project
BioSample	A database containing details of biological materials used in experimental investigation
BioSystems	A data repository to connect the records with literature and to facilitate analysis on biosystems data
Bookshelf	It is an online resources for accessing books and other related documents.
ClinVar	Archive of reports presenting the association in human variations and phenotypes, and supporting proof.
Conserved Domains	A resource for functional annotation of proteins.
dbGaP	This database contains the results from research done for interaction of human genotype and phenotype.
dbVAR	A database of genomic structural variation comprising information about large scale genomic variation, insertions, deletions, inversions and translocations.
EST	A database of short single-read transcript sequences used to evaluate gene expression, annotation and detect potential variation.
Gene	Integrated information for a large number of species. It has information about reference sequences. It also contains information such as pathways, maps, phenotypes, genome links, phenotypes etc.
Genome	Contains genome information and annotations, assemblies, maps, sequences and chromosomes.
GEO Datasets	This database stores submitter supplied records in addition to curated dataSets.
GEO Profiles	Profiles of gene expression from curated data.
GSS	Genome Survey Sequences (GSS), stores nucleotide sequences similar to EST's with genomic origin.
GTR	Genetic Testing Registry (GTR), a repository of comprehensive genetic test information which is voluntarily submitted by test contributors.
HomoloGene	Automatic detection of homologs among annotated genes of eukaryotes.
MedGen	It contains information about human medical genetics and other phenotypes having a genetic contribution.
MeSH	Medical Subject Headings (MeSH) is used for indexing research articles stored in PubMed.
Nucleotide	This database contains all the sequence data from different sources like GenBank, EMBL, and DDBJ.
OMIM	Database on Online Mendelian Inheritance in Man (OMIM). It has information related to mendelian disorders.
PopSet	A database of aligned nucleotide sequences collected to study the relatedness within a particular population.
Protein Clusters	An organized group of related protein sequences and its annotation information from refseq microorganisms.
PubChemBioAssay	A repository for storing biological tests of small molecules and siRNA reagents.
PubChem	A chemical molecule database with its biological activities.
PubMed	A database of citations and abstracts in the area of healthcare, nursing, dentistry, medicine and preclinical sciences.
PubMed Central	Contains full-text research articles submitted by authors or provided by the publishers.
dbSNP	Database of Single Nucleotide Polymorphism (SNP) and small scale variations.
SRA	Sequence Read Archive (SRA) contains data generated from the next generation sequencing experiments.
Structure	A Molecular Modeling Database (MMDB). It stores structures of proteins, DNA and RNA from PDB.
Taxonomy	Nomenclature and classification information for organisms from various available sequence databases.
UniGene	It divides sequences to form a non-redundant gene cluster. Every UniGene cluster represent a unique gene.

Table 5. Tools and Databases available at EMBL

Database/ Tools	Description
Clustal Omega	Multiple sequence alignment of DNA or protein sequences using hidden Markov model and seeded guide trees.
InterProScan	A software package that allows protein and nucleotide sequences to be examined against signatures (predictive models).
BLAST [protein]	Heuristic search to find statistically significant matches between input protein query and protein database
BLAST [nucleotide]	Heuristic search to find statistically significant matches between input nucleotide query and nucleotide database.
HMMER	Software to search sequence databases for homologs using profile hidden Markov models.
Ensembl	Genome browser for information retrieval from genomic data.
UniProt	Universal protein resource of protein sequence and functional information.
PDBe	Protein Data Bank in Europe, repository of experimentally obtained biomacromolecular structures
Europe PMC	Europe PMC repository provides access to literature related to life sciences.
Expression Atlas	A repository containing information on gene expression patterns in distinct biological conditions.
ChEMBL	Chemical database of biologically active molecules which show properties of a drug.

Table 6. Web Services available on EMBL-EBI

Activity	Web Services Available
Genomes	Ensembl BioMart, Ensembl Genomes REST API
Nucleotide sequences	ENA Browser
Protein sequences	PRIDE BioMart, UniProt.org, UniProtBioMart
Small molecules	ChEBI WS, PSICQIC (ChEMBL)
Gene expression	ArrayExpress, Gene Expression Atlas API
Molecular interactions	PSICQIC (IntAct)
Reactions, pathways and diseases	BioModels, PSICQIC (Reactome), Rhea
Protein families	InterProBioMart
Literature	Europe PMC Web Service
Ontologies	Ontology Lookup Service (OLS), QuickGO, SBO::Web Services, WSMIRIAM

DDBJ- All-Round Retrieval of Sequence and Annotation (DDBJ-ARSA)

DDBJ-ARSA is a keyword based search system implemented using XML on a high performance computing infrastructure. ARSA has been developed after detailed analysis of database structure of INSD collaboration and 23 other biological databases. The database are represented as XML files for executing search queries.

Entries from the databases can be retrieved using a program called *getentry.* This program is available on DDBJ which can execute query for retrieval using accession number provided. Some of the popular secondary databases available on web such as *Genome Information Broker (GIB)* databases, *Gene Trek in the Prokaryote Space (GTPS)* database and *Genes to Protein (GTOP)* database are developed and updated regularly by DDBJ. The GIB databases contain a family of complete genomes of microorganisms and viruses (GIBM and GIB-V), sequences from environmental samples (GIB-ENV) and sequences of the IS region (GIBIS). GTPS database is available online and has high quality open reading frames in prokaryote genomes.

Some analytical tools have also been developed by DDBJ that are available for use online or downloadable for stand-alone use. For example, DDBJ developed a stand-alone software called *GInforBIO* which can compare many genomes. DDBJ has also developed web services for calling them through computer networks. These web services have capability to run programs or execute queries in databases such as BLAST, CLUSTAL-W, GIB, GTOP, GTPS and so on. These web services can be very conveniently called from a java or perl program to perform desired computations for further analysis (Sugawara, 2007).

CONCLUSION

In this chapter, a wide range of biological databases available in public domain have been described. Few years ago, querying on these databases were not so user-friendly because of unavailability of advanced web based technologies. Now most of these databases are available online with very rich and easy to use web based applications. The main focus of the biological database web sites have been to provide graphical user interfaces (GUI) for search, and deliver quick results to the user. However, most of these web based interfaces do not have object-oriented technology implemented. Many research projects have been taken up for querying into object-oriented or semantic databases and, as a result, graphical query interfaces have been provided. Several efforts have also been made to formulate the queries to the databases and producing browser based exhaustive reports.

The most fundamental requirement to the biological research is the primary database. The important objectives of the biological databases are – faster information retrieval, analysis and discover knowledge out of it (Bhatt, Dey, & Ashour, 2017). The format of these databases are very important for development of effective retrieval system. As said earlier, a critical drawback of most of the biological databases is that most of them are having a flat file format. Need of interconnection between these databases is very frequent as entries in one database can be cross-linked to related entries in another database. Presence of different file formats in these databases have made interconnectivity between them a complex problem for the software developers. Another problem in the biological database is errors in sequencing and annotation. Redundancy is yet another problem in these databases. The reasons of the redundancies have been discussed earlier in this chapter. These redundancies can be reduced to a certain extent by merging redundant sequences into a single entry or store highly redundant sequences into a separate database.

REFERENCES

Anwar, N., & Hunt, E. (2009). Improved data retrieval from TreeBASE via taxonomic and linguistic data enrichment. *BMC Evolutionary Biology*, *9*(1), 93. doi:10.1186/1471-2148-9-93 PMID:19426482

Attwood, T. K., & Parry-Smith, D. J. (2002). *Introduction to Bioinformatics*. Singapore: Pvt. Ltd.

Bairoch, A., & Apweiler, R. (2000). The SWISS-PROT protein sequence database and its supplement TrEMBL. *Nucleic Acids Research*, *28*(1), 45–48. doi:10.1093/nar/28.1.45 PMID:10592178

Barrett, T. (2013). Gene Expression Omnibus (GEO). *The NCBI Handbook* (2nd ed.). Bethesda, MD: National Center for Biotechnology Information. Retrieved December 17, 2016, from https://www.ncbi.nlm.nih.gov/books/NBK159736/

Baxevanis, A. D. (2001). Information retrieval from biological databases. *Methods of Biochemical Analysis*, *43*, 155–185. doi:10.1002/0471223921.ch7 PMID:11449723

Baxevanis, A. D., & Francis Ouellette, B. F. (2005). *Bioinformatics - A Practical Guide to the analysis of Genes and Proteins* (3rd ed.). PHI Learning Private Limited.

Benson, D. A., Boguski, M. S., Lipman, D. J., Ostell, J., & Francis Ouellette, B. F. (1998). GenBank. *Nucleic Acids Research*, *26*(1), 1–7. doi:10.1093/nar/26.1.1 PMID:9399790

Bhatt, C., Dey, N., & Ashour, A. S. (2017). *Internet of Things and Big Data Technologies in Next Generation Healthcare.* Springer International Publishing. doi:10.1007/978-3-319-49736-5

Boutet, E., Lieberherr, D., Tognolli, M., Schneider, M., & Bairoch, A. (2007). UniProtKB/Swiss-Prot. *Methods in Molecular Biology (Clifton, N.J.), 406*, 89–112. PMID:18287689

Brooksbank, C. (2006). *Train online Bioinformatics for the terrified.* Retrieved December 20, 2016, http://www.ebi.ac.uk/training/online/course/bioinformatics-terrified

Brooksbank, C., Cameron, G., & Thornton, J. (2010). The European Bioinformatics Institutes data resources. *Nucleic Acids Research, 38*(Database), D17–D25. doi:10.1093/nar/gkp986 PMID:19934258

Cochrane, G., Karsch-Mizrachi, I., & Nakamura, Y. (2011). The International Nucleotide Sequence Database Collaboration. *Nucleic Acids Research, 39*(Database issue), D15–D18. doi:10.1093/nar/gkq1150 PMID:21106499

Cook, C. E., Bergman, M. T., Finn, R. D., Cochrane, G., Birney, E., & Apweiler, R. (2015). The European Bioinformatics Institute in 2016: Data growth and integration. *Nucleic Acids Research,* 1-7. doi: 10.1093/nar/gkv1352

Cooper, P., Landrum, M., Mizrachi, I., & Weisemann, J. (2010). *Entrez Sequences Help.* Retrieved December 17, 2016, from https://www.ncbi.nlm.nih.gov/books/NBK44863/

Drysdale, R (2008). FlyBase: a database for the Drosophila research community. *Methods Mol Biol., 420*, 45-59. doi: 10.1007/978-1-59745-583-1_3

Finn, R. D., Bateman, A., Clements, J., Coggill, P., Eberhardt, R. Y., Eddy, S. R., & Punta, M. et al. (2014). Pfam: The protein families database. *Nucleic Acids Research, 42*(Database issue), D222–D230. doi:10.1093/nar/gkt1223 PMID:24288371

Geer, R. C., & Sayers, E. W. (2003). Entrez: Making use of its power. *Briefings in Bioinformatics, 4*(2), 179–184. doi:10.1093/bib/4.2.179 PMID:12846398

Harris, T. W., Lee, R., Schwarz, E., Bradnam, K., Lawson, D., Chen, W., & Stein, L. D. et al. (2003). WormBase: A cross-species database for comparative genomics. *Nucleic Acids Research, 31*(1), 133–137. doi:10.1093/nar/gkg053 PMID:12519966

Henikoff, J. G., & Henikoff, S. (1996). Blocks database and its applications. *Methods in Enzymology, 266*, 88–105. doi:10.1016/S0076-6879(96)66008-X PMID:8743679

Huala, E., Dickerman, A. W., Garcia-Hernandez, M., Weems, D., Reiser, L., LaFond, F., & Rhee, S. Y. et al. (2001). The Arabidopsis Information Resource (TAIR): A comprehensive database and web-based information retrieval, analysis, and visualization system for a model plant. *Nucleic Acids Research*, *29*(1), 102–105. doi:10.1093/nar/29.1.102 PMID:11125061

Huerta-Cepas, J., Bueno, A., Dopazo, J., & Gabaldón, T. (2008). PhylomeDB: A database for genome-wide collections of gene phylogenies. *Nucleic Acids Research*, *36*(Database issue), D491–D496. PMID:17962297

Huerta-Cepas, J., Capella-Gutierrez, S., Pryszcz, L. P., Denisov, I., Kormes, D., Marcet-Houben, M., & Gabaldon, T. (2011). PhylomeDB v3.0: An expanding repository of genome-wide collections of trees, alignments and phylogeny-based orthology and paralogy predictions. *Nucleic Acids Research*, *39*(Database issue), D556–D560. doi:10.1093/nar/gkq1109 PMID:21075798

Huerta-Cepas, J., Capella-Gutiérrez, S., Pryszcz, L. P., Marcet-Houben, M., & Gabaldón, T. (2014). PhylomeDB v4: Zooming into the plurality of evolutionary histories of a genome. *Nucleic Acids Research*, *42*(Database issue), D897–D902. doi:10.1093/nar/gkt1177 PMID:24275491

Huerta-Cepas, J., Dopazo, H., Dopazo, J., & Gabaldón, T. (2007). The original phylogenetic pipeline used to reconstruct phylomes is described in: The human phylome. *Genome Biology*, *8*(6), R109. PMID:17567924

Kamal, S., Ripon, S. H., Dey, N., Ashour, A. S., & Santhi, V. (2016). A MapReduce approach to diminish imbalance parameters for big deoxyribonucleic acid dataset. *Computer Methods and Programs in Biomedicine*, *131*, 191–206. doi:10.1016/j.cmpb.2016.04.005 PMID:27265059

Kolesnikov, N., Hastings, E., Keays, M., Melnichuk, O., Tang, Y. A., Williams, E., & Brazma, A. et al. (2015). ArrayExpress update—simplifying data submissions. *Nucleic Acids Research*, *43*(Database issue), D1113–D1116. doi:10.1093/nar/gku1057 PMID:25361974

Lal, S. B., Pandey, P. K., Rai, P. K., Rai, A., Sharma, A., & Chaturvedi, K. K. (2013). Design and development of portal for biological database in agriculture. *Bioinformation*, *9*(11), 588–598. doi:10.6026/97320630009588 PMID:23888101

Lefranc, M. P. (2001). IMGT, the international ImMunoGeneTics database. *Nucleic Acids Research*, *29*(1), 207–209. doi:10.1093/nar/29.1.207 PMID:11125093

McWilliam, H., Li, W., Uludag, M., Squizzato, S., Park, Y. M., Buso, N., Cowley, A. P., & Lopez, R. (2013). Analysis Tool Web Services from the EMBL-EBI. *Nucleic Acids Research*, 1-4. doi:.10.1093/nar/gkt376

Munk, C., Isberg, V., Mordalski, S., Harpsøe, K., Rataj, K., Hauser, A. S., ... Gloriam, D. E. (2016). GPCRdb: The G protein-coupled receptor database – an introduction. *Br J Pharmacol., 173*(14), 2195-207. doi: 10.1111/bph.13509

O'Neill, S., & Curran, K. (2013). The Core Aspects of Search Engine Optimisation Necessary to Move up the Ranking. In K. Curran (Ed.), Pervasive and Ubiquitous Technology Innovations for Ambient Intelligence Environments (pp. 243-251). Hershey, PA: Information Science Reference. doi:10.4018/978-1-4666-2041-4.ch022

Payne, W. E., & Garrels, J. I. (1997). Yeast Protein database (YPD): A database for the complete proteome of Saccharomyces cerevisiae. *Nucleic Acids Research, 25*(1), 57–62. doi:10.1093/nar/25.1.57 PMID:9016505

Pillai, S., Silventoinen, V., Kallio, K., Senger, M., Sobhany, S., Tate, J., ... Lopez, R. (2005). SOAP-based services provided by the European Bioinformatics Institute. *Nucleic Acids Research, 33*, W25–W28. http://doi.org/<ALIGNMENT.qj></ALIGNMENT>10.1093/nar/gki491

Sanger, F. (1988). Sequences, sequences, and sequences. *Annual Review of Biochemistry, 57*(1), 1–28. doi:10.1146/annurev.bi.57.070188.000245 PMID:2460023

Schaller, A., Mueller, K., & Sung, B. (2008), Motorola's experiences in designing the Internet of Things. *Adjunct proceedings of the first international conference on the Internet of Things, Social-IoT Workshop 2008*, 82-85.

Schuler, G. D., Epstein, J. A., Ohkawa, H., & Kans, J. A. (1996). Entrez: Molecular biology database and retrieval systems. In Methods in Enzymology. San Diego, CA: Academic Press.

Sharma, A., Rai, A., & Lal, S. (2013). Workflow management systems for gene sequence analysis and evolutionary studies – A Review. *Bioinformation, 9*(13), 663–672. doi:10.6026/97320630009663 PMID:23930017

Singh, A., Sharma, A., & Dey, N. (2015). Semantics and Agents Oriented Web Personalization: State of the Art. *International Journal of Service Science, Management, Engineering, and Technology, 6*(2), 35–49. doi:10.4018/ijssmet.2015040103

Stein, L. D., & Thierry-Mieg, J. (1998). Scriptable Access to the Caenorhabditis elegans Genome Sequence and Other ACEDB Databases. *Genome Research, 8*(12), 1308–1315. PMID:9872985

Stretton, O. W. (2002). The First Sequence: Fred Sanger and Insulin Antony. *Genetics, 162*(2), 527–532. PMID:12399368

Sugawara, H. (2007). *DDBJ — Website to Deposit, Retrieve and Analyze Sequences and Annotations of Genes and Genomes*. Retrieved December 18, 2016, from http://www.asiabiotech.com/publication/apbn/11/english/preserved-docs/1115/1052_1054.pdf/

The UniProt Consortium. (2008). The Universal Protein Resource (UniProt). *Nucleic Acids Research, 36*(Database issue), D190–D195. doi:10.1093/nar/gkm895 PMID:18045787

Valentin, F., Squizzato, S., Goujon, M., McWilliam, H., Paern, J., & Lopez, R. (2010). Fast and efficient searching of biological data resources—using EB-eye. *Briefings in Bioinformatics, 11*(4), 375–384. doi:10.1093/bib/bbp065 PMID:20150321

Wagner, L., & Agarwala, R. (2013). UniGene. In The NCBI Handbook (2nd ed.). Bethesda, MD: National Center for Biotechnology Information (US). Available from https://www.ncbi.nlm.nih.gov/books/NBK169437/

Wu, C. H., Yeh, L.-S. L., Huang, H., Arminski, L., Castro-Alvear, J., Chen, Y., & Barker, W. C. et al. (2003). The Protein Information Resource. *Nucleic Acids Research, 31*(1), 345–347. doi:10.1093/nar/gkg040 PMID:12520019

Xiong, J. (2006). *Essential Bioinformatics. Texas A & M University*. doi:10.1017/CBO9780511806087

Chapter 11
Role of Social Networking Sites in Enhancing Teaching Environment

Singanamalla Vijayakumar
VIT University, India

Amudha J
VIT University, India

Vaishali Ravindra Thakare
VIT University, India

S. Bharath Bhushan
VIT University, India

V. Santhi
VIT University, India

ABSTRACT

In recent days, most of the academic institutions across the world understand the usefulness of social networks for teaching and learning. In general, information is being transferred across the world for multiple purposes in different aspects through social media networks. In academic environment to enhance the teaching and learning processes social media networks are used to greater extent. Researchers and academicians are making use of social media tools, specifically Facebook, Blogs, Google groups, SkyDrive and Twitter for teaching and research. Further, the academic performance of students has been tested statistically by teachers using Social Networking Sites (SNS). The study has been carried out to understand the role of SNS in teaching environment which reveals that students are accessing various social media tools for information sharing and personal interaction. Finally, it has been observed from the analysis that there is increasing demand for the role of SNS in future education perspective. In this chapter the role of SNS in teaching environment is carried out elaborated and presented.

DOI: 10.4018/978-1-5225-2483-0.ch011

1. INTRODUCTION

The social media networks take important role in general communication among people including teachers and students for academic purposes. In general, social media networks communication could be established for improving the academic activities such as teaching, learning, research and to carry out academic analysis to arrive at results. In this digital era, modern technologies with the use of social networking media are becoming important in our day to day life. This modern way of information sharing through social networks create a greater impacts in improving the performance of among academic people especially among youths. The performance improvement and knowledge skill developed using social networks is outlined in (Bureš, V., et al. 2016)'s work.

1.1. Overview

Recently, the virtual communication media is dominating most of the activities in students' day to day life – from play to leisure, school life, creating relations with family members, education with social activities. Indeed, media become so powerful that they can shape and influence the individual's attitudes, beliefs, values, and lifestyles. The communication media landscape for today's students includes print, radio, television, video games, computers, and the on-line technology of e-mail and various Internet applications. The various studies found that top leisure activities for teen students after school/college remain to be traditional media that is, watching TV and listening to the radio. However, there is an emerging prominence of technology-related activities like use of cell phones and Internet, indicating greater interest and participation in the technocentric life. New priorities among teen students, therefore, are hinged on the popularity of technology and connectivity.

The significant advancement in the field of electronic devices and networking has made the internet as an integral part of the students and teachers life. It has not only become as the largest information resource but as a rapid means of communication. It has a direct and dramatic impact on the academic life as students/teachers access internet for information retrieval, information sharing, entertainment, giving assignments online, posting queries in blogs over internet, discussions groups on SNS, etc. The most recent development is the social networking sites which have infiltrated, virtually every domain, including education. This evolution of social networking sites in education has transformed the teaching learning environment (Swara Kamal M. D., *et al.*2016). In universities both teachers and students use social networking sites to develop their teaching, personal learning and training through collaborative learning and production of knowledge.

1.2. Social Networking Sites (SNS)

SNSs are applications, is used to support a common space moving the borders of cultural norms for distribution benefits, collaborations, resource sharing, communications and interactions in a different way. Those are all activities of SNSs to be supporting on both the real and virtual social worlds, as they include offline and online interactions. This enhanced influence of social networking sites such as Facebook, Twitter, MySpace, LinkedIn, Ning, Xing, WhatsApp and etc have brought significant changes and replaced the conventional face-to-face learning and blackboard system. Such type of explosion of social network media and with their possibilities of networking brought modern techniques of teaching and learning environment (Quinn, D., *et al.* 2012).

1.3. Role of Students and Teachers in SNS

In present generation most of student's globally give details as 'natives of digital era' or 'members of the Internet generation'. They were born in the digital age and interacted with digital technology from their early age. For this reason, the modern professors who want to establish stronger relationships with their students, must, besides communication also improve the process of knowledge transfer by adjusting teaching strategies to the modern way of life that students live. Therefore, it is necessary to overcome the traditional way of learning by introducing and implementing virtual classrooms as innovative support to the education process in future.

Mostly, the larger educational system can be interest from the modification to allowed by teachers that too facilitated by the educational paradigms. This type of activities is allowing by the identified relationship with students as well as teachers respond and with intelligence and compassion to student and their learning (Abbott, 2005, Rodgers & Raider-Roth, 2006). In traditional paradigms of teacher-student communication challenges should be limited based on the traditional pattern teacher-student relationship modles and it's role. And, the some changes are difficult to inserting by the educational trust as they hysterically challenge long-established norms and traditions. Some of social networking sites, one is prominently building stones of the era 2.0, which is most salient example of the need to address unfamiliar educational scenarios.

The social networking sites (SNS) that are to construct for public users or semi-public profile and to build a personal inner network of connections (Boyd & Ellison, 2007). Mostly, the SNS have become an popular on the Internet websites and have been incorporated by many teenagers worldwide (Boyd, 2008; Ellison & Boyd, 2013; Lenhart, *et al.*, 2007). For example, the SNS pedagogical usages have been extensively discussed in different views of methods such as the instruction point view, possible learning mechanisms, and issues for formal and informal teaching and studying (e.g., Mazman & Usluel, 2010; Veletsianos, Kimmons, & French, 2013). In lack of research discussion should be discussed in another view that is related to use of SNS in education environment. Generally, this aspect as provided in social communications between students and teachers. But, this paper is discussing in unique view based on the literature review examining the relationships between the teachers and students. This communication should be provides to closely familiar with the SNS world. This chapter focuses the attention of interviews between the higher school students and teachers. Especially, as this communication has features that comes under the SNS use and perceptions (Boyd, 2014; Kärkkäinen, H., *et al.*, 2010). In future, most of the studies have explored facebook educational affordances in higher education studies that are relatively limited (Hew, 2011).

1.4. Research Agenda

The purpose of this study is to examine the role of social networking sites in teaching & learning environment and presents the findings synthesized from the survey conducted among university professors and students of various regions in Tamilnadu. In addition, the study effect of SNS on students life and how effectively SNS can be used for enhancing teaching and learning environment. Data was collected from an online survey and interviews and analyzed to discover the current status, practices tendencies and effects of using SNS in teaching and learning. Out of a total population of professors and students in India of around 250 students and professors from the universities and institution in Tamilnadu were randomly sampled, 138 took part in the survey. From these 138 participants, 38 were interviewed to gather additional data. In the following sections, the literature review is described first, followed by the research method presentation of the results, discussion of the findings and conclusion.

2. LITERATURE REVIEW

In the present generation, most widely increases the number of articles, can be implemented as sites whose primary purpose is to connect people using social networks. About, few of these studies are researched the influence of psychological factors in the use of social networks (Amichai-Hamburger and Vinitzky, 2010; Correa et al., 2010; Ryan and Xenos, 2011; Ross et al., 2009; Wilson et al., 2010). Very recent researches to be focused on the social networks issues such as user's privacy, technology development; social networks' structure (Debatin et al., 2009; Fogel and Nehmad, 2009). However, some of the researchers may have articulated the necessity to conduct a study that will be analyzes the use of social networks for educational purposes (Kabilan et al., 2010; Lockyer and Patterson, 2008; Mazman and Usluel, 2010; Roblyer et al., 2010). And also, few researchers are recommending that professors should be wary of the big invasion of social networking (Selwyn, 2009).

Generally, few studies have examined the influence of attractive social network like Facebook from a academic point of view. After this discussion they concluding that the ''online social network has a positive influence on student learning in academic environment'', because it helps the students to accept others easily, and thus more quickly adapt to the university culture which is here presented. Mazer et al. (2007) have described the analyses the influence of professors who are using Facebook profiles for cooperation with the students. Researchers have led them to the conclusion that students who cooperate with their professors in this way have greater motivation for learning and spread a positive climate in the classroom which can lead to better results in learning. Bowers-Campbell (2008) explains how teachers can use Facebook as a pedagogical tool for communication related to the interests and concerns of students. The author claims that it can increase self-efficacy in learning through increased communication with professors and other students through Facebook social network. However, professors should be cautious when posting content on a social network, because it can cause damage to their personal credibility (Mazer et al., 2007). In related review results may examine the influence of Facebook and it can have on the learning process of other things that can be of great benefit to students. Kabilan et al. (2010) squabble about that Facebook for provides a great help to using students in learning English language. Yang et al. (2011) discussed the necessities to conduct new empirical research for the use of Facebook, especially for educational purposes. Although, the Facebook is most widely used social network among college students, professors are not always ready to accept its use for the purpose of network for learning in the classrooms (Toetenela, 2014). In this context, Kalin (2012) discussed about realize the technology usages after knowing the benefits need to understand how students use the new technology in order to be able to follow the latest trends. However, other studies have found that there is a negative relation between the use of new technologies and academic outcomes in exams (Shapley et al., 2010). Bliuc et al. (2010) have shows the students who used assistive technology to find answers for questions with proper results/grades in conducting the exams. Recent technologies are more and more discussion to integral part of the new educational process that made for the visible differences in the results of students. Because, the huge wastage of senses to be uploading for commitment to learning (Junco, 2013). This topic is more and more popular to conducting the survey which can be useful to identify factors that may motivate students to adopt and use a number of tools of social networks, especially Facebook for educational purposes. Based on the above discussion the conclusions derived from this research will help us to clarify and improve the use of tools in social networks. This may be offering to us for educational purposes, the use of Facebook as virtual classroom, which will allow better adjustment of teaching strategies to modern needs of students.

The Voss A, et. al., 2008, had proposed an e-research model in which the resources are provided as services through dashboards with all operations that are essential. The end user can invoke the services through interface by submitting job.

Many different scientific workflow management systems may help us in processing data, computing resources and as well as variety of applications. The popular workflow systems such as Kepler (Ludäscher B, et. al. 2005), Taverna (Oinn T, et. al., 2004), Triana (Taylor I, et. al., 2004), Pegasus (Deelman E, et. al., 2007), ASKALON (Fahringer T, et. al., 2005), SWIFT (Zhao Y, et. al., 2007) and Pipeline Pilot (Yang X, et. al., 2010). These work flow systems performs better in terms of usability, automation, efficiency and reproducibility.

3. METHOD

3.1. Data Collection

Both quantitative data (via an online survey) and qualitative data (via interviews) were collected. The sample population chosen was the professors and students in the various universities and institution in Tamil Nadu. Out of a total population of around 250, 138 peoples have responded to the invitation and took part in the survey (Iahad, N.A., *et al.* 2012). Among these, 38 interviews were also conducted the survey and interview questions were designed based on the researchers' experiences and relevant literature review. The online survey questions were designed to find out the duration and purpose of using SNS, the use of SNS in teaching and learning, the effect of SNS in academic performance and the role of SNS in education in future. There were 20 questionnaires, which were multiple choice questions, matrix type questions, drop-down questions and textbox questions. Whenever, the face-to-face interviews were used to conducting the possible and e-mail communication was used to bridge the geographical distance when appropriate. Matrix type ranking questions were designed to explore in detail the benefits of SNS in academic performance. There were 6 interviewees who agreed to be interviewed.

3.2. Data Analysis

In the data analysis survey results are cleaned to reduce the invalid information and then summarized to generate categories or themes. This type of data was analyzed and studied to generate possible answers on research questions. The simple statistical information such as percentages was calculated for comparison purposes. In few related and similar results gathered from the online survey and published literature were compared and analyzed. While convenience samples could provide useful information, they would differ from an ideal sample that was randomly selected. The small sample size added further limitation to the data. These limitations were taken into consideration in the data analysis and interpretation. The researchers carefully examined all the data gathered from the interviews, and made sense as a whole. Mean while researchers used the new methods of coding to generate categories or themes according to the key points from the answers. Each individual answer was anonymously identified by a code. This can be considered for due to the page limitation, only a summary of the interview results is reported in this paper.

3.3. Researcher Variable Under Teaching Environment

The social networking sites are having useful for communicating the users studies purpose.

Characteristics included:

- Age.
- Gender.
- Marital status.
- Teaching experience [years].
- Seniority on SNS [years].
- Number of friends in SNS.

3.4. Attitudes Towards SNS Use in Teaching and Learning Environment

Some of the SNS users are discussing the following point in Teaching Environment.

1. In educational environment, most of the students and teachers are using for learning purpose.
2. There are many SNSs are provided in the entire world, to communicating the different researchers, teachers, and students through the social media networks.

3.5. Educational Environmental Benefits in Social Networking Sites

In recent days, social networks are provides a lot of information about the opportunities of educational society that can be accessed by everyone around the world wide. And also, provides the teaching and learning environment on the social media networks for improve academic environments. The internet and technology has completely included in education field; and ever, that has completely transformed into the SNS. The normal growth of SNS users are concentrating for their potential use of education and may have the conscious in SNS abilities in both team work association and active learning. Therefore, the educational effects of social networks are perspective affirmative in the teaching and learning environment. This cannot be achieved for only students and it may be offering the great opportunities for connecting between administrators and teachers. Using with SNS, the teachers as well as students can improve the involvement in educational environments. And also, to improve the ability of social technology should be provide enormous intelligence of association in the classroom and it makes good communication skills. For example, the University of Minnesota had done the great research on SNS like MySpace and Facebook, and also, initiate that the SNS impact on educational growth for students in higher studies.

In addition, that the literature reviews analysis can be shows as the usage of students that are using latest technology systems to update the web content. Through this achievement the creative work should be shared from one to another and also carry out the some responsible use information as well as technology. Usually, some of the students were also aware of professional networking opportunities through this SNS. The effective SNS benefits on educational environments as discussing below.

1. **EDMODO:** It is one of the largest SNS that has been used essentially for educational purpose. This can provide greater security for all its users as well as educational institutions. Edmodo encourages all other activities such as posting assignments, conducting surveys and sharing images and videos.
2. **ENGLISH BABY:** In this environment teaching aspects the English is main objective of English Baby website. This can be used most of users among the Chinese people in world wide. However, this site can be accessed through paying money.
3. **LIVEMOCHA:** Livemocha is a SNS that can be used for different environments are providing the website for educational users. As per the data analysis, this website consists the collection of course materials are available in more than 38 languages and it can be performing the review and posting the content.
4. **ACADMIA.EDU:** It is a scientific related website that can be introduced for scientists and the respective college students, especially researcher. Mostly, this platform is focused on academic researchers to share the research materials and research ideas to other website users. Using this website, the users can able to share their research papers with other users in the same field, have contact with experts in the field and get their help in a research. The website

also shows the number of people accessed the papers and their reviews to the users who post their research papers.

5. **EPERNICUS:** Epernicus is another social networking website, focuses on social networking aspect, built mainly for scientists and researchers. Unlike Acadmia.edu, it doesn't allow users to share their research papers and materials. It allows users to post questions and get suitable answers from recognized experts. The users of the website can participate on any topic related to science and research and hence the website is quite informative for its users.
6. **COURSE CRACKER:** This social network is communicating the peoples, who have interested to refinement of the learning process. The main aim of this website is to improve the educational experience of users by using latest web applications and web tools in various courses in digital world. This website provides the different course materials and also allows the users to post their course material, quizzes, assignments and other sources related to education and also give them permission to access the posted content.
7. **STUDENTS CIRCLE NETWORK:** This social network is a latest edition that provides an varoius kinds of social networking sites. And also, this website consist the course materials in the field of science, business, engineering, computing and humanities. This can having thousands of courses for learning both the students and teachers.
8. **9TH PERIOD:** The main theme of this network communication is introduces the digital tools for new technical courses. Thus, these activities are facilitating for the academic users like students, teachers and universities, through the Internet. This website allows users who have similar to interest and interact with each other without any discrepancies.
9. **THE SYNAPSE:** This site mainly designed for biology students and researchers all over the world. This website acts as a great source of the latest happenings and development in biology, generally built on the Ning platform.
10. **THE MOLECULAR FORCES:** It is another website built on the Ning platform that focuses on physics and chemistry students, teachers and researchers. Teachers can able to distribute their study materials and learning approaches in this website. The website also acts as a great platform for sharing and asking questions about new ideas.

The following are the most popular social networking websites that promote education:

1. **WIKIPEDIA:** Wikipedia is a most popularly using to providing the great repository of information about any field of research discussion as well as present methods of designing in the field of educational environment. Mostly,

this can be provides an information could be used for discussing many people's share their own views and opinions based on the network strategy environment review analysis. Also, they ask questions, review, modify, mention references, give feedbacks and share their knowledge gained from the article.

2. **FACEBOOK:** This is a world popular social networking site that has nearly billions of users are using all over the world. This site is considered to be an best website for promoting education learning mechanism. In this modern generation, you can find almost every student has an account in Facebook. The Facebook groups are formed for schools and classes and thus the website allows both the teachers and students to share their information, post queries and answers, set reminders about upcoming events, etc. The famous Facebook groups are available in Wikieducators, E-Learning in developing and developed countries, Teaching and Active Learning.
3. **LINKEDIN:** LinkedIn is one of the world popular website. But, this is created mainly for managing the business relationships and networking throughout world. This website is used by nearly a million of companies and professionals across the world. Not only LinkedIn educates its users, but also provides benefits to employers and job seekers.

4. RESULTS AND ANALYSIS

The survey is analysis as for the user's interview results that are presented and interpreted respectively with each dataset. For that, the demographic information of the respondents was gathered first. The respondents were male (50.00%) and female (50.00%); and most of them are professors of various fields. As most of them are professors of age above 30 years and from reputed institutions. It is reasonable to assume that they all have adequate computing skills to make of use SNS. Most of them (30%) use SNS for more than 8 hrs. Although the respondents have a reasonable level of experience with SNS, they do not have the same level of experience using SNS for teaching and learning.

Table 1 and Figure 1, shows the purpose of using SNS in teaching and learning environments. All 100.00% of respondents use SNS for information retrieval, 23.08% for teaching, 53.85 for research and 76.92% for entertainment.

Figure 2 shows the statistical analysis of teaching specification of teachers and Table 2 shows the responses in percentage i.e., for what purposes they use SNS, course preparation, giving assignments, guiding projects, providing feedback or communication. After analysing the responded data 62.50% teachers, use SNS for course preparation, 50% uses for guiding their student's projects, 12.50% for collecting feedback, and 62.50% for communication.

Figure 3 shows the statistical analysis of how SNS is helpful in teachers teaching. Based on questions (shown in Table 3) asked to the target population, the obtained data results in the following statistics shown in Figure 3. Similarly, Table 3 shows the percentage responses.

From the survey it is found that, 58.33% peoples answered yes to question "Do you use social media in teaching your courses?". 50% of the teachers rely on SNS for giving assignments,

72.73% of teachers are using SNS for posting contents related to the course outside class learning which is the great percentage for use of SNS by teachers. Additionally teachers are asking students to give their course related comments on course related posts through SNS, here 63.64% of teachers said yes for this question. Through this comments and posts students-teacher communication is getting stronger and efficient. Now days in various universities and colleges, SNS is established in education very well and this study conveys that, 63.64% of educational institutes are well established with SNS and its use. Moreover, through this survey, we have been asked to various teachers about benefits of SNS in education. So, 83.33% of teachers said that, SNS is beneficial in education.

Figure 4 shows the effect of SNS i.e., whether the effect of SNS is very negative, negative, No effect, very positive or positive. Table 4 shows the tabular representation of effect of SNS 61.54% answered as effect of SNS is positive in teaching and learning which is higher while, in case of grades and performance maximum i.e., 46.15% answered that there is no effect. And there is 50-50 probability of positive effect and no effect on student's attitude by learning through SNS (46.15%).

5. DISCUSSION

The e-learners experienced a significant improvement in the learning process than traditional methods. The social networking sites enable a great community platform to interact with wide number of peer learners. The peer learner comes with different innovative solutions in a short period of time. The learners can experience seamless deliver of course materials with better user satisfaction. The improved network technologies empower the communication with minimal error rate. The social network sites helps to engage the resource persons from all over the world at any time. The learners have convenience to take course at their preferred timings. The significant improvement is taken place at evaluation side; the evaluation is fast and precise. The results can be analysed graphically, which will ensure the learner to move in perfect way. The developers and course deliver organizations should take care about the bump between education and social activities.

Learning through social networking sites is a tremendous platform for the employed people. The SNS are alternative for distance education with enormous benefits. Common and ongoing participation and association within the context of the social network seemed to mitigate the problems traditionally facing online learners, such as isolation and lack of support, while contributing to a positive learning experience. The research is carried out on social networking sites like Facebook by university of Minnesota and they found that there is significant impact on students in high school. The principal investigator concluded that, 94 percent of the observed students used the Internet, 77 percent had their account on social networking sites and 82 percent of the students went online at home. The social networking sites helps to find employment by doing various activities like content updating, teaching and the development of projects. The SNS helps their students to teach in depth by collaborating through network by giving socially anxious and making students comfortable by interacting with their classmates. Applications like Twijector can project Twitter streams onto classroom walls. Students can create a live, interactive stream by Tweeting questions, clarifications, or responses about a topic.

The collaboration through the social networks will mitigate the issues faced in traditional online services such as positive learning experience, isolation and lack of support. As the content is delivered in form of multimedia, the content has good quality and learner can go through at any time with recurrent views. The content delivery sites should take care of the learner's privacy over the facilitators and peer students. The site interface helps the learners to spend more time and enhances the interaction with course content. The discovery education network and scholastic discussion forums provide a great space for learners to connect with their peers. These platforms provides more privacy to the facilitators and as well as learners than other social networking sites.

The teachers can collaborate with other persons from across the globe through social networking. The collaboration helps to enhance the teacher's skills and helps in getting updated information with new case studies. For example, you can now plan a virtual field trip, as discussed on our website earlier, with ease and accuracy. If you are planning a virtual trip to another country, you could get in touch with people from that country and understand their lifestyle, food habits and culture. The teachers will get exposure on web 2.0 technologies and which helps in lifelong learning process. The social networking sites are powerful tool for global harmony and engaging in cross cultural discussion. The learning through social networking sites helps to overcome all those activities and saves time and money. Students use social media day in and day out to interact with their peers and even teachers about class-related subjects. In a world where online engagement is important for businesses, these students are becoming experts at developing a sense of Internet presence.

However, despite of enormous advantages the negative aspects of social activities are prone to few registrations. The posting of facilitators and teachers in social media should be professional and it shouldn't be offending the public. The relation between teachers and student is not good compared with traditional class room teaching. The fake review to the site will result in losing the trust and results in losing wages. It is essential for teachers to remember that their actions on a public social network may be visible to students, parents, school districts and the media. The social networking sites help the teachers in various ways such as accessing the resources and collaborating with staffs, exchanging the e-content, good communication with parents and partnership with different schools and countries. Rather than viewing online social networks as locations that students visit to interact with one another, it may be more productive to evaluate which social networking features are valuable in day-to-day educational experiences, how such features are compatible with academic cultures and values, and how such features are used in real-world interventions.

6. CONCLUSION

The use of social networking sites are motivate to increase learning as well as a more active and collaborative methodologies in teaching environment. These methodologies are presented from the new perspective aspects that should favour the continuous exchange of ideas, as well as collaborative work strategies. In this way of analysis process is communicate peoples with group interaction and exchange of experiences (Ortíz, 2006; Davoli, Monari, & Eklund, 2009) as well as the content shared among members of the university institution is a constant variable.

There are many ways we can connect with students through SNS and by that, we use time outside course hours to communicate with them. SNS can be used as a supplemental tool in courses, because it is an environment student's feel familiar. Figure 5 and Table 5 shows the statistical and tabular analysis of role of SNS from survey conducted. And after analysing data, it has been noticed that 86.62% feels the role of SNS in future education perspective is increasing.

REFERENCES

Abbott, L. (2005). The nature of authentic professional development during curriculum-based telecomputing. *Journal of Research on Technology in Education*, *37*(4), 379–398. doi:10.1080/15391523.2005.10782444

Amichai-Hamburger, Y., & Vinitzky, G. (2010). Social network use and personality. *Computers in Human Behavior*, *26*(6), 1289–1295. doi:10.1016/j.chb.2010.03.018

Bentley, R., Bogart, R., Davis, A., Hurlburt, N., Mukherjee, J., Rezapkin, V., . . . Weiss, M. (2005). *A Framework for Space and Solar Physics Virtual Observatories*. Retrieved from hpde.gsfc.nasa.gov/VO_Framework_7_Jan_05.pdf

Bliuc, A. M., Ellis, R., Goodyear, P., & Piggott, L. (2010). Learning through face-to-face and online discussions: Associations between students conceptions, approaches and academic performance in political science. *British Journal of Educational Technology*, *41*(3), 512–524. doi:10.1111/j.1467-8535.2009.00966.x

Bowers-Campbell, J. (2008). Cyber pokes: Motivational antidote for developmental college readers. *Journal of College Reading and Learning*, *39*(1), 74–87. doi:10.1080/10790195.2008.10850313

Boyd, D. M. (2008). Why youth social network sites: The role of networked publics in teenage social life. In D. Buckingham (Ed.), *Youth, identity, and digital media* (pp. 119–142). Cambridge, MA: The MIT Press.

Boyd, D. M., & Ellison, N. B. (2007). Social network sites: Definition, history, and scholarship. *Journal of Computer-Mediated Communication*, *13*(1), 210–230. doi:10.1111/j.1083-6101.2007.00393.x

Bureš, V., Tučník, P., Mikulecký, P., Mls, K., & Blecha, P. (2016). Application of Ambient Intelligence in Educational Institutions: Visions and Architectures. *International Journal of Ambient Computing and Intelligence*, *7*(1), 94–120. doi:10.4018/IJACI.2016010105

Cisco. (2008). *Cisco reusable learning object strategy: designing and developing learning objects for multiple learning approaches*. Retrieved from http://business.cisco.com/

Debatin, B., Lovejoy, J., Horn, A., & Hughes, B. (2009). Facebook and online privacy: Attitudes, behaviors, and unintended consequences. *Journal of Computer-Mediated Communication*, *15*(1), 83–108. doi:10.1111/j.1083-6101.2009.01494.x

Deelman, E., Mehta, G., Singh, G., Su, M., & Vahi, K. (2007). Pegasus: mapping large-scale workflows to distributed resources. In I. Taylor, E. Deelman, D. Gannon, & M. Shields (Eds.), *Workflows for e-Science* (pp. 376–394). New York: Springer. doi:10.1007/978-1-84628-757-2_23

Duan, Q., Yan, Y., & Vasilakos, A. V. (2012). A Survey on Service-Oriented Network Virtualization Toward Convergence of Networking and Cloud Computing. Network and Service Management. *IEEE Transactions*, *9*(4), 373–392.

Ellison, N. B., & Boyd, D. (2013). Sociality through social network sites. In W. Dutton (Ed.), *The Oxford handbook of internet studies* (pp. 151–172). Oxford University Press.

Fahringer, T., Jugravu, A., Pllana, S., Prodan, R., Seragiotto, C. Jr, & Truong, H. (2005). ASKALON: A tool set for cluster and Grid computing. *Concurr Comput Pract Exp*, *17*(2–4), 143–169. doi:10.1002/cpe.929

Iahad, M., & Huspi. (2012). A blended community of inquiry approach: The usage of social network as a support for Course Management System.*International Conference on Computer & Information Science (ICCIS)*, 180-183.

Junco, R. (2013). Inequalities in Facebook use. *Computers in Human Behavior*, *29*(6), 2328–2336. doi:10.1016/j.chb.2013.05.005

Kabilan, M. K., Ahmad, N., & Abidin, M. J. Z. (2010). Facebook: An online environment for learning of English in institutions of higher education? *The Internet and Higher Education*, *13*(4), 179–187. doi:10.1016/j.iheduc.2010.07.003

Kalin, J. (2012). Doing what comes naturally? Students perceptions and use of collaborative technologies. *Int. J. Scholarship Teach. Learn.*, *6*(1), 1–21.

Kamal, Dey, Ashour, & Balas. (2016). FbMapping: An Automated System for Monitoring Facebook Data. *Neural Network World*.

Kärkkäinen, H., Jussila, J., & Väisänen, J. (2010). Social media use and potential in business-to-business companies' innovation. In *Proceedings of the 14th international academic mindtrek conference: Envisioning future media environments* (pp. 228-236). ACM.

Lenhart, A., Madden, M., Macgill, A. R., & Smith, A. (2007). *Teens and social media. Pew Internet and American Life Project.* Retrieved August 2012 from http://www.pewinternet.org/Reports/2007/Teensand-Social-Media.aspx

Ludäscher, B., Altintas, I., Berkley, C., Higgins, D., Jaeger, E., Jones, M., & Zhao, Y. et al. (2005). Scientific workflow management and the Kepler system. *Concurr Comput Pract Exp*, *18*(10), 1039–1065. doi:10.1002/cpe.994

Mazer, J. P., Murphy, R. E., & Simonds, C. J. (2007). Ill see you on Facebook: The effects of computer-mediated teacher self-disclosure on student motivation, affective learning, and classroom climate. *Communication Education*, *56*(1), 1–17. doi:10.1080/03634520601009710

Mazman, S. G., & Usluel, Y. K. (2010). Modeling educational usage of Facebook. *Computers & Education*, *55*(2), 444–453. doi:10.1016/j.compedu.2010.02.008

Mell, P., & Grance, T. (2009). *The NIST definition of cloud computing*. Retrieved from http://www.nist.gov/itl/cloud/upload/cloud-def-v15.pdf

Oinn, T., Addis, M., Ferris, J., Marvin, D., Senger, M., Greenwood, M., & Li, P. et al. (2004). Taverna: A tool for the composition and enactment of bioinformatics workflows. *Bioinformatics (Oxford, England)*, *20*(17), 3045–3054. doi:10.1093/bioinformatics/bth361 PMID:15201187

Quinn, D., Chen, L., & Mulvenna, M. (2012). Social Network Analysis-A Survey. *International Journal of Ambient Computing and Intelligence*, *4*(3), 46–58. doi:10.4018/jaci.2012070104

Rodgers, C. R., & Raider-Roth, M. B. (2006). Presence in teaching. Teachers and Teaching. *Theory into Practice*, *12*, 265–287.

Selwyn, N. (2009). Faceworking: Exploring students education-related use of Facebook. *Learning, Media and Technology*, *34*(2), 157–174. doi:10.1080/17439880902923622

Shapley, K. S., Sheehan, D., Maloney, C., & Caranikas-Walker, F. (2010). Evaluating the implementation fidelity of technology immersion and its relationship with student achievement. *The Journal of Technology, Learning, and Assessment*, *9*(4).

Stumme, G., Hotho, A., & Berendt, B. (2006). Semantic web mining: State of the art and future directions. *Web Semantics: Science, Services, and Agents on the World Wide Web*, *4*(2), 124–143. doi:10.1016/j.websem.2006.02.001

TAVERNA. (2010). *Taverna Workflow System*. Retrieved from http://www.taverna.org.uk/

Taylor, I., Shields, M., Wang, I., & Harrison, A. (2007). The Triana workflow environment: architecture and applications. In I. Taylor, E. Deelman, D. Gannon, & M. Shields (Eds.), *Workflows for e-Science* (pp. 320–339). New York: Springer. doi:10.1007/978-1-84628-757-2_20

Toetenela, L. (2014). Social networking: A collaborative open educational resource. *Computer Assisted Language Learning*, *27*(2), 149–162. doi:10.1080/09588221.2013.818561

Voss, A., Meer, E. V., & Fergusson, D. (2008). *Research in a connected world*. Retrieved from http://www.lulu.com/product/ebook/research-in-a-connected-world/17375289

Yang, X. (2011). QoS-oriented service computing: bring SOA into cloud environment. In X. Liu & Y. Li (Eds.), *Advanced design approaches to emerging software systems: principles, methodology and tools*. IGI Global USA.

Yang, X., Bruin, R., & Dove, M. (2010). *Developing an end-to-end scientific workflow: a case study of using a reliable, lightweight, and comprehensive workflow platform in e-Science*. doi:.21110.1109/MCSE.2009

Yang, Y., Wang, Q., Woo, H. L., & Quek, C. L. (2011). Using Facebook for teaching and learning: A review of the literature. Int. J. Continuing Eng. Edu. *Life-Long Learn.*, *21*(1), 72–86.

Zhao, Y., Hategan, M., Clifford, B., Foster, I., von, Laszewski, G., Nefedova, V., Raicu, I., Stef-Praun, T., & Wilde, M. (2007). Swift: fast, reliable, loosely coupled parallel computation. *Proceedings of 2007 IEEE congress on services (Services 2007)*, 199–206. doi:10.1109/SERVICES.2007.63

Compilation of References

Abbott, L. (2005). The nature of authentic professional development during curriculum-based telecomputing. *Journal of Research on Technology in Education*, *37*(4), 379–398. doi:10.1080/15391523.2005.10782444

Aghabozorgi, S. R., & Wah, T. Y. (2009). Dynamic modelling by usage data for personalization systems.*Proceedings of 13th International Conference on Information Visualization*, 450-455. doi doi:10.1109/iv.2009.111

Agrawal, R., Mannila, H., Srikant, R., Toivonen, H., & Verkamo, A. I. (1996). Fast discovery of association rules. *Advances in Knowledge Discovery and Data Mining, 12*(1), 307-328.

Agrawal, R., Imieliński, T., & Swami, A. (1993). Mining association rules between sets of items in large databases.*ACM SIGMOD Int Conf Manag Data*, *22*(2), 207–16. doi:10.1145/170035.170072

Alfred, R. (2008). *A Data Summarisation Approach to Knowledge Discovery*. University of York.

Alhenshiri, A. (2010). Web Information Retrieval and Search Engines Techniques. *Al-Satil Journal*, 55-92.

Aljandal, W., Bahirwani, V., Caragea, D., & Hsu, W. H. (2009). Ontology-Aware Classification and Association Rule Mining for Interest and Link Prediction in Social Networks. In *AAAI Spring Symposium: Social Semantic Web: Where Web 2.0 Meets Web 3.0* (pp. 3-8).

Alkhammash. (2016). *Designing Ontology for Association between Water Quality and Kidney Diseases for Medical Decision Support System*. VI International Conference Industrial Engineering and Environmental Protection 2016 (IIZS 2016), Zrenjanin, Serbia.

Alnoukari, M., & El Sheikh, A. (2011). Knowledge Discovery Process Models: From Traditional to Agile Modeling. *Business Intelligence and Agile Methodologies for Knowledge-Based Organizations: Cross-Disciplinary Applications*, 72-100.

Amichai-Hamburger, Y., & Vinitzky, G. (2010). Social network use and personality. *Computers in Human Behavior*, *26*(6), 1289–1295. doi:10.1016/j.chb.2010.03.018

Anand, S. S., & Büchner, A. G. (1998). Decision support using data mining. *Financial Times Management.*

Anand, D., & Niranjan, D. U. C. (1998). Watermarking Medical Images With Patient Information.*Proceedings of the 20th Annual International Conference of the IEEE Engineering in Medicine and Biology Society*, 703–706.

Anand, S. S., & Mobasher, B. (2005). Intelligent techniques for web personalization.*Proceedings of the 2003 International Conference on Intelligent Techniques for Web Personalization*, 1–36.

Androutsopoulos, I., Koutsias, J., Chandrinos, K. V., Paliouras, G., & Spyropoulos, C. D. (2000). An evaluation of naive bayesian anti-spam filtering.*Proceedings of the workshop on Machine Learning in the New Information Age.*

Anil, N.K., Kurian, S.B., Abahai, T. A. & Varghese, S.M. (2013). Multidimensional user data model for web personalization. *International Journal of Computer Applications*, *69*(12), 32-37.

Antoniou, G., & Van Harmelen, F. (2004). *A semantic web primer.* MIT press.

Antoniou, G., & Van Harmelen, F. (2004). Web ontology language: Owl. In *Handbook on ontologies* (pp. 67–92). Springer Berlin Heidelberg. doi:10.1007/978-3-540-24750-0_4

Anusaaraka: An Approach to Machine Translation. (n.d.). Retrieved from: http://sanskrit.uohyd.ac.in/faculty/amba/PUBLICATIONS/papers/hyd-anu-mt.pdf

Anusaarka. (n.d.). Retrieved from: http://www.anusaaraka.iiit.ac.in

Anwar, N., & Hunt, E. (2009). Improved data retrieval from TreeBASE via taxonomic and linguistic data enrichment. *BMC Evolutionary Biology*, *9*(1), 93. doi:10.1186/1471-2148-9-93 PMID:19426482

Armitage, L. H., & Enser, P. G. (1997). Analysis of user need in image archives. *Journal of Information Science*, *23*(4), 287–299. doi:10.1177/016555159702300403

Ashour, Sassi, Roy, Kausar, & Dey. (2016). MEDLINE Text Mining: An Enhancement Genetic Algorithm Based Approach for Document Clustering. In Applications of Intelligent Optimization in Biology and Medicine (pp. 267–287). Springer International Publishing.

Attwood, T. K., & Parry-Smith, D. J. (2002). *Introduction to Bioinformatics.* Singapore: Pvt. Ltd.

Baesens, B., Viaene, S., & Vanthienen, J. (2000). Post-processing of association rules.*The Sixth ACM SIGKDD International Conference on Knowledge Discovery and Data Mining (KDD'2000)*, 2-8.

Bairoch, A., & Apweiler, R. (2000). The SWISS-PROT protein sequence database and its supplement TrEMBL. *Nucleic Acids Research*, *28*(1), 45–48. doi:10.1093/nar/28.1.45 PMID:10592178

Balas, V. E., Dey, N., Ashour, A. D., & Pistolla, S. (2016). Image Fusion Incorporating Parameter Estimation Optimized Gaussian Mixture Model And Fuzzy Weighted Evaluation System: A Case Study In Time-Series Plantar Pressure Dataset. IEEE Sensors Journal, 1-15.

Baralis, E., & Chiusano, S. (2004). Essential classification rule sets. *ACM Transactions on Database Systems*, *29*(4), 635–674. doi:10.1145/1042046.1042048

Barnard, K., & Forsyth, D. (2001). Learning the semantics of words and pictures. In *Computer Vision, 2001. ICCV 2001. Proceedings. Eighth IEEE International Conference on* (Vol. 2, pp. 408-415). IEEE. doi:10.1109/ICCV.2001.937654

Barnard, K., Duygulu, P., & Forsyth, D. (2001). Clustering art. In *Computer Vision and Pattern Recognition, 2001. CVPR 2001.Proceedings of the 2001 IEEE Computer Society Conference on* (*Vol. 2*). IEEE.

Barnard, K., Duygulu, P., Forsyth, D., Freitas, N. D., Blei, D. M., & Jordan, M. I. (2003). Matching words and pictures. *Journal of Machine Learning Research*, *3*(Feb), 1107–1135.

Barrett, T. (2013). Gene Expression Omnibus (GEO). *The NCBI Handbook* (2nd ed.). Bethesda, MD: National Center for Biotechnology Information. Retrieved December 17, 2016, from https://www.ncbi.nlm.nih.gov/books/NBK159736/

Bates, J. (1994). Role of emotions in believable agents. *Communications of the ACM*, *37*(7), 122–125. doi:10.1145/176789.176803

Baumgarten, M., Mulvenna, M. D., Rooney, N., & Reid, J. (2013, April). Keyword-Based Sentiment Mining using Twitter. *International Journal of Ambient Computing and Intelligence*, *5*(2), 56–69. doi:10.4018/jaci.2013040104

Baxevanis, A. D. (2001). Information retrieval from biological databases. *Methods of Biochemical Analysis*, *43*, 155–185. doi:10.1002/0471223921.ch7 PMID:11449723

Baxevanis, A. D., & Francis Ouellette, B. F. (2005). *Bioinformatics - A Practical Guide to the analysis of Genes and Proteins* (3rd ed.). PHI Learning Private Limited.

Benson, D. A., Boguski, M. S., Lipman, D. J., Ostell, J., & Francis Ouellette, B. F. (1998). GenBank. *Nucleic Acids Research*, *26*(1), 1–7. doi:10.1093/nar/26.1.1 PMID:9399790

Bentley, R., Bogart, R., Davis, A., Hurlburt, N., Mukherjee, J., Rezapkin, V., . . . Weiss, M. (2005). *A Framework for Space and Solar Physics Virtual Observatories*. Retrieved from hpde.gsfc.nasa.gov/VO_Framework_7_Jan_05.pdf

Berkhin, P. (2006). A survey of clustering data mining techniques. In *Grouping multidimensional data* (pp. 25–71). Springer Berlin Heidelberg. doi:10.1007/3-540-28349-8_2

Berners-Lee, T., Hendler, J., & Lassila, O. (2001). The semantic web. *Scientific American*, *284*(5), 28–37. doi:10.1038/scientificamerican0501-34 PMID:11341160

Berry, M. J., & Linoff, G. (1997). *Data mining techniques: for marketing, sales, and customer support*. John Wiley & Sons, Inc.

Bharath Bhushan, S., & Pradeep Reddy, C. H. (2016). A Four-Level Linear Discriminant Analysis Based Service Selection in The Cloud Environment. *International Journal of Technology.*, *7*(5), 530–541.

Bhatt, C., Dey, N., & Ashour, A. S. (2017). *Internet of Things and Big Data Technologies in Next Generation Healthcare*. Springer International Publishing. doi:10.1007/978-3-319-49736-5

Bhowmick, P. K., Sarkar, S., & Basu, A. (2010). Ontology based user modelling for personalized information access. *International Journal of Computer Science and Applications*, *7*(1), 1–22.

Big data and analytics—an IDC four pillar research area, IDC, Technical Report. (n.d.). Retrieved November 1, 2016, from http://www.idc. com/prodserv/FourPillars/bigData/index.jsp

Biron, P., Malhotra, A., & Consortium, W. W. W. (2004). XML schema part 2: Datatypes. *World Wide Web Consortium Recommendation REC-xmlschema-2-20041028.*

Bliuc, A. M., Ellis, R., Goodyear, P., & Piggott, L. (2010). Learning through face-to-face and online discussions: Associations between students conceptions, approaches and academic performance in political science. *British Journal of Educational Technology*, *41*(3), 512–524. doi:10.1111/j.1467-8535.2009.00966.x

Bloedorn, E., Mani, I., & MacMillan, T. R. (1996). Machine Learning of User Profiles: Representational Issues.*Proceedings of AAAI 96,*433-438.

Bloehdorn, S., & Hotho, A. (2004, August). Boosting for text classification with semantic features. In *International Workshop on Knowledge Discovery on the Web* (pp. 149-166). Springer Berlin Heidelberg.

Bohannon, P., Fan, W., Flaster, M., & Narayan, P. (2005). Information preserving XML schema embedding.*Proceedings of the 31st international conference on Very large data bases.*

Boutet, E., Lieberherr, D., Tognolli, M., Schneider, M., & Bairoch, A. (2007). UniProtKB/Swiss-Prot. *Methods in Molecular Biology (Clifton, N.J.)*, *406*, 89–112. PMID:18287689

Bowers-Campbell, J. (2008). Cyber pokes: Motivational antidote for developmental college readers. *Journal of College Reading and Learning*, *39*(1), 74–87. doi:10.1080/10790195.2008.10850313

Boyd, D. M. (2008). Why youth social network sites: The role of networked publics in teenage social life. In D. Buckingham (Ed.), *Youth, identity, and digital media* (pp. 119–142). Cambridge, MA: The MIT Press.

Boyd, D. M., & Ellison, N. B. (2007). Social network sites: Definition, history, and scholarship. *Journal of Computer-Mediated Communication*, *13*(1), 210–230. doi:10.1111/j.1083-6101.2007.00393.x

Boyd, D., & Crawford, K. (2012). Critical questions for big data. *Information Communication and Society*, *15*(5), 662–679. doi:10.1080/1369118X.2012.678878

Brachman, R. J., Khabaza, T., Kloesgen, W., Piatetsky-Shapiro, G., & Simoudis, E. (1996). Mining business databases. *Communications of the ACM*, *39*(11), 42–48. doi:10.1145/240455.240468

Brin, S., Page, L., Motwani, R., & Winograd, T. (1998). *The Page Rank citation ranking: bringing order to the web*. Technical Report. Stanford University. Available on the Internet at http://dbpubs.stanford.edu:8090/pub/1999-66

Brooksbank, C. (2006). *Train online Bioinformatics for the terrified*. Retrieved December 20, 2016, http://www.ebi.ac.uk/training/online/course/bioinformatics-terrified

Brooksbank, C., Cameron, G., & Thornton, J. (2010). The European Bioinformatics Institutes data resources. *Nucleic Acids Research*, *38*(Database), D17–D25. doi:10.1093/nar/gkp986 PMID:19934258

Bruha, I., & Famili, A. (2000). Postprocessing in machine learning and data mining. *ACM SIGKDD Explorations Newsletter*, *2*(2), 110–114. doi:10.1145/380995.381059

Buccafurri, F., Lax, G., Rosaci, D., & Ursino, D. (2006). Dealing with semantic heterogeneity for improving web usage. *Data & Knowledge Engineering*, *58*(3), 436–465. doi:10.1016/j.datak.2005.06.002

Buitelaar, P., Eigner, T., & OntoSelect, T. D. (2004). A Dynamic Ontology Library with Support for Ontology Selection. *Proc. of the Demo Session at the International Semantic Web Conference*.

Bureš, V., Tučník, P., Mikulecký, P., Mls, K., & Blecha, P. (2016). Application of Ambient Intelligence in Educational Institutions: Visions and Architectures. *International Journal of Ambient Computing and Intelligence*, *7*(1), 94–120. doi:10.4018/IJACI.2016010105

Burge, P., Shawe-Taylor, J., Cooke, C., Moreau, Y., Preneel, B., & Stoermann, C. (1997, April). Fraud detection and management in mobile telecommunications networks. In *Security and Detection, 1997. ECOS 97., European Conference on* (pp. 91-96). IET. doi:10.1049/cp:19970429

Burl, M. C., Fayyad, U. M., Perona, P., Smyth, P., & Burl, M. P. (1994, June). Automating the hunt for volcanoes on Venus. In *Computer Vision and Pattern Recognition, 1994. Proceedings CVPR'94., 1994 IEEE Computer Society Conference on* (pp. 302-309). IEEE. doi:10.1109/CVPR.1994.323844

Cabena, P., Hadjinian, P., Stadler, R., Verhees, J., & Zanasi, A. (1998). *Discovering data mining: from concept to implementation*. Prentice-Hall, Inc.

Cannataro, M., Congiusta, A., Pugliese, A., Talia, D., & Trunfio, P. (2004). Distributed data mining on grids: Services, tools, and applications. *IEEE Transactions on System Man Cyber Part B Cyber.*, *34*(6), 51–65. PMID:15619945

Carmagnola, F., Cena, F., & Gena, C. (2011). User model interoperability: A survey. *User Modeling and User-Adapted Interaction*, *21*(3), 285–331. doi:10.1007/s11257-011-9097-5

Castells, P., Farnandez, M., & Vallet, D. (2007, February). An Adaptation of the Vector Space model for Ontology based Information Retrieval. *IEEE Transactions on Knowledge and Data Engineering*, *18*(2), 261–271. doi:10.1109/TKDE.2007.22

Chahal, P., Singh, M., & Kumar, S. (2013). Ranking of web documents using semantic similarity. *Proceedings of International Conference on Information Systems and Computer Networks (ISCON)*. doi:10.1109/ICISCON.2013.6524191

Chamiel, G., & Pagnucco, M. (2009). Ontology guided dynamic preference elicitation.*Proceedings of 3rd ACM Conference on Recommender Systems & the Social Web,*41-48.

Chandarana, P., & Vijayalakshmi, M. (2014). Big data analytics frameworks. *International Conference on Circuits, Systems, Communication and Information Technology Applications*, 430–434.

Chang, S., Smith, J., Beigi, M., & Benitez, A. (1997). Visual information retrieval from largedistributed online repositories. *Communications of the ACM*, *40*(12), 63–71. doi:10.1145/265563.265573

Chauhan, R., Goudar, R., Sharma, R. & Chauhan, A. (2013). *Domain Ontology based Semantic Search for Efficient Information Retrieval through Automatic Query Expansion*. Academic Press.

Cheng, Y., Qin, C., & Rusu, F. (2012). GLADE: big data analytics made easy.*ACM SIGMOD International Conference on Management of Data*, 697–700.

Chen, H., Chiang, R. H. L., & Storey, V. C. (2012). Business intelligence and analytics: From big data to big impact. *Management Information Systems Quarterly*, *36*(4), 1165–1171.

Chen, H., Du, X., Chen, X., & Xia, C. (2012). Query expansion model based on interest ontology.*Proceedings of International Conference on Information Management, Innovation Management and Industrial Engineering (ICIII)*.

Chen, K., & Liu, L. (2004). VISTA: Validating and refining clusters via visualization. *Information Visualization*, *3*(4), 257–270. doi:10.1057/palgrave.ivs.9500076

Chen, L., & Sycara, K. (1998). WebMate: A Personal Agent for Browsing and Searching.*InProceedings of the 2nd International Conference on Autonomous Agents* (pp 132-139). ACM Press. doi:10.1145/280765.280789

Cheptsov, A. (2014). Hpc in big data age: An evaluation report for java-based data-intensive applications implemented with Hadoop and OpenMP. *European MPI Users' Group Meeting*, 175-180.

Christos, F., & Douglas, W. (1995). *A Survey of Information Retrieval and Filtering Methods.* CS-TR-3514.

Cios, K. J., Teresinska, A., Konieczna, S., Potocka, J., & Sharma, S. (2000). Diagnosing myocardial perfusion from PECT bulls-eye maps-A knowledge discovery approach. *IEEE Engineering in Medicine and Biology Magazine*, *19*(4), 17–25. doi:10.1109/51.853478 PMID:10916729

Cisco. (2008). *Cisco reusable learning object strategy: designing and developing learning objects for multiple learning approaches*. Retrieved from http://business.cisco.com/

Coalition, D. S. (2002). DAML-S: Web service description for the semantic web. *Proceedings of ISWC.*

Cochrane, G., Karsch-Mizrachi, I., & Nakamura, Y. (2011). The International Nucleotide Sequence Database Collaboration. *Nucleic Acids Research*, *39*(Database issue), D15–D18. doi:10.1093/nar/gkq1150 PMID:21106499

Codd, E. F. (1970). A relational model of data for large shared data banks. *Communications of the ACM*, *13*(6), 377–387. doi:10.1145/362384.362685

Comaniciu, D., & Meer, P. (2002). Mean shift: A robust approach toward feature space analysis. *IEEE Transactions on Pattern Analysis and Machine Intelligence*, *24*(5), 603–619. doi:10.1109/34.1000236

Cook, C. E., Bergman, M. T., Finn, R. D., Cochrane, G., Birney, E., & Apweiler, R. (2015). The European Bioinformatics Institute in 2016: Data growth and integration. *Nucleic Acids Research,* 1-7. doi: 10.1093/nar/gkv1352

Cooper, P., Landrum, M., Mizrachi, I., & Weisemann, J. (2010). *Entrez Sequences Help*. Retrieved December 17, 2016, from https://www.ncbi.nlm.nih.gov/books/NBK44863/

Croft & Callan. (2016). *Lemur Project*. Retrieved http://www.lemurproject.org/

Croft, B., Metzler, D., & Strohman, T. (2010). *Search Engines: Information Retrieval in Practice*. Pearson Education.

da Costa, M. G., & Gong, Z. (2005, July). Web structure mining: an introduction. In *2005 IEEE International Conference on Information Acquisition*. IEEE.

Datta, R., Joshi, D., Li, J., & Wang, J. Z. (2008). Image retrieval: Ideas, influences, and trends of the new age.[CSUR]. *ACM Computing Surveys*, *40*(2), 5. doi:10.1145/1348246.1348248

Deb, S., & Zhang, Y. (2004). An overview of content-based image retrieval techniques. In *Advanced Information Networking and Applications, 2004. AINA 2004. 18th International Conference on* (Vol. 1, pp. 59-64). IEEE. doi:10.1109/AINA.2004.1283888

Debatin, B., Lovejoy, J., Horn, A., & Hughes, B. (2009). Facebook and online privacy: Attitudes, behaviors, and unintended consequences. *Journal of Computer-Mediated Communication*, *15*(1), 83–108. doi:10.1111/j.1083-6101.2009.01494.x

Decker, S., Melnik, S., Van Harmelen, F., Fensel, D., Klein, M., Broekstra, J., & Horrocks, I. et al. (2000). The semantic web: The roles of XML and RDF. *IEEE Internet Computing*, *4*(5), 63–73. doi:10.1109/4236.877487

Deelman, E., Mehta, G., Singh, G., Su, M., & Vahi, K. (2007). Pegasus: mapping large-scale workflows to distributed resources. In I. Taylor, E. Deelman, D. Gannon, & M. Shields (Eds.), *Workflows for e-Science* (pp. 376–394). New York: Springer. doi:10.1007/978-1-84628-757-2_23

Devedzic, V. (2002). Knowledge discovery and data mining in databases.Handbook of Software Engineering and Knowledge Engineering Vol. 1-Fundamentals, 615-637.

Dey, N., Samanta, S., Chakraborty, S., Das, A., Chaudhuri, S., & Suri, J. (2014). Firefly Algorithm for Optimization of Scaling Factors during Embedding of Manifold Medical Information: An Application in Ophthalmology Imaging. *Journal of Medical Imaging and Health Informatics*, *4*(3), 384–394. doi:10.1166/jmihi.2014.1265

Djaanfar, A. S., Frikh, B., & Ouhbi, B. (2012). A hybrid method for improving the SQD-PageRank algorithm.*Proceedings of Second International Conference on Innovative Computing Technology (INTECH)*, 231-238. doi:10.1109/INTECH.2012.6457747

Dou, D., Wang, H., & Liu, H. (2015, February). Semantic data mining: A survey of ontology-based approaches. In *Semantic Computing (ICSC), 2015 IEEE International Conference on* (pp. 244-251). IEEE. doi:10.1109/ICOSC.2015.7050814

Drysdale, R (2008). FlyBase: a database for the Drosophila research community. *Methods Mol Biol., 420*, 45-59. doi: 10.1007/978-1-59745-583-1_3

Duan, Q., Yan, Y., & Vasilakos, A. V. (2012). A Survey on Service-Oriented Network Virtualization Toward Convergence of Networking and Cloud Computing. Network and Service Management. *IEEE Transactions*, *9*(4), 373–392.

Eakins, J. P., B, J. M., & Graham, M. E. (1998). Similarity retrieval of trademark images. *IEEE Multimedia Magazine*, 53–63.

Edelstein, H. (2000). Building profitable customer relationships with data mining. In Customer Relationship Management (pp. 339-351). Vieweg+ Teubner Verlag.

Ehlert, P. (2003). *Intelligent User Interfaces: Introduction and Survey*. Research Report DKS03-01/ICE 01, Faculty of Information Technology and Systems, Delft University of Technology.

Eick, S. G., & Fyock, D. E. (1996). Visualizing corporate data. *AT&T Technical Journal, 75*(1), 74-86.

Ellison, N. B., & Boyd, D. (2013). Sociality through social network sites. In W. Dutton (Ed.), *The Oxford handbook of internet studies* (pp. 151–172). Oxford University Press.

Elloumi, M., & Zomaya, A. Y. (2013). *Biological Knowledge Discovery Handbook: Preprocessing, Mining and Postprocessing of Biological Data* (Vol. 23). John Wiley & Sons. doi:10.1002/9781118617151

Essa, Y. M., Attiya, G., & El-Sayed, A. (2013). Mobile agent based new framework for improving big data analysis.*International Conference on Cloud Computing and Big Data*, 381–386. doi:10.1109/CLOUDCOM-ASIA.2013.75

Fahringer, T., Jugravu, A., Pllana, S., Prodan, R., Seragiotto, C. Jr, & Truong, H. (2005). ASKALON: A tool set for cluster and Grid computing. *Concurr Comput Pract Exp, 17*(2–4), 143–169. doi:10.1002/cpe.929

Fallside, D. C., & Walmsley, P. (2004). XML schema part 0: primer second edition. W3C recommendation, 16.

Fan, J., & Li, D. (1998). An overview of data mining and knowledge discovery. *Journal of Computer Science and Technology*, *13*(4), 348–368. doi:10.1007/BF02946624

Fayyad, U. M., Piatetsky-Shapiro, G., & Smyth, P. (1996a, August). Knowledge discovery and data mining: towards a unifying framework. In KDD (Vol. 96, pp. 82-88).

Fayyad, U. M., Haussler, D., & Stolorz, P. E. (1996, August). KDD for Science Data Analysis: Issues and Examples. In *Proceedings of the 2nd International Conference on Knowledge Discovery and Data Mining*, (pp. 50-56).

Fayyad, U. M., Piatetsky-Shapiro, G., & Smyth, P. (1996b). The KDD process for extracting useful knowledge from volumes of data. *Communications of the ACM*, *39*(11), 27–34. doi:10.1145/240455.240464

Fayyad, U. M., Weir, N., & Djorgovski, S. (1993). SKICAT: A Machine Learning System for Automated Cataloging of Large Scale Sky Surveys. In *Proc. Tenth Intl. Conf. on Machine Learning* (pp. 112-119). doi:10.1016/B978-1-55860-307-3.50021-6

Feldman, D., Schmidt, M., & Sohler, C. (2013). Turning big data into tiny data: Constant-size coresets for k-means, PCA and projective clustering.*ACM-SIAM Symposium on Discrete Algorithms*, 1434–1453. doi:10.1137/1.9781611973105.103

Fensel, D., Lausen, H., Polleres, A., De Bruijn, J., Stollberg, M., Roman, D., & Domingue, J. (2006). *Enabling Semantic Web Services: Web Service Modeling Ontology*. Springer.

Fensel, D., van Harmelen, F., Horrocks, I., McGuinness, D. L., & Patel-Schneider, P. F. (2001). OIL: An Ontology Infrastructure for the Semantic Web. *IEEE Intelligent Systems*, *16*(2), 38–45. doi:10.1109/5254.920598

Finn, R. D., Bateman, A., Clements, J., Coggill, P., Eberhardt, R. Y., Eddy, S. R., & Punta, M. et al. (2014). Pfam: The protein families database. *Nucleic Acids Research*, *42*(Database issue), D222–D230. doi:10.1093/nar/gkt1223 PMID:24288371

Fisher, D., DeLine, R., Czerwinski, M., & Drucker, S. (2012). Interactions with big data analytics. *Interaction*, *19*(3), 50–59. doi:10.1145/2168931.2168943

Frankel, C., Swain, M., & Athitsos, V. (1996). *WebSeer: An image search engine for the world-wide web.* Technical Report 94-14, Computer Science Department, University of Chicago.

Franklin, S., & Graesser, A. (1996, August). Is it an Agent, or just a Program?: A Taxonomy for Autonomous Agents. In *International Workshop on Agent Theories, Architectures, and Languages* (pp. 21-35). Springer Berlin Heidelberg.

Furletti, B. (2009). *Ontology-driven knowledge discovery* (PhD Thesis). IMT Institute for Advanced Studies, Lucca, Italy.

Gao, Q., & Cho, Y. I. (2013). A multi-agent personalized ontology profile based query refinement approach for information retrieval. *Proceedings of 13th International Conference on Control, Automation and Systems (ICCAS)*. doi:10.1109/ICCAS.2013.6703997

Geer, R. C., & Sayers, E. W. (2003). Entrez: Making use of its power. *Briefings in Bioinformatics*, *4*(2), 179–184. doi:10.1093/bib/4.2.179 PMID:12846398

Gerber, A. J., Barnard, A., & Van Der Merwe, A. J. (2007). Towards a semantic web layered architecture. In *Proceedings of IASTED International Conference on Software Engineering (SE2007)* (pp. 353-362). Innsbruck, Austria: IASTED.

Gerber, A. J., Barnard, A., & Van der Merwe, A. J. (2007, February). Towards a semantic web layered architecture. In *Proceedings of the 25th conference on IASTED International Multi-Conference: Software Engineering. Innsbruck, Austria* (pp. 353-362). IASTED.

Gerber, A., Van der Merwe, A., & Barnard, A. (2008, June). A functional semantic web architecture. In *European Semantic Web Conference* (pp. 273-287). Springer Berlin Heidelberg.

Getoor, L. (2003). Link mining: A new data mining challenge. *ACM SIGKDD Explorations Newsletter*, *5*(1), 84–89. doi:10.1145/959242.959253

Gladun, A., Rogushina, J., Sanchez, G. F., Bejar, M. R., & Breis, F. T. J. (2009). An application of intelligent techniques and semantic web technologies in E-Learning environments. *Expert Systems with Applications*, *36*(2), 1922–1931. doi:10.1016/j.eswa.2007.12.019

Gobeill, J., Müller, H., & Ruch, P. (2007). Translation by Text Categorization: Medical Image Retrieval. Lecture Notes in Computer Science, 4730, 706-710.

Goker, A., & Davies, J. (2009). Information Retrieval: Searching in the 21st Century. John Wiley and Sons, Ltd.

Griffeth, D. N., & Velthuijsen, H. (1993). Win/Win negotiation among autonomous agents.*Proceedings of the 12th International Workshop on Distributed Artificial Intelligence*, 187-202.

Grobe, M. (2009). Rdf, jena, sparql and the 'semantic web'.*Proceedings of the 37th annual ACM SIGUCCS fall conference*.

Gruber, R. T. (1993). Toward principles for the design of ontologies used for knowledge sharing. *International Journal of Human-Computer Studies*, *43*(5-6), 907–928. doi:10.1006/ijhc.1995.1081

Grzymala-Busse, J. W. (2005). Rule induction. In Data Mining and Knowledge Discovery Handbook (pp. 277-294). Springer US. doi:10.1007/0-387-25465-X_13

Gudivada, V. N., & Raghavan, V. V. (1995). Content-based image retrieval systems. *IEEE Computer*, *28*(9), 18–31. doi:10.1109/2.410145

Haglin, D., Roiger, R., Hakkila, J., & Giblin, T. (2005). A tool for public analysis of scientific data. *Data Science Journal*, *4*, 39–53. doi:10.2481/dsj.4.39

Hall, J., Mani, G., & Barr, D. (1996). Applying computational intelligence to the investment process.*Proceedings of CIFER-96: Computational Intelligence in Financial Engineering*. Washington, DC: IEEE Computer Society.

Han, J., Kamber, M., & Pei, J. (2012a). Classification: Advanced methods. In Data mining: concepts and techniques. Elsevier.

Han, J., & Kamber, M. (2006). Classification and Prediction. In *Data mining: concepts and techniques* (2nd ed.; pp. 285–382). Elsevier.

Han, J., Kamber, M., & Pei, J. (2012b). *Data mining: concepts and techniques* (3rd ed.). Elsevier. doi:10.1007/978-1-4419-1428-6_3752

Haralick, R. M., Shanmugam, K., & Dinstein, I. H. (1973). Textural features for image classification. *IEEE Transactions on Systems, Man, and Cybernetics*, *3*(6), 610–621. doi:10.1109/TSMC.1973.4309314

Harris, T. W., Lee, R., Schwarz, E., Bradnam, K., Lawson, D., Chen, W., & Stein, L. D. et al. (2003). WormBase: A cross-species database for comparative genomics. *Nucleic Acids Research*, *31*(1), 133–137. doi:10.1093/nar/gkg053 PMID:12519966

Hatonen, K., Klemettinen, M., Mannila, H., Ronkainen, P., & Toivonen, H. (1996, February). Knowledge discovery from telecommunication network alarm databases. In *Data Engineering, 1996.Proceedings of the Twelfth International Conference on* (pp. 115-122). IEEE. doi:10.1109/ICDE.1996.492095

Haveliwala, T. H. (2002). Topic-sensitive PageRank.*Proceedings of the 11th International Conference on World Wide Web,*517–526.

Hawalah, A., & Fasli, M. (2011). A multi-agent system using ontological user profiles for dynamic user modelling.*Proceedings of International Conferences on Web Intelligence and Intelligent Agent Technology*, 430-437. doi:10.1109/WI-IAT.2011.76

Heflin, J. (2016). *An Introduction to the OWL Web Ontology Language*. Lehigh University.

Heflin, J., Hendler, J., & Luke, S. (1999). *SHOE: A knowledge representation language for internet applications. Technical CS-TR-4078*. Institute for Advanced Computer Studies, University of Maryland.

Hemalatha, et al. (n.d.). *A Computational Model for Texture Analysis in Images with Fractional Differential Filter for Texture Detection*. IGI Global.

Henikoff, J. G., & Henikoff, S. (1996). Blocks database and its applications. *Methods in Enzymology*, *266*, 88–105. doi:10.1016/S0076-6879(96)66008-X PMID:8743679

Hepp, M., Leymann, F., Domingue, J., Wahler, A., & Fensel, D. (2005). *Semantic business process management: A vision towards using semantic web services for business process management*. Paper presented at the e-Business Engineering, 2005. ICEBE 2005. IEEE International Conference on. doi:10.1109/ICEBE.2005.110

Hert, M., Reif, G., & Gall, H. C. (2011). A comparison of RDB-to-RDF mapping languages.*Proceedings of the 7th International Conference on Semantic Systems*.

Hewitt, C., Bishop, P., & Steiger, R. (1973, August). A universal modular actor formalism for artificial intelligence. In *Proceedings of the 3rd international joint conference on Artificial intelligence* (pp. 235-245). Morgan Kaufmann Publishers Inc.

Hiemstra, D., Arjen, P., & Vries, D. (2000). Relating the new languagemodels of information retrieval to the traditional retrieval models. CTIT technical report TR-CTIT.

Hinkelmann, K., Thönssen, B., & Wolff, D. (2010). Ontologies for E-government. In *Theory and applications of ontology: Computer applications* (pp. 429–462). Springer Netherlands. doi:10.1007/978-90-481-8847-5_19

Hipp, J., Güntzer, U., & Nakhaeizadeh, G. (2000). Algorithms for association rule mining—a general survey and comparison. *ACM SIGKDD Explorations Newsletter, 2*(1), 58-64.

Hollink, L., Schreiber, G., Wielemaker, J., & Wielinga, B. (2003, October). Semantic annotation of image collections. In Knowledge capture (Vol. 2). Academic Press.

Hoppe, A. (2013). Automatic ontology based user profile learning from heterogeneous web resources in a big data context.*Proceedings of the VLDB Endowment*, 6(12), 1428-1433. doi:10.14778/2536274.2536330

Hotho, A., Staab, S., & Stumme, G. (2003, November). Ontologies improve text document clustering. In *Data Mining, 2003. ICDM 2003. Third IEEE International Conference on* (pp. 541-544). IEEE. doi:10.1109/ICDM.2003.1250972

Huai, Y., Lee, R., Zhang, S., Xia, C. H., & Zhang, X. (2011) DOT: a matrix model for analyzing, optimizing and deploying software for big data analytics in distributed systems.*ACM Symposium on Cloud Computing*, 1-14. doi:10.1145/2038916.2038920

Huala, E., Dickerman, A. W., Garcia-Hernandez, M., Weems, D., Reiser, L., LaFond, F., & Rhee, S. Y. et al. (2001). The Arabidopsis Information Resource (TAIR): A comprehensive database and web-based information retrieval, analysis, and visualization system for a model plant. *Nucleic Acids Research*, *29*(1), 102–105. doi:10.1093/nar/29.1.102 PMID:11125061

Huerta-Cepas, J., Bueno, A., Dopazo, J., & Gabaldón, T. (2008). PhylomeDB: A database for genome-wide collections of gene phylogenies. *Nucleic Acids Research*, *36*(Database issue), D491–D496. PMID:17962297

Huerta-Cepas, J., Capella-Gutierrez, S., Pryszcz, L. P., Denisov, I., Kormes, D., Marcet-Houben, M., & Gabaldon, T. (2011). PhylomeDB v3.0: An expanding repository of genome-wide collections of trees, alignments and phylogeny-based orthology and paralogy predictions. *Nucleic Acids Research*, *39*(Database issue), D556–D560. doi:10.1093/nar/gkq1109 PMID:21075798

Huerta-Cepas, J., Capella-Gutiérrez, S., Pryszcz, L. P., Marcet-Houben, M., & Gabaldón, T. (2014). PhylomeDB v4: Zooming into the plurality of evolutionary histories of a genome. *Nucleic Acids Research*, *42*(Database issue), D897–D902. doi:10.1093/nar/gkt1177 PMID:24275491

Huerta-Cepas, J., Dopazo, H., Dopazo, J., & Gabaldón, T. (2007). The original phylogenetic pipeline used to reconstruct phylomes is described in: The human phylome. *Genome Biology*, *8*(6), R109. PMID:17567924

Iahad, M., & Huspi. (2012). A blended community of inquiry approach: The usage of social network as a support for Course Management System.*International Conference on Computer & Information Science (ICCIS)*, 180-183.

Jain, A. K., Murty, M. N., & Flynn, P. J. (1999). Data clustering: A review. *ACM Computing Surveys, 31*(3), 264–323. doi:10.1145/331499.331504

Jianmin, X., & Chang, L. (2012). Personalized Query Expansion Based on User Interest and Domain Knowledge. *Proceedings of Third Global Congress on Intelligent Systems (GCIS)*. doi:10.1109/GCIS.2012.70

Junco, R. (2013). Inequalities in Facebook use. *Computers in Human Behavior, 29*(6), 2328–2336. doi:10.1016/j.chb.2013.05.005

Juneja, D., Jagga, A., & Singh, A. (2015). A review of FIPA standardized agent communication language and interaction protocols. *Journal of Network Communications and Emerging Technologies, 5*(2), 179-191.

Juneja, D., Singh, A., Singh, R., & Mukherjee, S. (2016). A thorough insight into theoretical and practical developments in multiagent systems. International Journal of Ambient Computing and Intelligence.

Juneja, D., Singh, A., & Jagga, A. (2015, April). Knowledge Query Manipulation Language (KQML): Recap. *IFRSA's International Journal of Computing, 5*(2), 54–62.

Kabilan, M. K., Ahmad, N., & Abidin, M. J. Z. (2010). Facebook: An online environment for learning of English in institutions of higher education? *The Internet and Higher Education, 13*(4), 179–187. doi:10.1016/j.iheduc.2010.07.003

Kalin, J. (2012). Doing what comes naturally? Students perceptions and use of collaborative technologies. *Int. J. Scholarship Teach. Learn., 6*(1), 1–21.

Kamal, Dey, Ashour, & Balas. (2016). FbMapping: An Automated System for Monitoring Facebook Data. *Neural Network World.*

Kamal, S., Ripon, S. H., Dey, N., Ashour, A. S., & Santhi, V. (2016). A MapReduce approach to diminish imbalance parameters for big deoxyribonucleic acid dataset. *Computer Methods and Programs in Biomedicine, 131*, 191–206. doi:10.1016/j.cmpb.2016.04.005 PMID:27265059

Kantardzic, M. (2011). *Data mining: concepts, models, methods, and algorithms*. John Wiley & Sons. doi:10.1002/9781118029145

Kärkkäinen, H., Jussila, J., & Väisänen, J. (2010). Social media use and potential in business-to-business companies' innovation. In *Proceedings of the 14th international academic mindtrek conference: Envisioning future media environments* (pp. 228-236). ACM.

Kausar, N., Palaniappan, S., Samir, B. B., Abdullah, A., & Dey, N. (2016). Systematic Analysis of Applied Data Mining Based Optimization Algorithms in Clinical Attribute Extraction and Classification for Diagnosis of Cardiac Patients, Applications of Intelligent Optimization in Biology and Medicine Volume 96 of the series Intelligent Systems. *The Reference Librarian*, 217–231.

Kaya, M., & Alhajj, R. (2005). Genetic algorithm based framework for mining fuzzy association rules. *Fuzzy Sets and Systems*, *152*(3), 587–601. doi:10.1016/j.fss.2004.09.014

Keim, D. A. (2002). Information visualization and visual data mining. *IEEE Transactions on Visualization and Computer Graphics*, *8*(1), 1–8. doi:10.1109/2945.981847

Kekre, D. H., Thepade, S. D., Mukherjee, P., Wadhwa, S., Kakaiya, M., & Singh, S. (2010). Image retrieval with shape features extracted using gradient operators and slope magnitude technique with BTC. *International Journal of Computers and Applications*, *6*(8), 28–33. doi:10.5120/1094-1430

Kelly, D., & Teevan, J. (2003). Implicit feedback for inferring user preference: a bibliography. *ACM SIGIR Forum, 37*(2), 18-28.

Kelly, J., Vellante, D., & Floyer, D. (2014). *Big data market size and vendor revenues, Wikibon, Technical Report*. Retrieved November 1, 2016, from http://wikibon.org/wiki/v/Big_Data_Market_Size_and_Vendor_Revenues

Kitchin, R. (2014). The real-time city? Big data and smart urbanism. *GeoJournal*, *79*(1), 1–14. doi:10.1007/s10708-013-9516-8

Klösgen, W., & Zytkow, J. M. (2002). *Handbook of data mining and knowledge discovery*. Oxford University Press, Inc.

Kodi, T., Kumari, G. R. N., & Perumal, S. M. (2016). Review of CBIR Related with Low Level and High Level Features. *International Journal of Synthetic Emotions*, *7*(1), 27–40. doi:10.4018/IJSE.2016010103

Kohavi, R., & Tesler, J. D. (2001). *Method, system, and computer program product for visualizing a decision-tree classifier*. U.S. Patent No. 6,278,464. Washington, DC: U.S. Patent and Trademark Office.

Kolesnikov, N., Hastings, E., Keays, M., Melnichuk, O., Tang, Y. A., Williams, E., & Brazma, A. et al. (2015). ArrayExpress update—simplifying data submissions. *Nucleic Acids Research*, *43*(Database issue), D1113–D1116. doi:10.1093/nar/gku1057 PMID:25361974

Kollios, G., Gunopulos, D., Koudas, N., & Berchtold, S. (2003). Efficient biased sampling for approximate clustering and outlier detection in large data sets. *IEEE Transactions on Knowledge and Data Engineering*, *15*(5), 70–87. doi:10.1109/TKDE.2003.1232271

Koubarakis, M., Skiadopoulos, S., & Tryfonopoulos, C. (2006, December). Logic And Computational Complexity For Boolean Information Retrieval. *IEEE Transactions on Knowledge and Data Engineering*, *18*(12), 1659–1665. doi:10.1109/TKDE.2006.193

Krishna, K., & Murty, M. N. (1999). Genetic k-means algorithm. *IEEE Transactions on Systems, Man, and Cybernetics. Part B, Cybernetics*, *29*(3), 433–441. doi:10.1109/3477.764879 PMID:18252317

Krishnaswamy, C. R., Gilbert, E. W., & Pashley, M. M. (2000). Neural network applications in finance: A practical introduction. *Financial Practice and Education*, *10*, 75–84.

Ku Mahamud, K. R. (2013). Big data clustering using grid computing and ant-based algorithm.*International Conference on Computing and Informatics*, 6–14.

Kurgan, L. A., & Musilek, P. (2006). A survey of Knowledge Discovery and Data Mining process models. *The Knowledge Engineering Review*, *21*(01), 1–24. doi:10.1017/S0269888906000737

Lal, S. B., Pandey, P. K., Rai, P. K., Rai, A., Sharma, A., & Chaturvedi, K. K. (2013). Design and development of portal for biological database in agriculture. *Bioinformation*, *9*(11), 588–598. doi:10.6026/97320630009588 PMID:23888101

Laney, D. (2001). *3D data management: controlling data volume, velocity, and variety, META Group, Technical Report*. Retrieved November 1, 2016, from http://blogs.gartner.com/doug-laney/files/2012/01/ad949-3D-Data-Management-Controlling-Data-Volume-Velocity-and-Variety.pdf

Laskov, P., Gehl, C., Kruger, S., & Müller, K. R. (2006). Incremental support vector learning: Analysis, implementation and applications. *Journal of Machine Learning Research*, *7*, 19–36.

Lawrence, S., & Giles, C. L. (2000). Accessibility of information on the Web. *Intelligence*, *11*(1), 32–39. doi:10.1145/333175.333181

Le, D. N., Dey, N., & Nguyen, G. N. (2017). Machine Learning In Medical Imaging And Health Informatics. *Journal of Medical Imaging and Health Informatics*.

Lee,, T. B., Hendler, J., & Lassila, C. (2001). The Semantic Web. *Scientific American, 5*(1), 36.

Lee, M., & Kim, W. (2009). Semantic Association Search and Rank Method based on Spreading Activation for the Semantic Web. *Proceedings of the 2009 IEEE IEEM*, 1523-1527. doi:10.1109/IEEM.2009.5373086

Lefranc, M. P. (2001). IMGT, the international ImMunoGeneTics database. *Nucleic Acids Research, 29*(1), 207–209. doi:10.1093/nar/29.1.207 PMID:11125093

Lemos, M. (2004). *Workflow para bioinformatica* (Ph.D. Thesis). Programa de Pos-Graduacao em Informatica, Pontificia Universidade Catolica do Rio deJaneiro, Rio de Janeiro, Brazil. (in Portuguese)

Lempel, R., & Moran, S. (2000). The stochastic approach for link-structure analysis (SALSA) and the TKC Effect.*Proceedings of 9th International World Wide Web Conference*, 387-401. doi:10.1016/S1389-1286(00)00034-7

Lenhart, A., Madden, M., Macgill, A. R., & Smith, A. (2007). *Teens and social media. Pew Internet and American Life Project.* Retrieved August 2012 from http://www.pewinternet.org/Reports/2007/Teensand-Social-Media.aspx

Lent, B., Swami, A., & Widom, J. (1997, April). Clustering association rules. In *Data Engineering, 1997. Proceedings. 13th International Conference on* (pp. 220-231). IEEE. doi:10.1109/ICDE.1997.581756

Leung, K. W., Ng, W., & Lee, D. L. (2008). Personalized concept-based clustering of search engine queries. *IEEE Transactions on Knowledge and Data Engineering, 20*(11), 1505–1518. doi:10.1109/TKDE.2008.84

Li, W., Han, J., & Pei, J. (2001). CMAR: Accurate and efficient classification based on multiple class-association rules. In Data Mining, 2001. *ICDM 2001,Proceedings IEEE International Conference on* (pp. 369-376). IEEE.

Lieberman, H., & Liu, H. (2002, May). Adaptive linking between text and photos using common sense reasoning. In *International Conference on Adaptive Hypermedia and Adaptive Web-Based Systems* (pp. 2-11). Springer Berlin Heidelberg. doi:10.1007/3-540-47952-X_2

Lieberman, H., Rozenweig, E., & Singh, P. (2001). Aria: An agent for annotating and retrieving images. *Computer, 34*(7), 57–62. doi:10.1109/2.933504

Li, L., Yang, Z., Wang, B., & Kitsuregawa, M. (2007). Dynamic adaptation strategies for long-term and short-term user profile to personalize search. In G. Dong, X. Lin, W. Wang, Y. Yang, & J. X. Yu (Eds.), *Advances in Data and Web Management. Springer Berlin Heidelberg: LNCS 4505* (pp. 228–240). doi:10.1007/978-3-540-72524-4_26

Lin, M. Y., Lee, P. Y., & Hsueh, S. C. (2012). Apriori-based frequent item set mining algorithms on map reduce.*International Conference on Ubiquitous Information Management and Communication*, 76:1–76:8.

Li, T., Li, Q., Zhu, S., & Ogihara, M. (2002). A survey on wavelet applications in data mining. *ACM SIGKDD Explorations Newsletter*, *4*(2), 49–68. doi:10.1145/772862.772870

Liu, H., Sun, J., & Zhang, H. (2009). Post-processing for rule reduction using closed set. *Post-Mining of Association Rules: Techniques for Effective Knowledge Extraction*, 81-99.

Liu, B., Hsu, W., & Ma, Y. (1999, August). Pruning and summarizing the discovered associations. In *Proceedings of the fifth ACM SIGKDD international conference on Knowledge discovery and data mining* (pp. 125-134). ACM. doi:10.1145/312129.312216

Liu, S., Cui, W., Wu, Y., & Liu, M. (2014). A survey on information visualization: Recent advances and challenges. *The Visual Computer, 30*(12), 1373–1393. doi:10.1007/s00371-013-0892-3

Ludäscher, B., Altintas, I., Berkley, C., Higgins, D., Jaeger, E., Jones, M., & Zhao, Y. et al. (2005). Scientific workflow management and the Kepler system. *Concurr Comput Pract Exp*, *18*(10), 1039–1065. doi:10.1002/cpe.994

Lyman, P., & Varian, H. (2002). *How much information 2003?* Technical Report. Retrieved November 1, 2016, from http://www2.sims.berkeley.edu/research/projects/how-much-info-2003/printable_report.pdf

Manning, Raghavan, & Schütze. (2008). Introduction to Information Retrieval. Cambridge University Press.

Manola, F., Miller, E., & McBride, B. (2004). RDF primer. *W3C recommendation, 10*(1-107), 6.

Manola, F., Miller, E., & McBride, B. (2004). RDF primer. *W3C Recommendation, 10*, 1-107.

Mariscal, G., Marban, O., & Fernandez, C. (2010). A survey of data mining and knowledge discovery process models and methodologies. *The Knowledge Engineering Review*, *25*(02), 137–166. doi:10.1017/S0269888910000032

Markkula, M., & Sormunen, E. (2000). End-user searching challenges indexing practices in the digital newspaper photo archive. *Information Retrieval*, *1*(4), 259–285. doi:10.1023/A:1009995816485

Martens, W., Neven, F., Schwentick, T., & Bex, G. J. (2006). Expressiveness and complexity of XML Schema. *ACM Transactions on Database Systems*, *31*(3), 770–813. doi:10.1145/1166074.1166076

Matheus, C., Piatetsky-Shapiro, G., & McNeill, D. (1996). Selecting and Reporting What is Interesting: The KEFIR Application to Healthcare Data. In *AKDDM*. Cambridge, MA: AAAI/MIT Press.

Matos, E. E., Campos, F., Braga, R., & Palazzi, D. (2009). CelOWS: An ontology based framework for the provision of semantic web services related to biological models. *Journal of Biomedical Informatics*, *43*(1), 125–136. doi:10.1016/j.jbi.2009.08.008 PMID:19695346

Matthias, K., & Gerber, A. (2006). Fast composition planning of owl-s services and application. In *Web Services, ECOWS'06.4th European Conference on*. IEEE.

Ma, W. Y., & Manjunath, B. S. (1995, October). A comparison of wavelet transform features for texture image annotation. In *Proceedings of the 1995 International Conference on Image Processing* (Vol. 2). IEEE Computer Society. doi:10.1109/ICIP.1995.537463

Mazer, J. P., Murphy, R. E., & Simonds, C. J. (2007). Ill see you on Facebook: The effects of computer-mediated teacher self-disclosure on student motivation, affective learning, and classroom climate. *Communication Education*, *56*(1), 1–17. doi:10.1080/03634520601009710

Mazman, S. G., & Usluel, Y. K. (2010). Modeling educational usage of Facebook. *Computers & Education*, *55*(2), 444–453. doi:10.1016/j.compedu.2010.02.008

McCallum, A., & Nigam, K. (1998). A comparison of event models for naive Bayes text classification.*National Conference on Artificial Intelligence*, 41–48.

McWilliam, H., Li, W., Uludag, M., Squizzato, S., Park, Y. M., Buso, N., Cowley, A. P., & Lopez, R. (2013). Analysis Tool Web Services from the EMBL-EBI. *Nucleic Acids Research*, 1-4. doi:.10.1093/nar/gkt376

Meier, R., & Lee, D. (2009). Context-Aware Services for Ambient Environments (2009). *International Journal of Ambient Computing and Intelligence*, *1*(1), 1–14. doi:10.4018/jaci.2009010101

Mell, P., & Grance, T. (2009). *The NIST definition of cloud computing*. Retrieved from http://www.nist.gov/itl/cloud/upload/cloud-def-v15.pdf

Michael, S. L., Huijsmans, D. P., & Denteneer, D. (1996). *Content based image retrieval: KLT, projections, or templates*. Amsterdam University Press.

Middleton, S. E., Shadbolt, N. R., & Roure, D. C. D. (2004). Ontological user profiling in recommender systems. *ACM Transactions on Information Systems*, *22*(1), 54–88. doi:10.1145/963770.963773

Milojicic, D. (2000). Agent systems and applications. *IEEE Concurrency*, *8*(2), 22–23. doi:10.1109/MCC.2000.846190

Minio, M., & Tasso, C. (1996). User Modeling for Information Filtering on INTERNET Services: Exploiting an Extended Version of the UMT Shell.*Proceedings of UM96 Workshop on User Modeling for Information Filtering on the WWW.*

Moawad, I. F., Talha, H., Hosny, E., & Hashim, M. (2012). Agent-based web search personalization approach using dynamic user profile. *Egyptian Informatics Journal*, *13*(3), 191–198. doi:10.1016/j.eij.2012.09.002

Mokhtar, S. B., Raverrdy, P. G., Urbieta, A., & Cardoso, R. S. (2008). Interoperable Semantic and Syntactic Service for Ambient Computing Environment. Proceeding of Adhoc AMC.

Moukas, A. (1997). Amalthaea: Information Discovery and Filtering Using a Multiagent Evolving Ecosystem. *Applied Artificial Intelligence*, *11*(5), 437–457. doi:10.1080/088395197118127

Mukherjea, S., Hirata, K., & Hara, Y. (1997). Towards a multimedia world-wide web information retrieval engine. *Proceedings of the 6th International World-Wide Web Conference*, 177-188. doi:10.1016/S0169-7552(97)00046-9

Munk, C., Isberg, V., Mordalski, S., Harpsøe, K., Rataj, K., Hauser, A. S., ... Gloriam, D. E. (2016). GPCRdb: The G protein-coupled receptor database – an introduction. *Br J Pharmacol., 173*(14), 2195-207. doi: 10.1111/bph.13509

Murthy, S. K. (1998). Automatic construction of decision trees from data: A multi-disciplinary survey. *Data Mining and Knowledge Discovery*, *2*(4), 345–389. doi:10.1023/A:1009744630224

Nastar, C., Mitschke, M., Meilhac, C., & Boujemaa, N. (1998). A flexible content-based image retrieval system. Proceedings of the ACM International Multimedia Conference, 339–344.

Newsam, S., Sumengen, B., & Manjunath, B. S. (2001). Category-based image retrieval. In *Image Processing, 2001. Proceedings. 2001 International Conference on* (Vol. 3, pp. 596-599). IEEE. doi:10.1109/ICIP.2001.958189

Nie. (2010). *Cross-Language Information Retrieval*. Morgan & Claypool Publishers.

Noy, N. F., Crubezy, M., & Fergerson, R. W. (2003). Protege-2000: an open-source ontology-development and knowledge-acquisition environment.*Proceedings of AMIA Annu. Symp.*, 953.

Noy, N. F., Shah, N. H., Whetzel, P. L., Dai, B., Dorf, M., Griffith, N., & Musen, M. A. (2009). BioPortal: Ontologies and integrated data resources at the click of a mouse. *Nucleic Acids Research*, *37*(suppl 2), W170–W173. doi:10.1093/nar/gkp440 PMID:19483092

Nwana, H. S. (1996). Software agents: An overview. *The Knowledge Engineering Review*, *11*(03), 205–244. doi:10.1017/S026988890000789X

O'Neill, S., & Curran, K. (2013). The Core Aspects of Search Engine Optimisation Necessary to Move up the Ranking. In K. Curran (Ed.), Pervasive and Ubiquitous Technology Innovations for Ambient Intelligence Environments (pp. 243-251). Hershey, PA: Information Science Reference. doi:10.4018/978-1-4666-2041-4.ch022

Odella, F. (2016). Technology Studies and the Sociological Debate on Monitoring of Social Interactions. *International Journal of Ambient Computing and Intelligence*, *7*(1), 411–423. doi:10.4018/IJACI.2016010101

Oinn, T., Addis, M., Ferris, J., Marvin, D., Senger, M., Greenwood, M., & Li, P. et al. (2004). Taverna: A tool for the composition and enactment of bioinformatics workflows. *Bioinformatics (Oxford, England)*, *20*(17), 3045–3054. doi:10.1093/bioinformatics/bth361 PMID:15201187

ONeill, S., & Curran, K. (2011). The core aspects of search engine optimisation necessary to move up the ranking. *International Journal of Ambient Computing and Intelligence*, *3*(4), 62–70. doi:10.4018/jaci.2011100105

OWL-S Working Group. (2006). *OWL-S 1.2 Pre-Release*. Retrieved from http://www.ai.sri.com/ daml/services/owl-s/1.2/

Paha, I. N., Gulati, P., & Gupta, P. (2009). Ontology Driven Conjunctive Query Expansion based on Mining User Logs. *International Conference on Methods and Models in Computer Science*. doi:10.1109/ICM2CS.2009.5397960

Parastatidis, S. (2009). A Platform for All That We Know: Creating a Knowledge-Driven Research Infrastructure. In The Fourth Paradigm: Data Intensive Scientific Discovery. Academic Press.

Pasquier, N. (2009). Frequent closed itemsets based condensed representations for association rules. *Post-Mining of Association Rules: Techniques for Effective Knowledge Extraction*, 246-271.

Payne, W. E., & Garrels, J. I. (1997). Yeast Protein database (YPD): A database for the complete proteome of Saccharomyces cerevisiae. *Nucleic Acids Research*, *25*(1), 57–62. doi:10.1093/nar/25.1.57 PMID:9016505

Piatetsky-Shapiro, G. (1996). *Advances in knowledge discovery and data mining* (U. M. Fayyad, P. Smyth, & R. Uthurusamy, Eds.). Menlo Park, CA: AAAI press.

PigMix. (2015). Retrieved November 1st 2016 from https://cwiki.apache.org/confluence/display/PIG/PigMix

Pignotti, E., Edwards, P., Preece, A., Gotts, N., & Polhill, G. (2008). Enhancing workflow with a semantic description of scientific intent. *5th European Semantic Web Conference*, Tenerife, Spain. doi:10.1007/978-3-540-68234-9_47

Pillai, S., Silventoinen, V., Kallio, K., Senger, M., Sobhany, S., Tate, J., ... Lopez, R. (2005). SOAP-based services provided by the European Bioinformatics Institute. *Nucleic Acids Research, 33*, W25–W28. http://doi.org/<ALIGNMENT.qj></ALIGNMENT>10.1093/nar/gki491

Preethi, N., & Devi, T. (2013). New Integrated Case And Relation Based (CARE) Page Rank Algorithm. *International Conference on Computer Communication and Informatics (ICCCI)*. doi:10.1109/ICCCI.2013.6466260

Press, G. (2013). *$16.1 billion big data market: 2015 predictions from IDC and IIA, Forbes, Technical Report*. Retrieved November 1, 2016, from http://www.forbes.com/sites/ gilpress/2013/12/12/16-1-billion-big-data-market-2015-predictions-from-idc-and-iia/

Qiu, F., & Cho, J. (2006). Automatic identification of user interest for personalized search.*Proceedings of WWW*, 727-736. doi:10.1145/1135777.1135883

Quinn, D., Chen, L., & Mulvenna, M. (2012). Social Network Analysis-A Survey. *International Journal of Ambient Computing and Intelligence*, *4*(3), 46–58. doi:10.4018/jaci.2012070104

Ravindran, N., Liang, Y., & Liang, X. (2010). A labeled-tree approach to semantic and structural data interoperability applied in hydrology domain. *Information Sciences*, *180*(24), 5008–5028. doi:10.1016/j.ins.2010.06.015

Ravindra, P., & Anyanwu, K. (2014). Nesting Strategies for Enabling Nimble MapReduce Dataflows for Large RDF Data. *International Journal on Semantic Web and Information Systems*, *10*(1), 1–26. doi:10.4018/ijswis.2014010101

Razmerita, L., Angehrn, A., & Maedche, A. (2003). Ontology based user modeling for knowledge management systems. In *Proceedings of the 9th International Conference on User Modeling* (pp. 213–217). Springer-Verlag. doi:10.1007/3-540-44963-9_29

Reid, I. N., Brewer, C., Brucato, R. J., McKinley, W. R., Maury, A., Mendenhall, D., & Sargent, W. L. W. et al. (1991). The second palomar sky survey. *Publications of the Astronomical Society of the Pacific*, *103*(665), 661. doi:10.1086/132866

Remco, C. V., & Tanase, M. (2000). *Content-based image retrieval systems: A survey.* Technical Report UU-CS-2000-34, Utrecht University, Department of Computer Science.

Rennolls, K., & Al-Shawabkeh, A. (2008). Formal structures for data mining, knowledge discovery and communication in a knowledge management environment. *Intelligent Data Analysis*, *12*(2), 147–163.

Richardson, M., & Domingos, P. (2002). Advances in Neural Information Processing Systems: Vol. 14. *The Intelligent Surfer: Probabilistic Combination of Link and Content Information in PageRank*. MIT Press.

Rijsbergen, C. V. (1979). *Information Retrieval*. London: Butterworths.

Rocchio, J. J. (2010). *Relevance feedback in information*. The SMART Retrieval System, Experiments in Automatic Document Processing.

Rodgers, C. R., & Raider-Roth, M. B. (2006). Presence in teaching. Teachers and Teaching. *Theory into Practice*, *12*, 265–287.

Rui, Y., Huang, T. S., & Chang, S. F. (1999). Image retrieval: Current techniques, promising directions, and open issues. *Journal of Visual Communication and Image Representation*, *10*(1), 39–62. doi:10.1006/jvci.1999.0413

Russell, S. J., & Norvig, P. (2016). *Artificial Intelligence – A Modern Approach*. PHI.

Russom, P. (2011). *Big data analytics*. TDWI: Technical Report.

Rusu, O., Halcu, I., Grigoriu, O., Neculoiu, G., Sandulescu, V., Marinescu, M., & Marinescu, V. (2013). *Converting unstructured and semi-structured data into knowledge*. Paper presented at the Roedunet International Conference (RoEduNet), 2013 11th. doi:10.1109/RoEduNet.2013.6511736

Safarkhani, B., Mohsenzadeh, T. M., & Mojde, M. M. R. (2009). Deriving semantic sessions from semantic clusters. *Proceedings of International Conference on Information Management and Engineering*, 523-528. doi:10.1109/ICIME.2009.131

Sagayam, R., Srinivasan, S., & Roshni, S. (2012). A Survey of Text Mining:Retrieval, Extraction and Indexing Techniques. *IJCER*, *2*(5), 1443–1444.

Sagiroglu, S., & Sinanc, D. (2013). Big data: a review.*International Conference on Collaboration Technologies and Systems*, 42–47.

Sahoo, S. S., Halb, W., Hellmann, S., Idehen, K., Thibodeau Jr, T., Auer, S., . . . Ezzat, A. (2009). *A survey of current approaches for mapping of relational databases to rdf.* W3C RDB2RDF Incubator Group Report.

Saletore, V., Krishnan, K., Viswanathan, V., & Tolentino, M. (2014). *HcBench: Methodology, development, and full-system char- termination of a customer usage representative big data Hadoop benchmark*. Advancing Big Data Benchmarks.

Salton & McGill. (1986). Introduction to Modern Information Retrieval. McGraw-Hill, Inc.

Salton, G., & Buckley, C. (1998). Term weighting approaches in automatic text retrieval. *Information Processing & Management*, *24*(5), 513–523. doi:10.1016/0306-4573(88)90021-0

Salton, G., & McGill, M. (1983). *Introduction to Modern Information Retrieval*. McGraw-Hill.

Sambyal, , & Abrol, P. (2016). Feature based Text Extraction System using Connected Component Method. *International Journal of Synthetic Emotions*, *7*(1), 41–57. doi:10.4018/IJSE.2016010104

Sanger, F. (1988). Sequences, sequences, and sequences. *Annual Review of Biochemistry, 57*(1), 1–28. doi:10.1146/annurev.bi.57.070188.000245 PMID:2460023

Santofimia, M., Toro, X., & Villanueva, F. (2012). A Rule-Based Approach to Automatic Service Composition. *International Journal of Ambient Computing and Intelligence, 4*(1), 16–28. doi:10.4018/jaci.2012010102

Satyanarayana, A. (2014) Intelligent sampling for big data using bootstrap sampling and Chebyshev inequality.*IEEE Canadian Conference on Electrical and Computer Engineering*, 1–6. doi:10.1109/CCECE.2014.6901029

Schaller, A., Mueller, K., & Sung, B. (2008), Motorola's experiences in designing the Internet of Things. *Adjunct proceedings of the first international conference on the Internet of Things, Social-IoT Workshop 2008*, 82-85.

Schema-cache. (2010). Retrieved from http://schemacache.test.talis.com/

Schreiber, A. T., Dubbeldam, B., Wielemaker, J., & Wielinga, B. (2001). Ontology-based photo annotation. *IEEE Intelligent Systems, 16*(3), 66–74. doi:10.1109/5254.940028

Schuler, G. D., Epstein, J. A., Ohkawa, H., & Kans, J. A. (1996). Entrez: Molecular biology database and retrieval systems. In Methods in Enzymology. San Diego, CA: Academic Press.

Seetha, M., Muralikrishna, I. V., Deekshatulu, B. L., Malleswari, B. L., & Hegde, P. (2008). Artificial neural networks and other methods of image classification. *Journal of Theoretical & Applied Information Technology, 4*(11).

Selwyn, N. (2009). Faceworking: Exploring students education-related use of Facebook. *Learning, Media and Technology, 34*(2), 157–174. doi:10.1080/17439880902923622

Senator, T. E., Goldberg, H. G., Wooton, J., Cottini, M. A., Khan, A. U., Klinger, C. D., & Wong, R. W. et al. (1995). Financial Crimes Enforcement Network AI System (FAIS) Identifying Potential Money Laundering from Reports of Large Cash Transactions. *AI Magazine, 16*(4), 21.

Shadbolt, N., Hall, W., & Lee, T. B. (2006). The semantic web revisited. *IEEE Intelligent Systems, 21*(3), 96–101. doi:10.1109/MIS.2006.62

Shah, A., Adeniyi, J., & Al Tuwairqi, T. (2005). *An Algorithm for Transforming XML Documents Schema into Relational Database Schema. In Transformation of knowledge, information and data: theory and applications* (pp. 171–189). Idea Group Publishing. doi:10.4018/978-1-59140-527-6.ch008

Shapley, K. S., Sheehan, D., Maloney, C., & Caranikas-Walker, F. (2010). Evaluating the implementation fidelity of technology immersion and its relationship with student achievement. *The Journal of Technology, Learning, and Assessment*, *9*(4).

Sharma, A. K., & Juneja, D. (2006). BDI-based architecture of intelligent agents. *Proceedings of National Seminar on Emerging Trends in Network Technologies held at Career Institute of Technology and Management.*

Sharma, A., Rai, A., & Lal, S. (2013). Workflow management systems for gene sequence analysis and evolutionary studies – A Review. *Bioinformation*, *9*(13), 663–672. doi:10.6026/97320630009663 PMID:23930017

Shearer, C. (2000). The CRISP-DM model: The new blueprint for data mining. *Journal of Data Warehousing*, *5*(4), 13–22.

Shi, J., & Malik, J. (2000). Normalized cuts and image segmentation. *IEEE Transactions on Pattern Analysis and Machine Intelligence*, *22*(8), 888–905. doi:10.1109/34.868688

Shin, D., Lee, K., & Suba, T. (2009). Automated generation of composite Web services based on functional semantics. *Journal of Web Semantics*, *7*(4), 332–343. doi:10.1016/j.websem.2009.05.001

Shirkhorshidi, A. S., Aghabozorgi, S. R., Teh, Y. W., & Herawan, T. (2014). Big data clustering: a review.*International Conference on Computational Science and Its Applications*, 707–720.

Sieg, A., Mobasher, B., & Burke, R. (2007). Ontological user profiles for personalized web search. American Association for Artificial Intelligence, 84-91.

Sieg, A., Mobasher, B., & Burke, R. (2007). Learning ontology-based user profiles: A semantic approach to personalized web search. *IEEE Intelligent Informatics Bulletin*, *8*(1), 7–18.

Simon, P., Carles, S., & Nick, J. (1998). Agents that reason and negotiate by arguing. *J Logic Comput*, *8*(3), 261–292. doi:10.1093/logcom/8.3.261

Singh, A., Anand, P. (2013). State of Art in Ontology Development Tools. *International Journal of Advances in Computer Science & Technology*, *2*(7), 96-101.

Singh, A., Juneja, D. & Sharma, A.K. (2009). An extensive analysis of implementation issues in semantic web. *International Journal of Information Technology*, *5*(4), 67-74.

Singh, A., Juneja, D., & Sharma, K.A. (2010). General Design Structure of Ontological Databases in Semantic Web. *International Journal of Engineering Science and Technology, 2*(5), 1227-1232.

Singh, B., & Singh, H. K. (2010, December). Web data mining research: a survey. In *Computational Intelligence and Computing Research (ICCIC), 2010 IEEE International Conference on* (pp. 1-10). IEEE. doi:10.1109/ICCIC.2010.5705856

Singh, A., & Alhadidi, B. (2013, August23). Knowledge Oriented Personalized Search Engine: A Step towards Wisdom Web. *International Journal of Computers and Applications*, *76*(8), 1–9. doi:10.5120/13264-0744

Singh, A., & Anand, P. (2013). State of art in ontology development tools. *International Journal of Advances in Computer Science & Technology.*, *2*(7), 96–101.

Singh, A., Juneja, D., & Sharma, A. K. (2010). General design structure of ontological databases in semantic web. *International Journal of Engineering Science and Technology*, *2*(5), 1227–1232.

Singh, A., Juneja, D., & Sharma, K. A. (2011). Design of An Intelligent and Adaptive Mapping Mechanism for Multiagent Interface.*Proceedings of Springer International Conference on High Performance Architecture and Grid Computing (HPAGC'11)*, 373-384. doi:10.1007/978-3-642-22577-2_51

Singh, A., Sharma, A., & Dey, N. (2015). Semantics and Agents Oriented Web Personalization: State of the Art. *International Journal of Service Science, Management, Engineering, and Technology*, *6*(2), 35–49. doi:10.4018/ijssmet.2015040103

Singhai, N., & Shandilya, S. K. (2010). A survey on: Content based image retrieval systems. *International Journal of Computers and Applications*, *4*(2), 22–26. doi:10.5120/802-1139

Sirin, E. (2004). *OWLSAPI*. Retrieved from http://www.mindswap.org/2004/owl-s/api/

Skillen, K. L., Chen, L., Nugent, C. D., Donnelly, M. P., Burns, W., & Solheim, I. (2012). Ontological user profile modeling for context-aware application personalization. In J. Bravo, D. López-de-Ipiña, & F. Moya (Eds.), *Ubiquitous Computing and Ambient Intelligence*. Springer Berlin Heidelberg. doi:10.1007/978-3-642-35377-2_36

Smith, B., Ashburner, M., Rosse, C., Bard, J., Bug, W., Ceusters, W., & Leontis, N. et al. (2007). The OBO Foundry: Coordinated evolution of ontologies to support biomedical data integration. *Nature Biotechnology*, *25*(11), 1251–1255. doi:10.1038/nbt1346 PMID:17989687

Sosnin, P. (n.d.). Precedent-Oriented Approach to Conceptually Experimental Activity in Designing the Software Intensive Systems. *A Computational Model for Texture Analysis in Images with Fractional Differential Filter for Texture Detection*, *7*(1), 69-93.

Sosnovsky, S., & Dicheva, D. (2010). Ontological technologies for user modelling. *Int. J. Metadata. Semantics and Ontologies*, *5*(1), 32–71. doi:10.1504/IJMSO.2010.032649

Spaniol, M. (2014). *A Framework for Temporal Web Analytics*. Université de Caen.

Spanos, D.-E., Stavrou, P., & Mitrou, N. (2012). Bringing relational databases into the semantic web: A survey. *Semantic Web*, *3*(2), 169–209.

Srikant, R., & Agrawal, R. (1996). Mining sequential patterns: generalizations and performance improvements.*International Conference on Extending Database Technology: Advances in Database Technology*, 3–17. doi:10.1007/BFb0014140

Srivastava, J., Cooley, R., Deshpande, M., & Tan, P. N. (2000). Web usage mining: Discovery and applications of usage patterns from web data. *ACM SIGKDD Explorations Newsletter*, *1*(2), 12–23. doi:10.1145/846183.846188

Staab, S., & Studer, R. (Eds.). (2013). *Handbook on ontologies*. Springer Science & Business Media.

Stein, L. D., & Thierry-Mieg, J. (1998). Scriptable Access to the Caenorhabditis elegans Genome Sequence and Other ACEDB Databases. *Genome Research*, *8*(12), 1308–1315. PMID:9872985

Stolorz, P. E., & Dean, C. (1996, August). Quakefinder: A Scalable Data Mining System for Detecting Earthquakes from Space. In KDD (pp. 208-213).

Stolorz, P. E., Nakamura, H., Mesrobian, E., Muntz, R. R., Shek, E. C., Santos, J. R., . . . Farrara, J. D. (1995, August). Fast Spatio-Temporal Data Mining of Large Geophysical Datasets. In KDD (pp. 300-305).

Stretton, O. W. (2002). The First Sequence: Fred Sanger and Insulin Antony. *Genetics*, *162*(2), 527–532. PMID:12399368

Strohbach, M., Ziekow, H., Gazis, V., & Akiva, N. (2015). *Towards a Big Data Analytics Framework for IoT and Smart City Applications. In Modeling and Processing for Next-Generation Big-Data Technologies* (pp. 257–282). Springer.

Strohman, T., Metzler, D., Turtle, H., & Bruce Croft, W. (2005). *Indri: A language model based search engine for complex queries* (extended version). Technical Report IR-407. CIIR, CS Dept., U. of Mass. Amherst.

Stumme, G. (2006). Web Semantics: Science, Services and Agents on the World Wide Web 4. Semantic Web Mining State of the art and future directions, 124–143.

Stumme, G., Hotho, A., & Berendt, B. (2006). Semantic web mining: State of the art and future directions. *Web Semantics: Science, Services, and Agents on the World Wide Web*, *4*(2), 124–143. doi:10.1016/j.websem.2006.02.001

Sugawara, H. (2007). *DDBJ — Website to Deposit, Retrieve and Analyze Sequences and Annotations of Genes and Genomes*. Retrieved December 18, 2016, from http://www.asiabiotech.com/publication/apbn/11/english/preserved-docs/1115/1052_1054.pdf/

Sugiyama, K., Hatano, K., & Yoshikawa, M. (2004). Adaptive web search based on user profile constructed without any effort from users.*Proceedings of 13th International World Wide Web Conference (WWW '04)*, 675-684. doi:10.1145/988672.988764

Sumathi, C. P., Valli, R. P., & Santhanam, T. (2010). Automatic recommendation of web pages in web usage mining. *International Journal on Computer Science and Engineering*, *2*(09), 3046–3052.

Sycara, K. P. (1998). Multi-agent systems. AI Magazine, 79-92.

Taft, D. K. (2013). *Big data market to reach $40 billion by 2018, EWEEK, Technical Report*. Retrieved November 1, 2016, from http://www.eweek.com/database/big-data-market-to-reach-40-billion-by-2018.html

Tamma, V., & Payne, T. R. (2008). Is a semantic web agent a knowledge-savy agent? *IEEE Intelligent Systems*, *23*(4), 82–85. doi:10.1109/MIS.2008.69

Tamura, H., Mori, S., & Yamawaki, T. (1978). Textural features corresponding to visual perception. *IEEE Transactions on Systems, Man, and Cybernetics*, *8*(6), 460–473. doi:10.1109/TSMC.1978.4309999

TAVERNA. (2010). *Taverna Workflow System*. Retrieved from http://www.taverna.org.uk/

Taylor, I. J., Deelman, E., Gannon, D. B., & Shields, M. (2006). *Workflows for e-Science, Scientific Workflows for Grids* (1st ed.). Springer.

Taylor, I., Shields, M., Wang, I., & Harrison, A. (2007). The Triana workflow environment: architecture and applications. In I. Taylor, E. Deelman, D. Gannon, & M. Shields (Eds.), *Workflows for e-Science* (pp. 320–339). New York: Springer. doi:10.1007/978-1-84628-757-2_20

Tekin, C., & van der Schaar, M. (2013). Distributed online big data classification using context information.*Allerton Conference on Communication, Control, and Computing*, 1435–1442. doi:10.1109/Allerton.2013.6736696

The UniProt Consortium. (2008). The Universal Protein Resource (UniProt). *Nucleic Acids Research*, *36*(Database issue), D190–D195. doi:10.1093/nar/gkm895 PMID:18045787

Thomas, E., Pan, J. Z., & Sleeman, D. H. (2007, June). ONTOSEARCH2: Searching Ontologies Semantically. OWLED.

Thusoo, A., Sarma, J. S., Jain, N., Shao, Z., Chakka, P., Anthony, S., & Murthy, R. et al. (2009). Hive: A warehousing solution over a map-reduce framework. *VLDB Endowment*, *2*(2), 172–179.

Thuy, P. T. T., Lee, Y.-K., Lee, S., & Jeong, B.-S. (2007). *Transforming valid XML documents into RDF via RDF schema.* Paper presented at the Next Generation Web Services Practices, 2007. NWeSP 2007. Third International Conference on. doi:10.1109/NWESP.2007.23

Thuy, P. T. T., Lee, Y.-K., Lee, S., & Jeong, B.-S. (2008). *Exploiting XML schema for interpreting XML documents as RDF.* Paper presented at the Services Computing, 2008. SCC'08. IEEE International Conference on. doi:10.1109/SCC.2008.93

Thuy, P. T. T., Lee, Y.-K., & Lee, S. (2009). DTD2OWL: automatic transforming XML documents into OWL ontology.*Proceedings of the 2nd International Conference on Interaction Sciences: Information Technology, Culture and Human.* doi:10.1145/1655925.1655949

Toetenela, L. (2014). Social networking: A collaborative open educational resource. *Computer Assisted Language Learning*, *27*(2), 149–162. doi:10.1080/09588221.2013.818561

Toivonen, H., Klemettinen, M., Ronkainen, P., Hätönen, K., & Mannila, H. (1995). Pruning and grouping discovered association rules. *MLnet Workshop on Statistics, Machine Learning, and Discovery in Databases*, 47-52.

Tomar, D., & Agarwal, S. (2014). A survey on pre-processing and post-processing techniques in data mining. *International Journal of Database Theory & Application, 7*(4), 99–128. doi:10.14257/ijdta.2014.7.4.09

TONES Ontology Repository. (2010). Retrieved from http://owl.cs.manchester.ac.uk/repository/

Trajkova, J., & Gauch, S. (2004). Improving ontology-based user profiles. In *Proceedings of RIAO 2004* (pp. 380-389). University of Avignon.

Valentin, F., Squizzato, S., Goujon, M., McWilliam, H., Paern, J., & Lopez, R. (2010). Fast and efficient searching of biological data resources—using EB-eye. *Briefings in Bioinformatics, 11*(4), 375–384. doi:10.1093/bib/bbp065 PMID:20150321

Van Deursen, D., Poppe, C., Martens, G., Mannens, E., & Walle, R. (2008). *XML to RDF conversion: a generic approach.* Paper presented at the Automated solutions for Cross Media Content and Multi-channel Distribution, 2008. AXMEDIS'08. International Conference on. doi:10.1109/AXMEDIS.2008.17

Vigneshwari, S., & Aramudhan, M. (2012). A novel approach for personalizing the web using user profiling ontologies. *Proceedings of IEEE- Fourth International Conference on Advanced Computing*. doi:10.1109/icoac.2012.6416815

VISTRAILS. (2010). Retrieved from http://www.vistrails.org/index.php/Main_Page

Voss, A., Meer, E. V., & Fergusson, D. (2008). *Research in a connected world.* Retrieved from http://www.lulu.com/product/ebook/research-in-a-connected-world/17375289

Wagner, L., & Agarwala, R. (2013). UniGene. In The NCBI Handbook (2nd ed.). Bethesda, MD: National Center for Biotechnology Information (US). Available from https://www.ncbi.nlm.nih.gov/books/NBK169437/

Walia, E., & Verma, V. (2016). Boosting local texture descriptors with Log-Gabor filters response for improved image retrieval. *International Journal of Multimedia Information Retrieval*, 1-12.

Walia, E., & Verma, V. (2014, July). Wavelet-based Warping Technique for Mobile Devices.*Proceedings of the Third International Conference on Digital Image Processing and Vision (ICDIPV 2014)*, 27-34.

Wang, C., Zhang, L., & Zhang, H. J. (2008, July). Learning to reduce the semantic gap in web image retrieval and annotation. In *Proceedings of the 31st annual international ACM SIGIR conference on Research and development in information retrieval* (pp. 355-362). Singapore:ACM. doi:10.1145/1390334.1390396

Wang, , He, T., Li, Z., Cao, L., Dey, N., Ashour, A. S., & Shi, F. et al. (2016, October). Image Features based Affective Retrieval employing Improved Parameter and Structure Identification of Adaptive Neuro Fuzzy Inference System. *Neural Computing & Applications*. doi:10.1007/s00521-016-2512-4

Westerveld, T. (2000, April). Image retrieval: Content versus context. In *Content-Based Multimedia Information Access* (pp. 276–284). Le Centre De Hautes Etudes Internationales D'informatique Documentaire.

WfMC. (1999). *Workflow management coalition – Terminology and glossary*. Retrieved from http://www.wfmc.org/Download-document/WFMC-TC-1011-Ver-3-Terminology-and-Glossary-English.html

Whitman, M. W., & Mattord, H. J. (2011). *Principles of information security* (International 4th Edition). Thompson Course Technology.

Wiberg, . (2012). *Interaction Per Se: Understanding "The Ambience of Interaction" as Manifested and Situated in Everyday & Ubiquitous IT-Use*. IGI Global. doi:10.4018/978-1-4666-0038-6.ch007

Wirth, R., & Hipp, J. (2000, April). CRISP-DM: Towards a standard process model for data mining. In *Proceedings of the 4th international conference on the practical applications of knowledge discovery and data mining* (pp. 29-39).

Woerndl, W., & Groh, G. (2005). A proposal for an agent-based architecture for context-aware personalization in the semantic web. In *Proceeding of IJCAI Workshop Multi-agent information retrieval and recommender systems*. Edinburg, UK: UK-IJCAI.

Wonner, J., Grosjean, J., Capobianco, A., & Bechmann, D. (2012). Starfish: a selection technique for dense virtual environments.*ACM Symposium on Virtual Reality Software and Technology*, 101–104. doi:10.1145/2407336.2407356

Wooldridge, M., & Jennings, N. (1995). Intelligent agents: Theory and practice. *The Knowledge Engineering Review*, *10*(2), 115–152. doi:10.1017/S0269888900008122

WS-BPEL. (2007). *Web Services Business Process Execution Language Version 2.0*. Retrieved from http://docs.oasis-open.org/wsbpel/2.0/OS/wsbpel-v2.0-OS.html

Wu, C. H., Yeh, L.-S. L., Huang, H., Arminski, L., Castro-Alvear, J., Chen, Y., & Barker, W. C. et al. (2003). The Protein Information Resource. *Nucleic Acids Research*, *31*(1), 345–347. doi:10.1093/nar/gkg040 PMID:12520019

Xiong, J. (2006). *Essential Bioinformatics. Texas A & M University*. doi:10.1017/CBO9780511806087

Xu, H., Li, Z., Guo, S., & Chen, K. (2012). Cloudvista: Interactive and economical visual cluster analysis for big data in the cloud. *VLDB Endowment, 5*(12).

Xu, R., & Wunsch, D. (2009). *Clustering. Hoboken: Wiley-IEEE Press. Ding, C. & He, X (2004). K-means clustering via principal component analysis*. Paper presented at 21st International Conference on Machine Learning, Canada.

Xue, Z., Shen, G., Li, J., Xu, Q., Zhang, Y., & Shao, J. (2012). Compression-aware I/O performance analysis for big data clustering.*International Workshop on Big Data, Streams and Heterogeneous Source Mining Algorithms, Systems, Programming Models, and Applications*, 45–52. doi:10.1145/2351316.2351323

Yamamoto, C. H., de Oliveira, M. C. F., & Rezende, S. O. (2009). Visualization to assist the generation and exploration of association rules. *Post-Mining of Association Rules: Techniques for Effective Knowledge Extraction*, 224-245.

Yang, X., Bruin, R., & Dove, M. (2010). *Developing an end-to-end scientific workflow: a case study of using a reliable, lightweight, and comprehensive workflow platform in e-Science*. doi:.21110.1109/MCSE.2009

Yang, X. (2011). QoS-oriented service computing: bring SOA into cloud environment. In X. Liu & Y. Li (Eds.), *Advanced design approaches to emerging software systems: principles, methodology and tools*. IGI Global USA.

Yang, Y., Wang, Q., Woo, H. L., & Quek, C. L. (2011). Using Facebook for teaching and learning: A review of the literature. Int. J. Continuing Eng. Edu. *Life-Long Learn.*, *21*(1), 72–86.

Yates & Neto. (1999). *Modern Information Retrieval*. ACM.

Ye, F., Wang, Z. J., Zhou, F. C., Wang, Y. P., & Zhou, Y. C. (2013). Cloud-based big data mining and analyzing services platform integrating.*Proceedings of the International Conference on Advanced Cloud and Big Data*, 147–151. doi:10.1109/CBD.2013.13

Yuan, L. Y., Wu, L., You, J. H., & Chi, Y. (2014). Rubato DB: A highly scalable staged grid database system for OLTP and big data applications.*ACM International Conference on Conference on Information and Knowledge Management*, 1–10. doi:10.1145/2661829.2661879

Zaveri, A., Maurino, A., & Equille, L.-B. (2014). Web Data Quality: Current State and New Challenges. *International Journal on Semantic Web and Information Systems*, *10*(2), 1–6. doi:10.4018/ijswis.2014040101

Zhang, G. P. (2009). Neural networks for data mining. In Data mining and knowledge discovery handbook (pp. 419-444). Springer US. doi:10.1007/978-0-387-09823-4_21

Zhang, H. (2013), *A novel data pre-processing solution for large scale digital forensics investigation on big data* (Master's thesis). Norway.

Zhang, J., & Huang, M. L. (2013). 5Ws model for big data analysis and visualization. *International Conference on Computational Science and Engineering*, 1021–1028. doi:10.1109/CSE.2013.149

Zhang, L., Stoffel, A., Behrisch, M., Mittelstadt, S., Schreck, T., Pompl, R., & Keim, D. et al. (2012). Visual analytics for the big data era—a comparative review of state-of-the-art commercial systems.*IEEE Conference on Visual Analytics Science and Technology*, 173–182. doi:10.1109/VAST.2012.6400554

Zhao, Y., Hategan, M., Clifford, B., Foster, I., von, Laszewski, G., Nefedova, V., Raicu, I., Stef-Praun, T., & Wilde, M. (2007). Swift: fast, reliable, loosely coupled parallel computation. *Proceedings of 2007 IEEE congress on services (Services 2007)*, 199–206. doi:10.1109/SERVICES.2007.63

Zhao, J. M., Wang, W. S., Liu, X., & Chen, Y. F. (2014). *Big data benchmark - big DS*. Presented at Advancing Big Data Benchmarks.

About the Contributors

Aarti Singh is presently working as Asstt. Prof. in G.N.G. College, Yamuna Nagar, Haryana. She has a credible academic record, with various degrees like Ph.D. (Computer Science), M.Phil. (Computer Science), MCA, M.Sc. (Computer Science) and B.Sc. (Computer Science). Dr. Singh owes the credit of 72 published research papers in various International Journals of repute, with one Best Paper in an IEEE Conference. She has also participated in many International conferences within India and abroad. She is associated with many international conferences as editor and review committee member. Dr. Singh is associated with many journals as editorial board member and reviewer. Her research interests include Semantic Web, Agent Technology & Web Personalization.

Nilanjan Dey, PhD., is an Asst. Professor in the Department of Information Technology in Techno India College of Technology, Rajarhat, Kolkata, India. He holds an honorary position of Visiting Scientist at Global Biomedical Technologies Inc., CA, USA and Research Scientist of Laboratory of Applied Mathematical Modeling in Human Physiology, Territorial Organization Of- Sgientifig And Engineering Unions, BULGARIA, Associate Researcher of Laboratoire RIADI, University of Manouba, TUNISIA. He is the Editor-in-Chief of International Journal of Ambient Computing and Intelligence (IGI Global), US, International Journal of Rough Sets and Data Analysis (IGI Global), US, Series Editor of Advances in Geospatial Technologies (AGT) Book Series, (IGI Global), US, Executive Editor of International Journal of Image Mining (IJIM), Inderscience, Regional Editor-Asia of International Journal of Intelligent Engineering Informatics (IJIEI), Inderscience and Associated Editor of International Journal of Service Science, Management, Engineering, and Technology, IGI Global. He has 15 books and 200 international conferences and journal papers. https://www.researchgate.net/profile/Nilanjan_Dey3.

Amira S. Ashour, an Asst. Professor and Vice Chair of Computer Engineering Department of in Computers and Information Technology College, Taif University, KSA. Vice Chair of Computers Science Department of in Computers and Information Technology College, Taif University, KSA during 2006 till 2015. She is a Lecturer of Electronics and Electrical Communications Engineering, Faculty of Engg., Tanta University, Egypt. She got her Ph.D. in Smart Antenna (2005) in the Electronics and Electrical Communications Engineering, Tanta University, Egypt. She had her master in "Enhancement of Electromagnetic Non-Destructive Evaluation Performance Using Advanced Signal Processing Techniques," Faculty of Engineering, Egypt, 2000. Her research interests include Image Processing, Medical Imaging, Smart Antenna and Adaptive Antenna Arrays.

V. Santhi received her Ph.D in the field of Image Processing from VIT University, India. She did her M.Tech. in Computer Science and Engineering from Pondicherry University, B. Tech. in Computer Science and Engineering from Bharathidasan University, India. She is currently working as Associate Professor in School of Computer Science and Engineering, VIT University. Her publications are indexed in IEEE Computer Society, SPIE Digital Library, NASA Astrophysics Data Systems, SCOPUS, Thomson Reuter and ACM Digital Library. She is a reviewer of IEEE Transaction on Multimedia Security, IEEE Transaction on Image Processing, IET–Image Processing, International Journal of Information and Computer Security. She is member of IEEE Signal Processing Society, Computer Society of India and senior member of IACSIT. She has published many research findings in refereed Journals and in International Conferences. She has contributed many chapters and currently in the process of editing books. Her current research include Digital Image processing, Digital Signal Processing, Multimedia Security, Soft Computing, Bio-Inspired Computing, Remote Sensing.

* * *

Tauqir Ahmad is working as Associate Professor in Department of Computer Science & Engineering, University of Engineering and Technology (UET), Lahore from January 1999 – Present performing duties like Teaching and Research. Completed Doctor of Philosophy (Ph.D.) in the field of Computer Science from UET, Lahore on year 2012.

Bharath Bhushan is a Research Associate in the School of Information Technology and Engineering at VIT University in India. His research interests include Cloud Computing, Distributed Computing.

K. K. Chaturvedi is working as Senior Scientist (Computer Applications) in the Centre for Agricultural Bioinformatics (CABin) at ICAR - Indian Agricultural Statistics Research Institute, New Delhi, India. He is MCA from Madan Mohan Malaviya Engineering College Gorakhpur (UP) and Ph.D. (Computer Science) from University of Delhi, Delhi. He is involved in establishing the first data warehouse in Indian Agriculture and first supercomputing facility for Indian Agriculture as Advanced Supercomputing Hub for Omics Knowledge in Agriculture (ASHOKA). His areas of specializations are parallel algorithm, decision support system, data warehousing, mining software and biological repositories. He has published more than 40 research articles in national and international journals/conference proceedings of repute and large number of technical bulletins and popular articles. He is also the recipient of Scientist of the Year Award, Fellow of the Society for Scientific Development in Agriculture and Technology, South Asia Manthan Award by Digital Empowerment Foundation and editorial membership of many journals of repute. He visited Iowa State University and Cornell University, USA as visiting faculty. The more details about him are available at http://cabgrid.res.in/cabin/kkchaturvedi.aspx.

Mohammad Farooqi is a scientist at Centre for Agricultural Bioinformatics, ICAR-Indian Agricultural Statistics Research Institute. Experience in formulation and handling of research projects related to application of Statistics, Bioinformatics and Computer Application in agricultural research. Faculty member and research guide for the discipline of Bioinformatics and Computer Application at Post Graduate School of ICAR-Indian Agricultural Research Institute (ICAR-IARI) (Deemed National Agricultural University), New Delhi.

Akila Govindasamy completed her B.E in Computer Science and Engineering at Bharathidasan University at 1996 and M.E under Anna University in the year 2006. She completed her Ph.D in the year 2015 in the area of Bug Triage in Open Source Systems. She has acted as the Coordinator of an ACM-ICPS International Conference on Informatics and Analytics and is the Guest Editor of an Special Issue Special Issue on: "Image Processing and Analysis" for the Inderscience Journal of International Journal of Image Mining. She is also a Reviewer at several reputed journals like IET Software, International Journal of Advanced Intelligence Paradigms: Inderscience and IGI Global Journal of Organizational and End User Computing (JOEUC). She is the Principal Investigator of an UGC Minor Project. She has also delivered several Lectures at Short Term Training Programmes sponsored by TEQIP, QIP, etc.

Amudha J completed M.E in computer science in C. Abdhul Hakeem college of engineering and technology. Currently pursuing PhD in VIT University Vellore.

Vinoth Kumar Jambulingam, Research Associate, VIT University. He has completed his Master of Engineering in Rajalakshmi Engineering College from Anna Univeristy. Areas of Specialization: Data mining, Big Data and Privacy in Information Systems.

Mohit Jha is working as a Research Associate at Center for Agricultural Bioinformatics, ICAR - Indian Agricultural Statistics Research Institute, New Delhi. He received engineering. degree in information technology from Rajiv Gandhi Technical University, Bhopal in 2006 followed by M.Tech. in Bioinformatics from National Institute of Technology, Bhopal in 2008. He has worked as assistant professor at National Institute of Technology, Bhopal for 2 years. His research interests cover Large scale data analysis, Algorithm design and analysis, Graph Theory, Network Analysis and Data Mining.

Saruladha Krishnamurthy completed her B.E in Computer Science and Engineering at University of Madras at 1989 and M.Tech under Pondicherry University in the year 1997. She completed her Ph.D in the year 2012 in the area of Semantic similarity measures for ontology based Information Retrieval systems. She has acted as the Coordinator of an ACM-ICPS International Conference on Informatics and Analytics and is the Guest Editor of an Special Issue Special Issue on: "Image Processing and Analysis" for the Inderscience Journal of International Journal of Image Mining. She is also a Reviewer at several reputed journals like Springer Journal on Medical systems. She has 26 years of teaching experience. She is recognized supervisor in Pondciherry University. She has been Special Session organizer on information retrieval in International Conferences.She has organized several Faculty Development Programmes sponsored National funding agencies like AICTE,TEQIP. She has also served as resource person for Short Term Training Programmes sponsored by AICTE, TEQIP, QIP.

Raghvendra Kumar is working as Assistant Professor in Computer Science and Engineering Department at L.N.C.T Group of College Jabalpur, M.P. India. He received B. Tech. in Computer Science and Engineering from SRM University Chennai (Tamil Nadu), India, in 2011, M. Tech. in Computer Science and Engineering from KIIT University, Bhubaneswar, (Odisha) India in 2013, and pursuing Ph.D. in Computer Science and Engineering from Jodhpur National University, Jodhpur

(Rajasthan), India. He has published many research papers in international journal including IEEE and ACM. He attends many national and international conferences and also He Received best paper award in IEEE 2013 for his research work in the field of distributed database in Tamil Nadu. His researches areas are Computer Networks, Data Mining, cloud computing and Secure Multiparty Computations, Theory of Computer Science and Design of Algorithms. He authored many computer science books in field of Data Mining, Robotics, Graph Theory, Turing Machine, Cryptography, Security Solutions in cloud computing and Privacy Preservation.

Sanjeev Kumar has been a scientist for more than ten years at ICAR - Indian Agricultural Research Institute (ICAR-IARI), Pusa, New Delhi and more than five years at Centre for Agricultural Bioinformatics, ICAR - Indian Agricultural Statistics Research Institute, New Delhi. I was involved in designing and implementation of various research projects. My key role was that of a Statistician and Bioinformaticist with an active part in project formulation and implementation, data handling, data analysis, data-mining, simulation and modeling. As principal investigator of two projects, my role started with conceptualization, design and formulation and presentation of the concept. My role continues with overall planning, execution, management and monitoring of scientific, administrative as well as financial activities related to the project. As a faculty member, Agricultural Bioinformatics, I taught post graduate students of ICAR-IARI and guided number of M.Sc. and Ph.D. students in the capacity of member, research advisory committee.

Sushil Kumar is a Research Consultant in NRLMP project, Chhatishgarh at IIT Roorkee, India. He received his Ph.D. degree from IIT Roorkee, India in 2016. He has teaching experience of more than twelve years at M.L.N.College, Yamunanagar, India and G.N.K.I.T.M.S., Yamunanagar, India in the Department of Computer Science and Applications. He had been Offg. Director of G.N.K.I.T.M.S. from Aug. to Dec. 2009. His field of specialization includes Spatial Databases, 3D measurements with photographs, 3D printing, Internet of Things, Geo-tagging for professional use, Device programming (GPS, Digital Camera, Mobile, Total Station), GIS and surveying. He has earned more than 6 patents/copyrights, 12 research papers in international and national journals, conferences, seminars and workshops, etc.

Shashi Lal is working as a scientist (Computer Applications) in the Centre for Agricultural Bioinformatics at ICAR-Indian Agricultural Statistics Research Institute, New Delhi, India. He is B.Tech (Ag. Engg.), M.Sc. (Computer Applications) and Ph.D. (Information Technology). He has 22 years of experience in research, teaching and training in computer applications. His research area includes artificial neural network, software engineering, bioinformatics, data mining and statistical software development. He was also involved in various works for establishment of Bioinformatics and supercomputing facility in the institute. He has many research publications in various international & national journals.

Manisha Malhotra works as an Associate Professor in University Institute of Computing, Chandigarh University, Gharuan. She has published total 18 papers in various National / International Conferences, International Journal having indexed with Sci, Elsevier, Scopus, ACM. She has filed one patent that has been published in Indian Journal of Patent Office. She has credible record of various degrees like Ph.D (Computer Science & Applications), MCA (With Distinction), BSC (Computer Science)). She has certified in Cloud Computing. She has the members of various professional bodies like IEEE, CSI, IAENG. She also has the members of editorial boards of various journals.

Kaleem Razzaq Malik is the student of PhD in University of Engineering and Technology, Lahore, Pakistan and also have worked as instructor of Computer Science in Virtual University of Pakistan. He also have worked as Lecturer in Department of Software Engineering, Government College University Faisalabad, Pakistan from June 2013 - November 2015. He is now working as Assistant Professor in COMSATS Institue of Information Technology, Sahiwal Pakistan from December 2015 - Present performing duties like Teaching. Doing Doctor of Philosophy (Ph.D.) in the field of Computer Science from UET, Lahore since year 2011. His interests include, Computer Programming, Semantic Web and Databases.

Dwijesh Chandra Mishra is scientist, Centre for Agricultural Bioinformatics, ICAR - Indian Agricultural Statistics Research Institute (ICAR-IASRI), New Delhi, India (http://cabgrid.res.in/cabin/dcmishra.aspx). He did his Ph.D. in Agricultural Statistics from ICAR-Indian Agricultural Research Institute, New Delhi, India. He has more than 13 years of experience in research. He has several research papers in national and international journals of repute and also serving as faculty of Bioinformatics at ICAR-IASRI, New Delhi. He has also involved in developing course material for post graduate and Ph. D. in Bioinformatics. His current area of interests include computational biology, genome assembly, genomic data warehouse, transcriptomics, system biology, genomic selection and Genome Wide Association Studies (GWAS).

Raja Sekhar N received his Bachelor's in Computer Science and Engineering from JNTU Hyderabad, Andhra Pradesh, India in 2007 and his Master's in Computer Science and Engineering from JNTU Kakinada, Andhra Pradesh, India in 2011. He is currently a Research Scholar at VIT University, Vellore, India. His research interests include Smartgrid communications, Mobile Ad-hoc Networks, Computer Networks and Cloud Computing.

Sushil Kumar Narang did his Masters in Computer Applications from Dr. Ram Manohar Lohia University, Faizabad, India in 1995. He started his career as Lecturer at Department of Computer Science, M.L.N. College, Yamunanagar, India in 1996 and served there for Ten years. Presently He is working as Director IT at SAS Institute of IT & Research, Mohali, India. He carries over twenty years of teaching experience in the field of Computer Applications. He is a motivational speaker and content writer for various websites. He has delivered inspirational lectures at various corporate levels and institutions. He has written eight academic papers for national and International journals. His areas of expertise are Artificial Intelligence, Mobile application development and Core web programming.

Priyanka Pandey is working as Assistant Professor in Computer Science and Engineering Department at L.N.C.T Group of College Jabalpur, M.P. India. She received B.E. in Information Technology from TIE Tech (RGPV University), Jabalpur, MP, India, in 2013, M. Tech. in Computer Science and Engineering from TIE Tech (RGPV University), Jabalpur, MP, India. She published many research papers in international journal and conferences including IEEE. She attends many national and international conferences, her researches areas are Computer Networks, Data Mining, wireless network and Design of Algorithms.

Prasant Kumar Pattnaik, Ph.D. (Computer Science), Fellow IETE, Senior Member IEEE, is Professor at the School of Computer Engineering, KIIT University, Bhubaneswar. He has more than a decade of teaching research experience. Dr. Pattnaik has published numbers of Research papers in peer reviewed international journals and conferences. His researches areas are Computer Networks, Data Mining, cloud computing, Mobile Computing. He authored many computer science books in field of Data Mining, Robotics, Graph Theory, Turing Machine, Cryptography, Security Solutions in Cloud Computing, Mobile Computing and Privacy Preservation.

Anu Sharma is working as a scientist at ICAR - Indian Agricultural Statistics Research Institute, New Delhi, India and has seventeen years of experience in research, teaching and training in computer application in agriculture. She has completed MCA from Maharishi Dyanand University, Rohtak, India and currently pursuing Ph.D. Her research area is web personalization using ontology and semantic web, bioinformatics, data mining and statistical software development. She has many research publications in various international & national journals and conferences.

Vaishali Ravindra Thakare is a Research Associate in the School of Information Technology and Engineering, VIT University, Vellore. She received Bachelor of Engineering in Information Technology degree from Rashtrasant Tukdoji Maharaj Nagpur University, Nagpur in 2012. She has published research articles in peer-reviewed journals and in international conferences. Her area of interests includes cloud security and virtualization, security protocols in cloud computing, cloud computing architectures.

Vishal Verma is an Assistant Professor at Department of Computer Science, M. L. N. College, Yamunanagar, India. He received his Ph.D. in Computer Science from the Maharishi Markandeshwar University, Mullana, India in 2016. He is having rich experience of more than fourteen years in teaching blended with core research experience in computer graphics (lighting techniques, rendering techniques and their use in mobile devices), CBIR techniques, and knowledge discovery. He has a number of international journals and conference publications to his credit. He has participated in many reputed international conferences as a speaker, member of reviewing board, and also chaired a technical session in an international conference held in Australia.

Singanamalla Vijayakumar is a Research Associate in the School of Computer Science and Engineering, VIT University, Vellore. He received Bachelor of Engineering in Computer Science and Engineering, degree from Jawaharlal Nehru Technological University in 2011. His area of interests includes Image processing, SAR images, fuzzy logic.

Index

V

W

X

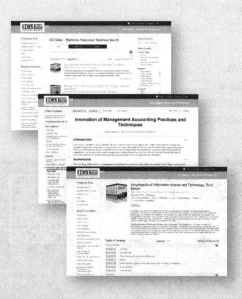

Printed in the United States
By Bookmasters